Computer Science and Ambient Intelligence

Computer Science
and
Ambient Intelligence

Edited by
Gaëlle Calvary
Thierry Delot
Florence Sèdes
Jean-Yves Tigli

First published 2013 in Great Britain and the United States by ISTE Ltd and John Wiley & Sons, Inc.

ISTE Ltd
27-37 St George's Road
London SW19 4EU
UK

www.iste.co.uk

John Wiley & Sons, Inc.
111 River Street
Hoboken, NJ 07030
USA

www.wiley.com

© ISTE Ltd 2013
The rights of Gaëlle Calvary, Thierry Delot, Florence Sèdes, Jean-Yves Tigli to be identified as the author of this work have been asserted by them in accordance with the Copyright, Designs and Patents Act 1988.

Library of Congress Control Number: 2012950237

British Library Cataloguing-in-Publication Data
A CIP record for this book is available from the British Library
ISBN: 978-1-84821-437-8

Printed and bound in Great Britain by CPI Group (UK) Ltd., Croydon, Surrey CR0 4YY

Table of Contents

Preface

In recent years, information and communication science and technology has witnessed spectacular advances owing to the groundbreaking nature of new materials, calculation processes and data sources. "Gray box" computers now only represent a small proportion of calculation resources and data sources. Indeed, more than 80% of processors are today integrated into various sophisticated devices. The number of sensors integrated into components with processing and signal transmission units has significantly increased. Each sensor is an active node in a system whose local processing capabilities make it possible to aggregate, sort and filter data or carry out more sophisticated processing.

Human–computer interaction has also significantly evolved. It is no longer simply confined to the traditional "screen, keyboard, mouse" settings, but permeates our everyday lives and activities. User interfaces (UIs) are no longer limited to graphics, nor to static contexts of use. Rather, they have become multimodal and are capable of adapting to dynamic contexts of use. With the mobility of the user, they migrate from one interactive space to another. While this vision is exciting in terms of usage, it raises significant challenges when engineering such UIs. These challenges are great since computing devices become more and more powerful and thus allow exploiting and mining huge databases. Anticipating and overcoming the risk of system hijacks are also a factor to be taken care of in these issues.

Transparency becomes a highly valuable quality for ensuring better access to resources at all levels of the system or corporation ("virtual", "in-network", and so on) making resources vulnerable to threats and attacks. Owing to the wide range of risks, from economic intelligence to protecting personal data, it is necessary to find the right balance between ensuring data protection and transparency of access to new autonomous resources in open environments. New challenges have emerged such as those relating to managing data access, ethics, and the well-known "precautionary principle", "Big data", "Big Brother"; the list is endless.

With such challenges, the growing diversity of dynamic services and smart objects raises new issues in the design, development and execution of software applications. These applications must be able to adapt to a software and hardware infrastructure, which is continuously and unpredictably changing. Prime examples of this include applications that follow the user as they move, such as those used in mobile phones, cars, houses, etc., which provide them with permanent access to services over a prolonged period of time. As such, the application must respond to variations in the context of use, while ensuring quality of service. Having simplified the distribution of software applications, middleware now facilitates the development of these applications by providing them with the ability to adapt. They must provide software mechanisms during run time that guarantee the permanent adaptation of the application to a changing context of use. These challenges will therefore increase significantly when faced with new uses in increasingly diverse, variable, and unpredictable contexts of use.

This book is the result of two CNRS (French National Center for Scientific Research) "Ambient intelligence" summer schools organized in July of 2009 and 2011. In line with the ethos of these schools, the present work aims to inform the lay reader of the challenges posed by this new field of research. Taking a holistic view, it covers various levels of abstraction, ranging from fundamental to advanced concepts and brings together the contributions of various specialists in the field, the majority of whom have carried out their research within the school.

This book features the main areas of computer science concerning ambient intelligence (e.g. human–computer interaction, middleware, networks, information systems, etc.). It is a multi-disciplinary advance with contributions originating from intelligent materials and ethics, the aim of which is to demonstrate the importance of integrated research, based on social sciences and technological advances. Such research is multi-disciplinary; the aim of which is mobilizing and bringing together expertise from each field to develop new theories. This book also pays tribute to the field's wide spectrum of applications with chapters focusing on health, transport, and even tourism. Teaching ambient intelligence is not addressed *per se*; rather, it is designed to provide a stimulating perspective to attest to the challenge of teaching within current frameworks due to the paradigm's interdisciplinary and contemporary nature and the lack of structures, platforms, and generic materials. Recent initiatives such as "FabLabs" are surely part of a response to this.

We would like to warmly thank all the authors who have contributed to the publication of this book. We also sincerely hope that you will have as much enjoyment reading their contributions as we have had in listening to their presentations during the two editions of the "ambient intelligence" summer school.

Gaëlle CALVARY, Thierry DELOT, Florence SÈDES and Jean-Yves TIGLI
November 2012

Chapter 1

Ambient Intelligence: Science or Fad?

1.1. Ambient intelligence: still young at 20 years

Ambient intelligence concerns the use of emerging technologies for computing, sensing, displaying, communicating and interacting to provide services in ordinary human environments. Different facets of this problem have been addressed under a variety of names, including ubiquitous computing, pervasive computing, disappearing computing, and the Internet of Things. Whatever the name, the field is defined by its core aim: to provide services and devices that can adapt to individual's needs and the social context. This includes diverse applications such as aiding people to adopt more energy-efficient lifestyles, improving the quality of life for the disabled, helping senior citizens remain independent, and aiding families with services for security, entertainment, and with tools for managing the cost of living.

Ambient intelligence is not a new concept. In 1988, only a few years after the introduction of the Macintosh computer and the French Minitel, Mark Weiser [WEI 91] identified the principal challenges under the name "ubiquitous computing". Weiser stated that technologies centered around daily activities would inevitably fade from view while becoming an imperceptible but ubiquitous component of ordinary life. Weiser contended that, although increasingly widespread, personal computing was the first of many steps in this process.

During the 1990s, researchers at IBM proposed the term *pervasive computing*. With this approach, emphasis was placed on technical challenges such as developing hardware and software techniques necessary for bringing computing into ordinary

Chapter written by Joëlle COUTAZ and James L. CROWLEY.

human environments. At around the same time, the European IST Advisory Group (ISTAG) put forth its vision of *ambient intelligence* [STA 03], leading to the creation of the *Disappearing Computer* program within the European Union's Fifth Framework Programme for Research and Technological Development. This period also saw the emergence of Philips Research's "Vision of the Future" [PHI 96] program and the creation of the Philips *HomeLab* designed to stimulate creativity through experimentation, to explore new opportunities for combining different technologies, to identify the socio-cultural significance of these innovations, and to make these concepts tangible, useful, and accessible to all.

During this period, a number of conferences, workshops, and journals were organized. The Ubicomp[1] conference, created from the mobile computing and smart environment communities, focuses primarily on user experience. The IEEE Pervasive and Percom[2] conferences have arisen from the "distributed computing" community, to focus on the challenges and technical solutions in distributed systems and networks. Within Europe, the EUSAI (*European Symposium on Ambient Intelligence*), later renamed AmI – *Ambient Intelligence*[3], was launched in 2002 with support from Philips Research. A scientific community has also emerged to address the topic of *context-aware computing*. While the concept of context is not new in computer science (nor in other fields), bringing computing into ordinary human environments raises a rich, new set of problems. Other aspects of this problem have also been explored, including collectives of artificial agents for ambient intelligence[4], the Internet of Things[5] and *Machine-to-Machine* (M2M), communicating objects, mobile computing, wearable computing[6], social computing, intelligent habitats and environments (towns, housing, roads, transport, architecture, etc.), *tangible and embedded interaction*[7], affective computing, human–robot interaction[8], and embedded systems.

In summary, Weiser's vision has been used to justify and define new research within an extremely diverse collection of fields. It is increasingly evident that such research cannot be carried out in isolation. Research in this area is fundamentally multi-disciplinary, requiring the assimilation of problems and concepts from a variety of specializations. From our perspective, in its current state, ambient intelligence is only the latest stage in the evolution of informatics as a scientific discipline. In the following chapters, we will provide an overview of the field in its current state.

---

1 www.ubicomp.org/. Ubicomp, created in 2001 as part of HUC 99 and HUC2k (*Handheld and Ubiquitous Computing*).
2 http://pervasive2008.org/, www.percom.org/.
3 www.ami-07.org/.
4 *Workshop Artificial Societies for Ambient Intelligence*, http://asami07.cs.rhul.ac.uk/.
5 www.internet-of-things-2008.org.
6 www.iswc.net/.
7 www.tei-conf.org/.
8 http://hri2007.org/.

1.2. A step forward in the evolution of informatics

Waldner [WAL 07] has summarized the evolution of computing by charting the continual miniaturization of electronic components, the spectacular increase in information processing and memory capacity, the omnipresence of networks, and the reduced costs of hardware production. In this approach, development of resources drives changes in the nature of computing. We carry out a parallel analysis using the changes in resources to predict developments in research. We will focus on three areas in particular: the availability of computing power as a critical resource, the individual as the focus of attention, and the physical and social worlds in relation to the digital world.

1.2.1. *Fifty years ago: the computer as an isolated critical resource*

Fifty years ago, computing machines were far too expensive and it was cumbersome to even imagine them being used in everyday homes, as shown in Figure 1.1. Access to computing was restricted to specialist operators and programs were carefully encoded on perforated "punch cards". Computing results were printed on reams of special fan-folded paper, with punch cards, magnetic tapes and removable disks used for long-term storage. At best, computing machines had around a megabyte of central memory. Computing networks and packet switching technologies for communications were an avant-garde area of research[9].

During this period, the user was a programmer specialized in scientific computing, statistics, and management applications (such as payroll). Programs were entered by a dedicated operator, who monitored the use of resources using a specific control language (*Job Control Language, JCL*). Any program that consumed more memory or printed more pages than what was anticipated was automatically terminated by the operating system and the programmer was responsible for declaring the required computing resources. The skill lay in being able to produce a correct program "from the start" using such techniques as memory overlays so that the program ran using the available central memory. The concept of virtual memory therefore became a subject of research. With the emergence of time-sharing systems, punching cards gradually disappeared in favor of personal terminals. These were initially built using TELEX terminals or "teletypes" that were eventually replaced by alphanumerical screens. Bit-mapped displays; however, were judged far too expensive because of memory costs.

---

9 Louis Pouzin, then a researcher at IRIA (later INRIA), and his team were responsible for the invention of packet-switching communications. Their datagramme technique was used within the Cyclade project, with a first network composed of hubs at IRIA, the CII and the IMAG in France. The first demonstration took place in 1973.

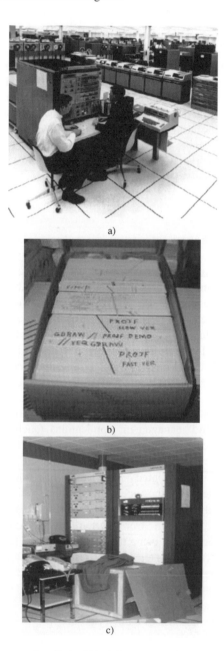

Figure 1.1. *a) A computer for all, the IBM 360, carrying out batch processing (at night) and time sharing (by day). b) A box of cards consisting of what can only be described as a very physical program! The program's procedures are given by lines and names written in pencil. c) The Cyclade hub at IMAG (Grenoble, France)*

The optimization of resources and "virtualization" (found today in *cloud computing*) remained the driving force in computing until researchers (North American, for the most part) turned their attention to the human component of the human–machine system. Indeed, as the cost of computing machines decreased, labor costs increasingly dominated the cost of computing.

1.2.2. *Thirty years ago: the user at the center of design*

The first CHI (*Computer–Human Interaction*) conference of the ACM[10] was organized in 1983. This conference, parallel with the first appearance of personal computers, marked the start of the pursuit of developing useful and usable applications for users. The user was no longer an experienced programmer, but a non-specialist using the computer as a tool for professional activities. An application was considered useful if it provided the functions expected by its user where it was said to ensure "functional conformity". A program was considered usable if the user interface (UI), which gives access to applicative functions, conformed to the cognitive, motor and sensory capabilities of the target user. This is known as "interactional conformity".

Computer scientists, whether academic or industrial, have, for too long, underestimated the cognitive dimension of the human user. Not only should a program provide her/him with the expected functions, but it should also provide access to these functions in a manner that respects the user's working procedures and abilities to perceive and reason. Not only should this arrangement conform to human thought processes, but it should also be made explicit to the user interface. It was only in 2010 that computing professionals recognized that the design of the human–computer interface was not simply a question of aesthetics, but an issue of user–computer conformity. By contributing concepts, theories and methods, cognitive psychology and ergonomics have played an important role in addressing this problem.

Methods used for user-interface design include participative and contextual design [BEY 98], iterative design (which is well adapted to the practice of "agile" programming), and scenario-based design [ROS 02]. These user-focused methods have given rise to a number of formalisms such as CLG [CAR 83], TAG [PAY 86] and ETAG [TAU 90], UAN [HAR 92], and CTT [PAT 97] to model the thought processes of target users in the form of task models (a tree structure with aims and sub-aims linked by composition operators or temporal relations). Such models go

---

10 CHI'83 followed the first workshop on the subject in Gaithersburg in March 1982, entitled *Human Factors in Computer Systems*.

beyond a simple *Use Case UML*, to specify the functional requirements and task sequences from a user perspective.

Example theories include the Model Human Processor [CAR 83] and Norman's direct correspondence principle [NOR 86], which state that there should be a clear correspondence between the psychological variables encountered by the user mentally and computing objects, as well as a direct correspondence between the internal state of the system in relation to the user and its representation by the user interface. These theories are, or at least should be, part of the toolkit of any competent computer scientist.

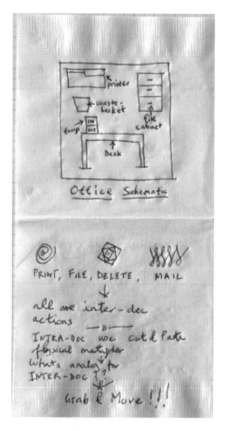

Figure 1.2. *In search of a graphic representation of the desktop metaphor, an idea already being used in the 1970s: sketch produced by Tim Mott at the end of the 1970s (taken from [MOG 06], p. 52). It shows the first generic commands: "Print, File, Delete, Mail, Cut and Paste, Grab and Move"*

Two complementary representations compete in modern user interface technologies: linguistic representations (including natural and artificial languages, as in the Unix Shell), and metaphorical interfaces based on the real world, such as with the desktop environment in modern personal computers. The WIMP (Window, Icon, Menu, Pointing) interaction paradigm, made possible by modern user interface toolkits, is a modern manifestation of the impact of the direct correspondence principle and its theoretical foundation in the Model Human Processor.

Ergonomics and cognitive psychology have also had a major impact on evaluation methods by suggesting protocols and metrics to assess human performance such as task performance duration and error rates. Although these methods are well elaborated and documented, in practice, software developers are still reluctant to integrate them into the software development process or, if they do so, evaluation is performed too late in the development process to have a real impact on system usability.

At the same time, the Internet, wireless networks, the web (which celebrated its 20th year in 2010), and web browsers are now used by nearly everyone. From a single computer, we have passed on to an era of "instantly connected" computing.

1.2.3. *The past decade: combining physical, social, and digital worlds*

In contrast to the previous era of computing, in which the desktop computer was the archetype, new technologies increasingly enable mobility and integration of digital systems into the ordinary physical objects. Ordinary objects are increasingly being fitted with technologies for computing, communications, sensing, actuation, and interaction. These devices are increasingly networked, forming a complex infrastructure creating a plethora of new services. Figure 1.3 demonstrates this trend in four images.

The examples in Figure 1.3 lead to three immediate observations: the polymorphism of the computer that weaves, both literally and figuratively, the digital into our everyday activities, from the useful to the pointless. In other words, the physical world has become a resource that can be shaped and (re)constructed by the individual, not only to be more efficient but also to improve the quality of our life, pleasure and experiences. This has resulted in the emergence of "funology" (i.e. the science of having fun) [BLY 03]. The user is no longer a subject limited to "consuming" applications imposed by the market, but can now take on the role of actor such as "DIYers" who construct and improve their living space using off-the-shelf components. Even the individual's ability to create has itself been surpassed by a new phenomenon, social networking [KRA 10], made possible by the universality of the Internet.

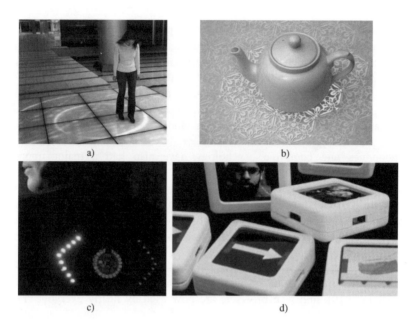

a)   b)

c)   d)

Figure 1.3. *Examples of services and devices: a) a light projection on a floor; b) the "history tablecloth" [GAV 06] that traces the movement of objects on it with a glowing ring gradually forming around the object and then progressively disappearing when the object is moved; c) an Arduino LilyPad application: personalization of a jacket fitted with an indicator showing changes in direction [BUE 08]; d) siftables that can be assembled in different ways to create new applications [MER 07]*

The social dimension of computing has in fact been an area of interest since the end of the 1980s[11]. The initial aim was to develop models, theories and digital systems, called groupware, designed to improve group activities in terms of production, coordination, and communication. With the web, the change in scale has led to new uses. Every individual, collective and community can now collect information, relate it, produce new information, and in turn share it with the rest of the world. Schneiderman [SHN 98] refers to this phenomenon with the mantra collect–relate–create–donate. Wikipedia is the most obvious example of a collective construction of encyclopedic knowledge. Other examples include the *Google Image Labeler*, which indexes images and *TopCoder* for thesocial production programs. The digital software stores, inspired by the Apple *App Store,* have led to changes in the software development process and have triggered new economic models and opportunities.

11 The first ACM conference on the subject *Computer Supported Collaborative Work* (CSCW) took place in 1987.

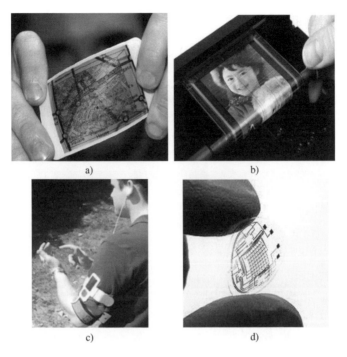

Figure 1.4. *Examples of devices integrating new ICT capabilities, device nanotechnology. a) A Gummi prototype (Sony), a bendable computer. Navigation across the screen is achieved by bending the surface [SCH 04]. b) A bendable OLED screen (introduced by Sony to the SID, Society for Information Display, 2010). c) Skinput applied to a music device: the finger pressure applied to the surface skin is sensed by an armband fitted with sensors [HAR 10]. d) A soft lens fitted with a circuit is placed directly on the surface of the eye*

Despite the constant avalanche of information, the human factor remains constant. The user remains a genuine bottleneck, and requires the invention of new interaction techniques to accommodate a growing flood of information. In this sense, gestural interaction and inertial measurement units in mobile telephones, physical interaction and motion sensing devices using real time 3D reconstruction such as Microsoft's Kinect muscular interaction, multipoint clear screens, and bendable objects are all noteworthy examples, as illustrated in Figure 1.4. These examples show that innovation requires the unprecedented cooperation ICT (information and communication technologies) and ICT–HSS (human and social sciences), from nanotechnologies to software engineering, and from the individual to all levels of society.

This brief overview indicates that we are entering into an era of radical change, which, in turn, raises a number of new challenges.

1.3. Extreme challenges

The scientific, technical and ethical challenges posed by ambient intelligence have been examined by a number of reports [COU 08, STA 03, PUN 05, WAL 07], specialized journals, conference sessions, and workshops. Research problems are generally organized as a stack of sub-domains shown in Figure 1.5. Three key challenges facing the field cover all of these domains: scalability, heterogeneity and dynamic adaptation. These three challenges arise from the fact that ambient intelligence pushes computing to its limits.

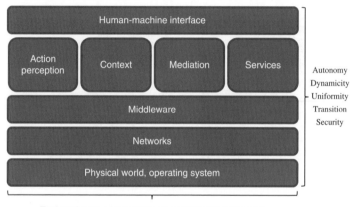

Figure 1.5. *Architectural overview of research themes in ambient intelligence*

1.3.1. *Multi-scale*

Changes in scale can lead to unexpected phenomena. For ambient intelligence, the challenge of scale results from the massive interconnection of a very large number of ordinary devices augmented with computing, sensing, actuation and interaction. The challenge lies in managing the co-existence of services and systems made possible by the interconnection of devices over a wide range of scales, from personal body-area networks based on wearable computing to city-wide and planetary scale systems. This challenge is greatly complicated by the heterogeneity resulting in part from technical challenges at each scale.

1.3.2. *Heterogeneity*

At any scale, a variety of possible solutions may be used to address competing technical challenges. In addition, each scale raises its own unique challenges.

Integrating devices with different programming frameworks can prove extremely complex. Integrating across scales makes integration even more challenging. While the field has seen concerted movements toward uniform standards, too often such efforts have been carried out in a vacuum, resulting in isolated silos of inter-operability. In such environments, dynamic adaptation is therefore impossible.

1.3.3. *Dynamic adaptation*

Dynamic adaptation, with its multiple facets, approaches and solutions has been examined for over a number of years in a variety of fields and research specialties (see Figure 1.5). For some researchers, the ultimate aim is an autonomous, safe, and secure system that does not require human intervention. For others, however, the user should remain involved, if desired. It is therefore necessary that "autonomous software compositions" provide users with interaction points at every level of abstraction in order to control the adaptation process if needed.

These problems have only been addressed in a piecemeal manner to date, constrained by the restricted view of a single specialty or area of application. It is therefore necessary to develop new technologies that are generic, enabling, and malleable. These technologies should be generic so that they can be applied to all contexts and allow the rapid development of services by professionals. Malleability is needed so that they can be organized and changed by the end user, as required, in a non-uniform, constrained, dynamic and multi-scale world[12]. This is not a question of creating a uniform and standardized world, but respecting diversity and the unexpected. For our part, the "malleable" constitutes a major challenge in coming years because we are placing the means to program (unconsciously), develop programs (without endangering life or property), and share them with others (like the *App Store* over social networks) in the hands of the end user.

1.4. Conclusion

In view of the above, is ambient intelligence a fad or an emerging scientific discipline? In line with Thomas Kuhn's definition, our analysis suggests that ambient intelligence does not have the status of a discipline[13] yet. If a scientific community is said to be organized around symposia and specialized reviews, it does not necessarily entail sharing a standard set of concepts and methods. Ambient intelligence is still "application driven" for its socio-economic benefits.

---

12 What Bell and Dourish call, in less technical terms, *a messy fragmented world* [BEL 06].
13 www.electroniques.biz/pdf/EIH200312110541038.pdf (in French).

For the foreseeable future, we believe that the response will be a progressive evolution of research processes and a collaborative approach toward a concrete and lasting integrated strategy. Indeed, each discipline and specialty progress by sharing information with other disciplines (it is a multi-disciplinary alliance that drives "collaborative" research projects) or new shared knowledge will arise from the integration of several disciplines and specialties, a pluri-disciplinary convergence, which is a challenge in itself. Human–machine interaction is a perfect example of the convergence between psychology, sociology, and computing. However, it has taken more than 20 years for it to be recognized as a discipline in its own right. It is therefore a question of time. Nevertheless, let us remember Alan Kay's well-known quote, "the best way to predict the future is to invent it!".

1.5. Bibliography

[BEL 06] BELL G., DOURISH P., "Yesterday's tomorrows: notes on ubiquitous computing's dominant vision", *Personal and Ubiquitous Computing*, 2006, www.ics.uci.edu/~jpd/ubicomp/BellDourish-YesterdaysTomorrows.pdf.

[BEY 98] BEYER H., HOLTZBLATT K., *Contextual Design*, Morgan Kaufman, San Francisco, 1998.

[BLY 03] BLYTHE M.A., OVERBEEKE K., MONK A.F., WRIGHT P.C. (ed.), *From Usability to Enjoyment*, Human Computer Interaction Series, vol. 3, Springer, New York, 2003.

[BUE 08] BUECHLEY L., EISENBERG M., CATCHEN J., CROCKETT A., "The LilyPad Arduino: using computational textiles to investigate engagement, aesthetics, and diversity in computer science education", *Proceedings of the SIGCHI Conference (CHI 2008)*, Florence, Italy, pp. 423–432, April 2008.

[CAR 83] CARD S.K., MORAN T.P., NEWELL A., *The Psychology of Human Computer Interaction*, Lawrence Erlbaum, Hillsdale, 1983.

[COU 08] COUTAZ J., CROWLEY J., Intelligence Ambiante : défis et opportunités, Document de réflexion conjoint du comité d'experts "Informatique Ambiante" du département ST2I du CNRS et du Groupe de travail "Intelligence Ambiante" du Groupe de concertation sectoriel (GCS3) du ministère de l'Enseignement supérieur et de la Recherche, DGRI A3, 2008. http://iihm.imag.fr/publs/2008/RapportIntellAmbiante.V1.2finale.pdf.

[GAV 06] GAVER W., BOWERS J., BOUCHER A., LAW A., PENNINGTON S., VILLAR N., "The history tablecloth; illuminating domestic activity", *DIS'06 Proceedings of the 6th Conference on Designing Interactive Systems*, ACM, New York, USA, pp. 199–208, 2006.

[HAR 10] HARRISON C., TAN D., MORRIS D., "Skinput: appropriating the body as an input surface", *Proceedings of CHI'10*, ACM, pp. 453–462, 2010.

[HAR 92] HARTSON R., GRAY P., "Temporal aspects of tasks in the user action notation", *Human Computer Interaction*, vol. 7, pp. 1–45, 1992.

[KRA 10] KRAUT R., MAHER M.L., OLSON J., MALONE T., PIROLLI P., THOMAS J.C., "Scientific foundations: a case for technology-mediated social participation theory", *IEEE Computer*, vol. 43, pp. 22–28, novembre 2010.

[MER 07] MERRILL D., KALANITHI J., MAES P., "Siftables: towards sensor network user interfaces", *Proceedings of the First International Conference on Tangible and Embedded Interaction (TEI'07)*, Baton Rouge, USA, pp. 15–17, Feburary 2007.

[MOG 06] MOGGRIDGE B., *Designing Interactions*, The MIT Press, Cambridge, MA, 2006.

[NAR 95] NARDI B., *A Small Matter of Programming, Perspectives on End User Computing*. The MIT Press, Cambridge, MA, 1995.

[NOR 86] NORMAN D., DRAPER S.W., *User Centered Design, New Perspectives on Human-Computer Interaction*, Lawrence Erlbaum, Hillsdale, 1986.

[PAR 09] PARVIZ B., "Augmented reality in a contact lens", *IEEE Spectrum*, September 2009.

[PAT 97] PATERNÒ F., MANCINI C., MENICONI S., "ConcurTaskTrees: a diagrammatic notation for specifying task models", *Proceedings of INTERACT 1997*, Sydney, Australia, pp. 362–369, 1997.

[PAY 86] PAYNE S., GREEN T., "Task-actions grammars: a model of the mental representation of task languages", *Human-Computer Interaction*, vol. 2, pp. 93–133, 1986.

[PHI 96] PHILIPS, Vision of the future, *Philips Corporate Design,* Eindhoven, V+K Publ., Bussum, Netherlands, 1996.

[PUN 05] PUNIE Y., "The future of ambient intelligence in Europe: the need for more everyday life", *Communications & Stratégies*, no. 57, 2005, www.idate.fr/fic/revue_telech/418/CS57_PUNIE.pdf.

[ROS 02] ROSSON M.B., CARROLL J.M., *Usability Engineering, Scenario-Based Development of Human Computer Interaction*, Morgan Kaufmann, San Francisco, 2002.

[SCH 04] SCHWESIG C., POUPYREV I., MORI E., "Gummi: a bendable computer", *Proceedings of CHI'2004*, ACM, pp. 263–270, 2004.

[STA 03] ST ADVISORY GROUP, *Ambient Intelligence: from Vision to Reality*, European Commission, 2003.

[SHN 98] SHNEIDERMAN B., "Relate-create-donate: a teaching/learning philosophy for cyber-generation", *Computers and Education*, vol. 31, no. 1, pp. 25–39, 1998.

[TAU 90] TAUBER M., "ETAG: extended task action grammar – a language for the description of the user's task language", *Proceedings INTERACT'90*, Elsevier, pp. 163–174, 1990.

[WAL 07] WALDNER J.B., *Nanocomputers and swarm intelligence*, ISTE Ltd., London and John Wiley & Sons, New York, 2007.

[WEI 91] WEISER M., "The computer for the twenty-first century", *Scientific American*, vol. 265, no. 3, pp. 66–75, 1991.

Chapter 2

Thinking about Ethics

As purveyors of ethical questions on safety and environmental hazards, risks relating to personal surveillance and privacy and the possibility of bettering mankind, information, and communication technologies in all their diversity and complexity raise the issue of evolution, far beyond the scope of a single technology. The consequences of miniaturization, invisibility and interaction of technologies with man, whether intended or not, have led to a surge in ethical reflection that reaches far beyond the scientific community and in which man as citizen is often a factor. Reflection on the ethical and social consequences of these technologies should neither be restricted to a single evaluation of risks and costs, nor to research into the social acceptance of new inventions. The interest, hope and beliefs that their developments engender civil society and the scientific community extend far beyond a mere rational analysis. Developed in a context of uncertainty with regard to their future consequences, a symbolic echo of ancient fears, technology, and its use provoke a collective emotional reaction that is often excessive or irrational. If an ethical enlightenment favors the emergence of a widely applicable solution for evaluating "reasonable doubt" in "proportionate and acceptable risk", this should be viewed from a perspective recognizing social value systems.

Strongly anchored in industry, these technologies form the frontier of science and its applications that are "at one with it" [KLE 08]. They are characterized by their significant complexity and interactions with other disciplines such as human and social sciences, biology or medicine. Based on action and immediacy, reflection and ethical dimensions are often incompatible with economic demands. For all that,

---

Chapter written by Anne-Marie BENOIT.

they are the carriers of social and political changes, which upset, sometimes unintentionally, the *status quo*. In their potential applications, they sometimes reach beyond the limits of the law, indicating future changes. It is in this muddle of contradicting imperatives that an ethical approach must "give sense to an ongoing experiment where we do not yet know the results and even highlight uncertainty" [KLE 08].

Technology is increasingly geared toward human identity in terms of fundamental rights by enabling us, under various restrictions, to process information relating to personal, sensitive[1], and biometric data that identify an individual on the basis of his/her physical, biological, or psychological characteristics (DNA, retina, iris, finger prints, hand contours, veins) and medical or behavioral (emotions) information. As such, can an ethical approach "appropriate" this data while respecting our fundamental rights? Do the values set out in and by a society change? Do technologies change the consensus on what is and what is not acceptable?

2.1. Ethics and fundamental rights

The increased capacity to collect data from a single person, track individuals in both public (stores, airports, etc.) and private spaces, and "profile" them using their individual behavior has led to the creation of laws and guidelines that restrict data collection. A new frontier has been crossed through the spread of technology and miniaturization, chips, "cloud computing", "the Internet of Things", or "pervasive computing", which have markedly influenced the human environment. The apparent insignificance of data, the priority given to objects over people, the logic of globalization (technological standardization based on an American concept of *privacy* without accounting for European principles protecting private life), and the risk of a lack of individual vigilance due to the presence and invisible activation complicating the situation[2]. The protection of private life, a fundamental component of human rights, is becoming a challenge in the development of technologies. Indeed, if the right to private life involves protecting aspects of personal life, it is also a highly vague right whose recognition is left to judges who base their decisions, in part, on European Community legislations such as the Convention for the Protection of Human Rights and Fundamental Freedoms (article 8), the

---

1 Article 8 of the reused French law of 6 January 1978 sets out a number of stipulations regarding sensitive data: "It is prohibited to collect or process personal data which, either directly or indirectly, reveal the racial or ethnic origins, the political, philosophical or religious opinions or the membership of trade unions of persons, or which relate to the health or sexual life of these persons".
2 Opinion of PH. Lemoine, CNIL Commissioner.

Amsterdam Treaty (November 10, 1997), directives 95/46/EC[3] on the protection of personal data in Europe, or even the European Union Charter of Fundamental Rights, Article 8 of which states that everyone has the right to have respect for their personal data. It is therefore the responsibility of judges to not only respect private life, but also to protect it.

These technologies, combined with an industrial, economic, and competitive world in daily life, cause not entirely unfounded fears in civil society. The invisibility of data collection, which can be done without the knowledge or consent of those involved or the notification of purpose; the interoperability, which means that this data can be read by several individuals; profiling individuals, segmentation, discrimination, and exclusion are some of the repercussions that must be considered when evaluating risk. These risks are even harder to appreciate when there is uncertainty about these new technologies. Assistive technology designed to improve daily life for those with disabilities can also be used as a potential surveillance technology. Fears have been raised and fed by the potential endlessness of these technologies in terms of security, for example web profiling or the use of different bio-identification tools such as chips placed in the human body. These technologies and the amalgamation of several technologies (biology, cognitive sciences, etc.) are becoming embedded within the entirety of our social fabric. Authors have described the interaction paradigm in ubiquitous computing as the "processing of information becoming dissolved within behavior". Human relationships shaped by software, chips, and nano-objets lead the individual to more or less consciously abdicate their right to privacy, the integrity of their individual liberty, and dignity.

Is this a catastrophic scenario for man or a "seductive promise"? The uncertainty of these technologies and the "improved human" paradigm have regularly fed fears often expressed by the scientific community or the media. Even if some fears appear to be unfounded today, such as the imminent arrival of a world controlled by robots, resulting in a fusion of the human central nervous system and machines, others should not be disregarded. Transplants of computer implants into the human body to compensate for a loss in physical capabilities or function by restoring damaged functions "contribute to the promotion of human dignity whilst representing a risk which must be considered"[4]. According to this perspective, respect for human dignity is a basic human right. It is, along with liberty, one of the principal frames of

3 Directive 95/46/CE from the European Parliament and Council from October 24, 1995 relating to the physical protection of individuals with regard to the treatment of data of a personal nature and the free circulation of this data.
4 The ethical aspect of TIC implants in humans – opinion of the European Group on Ethics in Science and New Technology (EGE), http://ec.europa.eu/bepa/european-group-ethics/docs/publications/ict_final_22_february-adopted.pdf. On March 22nd 2011, the President of the European Commission asked the EGE to produce a report on the ethical implications of information and communication technologies.

reference governing activity relating to progress in research. Given the uncertainty of technology, it is necessary to seek, as far as possible, a balance between "the reasonable and the relative".

2.2. Ethics and values

As E. Klein, A. Grinbau and V. Bontems have highlighted in relation to nano-sciences "the reference to ethics has become a sort of pervasive code against which every new question must be measured" [KLE 08]. Who, which organizations, an ethical committee, can claim to set out society's values? The "incomplete" quantification of risks carried out by both scientists and policy makers and the cost-benefit projections made by financiers and industry are not sufficient to measure the potential future consequences of technology.

In terms of policy makers, the creation of regulations that enable better practical adaptation brings citizens into public debate via opinion polls, the creation of user associations, professionals, or professional practices (good practice codes, good behavior codes, recommendations, codes of ethics). Regulation, as a model for technological "ethical governance", is based on the observation of proven social phenomena and reasonable transactions with regard to values and beliefs driven by these phenomena. The reality is more deceptive because regulation, which is based only on the present, comes from a tangle of origins and sources (citizens, professionals, policy makers, etc), ethics comities, and ethical spaces that give piecemeal, segmented and hard-to-implement recommendations.

Ethics cannot be reduced to the simple regulation and management of risks. It raises questions and provokes reflection on the human condition in civil society whose uncertainties and risks are immeasurable since the future is obviously difficult to predict. Since Max Weber there has been a distinction in numerous theories between the ethics of responsibility and the ethics of the discussion developed by Habermas. While in the ethics of responsibility, if the consequences are attributable to an action, man should, as far as he can predict, place himself in a situation to anticipate potential problems. In the ethics of discussion, it is, however, essential that people can exchange rational arguments about their interests in a public space of free discussion, which will give rise to new norms and common interests.

None of these approaches to ethics is intellectually satisfying. Both tend to impose the principle of precaution as being a basic element of the "ethics of the future"[5]. The boundaries of the precaution principle were progressively set out over

---

5 Borrowed from Hans Jonas.

the course of the 1990s from a fluid concept developed in the 1970s around nuclear energy. It is out of concern for preserving the future that this principle recognizes the need and legitimacy of not waiting for scientific certainty to engage preventive actions. For example, in France, the *Law Barnier* relating to environmental protection calls for "in the absence of certainty, considering the scientific and technical information available [and] the adoption of effective and proportionate measures to prevent the risk of serious and irreversible damage to the environment at an economically acceptable cost"[6]. Recognition of this principle, which has also been extended to health, has reversed the label of guilt from the victim to the alleged perpetrator of any harm caused.

In this sense, the precaution principle allows us to justify a scientific approach and restrict technologies to only those risks that can be objectively measured. It is, however, not possible in a situation of uncertainty or lack of knowledge around potential or even probable harm. Beyond this principle and its definition, the scientific community has a responsibility to take on the role of the researcher. Should they, therefore, be given preferential treatment in comparison to the lay observer in terms of ethics? Does the scientific community have an obligation to inform policy makers and citizens of the risks where no evaluation is foreseeable or even possible? Is it possible to make decisions as to what is desirable and what is not?

Is there, outside of technological ethics, an ethics specific to researchers that releases them from their liberty and, as a consequence, responsibility? Is there, at the margin of technological ethics, an ethics relieving researchers of their liberty and, as a result, their responsibility? The act of "whistle blowing"[7], a new factor in risk management, allows scientists, who discover elements that they consider to be potentially harmful for humans, society, or the environment, to bring them to the attention of officials, organizations, or the media, sometimes against the wishes of their superiors. Do these technologies present a genuinely new perspective for ethics? Should we rethink ethics in relation to the specific properties of these technologies? In the section entitled "Challenges", the 30th CNIL report (2010) [COM 10] responds directly to these issues by proposing to increase data protection against a framework of shared and common ethics. However, when individuals waive some of their privacy in return for "real or imagined benefits", in the name of security, for example, allowing their biometric data to be collected, the response must be negative. The consent of those concerned does not remove the need for an ethical reflection on information and communication technology. The requirement to consider human dignity is an absolute principle, the consent of which does not remove the need to acknowledge this or justify its infringement.

---

6 French law no.95–101 from February 2, 1995 relating to environmental protection.
7 F. Chateauraynaud and D. Torny have also used the term "whistleblower".

Paradoxically, the gravity of the "judicial crisis" left in the wake of these unprecedented technologies can also be questioned. Indeed, on examination of preparatory work for laws concerning freedom of information or annual reports by information commissions, the admission of powerlessness against the extent of upheaval caused is shocking. If doctrine has shown that the fantasy of fixed law lives on, there is no more important a challenge than conforming to norms and values that are evolving at a different rate.

2.3. Ethics and future perspectives

In a competitive economic world characterized by constant redefinition of values, ethics should not delay or "paralyze" the development of technology, neither in the present nor, even more so, in the future. Each research project should be subject to an ethical discussion, which should be expressed more through the type of approach taken rather than its affirmed and quickly outdated principles.

These increasingly "invasive" technologies are blurring the boundary between man and his environment. By their irreversible nature, they modify man's conditions of living by modeling, simplifying, and making them easier. They have also encountered challenges both in the public arena as well as in the private sphere. However, fears arise when these technologies affect human nature. The notion of human dignity is the single "benchmark" that allows us to distinguish between what is acceptable and unacceptable for an individual.

Beyond these demands, ethics is not declared; rather it is transmitted and taught. It can only be the result of clearly affirmed desires to integrate it into an approach to research without falling into the pitfall of "DIY ethics". While ethics in science and technology, which directly relies on philosophy, raises questions without often providing a response, "applied ethics" or an ethical approach allows us to balance "in equal measure" the various interests of social actors in a rational consensus.

2.4. Bibliography

[COM 10] COMMISSION INFORMATIQUE ET LIBERTÉ, 30e rapport, La Documentation Française, Paris, pp. 61–63, 2010.

[COU 99] COUR DE CASSATION, 1e chambre civile, 16 July 1998, note, Jurisprudence, Dalloz, Paris, p. 541, 1999.

[GRE 06] GREENFIELD A., *Dawning Age of Ubiquitous Computing*, Peachpit Press, Berkerley, 2006.

[KLE 08] KLEIN E., GRINBAUM A., BONTEMS V., "Nanosciences: les enjeux d'un débat", *Le Débat*, vol. 1, no. 148, 2008.

Chapter 3

Sensor Networks

3.1. MAC layers for wireless sensor networks

Energy consumption is one key feature of wireless sensor networks. A whole field of research has been dedicated to reducing radio usage since radio transceivers are a huge source of energy consumption. Since medium access control is closely related to the energy performance of wireless sensor networks, several medium access protocols (MAC protocols or, more commonly, MAC layers) have been proposed throughout the literature.

This chapter will examine the different techniques used to access medium radio in wireless sensor networks. This section will not attempt to provide an exhaustive overview given the vast body of literature on the subject. We will also not detail all the protocols presented in the literature nor all current standards. For a more extensive overview, Bachir *et al.* [BAC 10] summarize and describe a large proportion of the protocols and techniques to which we will refer in detail.

3.1.1. *Challenges at MAC level*

Medium access control for wireless sensor networks must respond to a simple objective. The MAC sub-layer of OSI model is responsible for the efficient and fair distribution of medium radio usage. For a correct MAC layer design for wireless sensor networks and to respond to this objective, the MAC layer must have the following characteristics:

Chapter written by Jean CARLE, Michaël HAUSPIE, Nathalie MITTON, Tahiry RAZAFINDRALAMBO and David SIMPLOT-RYL.

Energy efficiency: the MAC sub-layer must reduce energy consumption at each sensor. This characteristic is important because wireless sensors are built with batteries that are difficult, if not often impossible, to replace once the network has been deployed.

Latency: latency is often linked to the requirements of the application being used. While detecting events where sending an urgent message to a central operator is necessary, reduced latency is required. Latency is often tied to the concept of real time in sensor networks.

Throughput: throughput is also related to the application. Surveillance applications often require a strong temporal resolution, which demands a large quantity of data from the sensors. For this type of application, it is therefore necessary to provide higher throughput at MAC level.

Fairness: fairness is an intrinsic characteristic a MAC protocol must possess. It is necessary in a wireless sensor network that the central entity (sink) receives the data from each sensor fairly.

The need for these characteristics is strongly related to the application in question, irrespective of energy consumption and fairness. It should be noted that it is very difficult to have an MAC layer which possesses all these characteristics, therefore often entailing a certain level of compromise.

3.1.2. *Energy consumption*

Energy consumption is the reason for designing specific MAC protocols for wireless sensor networks. There are four main sources of energy consumption at MAC level:

– collisions or, more generally, packet losses represent the main source of energy consumption because a lost packet must be retransmitted the majority of the time. In addition, retransmission increases latency;

– the reception of a packet by a sensor, which is not the intended destination, also represents a large source of energy loss;

– control packets, which are often used for network maintenance and are regularly sent by sensors, result in loss of energy because they can sometimes be less useful than data packets;

– actively listening to the radio channel without receiving data consumes as much energy as receiving it.

3.1.3. *Parameters for evaluating a MAC layer*

The number of MAC protocols proposed in the literature requires the use of common parameters to evaluate and compare their performance. The following are the main parameters to be considered:

– Energy consumption: this often takes the form of joules/bits and is calculated as the ratio between the total amount of energy consumed over the total number of useful bits of transmitted data. The smaller this value, the more effective the protocol is.

– Delivery rate: this is the number of packets received (by the final destination) over the number of packets transmitted for this destination.

– Latency or delay: this is the average time taken for a packet to travel from its source to its destination.

– Throughput: this is the amount of useful data received per unit of time.

3.1.4. *MAC Protocols*

MAC protocols in sensor networks can be classified according to two categories: contention protocols and explicit scheduling protocols. The latter prevent collisions and enable active listening on the channel for useless receptions. However, this requires strict sensor synchronization. On the other hand, contention protocols do not have a synchronization aspect and are tolerant to changes in topology but do not prevent collisions or active listening on the radio channel.

The IEEE 802.11[IEE 99] standard is a contention-based protocol. The energy-saving part described in the standard, PSM (*Power Save Mode*), reduces active listening on the channel by authorizing sensors to turn off their radio transmitter. The need for synchronization in using PSM makes the use of IEEE 802.11 in multi-hop sensor networks difficult. The IEEE 802.15.4 standard [IEE 03] is similar to 802.11, but focuses on the energy aspect which requires synchronization.

PAMAS [SIN 98] is one of the first protocols allowing sensors to completely turn off their radio transmitters to save energy. This protocol uses two radio interfaces, one for data packets and the other for control packets. The use of these two interfaces increases sensor cost considerably and MAC layer complexity. It should also be noted that the energy consumed in the transition between off and on mode for the transceiver is not significant.

S-MAC [YE 02] is a protocol based on the issue raised in 802.11. In this MAC protocol, sensors change from sleep mode to listening mode to reduce energy consumption. A temporal framework is defined by S-MAC and contains a listening period in which sensors can initiate communication using control packets (RTS, CTS,

SYNC) and a period where the sensors can turn off their radio. S-MAC does, however, exhibit problems during the listening period, which consumes energy even if no data are being transmitted.

An improvement on the ALOHA protocol [ABR 70] is proposed in [ELH 02], which adds a preamble sampling technique. This protocol proposes that each transmitter sends a preamble before transmitting data. Each sensor can therefore be synchronized on this preamble to receive the message. To save energy, the potential receivers show themselves for a short period to listen if a preamble is transmitting and returns to off mode if not. If a preamble is received, the receiver continues to listen to the medium radio until the data is received.

WiseMAC [ENZ 04] combines the explicit scheduling and preamble sampling approaches. The sensors use two channels, one with explicit scheduling to access the data channel and the other with preamble sampling to access the control channel. WiseMAC adapts to traffic flow and has superior performance to that of S-MAC.

B-MAC [POL 04] is similar to the solution presented in [ELH 02]. However, in B-MAC, the length of the preamble is a protocol of the parameter and can be modified. B-MAC is therefore a trade-off between delay, throughput, and energy consumption.

In this section we have introduced some of the MAC layers proposed in the literature. [BAC 10] provides a more extensive overview of current work in the field. Over recent years, a large number of protocols have emerged in the literature. However, there are still several other aspects that must be considered while creating or improving existing protocols such as security, mobility, and real-time aspects.

3.2. Topology control

In the case of wired networks, the network's structure is fixed in advance and does not (or at least to a very small extent) evolve over time. As such, ensuring connectivity in a fixed structure is a question of material maintenance (node or failed link) or controlling congestion (avoiding or repairing digital gridlocks).

In the case of dynamic networks, the communication structure is no longer fixed but is variable over time. There are a number of reasons for this:

Mobility: physical communication connections change according to the distance between nodes. The neighborhood of each node u (defined as the set of nodes with a direct radio connection with u) and therefore the network's structure, is, as a result, modified.

Loss of nodes: this can occur due to breakdowns in the material, batteries which are too weak, or even voluntary standby (for conserving energy, for example).

Appearance of nodes: this can occur when a node which was previously in standby is turned on or when new nodes are deployed.

Environment: on the one hand, wireless communications are subject to electromagnetic hazards. On the other, a growing number of nodes in a communication zone will increase interference which therefore limits the consequences of communication connections.

Topology control aims to manage all these phenomena in order to ensure connectivity in the graph associated with the network. It can also be used to simplify the associated graph. For example, the selection of edges to obtain a spanning tree (used by some distributed algorithms) or a spanning planar sub-graph (graph containing all the nodes of the network with no intersection between edges) used, for example, in geographic routing (see section 3.3.3).

Topology control uses techniques to maintain connectivity and reduce the number of edges in the graph associated with the network. In the next section, we will introduce a technique for reducing the number of edges by adjusting the communication range. The following section will explain the notion of managing the surveillance coverage zone using sensor networks. This involves activity scheduling, that is, managing the activation and standby of nodes in an optimization optic of the network's life span.

For an alternative perspective on topology control, see Santi [SAN 05] or chapters in [FRE 08, MIT 09, SIM 05].

3.2.1. *Range adjustment*

Range adjustment consists of adapting the communication range for each node. This "*filters the neighborhood*" by eliminating neighbors, thereby limiting interference and conserving energy. Reducing interference limits the retransmission of messages which in turn preserves various resources (processor, memory, energy, bandwidth) in the nodes and network and provides better network performance (reduced delay and jig, better output, etc.). Adjusting its range reduces the energy consumption of the nodes since the further a node transmits, the more energy it requires. To calculate energy cost for a node to transmit to a distance r, we commonly use the following formula proposed in [ROD 99]:

$$cost(r) \quad = \quad \begin{cases} r^\alpha + c & \text{if } r \neq 0 \\ 0 & \text{otherwise} \end{cases} \qquad [3.1]$$

where c is a constant symbolizing the cost of processing the signal and α is a real constant (≥ 2) representing the disappearance of the signal. Note, however, that for this formula to be completely exact, the cost must again be multiplied by a value that accounts for packet size.

As such, when radio chips allow it, the network depends on how its nodes adjust their range. A change of range can take place in a general and permanent way or for a specific application. In permanent cases, each node adapts its range to reduce its number of neighbors (nodes with which it can directly communicate) to reduce the size of neighborhood tables (and therefore an increase in memory), to accelerate calculations (increase in processing) and reduce collisions and interference while ensuring that the network remains connected as a whole. To do so, we generally use neighborhood reduction graphs which are subgraphs of the original graph G. They are designed to maintain connectivity with G and are calculated in a both local and a distributed way, that is only using topological information about its neighborhood to one or two jumps (links to and between neighbors) or to only one jump if we know the node's geographical positions. There are several of these graphs in the literature, but the two most commonly used are the Gabriel graph (GG) and the relative neighborhood graph (RNG) [TOU 80]. The Gabriel graph retains an edge between the nodes u and v if there is a node w in the disk with a diameter of uv, as shown by Figure 3.1.

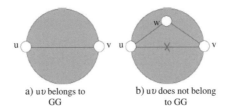

a) uv belongs to
GG

b) uv does not belong
to GG

Figure 3.1. *Illustration of the Gabriel graph*

The RNG, however, uses any weight on its edges. In every triangle uvw, it retains the edge with the strongest weight. If the weight used is the edge's Euclidean distance, it will retain the edge uvw if, and only if, there is a node w in the disk with a radius of uv, as shown in Figure 3.2. In the latter case, we have the following relationship $\text{RNG}(G) \subseteq \text{GG}(G) \subseteq G$.

Figure 3.3 provides an example of a unitary graph a) from which the Gabriel b) and relative neighborhood c) graphs have been extracted. Based on the calculation of this subgraph, each node will adjust its range in order to join its most distant neighbor in this subgraph. With the range reduced, it does the same for the other neighbors and the network's connectivity is guaranteed.

Range adjustment is also used on a case-by-case basis. It is notably used by certain routing algorithms [ELH 09, SAN 06, STO 04b], as explained in section 3.3.3

or diffusion algorithms (see section 3.3.1). The idea is that when a node u needs to broadcast or transmit a message, it selects the neighbor(s) v to whom it will transmit the message based on an energy criterion. Once the node(s) v has(ve) been selected, u adjusts its range so that it reaches all or only the node(s) v. This allows us to limit the number of nodes receiving the message when they are not affected by it and optimize energy consumption throughout the network.

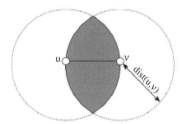

Figure 3.2. *Calculation of an RNG with Euclidean distance: if a node w exists in the gray zone, the edge (u, v) will not belong to the RNG graph*

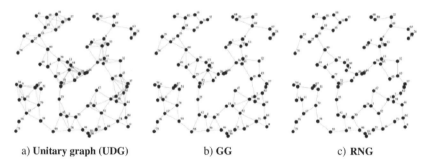

a) **Unitary graph (UDG)**   b) **GG**   c) **RNG**

Figure 3.3. *A unitary graph with its associated GG and RNG sub-graphs*

3.2.2. *Spanning*

One of the main characteristics that marks out *ad hoc* networks from sensor networks (or actuators) are the materials used. Indeed, as with *ad hoc* networks, sensor networks have nodes with memory, calculation, and communication capacities, but they also have the capacity to sense the physical environment around the sensor(s) fitted in the nodes and, in the case of actuators, the ability to modify this environment (move an object, send an antidote to the right place, emit a sound, etc.). It is this characteristic which characterizes these new networks and which raises the coverage problem that we will discuss here.

3.2.2.1. *Different coverages*

Standard coverage in wireless networks refers to communication links which transmit data between all the nodes in the network, either directly, where we talk about one-hop communication, or indirectly where we speak of multi-hop communication.

3.2.2.1.1. Single coverage

However, coverage for sensor networks raises the question of the quality of surveillance in a geographic zone by a set of sensors organized in network [HUA 05, MEG 01] in order to map the environment, follow objects, and/or detect abnormal events. For instance, a sudden increase in temperature associated with a fall in hygrometric degree can indicate a fire, and an alarm may sound at the appropriate fire station.

As such, as illustrated in Figure 3.6, spanning a zone in the context of sensor networks entails ensuring its surveillance with its level of reliability depending on the application (a form of quality of service). To allow surveillance to continue for as long as possible, it is necessary to optimize node use. We therefore want to minimize the number of active nodes required for this surveillance and put others in standby to conserve energy. They will be used to replace broken-down nodes and as such lengthen the duration of effective surveillance.

3.2.2.1.2. Multiple coverage

For economic reasons, materials are not perfect, and due to the as-yet insufficient knowledge of good materials, the activities carried out by a sensor are still fairly basic [GAU 06]. Therefore, it may be interesting to have several active nodes on the same zone at the same time. A basic definition of multiple coverage is as follows: we have a k-coverage if every geographic point in the zone being monitored is covered by k sensors.

Each active node analyzes its environment, either regularly for continuous surveillance, or is triggered by a specific event (e.g. to reinforce existing surveillance). Each node has a partial and localized view of the zone. The network organization for nodes participating in sensing and the implemented communication protocol allow those collecting information, also known as a sink nodes, to have a digital view of the monitored area [AKY 02]. With this in mind, some issues may be the surface and quality of a sensor's surveillance zone. A number of models have been proposed to respond to these questions.

3.2.2.2. *Models*

Isotropic models are those most frequently used in the literature, several examples of which are provided in Figure 3.4. Due to the absence of precise information about the material (e.g. detailed characteristics and position on the node) and on the physical environment, it is not possible to obtain a realistic sensing model. Figure 3.5 gives an example of an experimental model carried out in open parking with infrared sensors, which shows anisotropy in a real-life situation. Figure 3.5 shows, for a single sensor (the object numbered as 0), the differences between an isotropic model (the unit disk model, Figure 3.4) and a more realistic model, where some states (in this case objects 1 and 4) will be treated differently.

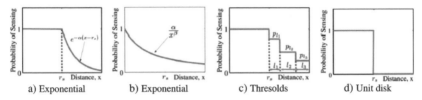

a) Exponential   b) Exponential   c) Thresolds   d) Unit disk

Figure 3.4. *Isotropic models for a sensor's detection zone [HWA 07]*

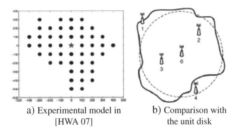

a) Experimental model in   b) Comparison with
[HWA 07]   the unit disk

Figure 3.5. *Irregularities at the edge of an infrared sensor's zone*

This confirms that practical studies are a necessary step. However, theoretical studies still remain essential for upstream optimization of management protocols in the coverage area. In the rest of this chapter, we will assume that nodes have sensors adapted to their desired aim (temperature, light or sound power, vibration, density of harmful gases, measure of electromagnetic fields, etc.). For simplicity, we will suppose that each node allows surveillance in a circular zone in which it is the center.

3.2.2.3. *Different coverage qualities*

R_S^i is the sensing radius of the node i, $\mathcal{N}$ is the set of nodes in the network, and $\mathcal{A}$ the zone in which surveillance is being carried out. When zone $\mathcal{A}$ is completely covered, every point, p, of $\mathcal{A}$ is covered by at least one node in the network (Figure 3.6): $\forall p \in \mathcal{A}, \exists i \in \mathcal{N} \mid d(p,i) \leq R_S^i$, where $d(p,i)$ is the distance function between p and the node i.

Some applications do not require complete spanning. Gaps in coverage (Figures 3.6 and 3.6) are acceptable. This is the case with, for example, surveillance of static and persistent events (extended over time such as a fire in a warehouse) or over space (surface or volume greater than that of the sensor such as a gas leak). For the surveillance of mobile objects, a non-closed partial coverage (Figure 3.6) is not sufficient. We cannot, therefore, guarantee, at a given moment, the position of an object that is in a gap of open coverage at a previous point (for instance, the object could be out of the area). However, if gaps in coverage are closed (Figure 3.6 where the contour is completely covered), we can therefore at least ensure that the object is still in the zone or we can count the tracked objects.

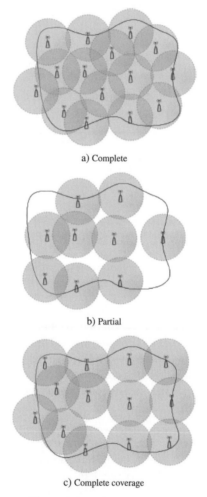

a) Complete

b) Partial

c) Complete coverage

Figure 3.6. *Different coverage*

Several constraints are related to this problem of coverage, the main constraints being that of connectivity and energy consumption. The first constraint is very significant and occurs for several reasons. A reason is structural since, without connectivity, there is no communication and therefore no network. The second reason is more applicative. This is because sensor networks are typically used either to signal specific phenomena (fire, a leak of toxic gas, intrusion, etc.) or to monitor mobile objects on the ground (e.g. car tracking). Connectivity is therefore required each time we want to propagate information to other nodes, in particular toward sinks that collect and analyze data for the entire zone.

In terms of energy constraints, these are important due to the use of batteries. The node's life span, and therefore the network itself, is limited as the materials involved are small and costly. In addition, the replacement of batteries is a costly process because it requires external (often human) intervention. This replacement is not always desirable or even possible, for example, in case of deployment in inaccessible or dangerous zones (mountains, underwater, concrete encased sensors, behind enemy lines, etc.). The network must therefore respond to the demands of the application for as long as possible without external intervention. The energy resource is thus an important parameter for which the material and the entire chain of protocols (coverage protocols included) must be taken into account. During deployment, redundancy is also used to balance energy consumption between sensors.

Note that in the context of networks with low ressources, in terms of memory, energy and communication, only the use of distributed protocols based on local knowledge of topology is recommended because they generate less traffic and use less memory than centralized or standard distributed algorithms. The result is that they are often less efficient because their rules are based on a restricted knowledge of the topology.

3.2.2.4. *Coverage protocols*

PEAS [YE 03] uses a probabilistic approach. Each node decides to go into standby if it has at least one sufficiently close neighbor. To ensure a good level of coverage, the threshold distance must be far less than the surveillance radius (threshold $\leq \frac{R_S}{1+\sqrt{5}}$ for a probability of coverage close to 1). The active nodes remain so until all their energy has been used. The nodes in standby take over as active nodes turn off. The advantage is that each node only needs the distance with its neighbors.

A method based on Markov chains is proposed in [YEN 07]. The analysis shows that it is possible to change the standby probability of the nodes in order to ensure total coverage (in probability) at the same time as connectivity of the network. The advantage is that this takes place irrespective of the relationship between R_C (communication radius) and R_S (sensing radius). Nevertheless, any change in configuration requires complex readjustments, which could present an obstacle to use in highly dynamic networks.

In [TIA 02, TIA 05], the solution is determinist and is based on the knowledge of neighbors, their positions, and their coverage. A node will decide to go into standby if there are enough neighbors to cover its own zone. In addition, this requires synchronization of the network and a management of a unique key for each node. If coverage is complete in this protocol, the connectivity constraint becomes useless. The connectivity constraint is cleared by making hypotheses on the characteristics of the materials used: all the nodes must be equal (same communication radius R_C and sensing radius R_S) and verify $R_C \geq R_S$, which ensures the network's connectivity [XIN 05]. If the relationship $R_C/R_S \geq 1$ is possible at time of the network's deployment, it will change (and could be inverted) at a different speed for each node. Thus, the radii's homogeneity hypothesis will be incorrect. Errors in transmission will also affect the overall performance [GAL 06].

Based on the same principle of evaluating neighbors' positions, [CAR 05a] proposes considering connectivity at the same time as coverage without dependency between communication and surveillance radii. A heuristic on the relay selection, in the same way as with multi-point relays, increases the network's life span and transmission errors, thanks to the (lower) number of messages generated, and also gives a better resistance to message loss [GAL 08].

3.2.2.5. *Protocols for multi-coverage*

All the protocols presented until now have attempted to reduce the number of active nodes. Measures carried out by a sensor are not always few (due to the lack of materials or the non-existence of good materials). Due to this, it may be better to have several nodes carry out sensing on a single zone at the same time.

If we have enough nodes (we will call n this number of nodes), multiple coverage can be achieved by carrying out the chosen coverage method several times and taking care to exclude the nodes used in the previous execution. We therefore talk about multi-coverage using layers, giving k disjoint subsets of n_i nodes ($i \in \{1, 2 \ldots, k\}$, $\sum_i n_i \leq n$) for k single coverage. However, this intuitive method for solving the multiple coverage problem respects a more precise definition than multiple coverage. Indeed, it uses disjoint sets which are not obligatory for obtaining coverage of all the geographic points with k sensors.

The majority of contributions focusing on multiple coverage are not localized. They often consist of centralized solutions which are transformed into distributed versions requiring information on several jumps (number of intermediary transmissions to reach a given node) [ABR 04, AMM 09, TIA 05, ZHO 04]. A large majority are also extensions of single-coverage methods [GAL 07, GAL 08, TIA 05].

3.3. Routing

Routing is the mechanism by which paths are selected in a network to move data from a sender to one or several destinations. While high performing and effective in wireless networks, routing proves to be a more difficult task in sensor networks due to, on the one hand, sensors' hardware constraints (lack of memory, limited calculation capacity, battery life) and, on the other, the medium radio range which means that two non-connected nodes do not know each other. When the message is sent to all the nodes in the network, it is called broadcasting. This is what we will discuss in section 3.3.1. When the message is destined for a single receiver, we speak of unicast routing. There are several families of unicast routing protocols for sensor networks, which include 1) "classic" protocols taken from *ad hoc* networks and 2) protocols based on the geographic position of nodes. These two types of routing will be examined in the rest of this chapter.

3.3.1. *Broadcast*

Broadcast consists of sending a message from a source node toward all other nodes in the network. This a tool used by classic routing protocols (see section 3.3.2 for an explanation of routing). The simplest approach for disseminating a message is blind flooding: when a node receives the transmitted message for the first time, it retransmits it to its neighbors. This mechanism imposes enormous strain on the network, causing a number of messages and collisions, requiring a lot of energy and bandwidth [NI 99]. It is for this reason that such a mechanism cannot be applied to dense or WAN networks. This requires the use of more intelligent broadcast protocols which reduce the number of retransmissions required and only allow a subset of nodes to transmit.

The approaches examined initially suppose that nodes are not able to adjust their range and have tried to determine a set of "dominant" nodes. In order for all the nodes in the network to receive the message, each of the nodes must be either dominant or the neighbor of at least a dominant node. The difficulty is therefore in finding this kind of connected dominating set of a minimum size, which also minimizes the number of redundant receptions of a message retransmitted by this set. This problem is shown to be NP-difficult [GAR 79]. Various works have focused on constructing this set through different means. Some are based on electing a leader for each node. A node neighboring several leaders is said to be a gateway and the leaders and gateways constitute the dominating set [CHI 96, EPH 87, GER 95]. Other approaches proceed by elimination. This is the case with the solution proposed in [WU 01], and reformulated in [CAR 04a] as follows: a node u is not dominant if the set of its neighbors with greater priority[1] is connected and covers the set of neighbors of u.

---

1 The node identifier can be considered as a priority.

The dominating sets can therefore be used for several types of applications (deployment, routing, auto-organization), but where their only use is broadcast, it raises the problem of fairness of charge for nodes in the network. Indeed, a dominating set is constructed independently of the message source. The set is the same irrespective of the source and, as a result, it is always the same nodes which are used for broadcast and which exhaust their resources. Some approaches have therefore proposed solutions where relayers depend on the source of the message. This is the case with, for example, Multi Point Relay (MPR) [QAY 02] developed in the OLSR routing protocol (see section 3.3.2).

Optimal selection of MPR is an NP-complete problem [JAC 02]. We will examine here the most frequently used algorithm, the *Simple Greedy MPR Heuristic* [QAY 02]. Each node chooses its MPR from its 1-hop neighbors in order to span all its 2-hop neighbors in exactly 2 hops. The MPR selection algorithm is split into two stages. The first stage selects the node v which spans the neighboring "isolated nodes" within two hops. A node that is isolated in relation to u is a 2-hop neighbor, which only has a single 1-hop neighbor shared with u, which we will call v. This is the case with, for example, v_4 and v_8 in Figure 3.7, which are the isolated nodes for u (u does not know the connection between v_8 and v_9). These isolated nodes must necessarily belong to the set of MPRs in u for the 2-neighbor to be completely spanned. $MPR_1(u)$ is the set of MPRs of u selected during this first stage (nodes v_6 and v_7 in Figure 3.7). The second stage selects the neighbors of u which do not belong to $MPR_1(u)$ and spans the maximum number of 2-hop neighbors not already spanned by $MPR_1(u)$.

For example, in Figure 3.7, the nodes v_3 and v_4 still need to be spanned. To do so, u has the choice between the nodes v_1, v_2 and v_5. The node v_1 spans the set of nodes remaining rather than the others, it becomes an MPR of u. The second stage is repeated until all the 2-hop neighbors of u are spanned. Several algorithms have therefore been proposed to reduce the number of MPRs selected per node (and therefore the number of retransmissions) but since the algorithm's first stage is necessary and selects a greater proportion of MPRs (more than 75% according to [BUS 05]), these variants only give small improvements. The authors of [KHA 10, MOR 06] have relaxed this strong constraint to propose variants that enable better performance in terms of QoS. By allowing a 1- or 2-hop neighbor to reach a neighbor via several intermediaries that offer better QoS criteria (the selection of MPRs is thefore governed by calculating better paths on a neighbor with different criteria such as delay or bandwidth), these new propositions significantly increase the QoS performance of selected routes while reducing the number of selected MPRs per node. In Figure 3.7, if we suppose that the weight on the edges represents the bandwidth value, we see that in two hops, the node v_4 could benefit from a bandwidth of 4 (uv_1v_4) while there is a 3-hop path $uv_1v_5v_4$, which gives a bandwidth of 5 and which will be found by [KHA 10].

The authors of [STO 02] have proposed another kind of algorithm based on eliminating neighbors called *Wait and See*. On receiving the transmitted message, a node waits for a random period of time where it waits to see if one of these neighbors retransmits the message and, if so, which of its neighbors receive this information. If, at the end of the wait period (and only in this case), there are nodes among the neighbors which have not received the message, then it transmits the message. The authors of [CAR 03] have also proposed an improvement on this algorithm focusing on the RNG (see section 3.2.1) rather than the real graph.

These diagrams, based on eliminating neighbors (*Wait & See* and *Wait & See* based on RNG), obtain excellent performance in terms of the number of transmissions and receptions, but entail significant latency in the broadcast process due to the random wait period of each node.

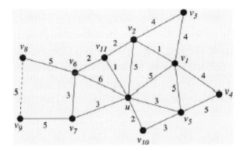

Figure 3.7. *Example MPR selection*

All these approaches have a common feature in that they do not account for the fact that some nodes can adjust their range. This is not the case in [CAR 03, WIE 00] and [CAR 04b], which use range adaptation and topology control to increase broadcast performance. Each node adjusts its range to reach the node furthest from a subgraph, the minimum tree spanning for [WIE 00] (which has the disadvantage of being centralized), the RNG for the RBOP protocol [CAR 03], or the LMST for LBOP [CAR 04b]. On receiving the message, each node retransmits in the same way. These techniques have obtained good performance in terms of energy use.

Other approaches use range adaptation to construct a broadcast tree that optimizes energy costs. The original idea is the centralized *broadcast incremental power protocol* (BIP protocol) [WIE 00]. The tree's root is a source node fixed in advance with the calculation of a new tree being required when this node changes. The main idea is to consider the natural advantage of omni-directional wireless transmissions for broadcast: a message transmitted by a node u with a range $r(u)$ is received by *all* the neighbors of u in the radio range. The tree is constructed greedily. At each stage, we insert a node (which is not yet in the tree) into the tree requiring the least additional power to be spanned and the corresponding edge. For example, in Figure 3.7, if the source is the node u, we will add the node $v_1 0$, the edge uv_{10} being the shortest and therefore the most energy efficient. Subsequently, for each neighbor of u and v_{10}, we calculate the least costly solution to insert into the tree. For example, to join the node v_5, BIP will see if it is better to add the tree $v_{10}v_5$ or extend the range of u so that the edge uv_5 is in a tree. This maintains the edge uv_{10} due to the omni-directional nature of the radio transmission, and the tree is calculated. Each node then adjusts its range in order to join its neighbors in the tree. If we refer to the energy model given by equation [3.1], the existence of the constant c entails the creation of a new transmission since a node that has not transmitted yet may be more costly than increasing the range of a node which has already transmitted (and which has therefore paid the cost of this constant).

The authors of [ING 08] have proposed a distributed and localized version of this algorithm called *localized broadcast incremental power protocol* (LBIP). In LBIP, each node only knows its k-hop neighbors. As such, the source nodes apply BIP in its k-hop neighborhood (in general, $k = 2$) and transmit the message locally by inserting the list of internal nodes in the tree, which it has calculated using the associated range. On receiving the message, these same nodes repeat the algorithm based on the results provided by the previous relay. In functioning in this way, a broadcast structure is constructed incrementally from multiple small, locally calculated BIP trees.

3.3.2. *Classic routing*

Routing protocols for "classic" sensor networks are, in general, designed as a basis for *ad hoc* networks. There are normally two major families of "classic" routing protocols in the literature:

Proactive: the routes to all the nodes in the network are established and maintained permanently on each node. The advantage of this kind of process is that a route is available immediately, irrespective of the destination. The disadvantages are the size of routing tables to be maintained on each node (size in $O(n)$ if n is the number of nodes in the network) and the number of control messages to be sent periodically to update all the routes that have not yet been used.

Reactive: the routes are built on demand. The advantage of this kind of protocol is that it reduces the average size of routing tables and does not periodically send route request messages. The disadvantage is that when routing is necessary, searching for the route at the node destination can take a long time, entailing significant latency and requiring a flood of the network.

3.3.2.1. *Proactive routing protocols*

In proactive routing, each node maintains a permanent overview of the network. The basic principles of all protocols are the same. They are based on periodically sending Hello messages as happens with some routing protocols in the wire (OSPF [MOY 94]) to communicate their presence and often their neighborhood table. Each node therefore learns of the existence of all the nodes in its range (its neighbors) with additional information on other links.

Protocols differ in the way routes are calculated, information is stored (entire route or just the next hop), transmitted (complete or limited flooding) and maintained (sent periodically or only during important modifications). The nodes establish routing tables in two ways using:

– BellmanFord distance vectors (such as DSDV [PER 94], WRP [MUR 96]). The nodes transmit, using Hello packets, their routing table in which each node is associated with its distance according to the number of hops. Regular updates between the nodes communicate modifications in topology. The algorithm collects the distances in order to maintain information on the network's topology. This method generally suffers from a loop creation phenomenon, which explains why it is less commonly used. DSDV [PER 94], however, overcomes this problem by using sequence numbers to identify the date the information is received.

– Dijkstra state links [DIJ 59] (such as OLSR [CLA 03], GSR [CHE 98], and Fish-eye state routing [GER 02, PEI 00]). The nodes send the state of the relationship separating it from other nodes to their neighbors (their neighborhood table only) and not the number of hops separating it from every other node in the network. In this way, each node can produce a map of the network's state and, as a result, choose the most appropriate route for a message at any given moment;

The most recent protocols are generally based on state-link algorithms because this method exchanges less information which generates smaller packets that are therefore transmitted with fewer errors and use less bandwidth and energy meaning that routes are calculated more quickly. In all cases, Hello messages still containing the node identifier are periodically sent. Other information is added to these messages depending on the protocol. The majority of proactive protocols transmit information designed to calculate routes only when there are changes in the link or distance. This method can be optimized as FSR [GER 02, PEI 00] has done or ZHLS [HAM 06]; for example, in the following way. The closer the neighbors are, the more frequently topological information concerning them is sent. As such, the precision of routes decreases with distance. The idea is that a node a wanting to join a distant node b only has imprecise information about b, but does at least know the direction in which to send the message. The closer to the node we are, the more precise the maintained routes are. This type of algorithm allows easier scaling due to the fact that it limits the transmission of maintenance messages in the area. Algorithms also differ in the way that routing information is transmitted in the network. This aspect is not always considered in algorithms that rely on one of the diffusion methods developed in section 3.3.1.

The most commonly used and deployed routing algorithm today is the *Optimized Link-State Routing* (OSLR) protocol [CLA 03], which, as its name indicates, is a state-link routing. OSLR is a standardized protocol at the IETF. OLSR has introduced an optimized transmission using multi-point relays (MPR) as described in section 3.3.1. OLSR periodically transmits TC (*Topology Control*) packets containing only the list of MPRs from a node, the latter being only those authorized to relay information.

3.3.2.2. *Reactive routing protocols*

Reactive routing protocols construct a route on demand. In contrast to proactive protocols, they do not always require the use of Hello packets. However, they do always need a flooding mechanism and all the links must be bidirectional. The source transmits its message to all its neighbors which retransmit the received packet. Only the destination does not retransmit the message. As such, transmission continues after being received by the destination that uses up all the network's bandwidth and the nodes' energy. Protocols differ mainly in terms of information stored throughout flooding, the chosen route mechanism, and the way in which information is protected to limit route demands. In some cases, as with *Dynamic Source Routing* (DSR) [JOH 01], the entire route is determined by the source to the destination. For example, in Figure 3.8, the node *a* seeks the node *b*. It transmits a "*Route Request*" (RR) in which all the intermediary nodes enter their identifier into the message before relaying it. The message therefore arrives at *b*, which stops flooding, extracts the packet route, and includes it in the message and sends it to *a* in the form of a "*Route Reply*". Contrary to the "*Route Request*", the "*Route Reply*" does not flood the network but follows the route prescribed by *b* (Figure 3.8). In order to limit the discovery of routes, the nodes participate in discovering *b* for *a*, and also store information as the message is transmitted. For example, in Figure 3.8, the intermediary nodes extract routes toward the other nodes in the "*Route Reply*". This is, for example, what has allowed the node *e* in Figure 3.8 to stop flooding and send a "*Route Reply*" because it had an instruction route for the node *b*.

Including the route in the message does not allow the large-scale use of these kinds of protocol. The packet grows with the size of the route which generates a growing use of bandwidth, memory required in the nodes, and energy resources. It is for this reason that other algorithms such as AODV [PER 03] only store the first hop on the list as well as the distance in the number of hops. In the same way, the nodes discover routes providing them with information contained in the "*Route Reply*".

Maintaining routes is generally carried out by nodes. Each node on a route is responsible for the link that separates it from its next neighbor on the path. If the link breaks, depending on the algorithm, an error message can be sent directly to the source, as [JOH 01] has done, or a local reconstruction (by localized flooding) is initiated and only in case of failure is the source notified [PER 03].

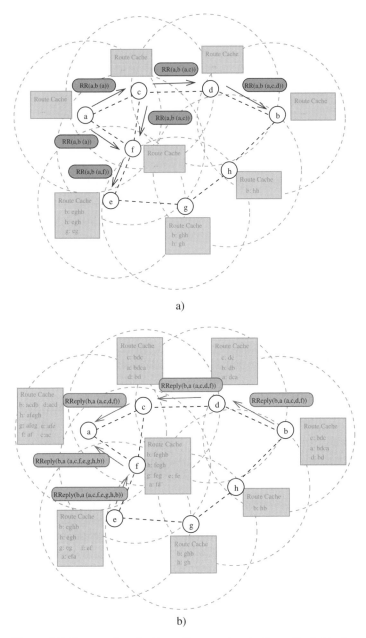

Figure 3.8. *Propagation of a Route Request a) and a Route Reply b) of a toward b in DSR. The gray squares represent the instruction for each node, the rounded boxes being the message content on a link*

In all these cases, the management of instructions/routing tables is complex because storing unbeneficial information for too long requires memory while suppressing it too quickly generates new route discoveries, which could have been avoided. AODV is currently the most commonly used reactive protocol and is the standard at IETF. However, there are a number of variations of AODV and DSV such as *Temporary Ordering Routing Algorithm* (TORA) [PAR 01], for example, which aims to store several paths. For example, in Figure 3.8, the node a can maintain the routes $acdb$ and $afegb$ toward b with TORA while the DSR only maintains the shortest. This introduces an additional cost in terms of memory and maintenance, but increases transmission reliability. Others such as *Signal Stability-based Routing* (SSR) [DUB 97] favor one route over another based on the strength of the signal received on each link.

3.3.3. *Geographic routing*

The complexity of control messages and the size of memory required in geographic routing protocols is, in the majority of cases, $O(1)$, without accounting for the complexity due to the construction of geographic coordinates if this construction is necessary/exists. It is this reduced complexity, among other factors, which has motivated the design of routing protocols using sensors' coordinates. In addition, the low cost of GPS and applications requiring an increasing number of sensors have only reinforced the need for the use and design of these protocols.

Geographic routing is based on several hypotheses:

– each sensor knows its position;

– each sensor knows the position of its neighbors;

– each sensor knows the coordinates (real or virtual) of each of its neighbors.

Geographic routing protocols use information on geographic location coordinates from a sensor to make decisions about routing. This geographic information is generally provided by a positioning system such as GPS or obtained using successive interpolations using the positions of neighboring sensors. A number of protocols also propose constructing virtual coordinates, which are more or less close to real coordinates.

3.3.3.1. *Properties of geographic routing*

The basic principle of geographic routing is based on the distance between the source and its destination. The routing decision is made so that the sensor selected as being the next jump is closer in terms of distance from the destination than the sensor in question. Note that in some cases there is no closer sensor than the sensor in question.

This routing principle obtains the following properties which allow the scaling and use of these kind of protocols in restricted environments:

Localized: only local information is required to make the routing decision. This information includes the position of the sensor possessing the packet, the position of this sensor's neighbors, and the position of the destination. The location of information required for the routing decision enables easier scaling of geographic routing protocols.

Distributed: all the sensors run the same algorithm. Again, this property increases resistance for better scaling.

Memoryless: sensors, in contrast to normal routing nodes, do not need to maintain the routing table. In addition, it is also not necessary to include additional information in the packet.

3.3.3.2. *Principles and challenges*

The majority of geographic protocols proposed in the literature are greedy. In these protocols, the routing decision is made so that the sensor chosen as the next hop is the closest in terms of distance to the destination [BEN 09, CAR 05b, FIN 87, TAK 84]. These protocols differ by the real ([FIN 87, TAK 84]) and virtual coordinates systems ([BEN 09, CAR 05b]) used. Greedy routing does, nevertheless, pose delivery guarantee problems because in some cases there is no sensor closer to the destination than the sensor in question.

Despite the simplicity of greedy geographic routings, several fundamental problems are raised, particularly when this routing is applied to wireless sensor networks. Beyond the problem of obtaining positions, two objectives must be attained, irrespective of the system of coordinates used:

Delivery rate: contrary to normal routing, in wireless networks, geographic routing does not systematically guarantee delivery of a packet even if a path between the source and the destination exists. Solutions to guarantee delivery have been proposed in FACE by Stojmenovic *et al.* [BOS 99], for example. This solution relies on graph planarization[2] while remaining local. The use of the subgraph extracted after planarization prevents deadlock during routing. Note that this planarization is only effective when using real geographic coordinates. Chavez *et al.* propose LTP in [CHA 07] which guarantees the delivery of packets by using a system of virtual coordinates based on the construction of a tree. The two approaches cited above have a shared problem. This is because the length of routes created by routing is far from being optimal, which increases energy consumption during routing. An improvement of FACE, which is only required in case of routing failure, has been proposed in GFG [STO 04a].

---

2 See section 3.2.1.

Energy: as mentioned in previous sections, reducing energy consumption is one of the strongest constraints on sensor networks. It must be conserved throughout the protocol stack and routing is no exception to this. Stojmenovic *et al.* in [STO 01] have calculated the optimum transmission range, which minimizes energy consumption while transmitting a message. The choice of next hop can therefore be influenced by this optimum range. The mechanisms of energy conservation have been applied to greedy routing protocols for each type of real [STO 04b] and virtual VCost [ELH 07] coordinates and have been extended to delivery guaranteeing protocols. It is with this in mind that EtE [ELH 09], a protocol using real geographic coordinates, has been proposed. In this protocol, the next hop is that which minimizes the ratio of energy cost and progress (*Cost Over Progress*) carried out at the final destination. Note that EtE also guarantees delivery because it relies on the same principles introduced in FACE to combat deadlock. Hector [MIT 08], proposed by Mitton *et al.*, is a geographic routing protocol using virtual coordinates, which is energy efficient and guarantees delivery. Hector uses a dual system of coordinates, such as that proposed in LTP [CHA 07] and another relying on anchors such as those proposed in [CAR 05b]. This combination guarantees delivery using LTP without having to increase the length of routes thanks to VCap. It is presupposed in Hector that each sensor can evaluate the real distances with its neighbors thanks to *Received Signal Strength Indicator* (RSSI) based evaluation or another system. It is therefore possible to apply the same rules for choosing the next hop as those used in EtE.

	Exact positions	Virtual positions
Energy efficiency (EE)	COP [KUR 06] NFP [HOU 86]	VCost [ELH 07]
Delivery guarantee (DG)	GFG [BOS 99]	LTP [CHA 07], [LIU 06] ABVCap [TSA 07]
EE+GL	SPFSP [SAN 06] EtE [ELH 09]	HECTOR [MIT 08]

Table 3.1. *Classification of geographic routing protocols*

3.3.3.3. *Summary*

Table 3.1 classifies some of the geographic routing protocols proposed in the literature according to their properties. For further reading on geographic routing protocols, see [MIT 10] and the bibliography.

3.4. Deployment of sensor networks

The aim of this section is to provide the reader with methods and recommendations for successfully identifying a solution to her/his real-life application.

The hardware used in sensor networks is very different to that generally encountered by developers. Since developers usually create user applications or operating system modules, having always worked on a desktop platform is not a sufficient preparation for this kind of software. As such, we will examine the notable differences encountered while working with sensors and their impact on the development cycle.

3.4.1. *Knowing the hardware*

We will examine a number of points of which developers of sensor network solutions must be aware. The majority of examples in this section will be focused on MSP430 microcontroller [TEX 06], which is commonly used in sensor network platforms.

The majority of microcontrollers available for sensors have limitations which distinguish them significantly from a normal computer. What is initially most apparent is their low calculatory power and very limited memory[3] (whether volatile or not). These limitations must be taken into consideration when designing a protocol or a system component.

The solution must be simple and only be used for operations requiring low calculation power. Generally, microcontrollers do not have a floating calculation use with reduced functioning frequency and a simplified architecture which favors low energy consumption on basic power. It is therefore important to limit the number of floating point calculations which, if they can be emulated using calculation units in integer numbers, significantly monopolize the microcontroller and consume a lot of energy.

Due to the low amount of available working memory, it is better to develop solutions with only a minimum number of states. In the case of routing, for example, it would be easier to use a protocol which does not retain the routing table but only information on the sensor's neighborhood. The low amount of available memory emphasizes an often-ignored problem with desktop computers, that of memory fragmentation. Successive allocations and dynamic cleaning leave the memory in such a fragmented state that it is quickly impossible to find a contiguous zone big enough for the application or system to continue to function normally. Using memory piecemeal and limiting dynamic allocations as far as possible will be essential in any development.

Another recurrent problem which must be considered is that of memory access, particularly when this consists of packing or unpacking the packets for a network

---

3 The memory in a sensor is generally a million times smaller than that of a desktop computer.

protocol. A number of microcontrollers such as MSP430 or the majority of ARM processors [ARM 00] have limitations with respect to data alignment. In the MSP430, for example, reading a word (16 bits of data) can only be done on an even address. If the 16 bit value that we want to obtain is stored at an odd address, it is mandatory to read it byte per byte and reconstruct the 16 bit word. Let us take the following packet as an example:

Data	00	AB	AA	FE	42	76	82	40
Address	0	1	2	3	4	5	6	7

If we want to read the 16 bit word at address 3 (composed of bytes 3 and 4), the following C code will not be valid:

```
/* pointer to the start of data */
unsigned char *data = (unsigned char*) 0;
/* pointer to the word to read */
unsigned short *shortptr = (unsigned short *)(data +3);
/* value read */
unsigned short val = *shortptr;
```

This code, which is perfectly viable for a normal microprocessor (and which will compile without issue, even on the MSP430), will face alignment problems. The microcontroller will simply ignore the least significant bit at the address, which will transform data + 3 into data + 2 when the value is read. The viewed word will therefore be 0xFEAA instead of 0x42FE[4].

To correctly read the desired value, it is preferable to use the following code:

```
unsigned char *data = (unsigned char*)0;
unsigned short val = data[3] | (data[4] << 8);
```

As we can see here, knowing the *endianness*[5] of the microcontroller, and that used in the data, is also of utmost importance.

These recommendations are only general examples (although valuable for the majority of controllers). Before beginning to develop a solution, it is important to take the time to read and compare the specifications of the microcontroller and the platform being used.

---

4 The MSP430 is *little endian* and therefore the least significant byte is found at low address.

5 A term indicating the order in which the bytes of a word are stored in the memory.

3.4.2. *Development process*

The development process is also very different for sensors. Firstly, for the majority of systems, the sensor's means of transmitting information to the developer are highly limited. In general, the latter are limited to making LEDs[6] blink and sending the information to the serial port. The distributed network of sensor networks also amplifies this difference. If it is often possible to carry out the program step by step with a program such as GDB [GDB10], the other sensors in the network will not cease to function. It is therefore difficult to correct failing behavior in the system or the protocol.

To overcome these limitations, it is even more important to use appropriate software development methods. We can, for example, cite unit tests [HAM 04], code reviews, binomial programming (if possible), etc. Each component in the system must be tested and validated before being used as the basis for every other element. This is as significant as it is common to see a problem appear only after several hours of execution due to a non-verified test case.

The use of simulators (such as WSIM [FRA 07]) can greatly help development. Launching a system or running a program is often much faster than doing so on the sensor and the control provided by the simulator is more important. In the case of WSIM, it is possible to execute the network step by step by keeping them synchronized. It is also easier to find which part of the program is stopping a vital component in the system. Since sensors often do not have MMUs[7], the system is not capable of detecting if an application has written internal data in its structures.

3.4.3. *Ensuring stability*

Another aspect which sets applications in sensor networks apart is that, once deployment is carried out, human intervention is often impossible. In addition to changing batteries, this impossibility also forces the system to function, whatever may happen. While the sensor has energy, the system *must* function. On a desktop computer, an application which stops unexpectedly is not an unsolvable problem. At worst, the user loses part of their work but, if saved regularly, it is only necessary to restart the program to continue. In the case of a sensor network, if the system stops, it needs to be able to restart automatically. The majority of platforms have a *watchdog* mechanism. A *watchdog* is a hardware component[8] which restarts the system if it does not carry out an operation regularly. In general, the operation consists in writing in a

---

6 LED: *light-emitting diode.*

7 *MMU*: *Memory Management Units.*

8 Or a program but they are less reliable.

particular register of the microprocessor, linked to the *watchdog*. If this writing is not carried out within a certain amount of time, the microprocessor restarts.

However, only the microprocessor is generally restarted by the watchdog which differentiates a hot restart from a cold restart, for example startup of the whole platform.

Particular care should be taken with the system's initialization code and devices, in particular. For example, if the radio receives a packet during the microprocessor's reinitialization, it is important that the system parametrizes the radio correctly at restart. If this does not happen, the radio will require reading (to recover the packet's data) and will remain stuck in this state. The microprocessor will never be noted and will therefore not receive any packets and the system is isolated from the other sensors.

3.4.4. *Preparing for deployment*

Despite all care taken during development, the deployment phases, strictly speaking, can always bring a number of surprises. It is important to prepare the deployment phase on a large scale using a series of laboratory-proven tests. Testing the system with two or three sensors on a desk is nowhere near comparable with wider deployment where the network is composed of several dozen sensors. Before proceeding to actual deployment, it should be ensured that the system can function for several days. This will, in addition, provide an estimation of the life span of the sensor batteries and allow adjustments if consumption is too much.

To ensure the success of these tests, it is important to obtain as much information as possible and measure and collect different parameters from the system. How many packets have been received, transmitted or rejected by the routing protocol? How long has the microcontroller been in standby? Is this the same for the radio interface? How many times has the *watchdog* had to restart the system? Has the restart been carried out properly? All this information allows incorrect behavior to be detected and the system to be modified to create an optimum version before actual deployment. The SensLAB [SL10] project can help to prepare for deployment by proposing a complete test environment in which important operations (programming sensors, collecting information) are automatized. In addition, this kind of platform is an excellent compromise between small-scale laboratory tests and large-scale practical deployment.

The environment in which deployment takes place can also strongly affect the system's operating conditions. This is because the quality of the radio channel can differ greatly from that of the laboratory. Small-scale deployments in a real environment can also save time by detecting problems related to the eventual environment.

Before starting the system, it should also be considered whether it serves its final purpose to deactivate all the unbeneficial *debugging* information for final operation. If the LEDs are useful for showing the system's state during the development phase, their energy consumption cannot be ignored and their use may greatly alter the final life span of the network. The same also applies to the other components such as, for example, the serial port.

For further information on deployment, see [BAR 08].

3.5. Bibliography

[ABR 70] ABRAMSON N., "THE ALOHA SYSTEM another alternative for computer communications", *AFIPS '70 (Fall) Proceedings of the Novembre 17-19, 1970, Fall Joint Computer Conference*, New York, NY, USA, ACM, pp. 281–285, 1970.

[ABR 04] ABRAMS Z., GOEL A., PLOTKIN S., "Set k-cover algorithms for energy efficient monitoring in wireless sensor networks", *Proc. of the 3rd Int'l Symp. on Information Processing in Sensor Networks (IPSN'04)*, Berkeley, CA, USA, pp. 424–432, 2004.

[AKY 02] AKYILDIZ I.F., SU W., SANKARASUBRAMANIAM Y., CAYIRCI E., "Wireless sensor networks a survey", *Computer Networks*, vol. 38, no. 4, pp. 393–422, 2002.

[AMM 09] AMMARI H.M., GIUDICI J., "On the Connected k-Coverage Problem in Heterogeneous Sensor Nets The Curse of Randomness and Heterogeneity", *Proc. of the Int'l Conf. on Distributed Computing Systems (ICDCS'09)*, vol. 0, pp. 265–272, IEEE Computer Society, 2009.

[ARM 00] ARM, ARM9TDMI Technical Reference Manual, 2000.

[BAC 10] BACHIR A., DOHLER M., WATTEYNE T., LEUNG K., "MAC Essentials for Wireless Sensor Networks", *Communications Surveys Tutorials, IEEE*, vol. 12, no. 2, pp. 222–248, second 2010.

[BAR 08] BARRENETXEA G., INGELREST F., SCHAEFER G., VETTERLI M., "The Hitchhiker's Guide to Successful Wireless Sensor Network Deployments", *Proceedings of the 6th ACM Conference on Embedded Networked Sensor Systems (SenSys 2008)*, Raleigh, NC, USA, November 2008.

[BEN 09] BENBADIS F., PUIG J.-J., DE AMORIM M., CHAUDET C., FRIEDMAN T., SIMPLOT-RYL D., "Jumps: Enhanced hop-count positioning in sensor networks using multiple coordinates.", *Ad Hoc & Sensor Wireless Networks*, vol. 2, 2009.

[BOS 99] BOSE P., MORIN P., STOJMENOVIC I., URRUTIA J., "Routing with guaranteed delivery in ad hoc wireless networks", *Proc. of the 3rd Int. Workshop on Discrete Algorithms and Methods for Mobile Computing and Comm. (DIAL-M)*, Seattle, WA, USA, pp. 48–55, August 1999.

[BUS 05] BUSSON A., MITTON N., FLEURY E., "An analysis of the MPR selection in OLSR and consequences.", *The fourth Annual Mediterranean Ad Hoc Networking Workshop, MED-HOC-NET 05*, Ile de Porquerolles, France, June 2005.

[CAR 03] CARTIGNY J., INGELREST F., SIMPLOT D., "RNG relay subset flooding protocols in mobile ad hoc networks", *International Journal of Foundations of Computer Science*, vol. 14, no. 2, 2003.

[CAR 04a] CARLE J., SIMPLOT-RYL D., "Energy efficient area monitoring by sensor networks", *IEEE Computer Magazine*, vol. 37, pp. 40–46, 2004.

[CAR 04b] CARTIGNY J., INGELREST F., SIMPLOT-RYL D., STOJMENOVIĆ I., "Localized LMST and RNG Based Minimum-Energy Broadcast Protocols in Ad Hoc Networks", *Ad hoc Networks*, vol. 3, no. 1, pp. 1–16, January 2004.

[CAR 05a] CARLE J., GALLAIS A., SIMPLOT-RYL D., "Preserving Area Coverage in Wireless Sensor Networks by using Surface Coverage Relay Dominating Sets", *Proc. 10th IEEE Symposium on Computers and Communications (ISCC 2005)*, Cartagène, Spain, 2005.

[CAR 05b] CARUSO A., CHESSA S., DE S., URPI A., "GPS free coordinate assignment and routing in wireless sensor networks", *Proc. of the 24th Conference of the IEEE Communications Society (INFOCOM)*, vol. 1, pp. 150–160, March 2005.

[CHA 07] CHAVEZ E., MITTON N., TEJEDA H., "Routing in wireless networks with position trees", *Proc. of the 6th International Conference on AD-HOC Networks & Wireless (Ad Hoc Now)*, Morelia, Mexico, September 2007.

[CHE 98] CHEN T.-W., GERLA M., "Global state routing a new routing scheme for ad-hoc wireless networks", *Proc. IEEE Int'l Conf. on Communications, (ICC 1998)*, Atlanta, GA, USA, pp. 171–175, 1998.

[CHI 96] CHIANG C., WU H., LIU W., GERLA M., "Routing in clustered multihop, mobile wireless networks with fading channel", *ICCS/ISPACS'96*, Singapore, November 1996.

[CLA 03] CLAUSEN T., JACQUET P., LAOUITI A., MUHLETHALER P., QAYYUM A., VIENNOT L., OLSR - Optimized Link State Routing Protocol, October 2003, RFC 3626.

[DIJ 59] DIJKSTRA E., "A note on two problems in connection with graphs", *Numer. Math.*, vol. 1, pp. 269–271, 1959.

[DUB 97] DUBE R., RAIS C.D., WANG K.-Y., TRIPATHI S.K., "Signal Stability-based adaptive routing (SSA) for ad hoc mobile networks", *IEEE Personal Communications Magazine*, IEEE, pp. 36–45, February 1997.

[ELH 02] EL-HOIYDI A., "Aloha with preamble sampling for sporadic traffic in ad hoc wireless sensor networks", *Communications, 2002. ICC 2002. IEEE International Conference on*, vol. 5, pp. 3418–3423, 2002.

[ELH 07] ELHAFSI E. H., MITTON N., SIMPLOT-RYL D., "Cost over progress based energy efficient routing over virtual coordinates in wireless sensor networks", *Proc. of IEEE International Workshop From Theory to Practice in Wireless Sensor Networks (t2pWSN)*, Helsinki, Finland, 2007.

[ELH 09] ELHAFSI E., MITTON N., B.PAVKOVIC, SIMPLOT-RYL D., "Energy-aware georouting with guaranteed delivery in wireless sensor networks with obstacles", *Int. Jour. of Wireless Information*, vol. 16, no. 3, 2009.

[ENZ 04] ENZ C. C., EL-HOIYDI A., DECOTIGNIE J.-D., PEIRIS V., "WiseNET an ultralow-power wireless sensor network solution", *Computer*, vol. 37, no. 8, pp. 62–70, IEEE Computer Society Press, 2004.

[EPH 87] EPHREMIDES A., WIESELTHIER J., BAKER D., "A design concept for reliable mobile radio networks with frequency hoping signaling", *Journal of IEEE*, pp. 56–73, 1987.

[FIN 87] FINN G., Routing and Addressing Problems in Large Metropolitan-scale Internetworks, Report no. ISI/RR-87-180, Information Sciences Institute (ISI), 1987.

[FRA 07] FRABOULET A., WSIM / Worldsens Simulator, 2007.

[FRE 08] FREY H., SIMPLOT-RYL D., "Localized topology control algorithms for ad hoc and sensor networks", *Handbook of Applied Algorithms*, pp. 439–464, Wiley, 2008.

[GAL 06] GALLAIS A., PARVERY H., CARLE J., GORCE J.-M., SIMPLOT-RYL D., "Efficiency impairment of wireless sensor networks protocols under realistic physical layer conditions", *Proc. 10th IEEE International Conference on Communication Systems (ICCS 2006)*, Singapore, 2006.

[GAL 07] GALLAIS A., CARLE J., "An adaptive localized algorithm for multiple sensor area coverage", *Ad Hoc & Sensor Wireless Networks journal (AHSWN)*, vol. 4, no. 3, pp. 271–288, 2007.

[GAL 08] GALLAIS A., CARLE J., "Performance evaluation and enhancement of surface coverage relay protocol", *Proc. 7th Int'l IFIP-TC6 Networking Conf. on AdHoc and Sensor Networks, Wireless Networks, Next Generation Internet (Networking'08)*, Singapore, pp. 124–134, 2008.

[GAR 79] GAREY M. R., JOHNSON D. S., *Computers and Intractability a Guide to the Theory of NP-completeness*, W.H. Freeman & Company, New York, USA, 1979.

[GAU 06] GAURA E., NEWMAN R., *Smart MEMS and Sensor Systems*, World Scientific, 2006.

[GDB 10] "GDB The GNU Project Debugger", http//www.gnu.org/software/gdb, 2010.

[GER 95] GERLA M., TSAI J. T.-C., "Multicluster, mobile, multimedia radio network", *ACM/Baltzer Journal of Wireless Networks*, vol. 1, no. 3, pp. 255–265, July 1995.

[GER 02] GERLA M., HONG X., PEI G., Fisheye State Routing Protocol (FSR) for Ad Hoc Networks, 2002, IETF MANET Working Group, Internet Draft.

[HAM 04] HAMILL P., *Unit Test Frameworks*, O'Reilly, First edition, 2004.

[HAM 06] HAMMA T., KATOH T., BISTA B., TAKATA T., "An efficient ZHLS routing protocol for mobile ad hoc networks", *Proc. of DEXA Workshops*, pp. 66–70, 2006.

[HOU 86] HOU T.-C., LI V., "Transmission range control in multihop packet radio networks", *Communications, IEEE Transactions on [legacy, pre - 1988]*, vol. 34, no. 1, pp. 38–44, 1986.

[HUA 05] HUANG C.-F., TSENG Y.-C., "The coverage problem in a wireless sensor network", *Mobile Networks and Application*, vol. 10, no. 4, pp. 519–528, Kluwer Academic Publishers, 2005.

[HWA 07] HWANG J., GU Y., HE T., KIM Y., "Realistic sensing area modeling", *Proc. of the 26th Annual IEEE Conf. on Computer Communications (INFOCOM 2007)*, pp. 2421–2425, 2007.

[IEE 99] IEEE, IEEE 802.11, Local and metropolitan area networks - Specific requirements Part 11 Wireless LAN Medium Access Control (MAC) and Physical Layer (PHY) specifications, IEEE standard, 1999.

[IEE 03] IEEE, IEEE 802.15.4-2003 standard for information technology - telecommunication and information exchange between systems - lan/wan - part 15.4 Wireless medium access control (mac) and physical layer (phy) specifications for wireless personal area networks (lr-wpam). IEEE standard, 2003.

[ING 08] INGELREST F., SIMPLOT-RYL D., "Localized broadcast incremental power protocol for wireless ad hoc networks", *Wireless Networks*, vol. 14, no. 3, pp. 309–319, 2008.

[JAC 02] JACQUET P., LAOUITI A., MINET P., VIENNOT L., "Performance of multipoint relaying in *ad hoc* mobile routing protocols", *Networking*, Pisa, Italy, 2002.

[JOH 01] JOHNSON D., MALTZ D. A., BROCH J., "DSR the dynamic source routing protocol for multi-hop wireless ad hoc networks", *Ad Hoc Networking*, vol. 5, pp. 139–172, Addison-Wesley, 2001.

[KHA 10] KHADAR F., MITTON N., SIMPLOT-RYL D., "Towards an efficient QoS based selection of neighbors in QOLSR.", *Proc. 3rd International Workshop on Sensor Networks (SN)*, Gênes, Italy, June 2010.

[KUR 06] KURUVILA J., NAYAK A., STOJMENOVIC I., "Progress and location based localized power aware routing for ad hoc sensor wireless networks", *IJDSN*, vol. 2, pp. 147–159, 2006.

[LIU 06] LIU K., ABU-GHAZALEH N., "Stateless and guaranteed geometric routing on virtual coordinate systems", *Proc. of the IEEE Int. Conference on Mobile Adhoc and Sensor Systems (MASS)*, pp. 340–346, October 2006.

[MEG 01] MEGUERDICHIAN S., KOUSHANFAR F., POTKONJAK M., SRIVASTAVA M.B., "Coverage problems in wireless ad-hoc sensor networks", *Proc. of the 20th Annual IEEE Conf. on Computer Communications (INFOCOM 2001)*, pp. 1380–1387, 2001.

[MIT 08] MITTON N., RAZAFINDRALAMBO T., SIMPLOT-RYL D., STOJMENOVIC I., "Hector is an Energy effiCient Tree-based Optimized Routing protocol for wireless networks", *Proc. of the 4th International Conference on Mobile Ad-hoc and Sensor Networks (MSN)*, Wuhan, China, December 2008.

[MIT 09] MITTON N., INGELREST F., SIMPLOT-RYL D., "Découverte de voisinage et contrôle de topologie", in FLEURY E., SIMPLOT-RYL D., *Réseaux de capteurs théorie et modélisation*, Hermes-Lavoisier, 2009.

[MIT 10] MITTON N., RAZAFINDRALAMBO T., SIMPLOT-RYL D., "Position-based routing in wireless ad hoc and sensor networks", *Theoretical Aspects of Distributed Computing in Sensor Networks*, Springer, 2010.

[MOR 06] MORARU L., SIMPLOT-RYL D., "QoS preserving topology advertising reduction for OLSR routing protocol for mobile ad hoc networks", *Proc. 3rd Wireless On demand Network Systems and Services (WONS 2006)*, Les Ménuires, France, 2006.

[MOY 94] MOY J., *OSPF - Open Shortest Path First*, March 1994, RFC 1583.

[MUR 96] MURTHY S., GARCIA-LUNA-ACEVES J. J., "An efficient routing protocol for wireless networks", *Mob. Netw. Appl.*, vol. 1, no. 2, pp. 183–197, Kluwer Academic Publishers, 1996.

[NI 99] NI S., TSENG Y., CHEN Y., SHEU J., "The Broadcast Storm Problem in a Mobile Ad Hoc Network", *Proceedings of the Fifth Annual ACM/IEEE International Conference on Mobile Computing and Networking*, pp. 151–162, 1999.

[PAR 01] PARK V., CORSON S., *Temporally-Ordered Routing Algorithm (TORA)*, June 2001, Internet Draft.

[PEI 00] PEI G., GERLA M., CHEN T.-W., "Fisheye state routing a routing scheme for ad hoc wireless networks", *Proc. IEEE Int'l Conf. on Communications, (ICC 2000)*, vol. 1, New Orleans, LA, USA, pp. 70–74, 2000.

[PER 94] PERKINS C. E., BHAGWAT P., "Highly dynamic destination-sequenced distance-vector routing (DSDV) for mobile computers", *SIGCOMM Comput. Commun. Rev.*, vol. 24, no. 4, pp. 234–244, ACM, 1994.

[PER 03] PERKINS C., BELDING-ROYER E., DAS S., *Ad hoc On-Demand Distance Vector (AODV) Routing*, July 2003, IETF. RFC 3561.

[POL 04] POLASTRE J., HILL J., CULLER D., "Versatile low power media access for wireless sensor networks", *SenSys '04 Proceedings of the 2nd International Conference on Embedded Networked Sensor Systems*, New York, NY, USA, ACM, pp. 95–107, 2004.

[QAY 02] QAYYUM A., VIENNOT L., LAOUITI A., "Multipoint relaying An efficient technique for flooding in mobile wireless networks", *HICSS'02*, Hawai, USA, January 2002.

[ROD 99] RODOPLU V., MENG T., "Minimizing energy mobile wireless networks", *IEEE Journal on Selected Areas*, vol. 17, no. 8, pp. 1333–1347, 1999.

[SAN 05] SANTI P., "Topology control in wireless ad hoc and sensor networks", *ACM Comput. Surv.*, vol. 37, no. 2, pp. 164–194, 2005.

[SAN 06] SANCHEZ J. A., RUIZ P. M., "Exploiting local knowledge to enhance energy-efficient geographic routing", *MSN*, Hong Kong, China, 2006.

[SIM 05] SIMPLOT-RYL D., STOJMENOVIC I., WU. J., "Energy efficient backbone construction, broadcasting, and area coverage in sensor networks", *Handbook of Sensor Networks*, John Wiley & Sons, 2005.

[SIN 98] SINGH S., RAGHAVENDRA C. S., "PAMAS–power aware multi-access protocol with signalling for ad hoc networks", *SIGCOMM Comput. Commun. Rev.*, vol. 28, no. 3, pp. 5–26, ACM, 1998.

[SL 10] Senslab Very large scale open wireless sensor network testbed, http//www.senslab.info, 2010.

[STO 01] STOJMENOVIC I., LIN X., "Power-aware localized routing in wireless networks", *IEEE Trans. Parallel Distrib. Syst. (TPDS)*, vol. 12, no. 11, pp. 1122–1133, IEEE Press, 2001.

[STO 02] Stojmenovic I., Seddigh M., Zunic J., "Dominating sets and neighbor elimination-based broadcasting algorithms in wireless networks", *IEEE TPDS*, vol. 13, no. 1, January 2002.

[STO 04a] Stojmenovic I., Datta S., "Power and cost aware localized routing with guaranteed delivery in wireless networks", *Wireless Comm. and Mobile Compt.*, vol. 4, no. 2, pp. 175–188, 2004.

[STO 04b] Stojmenovic I., Datta S., "Power and cost aware localized routing with guaranteed delivery in wireless networks", *Wireless Comm. and Mobile Compt.*, vol. 4, no. 2, pp. 175–188, 2004.

[TAK 84] Takagi H., Kleinrock L., "Optimal transmission ranges for randomly distributed packet radio terminals", *IEEE Transaction on Communications*, vol. 22, no. 3, 1984.

[TEX 06] Texas Instruments, MSP430x1xx Family User's Guide, 2006.

[TIA 02] Tian D., Georganas N. D., "A coverage-preserving node scheduling scheme for large wireless sensor networks", *Proc. of the 1st ACM Int'l Workshop on Wireless Sensor Networks and Applications (WSNA 2002)*, pp. 32–41, 2002.

[TIA 05] Tian D., Georganas N.D., "Connectivity maintenance and coverage preservation in wireless sensor networks", *Ad Hoc Network*, vol. 3, no. 6, pp. 744–761, 2005.

[TOU 80] Toussaint G., "The relative neighborhood graph of a finite planar set", *Pattern Recognition*, vol. 12, no. 4, pp. 261–268, 1980.

[TSA 07] Tsai M.-J., Yang H.-Y., Huang W.-Q., "Axis-based virtual coordinate assignment protocol and delivery-guaranteed routing protocol in wireless sensor networks", *Proc. of the 26rd Conference of the IEEE Communications Society (INFOCOM)*, vol. 1, pp. 2234–2242, May 2007.

[WIE 00] Wieselthier J., Nguyen G., Ephremides A., "On the construction of energy-efficient broadcast and multicast trees in wireless networks", *Proceedings of the Annual Joint Conference of the IEEE Computer and Communications Societies (INFOCOM)*, Tel Aviv, Israel, March 2000.

[WU 01] Wu J., Li H., "A dominating set based routing scheme in ad hoc wireless networks", *Telecommunications Systems*, vol. 3, pp. 13–36, 2001.

[XIN 05] Xing G., Wang X., Zhang Y., Lu C., Pless R., Gill C., "Integrated coverage and connectivity configuration for energy conservation in sensor networks", *ACM Trans. Sensor Network*, vol. 1, no. 1, pp. 36–72, 2005.

[YE 02] Ye W., Heidemann J., Estrin D., "An energy-efficient MAC protocol for wireless sensor networks", *INFOCOM 2002, Twenty-First Annual Joint Conference of the IEEE Computer and Communications Societies, Proceedings, IEEE*, vol. 3, pp. 1567–1576, 2002.

[YE 03] Ye F., Zhong G., Cheng J., Lu S., Zhang L., "PEAS A robust energy conserving protocol for long-lived sensor networks", *Proc 23rd Int'l Conf. on Distributed Computing Systems (ICDCS 2003)*, pp. 28–37, 2003.

[YEN 07] YENER B., MAGDON-ISMAIL M., SIVRIKAYA F., "Joint problem of power optimal connectivity and coverage in wireless sensor networks", *Wireless Networks*, vol. 13, no. 4, pp. 537–550, Kluwer Academic Publishers, 2007.

[ZHO 04] ZHOU Z., DAS S., GUPTA H., "Connected K-Coverage Problem in Sensor Networks", *Proc. of the Int'l Conf. on Computer Communications and Networks (ICCCN'04)*, Chicago, IL, USA, pp. 373–378, 2004.

Chapter 4

Smart Systems, Ambient Intelligence and Energy Sources: Current Developments and Future Applications

4.1. Introduction

Ubiquity and mobility are at the heart of the current revolution in the way we use technology. Portable information tools such as *smartphones* have had enormous success and shape everyday computing technology with their adapted features, which are available at any time (although this is a matter of debate[1]), any place or circumstance. Ubiquity and mobility have become a reality with the arrival of these new electronic companions.

Accelerometers, gyroscopes, compasses and GPS, as well as embedded devices allow us to locate and navigate more accurately, provided that access to an energy source can be found easily. As such, having enough portable energy becomes a necessity that hampers conventional sources and batteries' current limitations. In this chapter, research in the field of generating and storing energy (such as *energy harvesting* via pressure on the sole of shoes, backpacks, or military packs during exercises) will be examined in order to evaluate it's "physical" and very real limitations, in the hope of never having to replace their batteries.

Chapter written by Georges AKHRAS and Florence SÈDES.
1   www.greenit.fr/article/bonnes-pratiques/comment-sauver-la-batterie-de-votre-smartphone-3137 (in French only).

However, reality has caught up and this field is no longer only an academic area of research. The Japanese company SoundPower Corp. manufactures tiles, panels, paving stones and carpets that light up when subjected to pressure (www. soundpower.co.jp/products/products1.html). It is on the basis of this development that Alexandre Marciel, Deputy Mayor of Toulouse, in charge of public lighting in the city, has pinpointed that "energy is wasted in public space (lost movement) and a potential opportunity to recover some of it". Marciel has therefore focused on a limited but important area: "capturing gravitational energy produced by foot movement to transform it into electrical energy for public lighting". After contacting several English-speaking laboratories and with the lighting technical services of Toulouse, it was decided to develop an innovative way of producing a ground energy generator for public lighting. The city has therefore altered a Dutch product from its original function, *the sustainable dance floor*, retro-lit slabs that light up from dancers' movements jumping on a particular spot, a product used in nightclubs that has been adapted to standard LED streetlights. In terms of initial results, 60 W in 10 s, which is enough energy to power a streetlight for normal functioning, is produced by walking normally over 8 m; although research is underway to improve energy performance: 10 m^2 of public space would be enough to provide a lamp with 75 W all night with normal steps. This device could be linked to motion-sensitive lamps.

Toulouse was the first city in the world to test this new energy source, though more basic applications have been tested in Japan. Based on research into energy autonomy, the design of intelligent materials opens the way for research into wearable computers (clothing) and intelligent textiles. New modes of interaction and therefore new behavior have appeared, thanks to the wide integration of sensors into objects, textiles, tools, etc., which have changed the very notion of interaction. The aim is to replace classic interfaces with much more subtle, "natural" interfaces. While interaction has been highly localized and interfaced by specialized physical devices such as keyboard, screen, and mouse in the past, interaction has today become ubiquitous and mobile. Natural interaction has become a reality, supported by smart devices, systems and structures. The developments initiated by these materials and structures will be examined later. The results of this research can now be found in our hands, homes, cars and clothes: an interdisciplinary approach, centered resolutely on information, the user, and the advances in material science is emerging in line with current expectations, as we will attempt to illustrate in this chapter.

4.2. Did you say "smart systems"?

The origins of smart systems lie in a field of research that envisioned devices and materials that could mimic human muscular and nervous systems. The basic idea is to produce non-biological structures that will achieve the optimum functionality observed in biological systems through emulating their adaptive capabilities and integrated design.

These systems are fitted with partly or fully integrated sensors and actuators.

There are two categories: passive systems or structures that respond to a stimulus without electronic assistance or return systems and those that are active and use feedback to accelerate recognition and response time. These systems or structures also have the ability to adapt to a stimulus without external intervention, electronic assistance, or a return system. The high-end system is the smart system that uses sensors, actuators and return systems to anticipate and adjust its behavior.

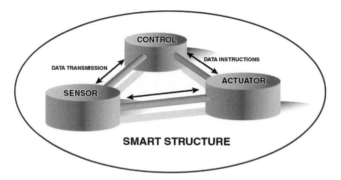

Figure 4.1. *Basic components of a smart structure*

A smart system is a system equipped with sensors and actuators with the innovative ability to perform intelligent actions. Figure 4.1 presents the basic components of a smart system [AKH 00]: *their equivalents in the human body appear in brackets*:

1) data acquisition (*tactile sensing*): collect the required raw data needed for an appropriate control and monitoring of the structure;

2) data transmission (*sensing nerves*): forward the raw data to the local and central command and control units;

3) command and control center (*brain*): analyze the data, reach the appropriate conclusion, and determine the specific actions;

4) data instructions (*motor nerves*): transmit the decisions and the associated instructions back to the actuators;

5) controlling devices (*muscles*): take action by triggering the controlling devices/units.

4.2.1. *Smart materials*

Sensors and actuators in smart systems are generally made of smart materials. These materials can be classified according to their type and characteristic function: piezoelectric, magnetostrictive, electrostrictive, ferromagnetostrictive, magnetorheological or electrorheological, shape memory alloys or polymers, and intelligent fiber optics, to mention but a few.

Combining two or more materials to utilize *synergistically* the best properties of their individual constituents is the ultimate objective of any smart composite material.

By their very nature, smart composite structures lead to either a reduction in production and usage costs or a marked improvement in performance. Their potential advantages include:

– increased comfort by reducing noise and vibrations;

– prolonged structural lifespan of systems and components;

– growth in precisions and operational capacity;

– improved performance;

– new applications.

The production of these composites is designed to further develop, improve or increase the product's functions and/or capabilities; for example, in terms of flexibility, rigidity, resistance, etc. The arrival of nanotechnologies has enabled the development of increasingly smaller devices, embedded and integrated into the environment, portable, even woven into clothing fibers.

With particular intrinsic and/or extrinsic capacities, emerging smart materials have special functions that allow them:

– to adequately respond to any internal and/or external stimuli in their environments;

– to adapt their function in accordance with these changes.

These new products provide optimal responses to extremely complex problems. For example, detecting problems at the start or adapting their response in reaction to unpredicted conditions and improving the system's lifespan and its lifecycle. In addition, exercising better control by minimizing distortion and increasing precision will also improve more than one product or structure. Better preventive maintenance and consequently better efficiency in systems are also potential advantages.

4.2.2. *Sensors and actuators*

Sensors and actuators are designed according to the nature of the phenomenon being monitored or their desired function (magnetic, thermal, optic, radiation, mechanical, or chemical reaction) as well as the type of results sought after (thermal, magnetic, electric, optical, or mechanical). Other characteristics also come into play: the size, configuration and mechanical properties of the interface required; environmental conditions (thermal, magnetic, electrical, or corrosion); as well as the geometry and mechanical properties of the interface. Finally, the operational properties of the acquired data (sensitivity, bandwidth, linearity, standard length, scope) and/or actuator properties (displacement, force generation, hysteresis, response time, bandwidth, etc.) are also determinant factors.

4.2.3. *Command and control unit*

The command and control unit manages routine operations and monitors the safety and integrity of the system within a communication network that can be functioning in real time. This unit also controls sensors, actuators, as well as non-destructive integrated evaluation instruments. It can also monitor operational and control devices. It is the brain of the smart structure which fulfills two basic distinct functions: a processing function and an analysis function. This requires the use of special algorithms based on artificial intelligence, pattern recognition and fuzzy logic neural networks to process raw data. Expert systems are also used to collect, manage, classify and store data.

4.2.4. *Managing data and security*

To be truly effective, smart systems require fairly significant computer resources. The cloud cluster model, the unavoidable *cloud*, is attractive because it allows a drastic reduction in costs, thanks to the virtualization of managing the storage, analysis, and archiving of information. This almost unlimited flexibility of communication provides availability and highly efficient handling of data and information.

However, since these systems deal with users' personal data, a strong warning is in order. The introduction of these new technologies should not, in any way, infringe users' private lives [ALK 08]. For this type of application, effectively managing information accessibility to ensure absolute security is essential. Without an absolute guarantee, we should not use these new technologies, but well established secure systems [ALK 09].

By its very nature, the technology of smart systems is a highly multi-disciplinary domain involving interdisciplinary teams. Unimpeded operation of these systems requires a lot of energy (electricity, batteries, etc.). This state of affairs may explain the slow progress made in their applications. However, since the dawn of *energy harvesting*, new avenues have opened up.

Rather than concentrating on improving battery technology, numerous academic or industrial research teams have explored more environmentally-friendly means of generating/collecting energy. The principle consists of collecting energy on location from renewable resources: solar, wind, hydro, electromagnetic, electrostatic, wave, tidal, ocean thermal sources, and particularly from human movement and vibration. This latter approach is the most promising for autonomous approaches.

4.3. Energy harvesting[2]

Storing energy for later use has become a device that we use daily, such as, for example lighting balconies or garden paths at night within the context of street safety with devices that recharge during the day and light up at night.

More pioneering, but still at the prototype stage, are dynamic devices based on movement or vibrations. This entails storing "ambient" energy from movement or vibrations, which is currently lost or even suppressed or removed. The question therefore lies in the maximum quantity of energy available in potential vibration sources and comparing the effectiveness of different vibrations for electricity conversion methods.

The potential applications are unlimited: as such the device used in Toulouse, mentioned in the introduction will be the subject of further research to build automatic road tolls where vehicle movement determines ticket distribution and payment machines.

4.3.1. *Initial applications*

The "ingenious" idea of collecting energy from walking to give autonomy to pedestrians has taken the form of several different prototypes. The first of its kind, fitted in the sole of shoes, was developed by MIT in 1998. It could generate between 60 and 250 mW during normal walking. Several better performing models have since appeared.

---

2 www.energyharvesting.net.

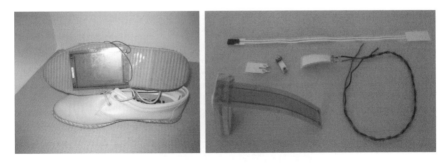

Figure 4.2. *Shoes equipped to generate electricity and their basic components*

Fitting a mechanism that moves inside a walker's backpack generates around 45 mW when walking at around 3–4 km/h (see Figure 4.3).

Other devices are based on dynamics, such as the knee bracelet (see Figure 4.4).

Figure 4.3. *A walker with an energy-generating backpack*

Given the current trend for recycling, some research has sought to evaluate the possibility of recycling "ambient" electromagnetism by sending these signals to supply low-power electronic devices: http://theinstitute.ieee.org/technology-focus/technology-topic/harvesting-energy-out-of-thin-air (October 2011). In the same vein, there is an abundance of research into low, even "ultra-low" consumption devices.

Figure 4.4. *Energy-generating knee bracelet*

4.3.2. *Second generation*

If, as mentioned previously, several examples of energy generation using human movement and vibration are possible, it becomes quickly evident that the power produced is too minimal to be able to be satisfactorily and effectively used in real applications. This statement has cooled the enthusiasm of even the most enthusiastic researchers and the majority of these prototypes have remained in the laboratory. Furthermore, it appears that storing these small quantities is neither industrially practical nor feasible.

The very recent arrival of sensors, actuators and new devices (iPads, iPhones, GPS, etc.) with low or very low energy consumption has reignited hopes and opened the way for exploiting this technology to power these new tools.

4.3.3. *Managing systems, processes and energy*

The aim of this research is to identify parameters that can be used to effectively manage processes in terms of energy consumption and then use them to reduce the energy impact of infrastructures. This entails measuring, estimating and modeling energy consumption and theoretical models for ordering tasks according to energy criteria (see the site "green programming" www.ecoinfo.cnrs.fr/spip.php?rubrique41 (in French only).

4.4. Wearable computers and smart fibers

The idea that a small amount of energy can power a light-emitting diode (LED) or a tool with simplified functions such as sensors or transmitters is highly promising because they can be used without batteries/cumbersome storage systems. From this, the concept of fibers, materials, or smart coatings has emerged.

Some smart materials contain microcapsules distributed throughout their fibers, which contain solid or liquid products that can react to light, temperature, or friction and release their content when the item of clothing is used in a specific context. "Caring" clothing or textiles have also been proposed, which, having detected signals in the human body and the environment, in turn become thermo regulators, antibacterial, anti-UV, antimagnetic, anti-stress, medication or scent releasing (micro-encapsulation), non-friction, anti-tasks, etc. Even more significantly, some can react according to prerecorded data, which can, for example, change color when it detects an allergenic product.

As a result, a "portable" computer can take the form of a comfortable and machine washable t-shirt that can be worn all day like any other kind of clothing. Some devices are designed for medical use or monitoring: sensors are fitted in the fibers of organs being monitored (chest, abdomen, etc.) which continually analyze pulse or heart rhythm, for example.

Dangerous occupations may also benefit with, for example, a fireman's jacket that can not only monitor external risks (external temperature, presence of toxic gas, etc.) but also react to the detection of signs of distress or malfunction by monitoring vital parameters (body temperature, breathing, heart rhythm). Again, smart textiles can be used for treatment: the fibers release, via microcapsules, an antiseptic or another kind of medical substance adapted to the situation or detected problem; for example, dressings fitted with microprocessors that can continuously diagnose wounds and deliver drugs for them.

In the same vein, a young Norwegian student, Anne Britt Torkildsby, focusing on the aging population, has created a smart undergarment, ARMS, designed to help people, mostly senior, to recover from a stroke by supporting the muscles using electrical impulses emitted by the fabric. ARMS behaves like any other underwear. In addition to its design, its main function is to increase the control, force and functional capabilities. The internal layer of the textile detects the user's muscle movements. The information is then processed by a microsystem that communicates with the second layer of the material fitted with a network of electrodes. These, in turn, activate a pocket filled with gel comprising electroactive polymers that help the muscles function.

Scientists in Singapore have developed a high-tech shirt that transmits an electronic alert when a senior citizen falls over, as indicated in the local daily newspaper *The Straits Times*. This new generation of shirt uses Bluetooth wireless technology. When a fall occurs, the shirt sends an alert to the family or next of kin (telephone call, text message, or even e-mail).

At the cardiovascular pathology conference, the San Raffaele University Hospital announced the development of a gym suit for cardiac patients that allows doctors to monitor patients remotely. The principle of this machine-washable item is that it can remotely control, at any time in the day, the patient's vital signs, heartbeat, breathing, movement and temperature. Called "Wealthy" (*Wearable Health Care System*), the combination is revolutionary due to its components, "multifunctional materials obtained by mixing classic, breathable, and elastic materials with electrophysical properties which allow its wearer's vital signs to be taken and recorded". A box weighing around 150 g is fitted in the outfit. It uses GPRS technology to transmit data to a listening station in the hospital's coronary department "in order to spare the patient tedious hospital visits for regular monitoring with electrode devices".

Of course, this clothing is still at an experimental stage and will not appear on the market for a number of years. However, bit by bit, the concept of smart materials is being developed. We can fit shirts with MP3 and GPRS readers. Materials with a soyaprotein base for its antibacterial properties and ability to combat humidity have also been developed. The American Military is currently developing a fabric that can change color according to its surroundings, administer medication, and solidify in case of a breach.

Another example is smart prosthetics, which, by controlling knee movements with angular position sensors and pressure, collect data and uses them for the overall analysis of potential actions.

The possibility, based on human movement and vibrations without batteries, of generating energy and powering the previous applications in real time will accelerate the implementation and development of new uses.

4.5. Other applications

Smart materials are employed to offset noise or vibrations (vehicles, ventilators, air conditioning, propellers, etc.). In the leisure industry, this has led to the introduction of new generations of golf clubs, baseball bats, as well as skis or surfboards, bike frames, handlebars, etc. More solid tennis rackets have also been designed that prevent tennis elbow by absorbing vibrations, thus giving the player more power. In transportation (automobiles, aeronautical, trains etc.), smart composites have been used to reduce noise and suppress, or at least decrease, vibrations in structural components: controlling or optimizing their operation and eventually improving performance. Helicopters, for example, are probably the aircraft with the highest amount of vibration. Suppressing or decreasing these vibrations is complicated. The *Smart Material Actuated Rotor Technology* (SMART) by Boeing has managed to reduce vibration by 80%, a decrease of 10 decibels (dB) in the noise generated by the sound of vortex blades on landing, a gain of 10% in rotor performance, and an automatic alignment of blades in flight [BOE 11, CHE 06, HEI 09, STR 04, STR 05]. Eurocoptor has developed a similar system and hopes to put it into operation soon [WIC 04]. The "Ultraquiet cabin" system developed by Ultra Electronics Ltd. is used in Saab and Bombadier platforms (www.ultraquiet.com). There are also a number of military projects: www.flugrevue.de/de/militaer/fluggeraet-hersteller/news-in-brief.3544.htm.

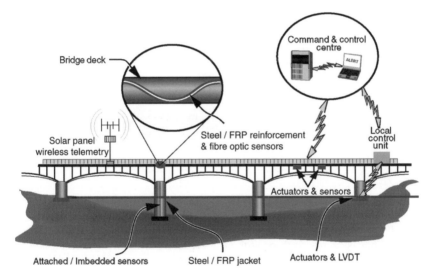

Figure 4.5. *Components of a smart bridge*

In several areas of civil engineering, the use of fiber optics, wireless telemetry, and semi-active damper control has helped monitor movement and deflections due to earthquakes or wind in buildings. This therefore allows the safety of buildings and wind turbines to be monitored. For example, the device is used to monitor deformation or vibrations in a cracked bridge in Berlin (Germany) or to observe the movement of joints between concrete panels in Germany and Switzerland; vibrations and corrosion in a number of US and Canadian bridges are monitored using this method as well as rock falls in mooring cables in Swiss tunnels; lastly, it is also used to monitor a number of bridges and buildings in Japan. Figure 4.5 shows a rough sketch of a smart bridge [AKH 97, AKH 98].

Composites are now widely used in the aerospace industry. They offer undeniable advantages in relation to metal alloys (reduced weight, better rigidity, resistance to corrosion). Boeing and Airbus are working on increasing the percentage of composites in their fleets. However, the reaction of these composites to solicitations and vibrations requires monitoring and special inspections. Smart composites can respond advantageously to this task. Sensors and actuators can be integrated into layers of composites with minimal effect on their general integrity [BAR 04, IHN 04, SMA 11, ZHO 06] (see Figure 4.6).

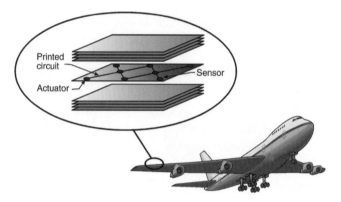

Figure 4.6. *Integration of smart materials in a composite structure*

Autonomous smart systems are also used in a number of stealth applications. Several types of ground, sea or air-smart vehicles are currently being developed. These transport systems, with or without a crew, are fitted with sensors, actuators, and refined commands to improve their main functions, control, and performance.

4.6. Conclusion

Smart technologies present a potential unlimited opportunity for engineering applications. As such, an initial aspect concerns optimizing the response of complex systems such as preventative warning systems, improving survival conditions, and adapting response to react to unpredicted conditions. A second axis concerns otherwise unachievable improvements such as minimizing distortion and increasing precision or ensuring better control. Lastly, preventative maintenance and performance optimization functions are also a possibility.

The field of smart materials and structures is, by its very nature, highly interdisciplinary in terms of fundamental sciences as well as applied sciences: aeronautics, embedded, domestic, etc. While the science of smart materials is developing rapidly, industrial and public applications are still fairly timid attempts.

This is a significant area of investigation: the smart processing of regular and ambient data is designed to encourage optimum functioning in ambient systems in their respective environments. It is on the basis of this single condition that we speak of *smart environments* beyond merely "smart" or *sentient computing*, reminiscent of Cook and Das' definition [COO 05]:

"A small world where all kinds of smart devices are continuously working to make inhabitants' lives more comfortable". Nothing to do with "Big Brother"!

The challenge of ambient intelligence and situated computing lies in the development of calculatory devices that have a perfect autonomy to adapt, detect, interpret and respond to the user's intelligent environment. At the same time, these kinds of devices are currently energy greedy because they are designed without consideration of these constraints and therefore more effective research strategies must be employed to ensure energy autonomy in large-scale systems.

There are still reservations about these technological limitations because the way we deal with the uncertain is still an issue. The quality of real-world information and the relevance of its treatment are problems. Having too much confidence in sensors may risk falsifying our ability for judgment. In parallel with these engineering considerations, a socio-psycho-ergonomic dimension arises: an ethical approach in sustainable development is a necessity if we are to listen to the concerns of citizens. Nanotechnology has gained the mistrust of experts in "Green IT" alongside the challenges relating to ensuring respect for private life.

New challenges have also emerged such as providing energy efficiency tools in fields such as electrical networks, transport, food distribution and town planning: sustainable development has led to the development of depolluting concrete coated with CO_2-absorbent paint.

Beyond this, we are seeing new operatory paradigms emerge via these materials such as quantum computing to charge networks and other saturated channels that may be potentially increasingly used to treat data flow reliably in real time. Monitoring, recording and diagnosing complex systems require rethinking our approach to systems that are still too centralized and fragile: autonomous adaptation is the future.

4.7. Bibliography

[AKH 97] AKHRAS G., Smart structures and their applications in civil engineering, Civil Engineering Report, CE97-2, RMC, Kingston, Ontario, Canada, 1997.

[AKH 98] AKHRAS G., How smart can a bridge be?, Atelier Canado-Taïwanais sur les ponts à moyenne et à longue portée, Taipei, Taiwan, 9–11, March 1998.

[AKH 00] AKHRAS G., "Smart materials and smart systems for the future", *Canadian Military Journal*, vol. 1, no. 3, pp. 25–31, 2000.

[ALK 08] AL KUKHUN D., SÈDES F., "Adaptive solutions for access control within pervasive healthcare systems", *International Conference on Smart homes and Telematics (ICOST 2008)*, Ames, IA, USA, 28 June–02 July 2008, vol. 5120, HELAL S., MITRA S., WONG J., CHANG K., MOUNIR M. (eds), Lecture Notes in Computer Science, Springer, pp. 42–53, June 2008.

[ALK 09] AL KUKHUN D., SÈDES F., "La mise en œuvre d'un modèle de contrôle d'accès adapté aux systèmes pervasifs. Application aux équipes mobiles gériatriques", *Document Numérique*, vol. 12, no. 3, Hermès, pp. 59–78, December 2009.

[BAR 04] BARTELDS G., HEIDA J.H., MCFEAT J., BOLLER C., "Introduction", in STASZEWSKI W., BOLLER C., TOMLINSON G. (dir.), *Health Monitoring of Aerospace Structures*, IOP Publishing, John Wiley & Sons, West Sussex, pp. 29–73, 2004.

[BOE 11] BOEING OFFICIAL WEBSITE, 2011, www.boeing.com/news/releases/2004/q2/nr_040518t.html.

[CHE 06] CHEN Y., WICKRAMASINGHE V., ZIMCIK D.G., "Development of adaptive seat mounts for helicopter vibration suppression", *Cansmart 2006, International Workshop Smart Materials and Structures*, Toronto, Canada, pp. 9–19, 2006.

[COO 05] COOK D., DAS S., *Smart Environments: Technologies, Protocols, and Applications*, Wiley, Hoboken, 2005.

[HEI 09] HEINZ J.C., "Investigation of piezoelectric flaps for load alleviation using CFD", *Riso-R-1702*, National Laboratory for Sustainable Energy, Technical University of Denmark, 2009, www.risoe.dtu.dk/.

[IHN 04] IHN J.B., CHANG F.K., "Detection and monitoring of hidden fatigue crack growth using a built-in piezoelectric sensor/actuator network: II. validation using riveted joints and repair patches", *Smart Materials and Structures*, vol. 13, pp. 621–630, 2004.

[SMA 11] SMART Layer® is a registered trademark of Acellent Technologies Inc., 2011, www.acellent.com.

[STR 04] STRAUB F.K., KENNEDY D.K., DOMZALSKI D.B., HASSAN A.A., NGO H., ANAND V., BIRCHETTE T., "Smart material actuated rotor technology – SMART", *Journal of Intelligent Material Systems and Structures*, vol. 15, pp. 249–260, 2004.

[STR 05] STRAUB F., KENNEDY D., "Design, development, fabrication and testing of an active flap rotor system", *61st AHS Annual Forum*, Grapevine, Texas, June 2005.

[WIC 04] WICKRAMASINGHE V., ZIMCIK D., CHEN Y., "A novel adaptive structural impedance control approach to suppress aircraft vibration and noise", *RTO AVT Symposium on "Habitability of Combat and Transport Vehicles: Noise, Vibration and Motion"*, Prague, Czech republic, published in RTO-MP-AVT-110, pp. 16–1 to 16–13, 2004.

[ZHO 06] ZHONGQING S., XIAOMING W., ZHIPING C., LIN Y., DONG W., "A built-in active sensor network for health monitoring of composite structures", *Smart Materials and Structures*, vol. 15, pp. 1939–1949, 2006.

Chapter 5

Middleware in Ubiquitous Computing

5.1. Middleware

The growing complexity of applications as well as advances in the calculation capabilities of computer materials requires heavy investment during their development. It is difficult to maintain and develop autonomous or context-adapted applications when the code that manages non-operational functions is mixed with the operational code. This is called a "laissez-faire" design approach [SAT 96]. With the vast expansion of distributed architectures 20 years ago, middleware emerged. This provides a transparent, comprehensive view of the set of distributed resources with which it can interact. The mechanisms for managing distributions are therefore taken out from applications to propose reusable and generic solutions. We will first examine the key developments in software and computer environments (section 5.2) and then discuss the main properties of middleware in ubiquitous computing (section 5.3).

5.2. Development of middleware with new computer environments

Following the *mainframe* era of bulky, multiuser devices, the development of microelectronics has reduced the size and cost of computers. Computer networks could therefore be created to benefit from greater computing power and more significant storage space. These computers could solve more complex problems and spread the use of various resources. Distributed computing (section 5.2.1) was the

---

Chapter written by Vincent HOURDIN, Nicolas FERRY, Jean-Yves TIGLI, Stéphane LAVIROTTE and Gaëtan REY.

first to propose middleware to facilitate the development of applications based on complex and non-functional mechanisms, such as network distribution, and foster the reusability of these mechanisms.

As a result, the miniaturization and popularization of wireless networks and various interactions with the physical environment and the user have resulted in mobile computing (section 5.2.2), context-sensitive computing (section 5.2.3) and ubiquitous computing (section 5.2.4). Middleware has developed in a similar way and has gradually integrated new functions (Figure 5.1).

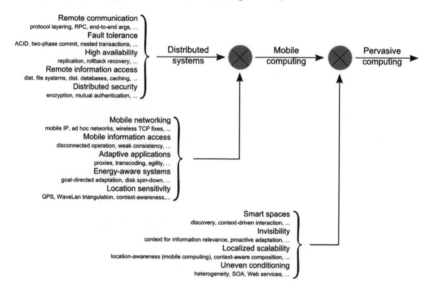

Figure 5.1. *Taxonomy of research problems in ubiquitous computing [SAT 01]*

5.2.1. *Distribution*

Issarny *et al.* [ISS 07] provide a precise definition of the term middleware as being a program layer situated between the application and the operating system in relation to the network. We therefore speak of network middleware, which is designed to facilitate the creation of distributed applications, provide a high level of abstraction on network problems and allow developers to create distributed applications while focusing on distribution-related constraints.

To facilitate the integration of applications, middleware provides mechanisms for their coordination [ISS 07]. Different message-based protocols such as MOM (Message Oriented Middleware) [EUG 03], tuple protocols such as Linda [GEL 85], or even procedure calls on distant hosts such as RPC (Remote Procedure Call) [SRI 95] have been proposed. With the appearance of object-oriented programming, RPCs are evolving and communications are made between remote objects such as with Java-RMI (Remote Method Invocation) or DCOM (Distributed Component Object Model). Some types of middleware enable communications over heterogeneous protocols such as CORBA [WAN 01]. The CORBA bus sends requests from the client application toward the object by masking problems of heterogeneity such as data format (marshalling) or communication protocols. Other constraints are also integrated into this middleware, such as, for example, security or fault tolerance.

Design approaches for applications are evolving and are increasingly moving toward "transparent" approaches [SAT 96]. These consist of externalizing the mechanisms related to non-functional concerns from these applications (security, monitoring, transaction, etc.) and, as a result, implementing them in middleware.

More than being merely a means of hiding distribution, middleware has been defined in more detail as follows: "Middleware is a software layer between the network operating system and the application. It provides reusable and well-known solutions to frequently encountered problems such as heterogeneity, interoperability, security, and reliability" [ISS 07].

5.2.2. *Mobility*

Besides being governed by material developments, new challenges have arisen for middleware in various fields such as grid or mobile computing. They are designed to propose increasingly complex mechanisms for applications. With the miniaturization of computing materials, an increasing number of smart and mobile objects are becoming part of our daily environment. In addition to the problems found in middleware in distributed computing, there are the constraints created by the mobility of these objects. LIME [MUR 01] is an example of middleware that accounts for this physical and logical mobility of applications, as well as supporting them. It highlights an initial challenge of consistency in shared data. However, disconnections are no longer considered malfunctions but a normal mode of operation [MAS 02]. For example, the CARMEN middleware [BEL 03] centers on connection problems inherent to wireless connections. Communications that were normally synchronous are becoming mostly asynchronous to offer better distributions between the different entities of a network.

Middleware must therefore be able to dynamically and quickly consider the appearance and disappearance of mobile devices.

Furthermore, a first type of information about the application's environment becomes essential: its location. Equally, information relating to the system becomes critical such as autonomy or even bandwidth. The MobiPADS middleware [CHA 03] proposes a series of mechanisms used to consider the internal state of the mobile device. CARISMA (Context-Aware Reflective Middleware System for Mobile Application) [CAP 03], is a mobile reflexive middleware, which is context sensitive. It monitors two types of contextual information: device-related and environment-related information, which also encompass other types of information.

5.2.3. *Context awareness and adaptation*

In parallel with this, and as a result of miniaturization, a multitude of sensors that can be distributed in the physical environment has given rise to context-aware computing. Mechanisms for context awareness have been borrowed from other applications and considered via a cross-disciplinary approach [DAV 06, SAL 99]. Middleware has introduced mechanisms ranging from context perception to application's adaptation.

In this field, two types of middleware have emerged. Firstly, middleware such as the Context Toolkit [SAL 99], Context Fabric [HON 02], SOCAM [GU 05], ACoMS [HU 08], Contextors [REY 05], and CoWSAMI [ATH 08] have factorized mechanisms for observing context (context perception). Most of them propose gathering, storage and processing mechanisms for contextual information. However, the observation of context remains a sub-problem in context awareness. As shown in SAFRAN [DAV 06], adapting application behavior is also a cross-disciplinary concern, which is part of accounting for context [BOT 07]. Middleware is therefore increasingly adopting these functions, ranging from context gathering to adapting the application's behavior.

5.2.4. *Ubiquitous computing*

Ubiquitous computing is the result of a combination of mobile computing and context awareness, taking and combining concepts from both worlds. Middleware in ubiquitous computing relies on a set of potentially distributed, heterogeneous, and mobile resources, providing contextual information with dynamics suitable for context adaptation. Various middleware have attempted to address these problems and are generally focused specifically on one of them.

Amigo [VAL 05], for example, focuses on the integration of several communication and discovery protocols to consider as many heterogeneous entities as possible. Aura [SOU 02] addresses the problem of user-task migration, while Gaia [ROM 02] proposes a centralized system based on an operating system model. RCSM [YAU 02], in contrast, focuses more specifically on adaptation mechanisms.

The previous definition of middleware can be therefore amended as follows: middleware is a software bridge between a variable software infrastructure and an applicative model, providing a set of mechanisms that responds to the non-functional tasks underpinning applications.

This maintains application functions irrespective of changes in its infrastructure and environment. Middleware therefore provides a number of responses to these various concerns (Figure 5.2).

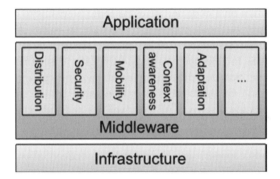

Figure 5.2. *Middleware in ubiquitous computing*

In this section, we will focus on middleware in ubiquitous computing. In section 5.3, we will examine in further detail the features that it must fulfill and what this entails for middleware.

5.3. Main properties of middleware in ubiquitous computing

The main properties and features of middleware, which can be considered as a prerequisite of ubiquitous computing applications, have already been widely studied [COS 08, NIE 04, TIG 09b]. In the following sections, we will list their main properties by explaining how they are involved at the heart of middleware and their consequences for the application.

5.3.1. *Heterogeneity and interoperability*

In a ubiquitous computing environment, numerous devices and software entities created by different designers or companies are available. They often use different data representations, programming languages, protocols, and means of communication. Middleware must, as far as possible, enable applications to communicate with different entities transparently. Managing heterogeneity gives middleware interoperability abilities.

Heterogeneity occurs at two levels. Technological heterogeneity at the material or software level is the most obvious. To facilitate interoperability between technologically heterogeneous entities, it is necessary to use standards such as public interfaces or standardized communication mechanisms. A solution at a software level is to communicate using a shared API and a unified binary format [COS 08] to distribute the middleware over different devices. Another solution is to execute the heart of the application on a node and delegate some functions to other mobile nodes by, for example, carrying out requests. To do so, it is desirable to use shared communication standards such as CORBA or web services to allow the code based on various languages to interoperate. In the opposite case, the middleware must carry out conversions between different entities, as done by Amigo [VAL 05]. An abstract representation of the entities is manipulated by the application and the middleware manages the discovery of these entities and their communication in its protocols.

Heterogeneity also appears at a semantic level. Indeed, even if the problem of technological heterogeneity is resolved, the various devices or available software services do not necessarily have a well-known semantics. In ubiquitous computing, all the software entities are not necessarily known at the design stage. It is therefore necessary to integrate them into applications as and when they are available. In order to carry out such processes, their semantics must be known. A mechanism indicating the entities' semantics must therefore be provided by the middleware. There are two main strategies:

– constraining the entities included in the application to a predefined list, as is the case with UPnP profiles, for example. All the entities must conform to predefined and standardized interfaces and therefore with a well-known semantics at the design stage;

– defining a semantic description standard, based on an ontology shared by all the elements in the system. In this case, the entities must provide a description of their semantics, which is not the case in current industrial products.

Even if the semantics of a device or software entity is known, it may be designed to fulfill a specific function but used for another. For example, a keypad on a mobile phone can be used to enter a number or can serve as a remote to switch on a light. In addition, the semantics of these two features are not necessarily expressed in the same way. We therefore speak of an ontology alignment problem.

5.3.2. *Scalability*

Ubiquitous computing systems are generally initially designed in a restricted environment called an ambient space containing a small number of users. Scalability entails considering a system with a large number of users and including several ambient spaces that are available anywhere. The distribution or replication of some systems is therefore mandatory to avoid a bottleneck. This argument responds to a need for centralization to improve system performance such as, for example, the distribution of authenticated encryption keys [LEE 07].

The management of large-scale contextual information is a major concern in terms of communication efficacy [DEV 10], which is directly linked to the energy consumption of embedded or mobile devices. Communication with remote resources must be reduced [COS 08] to support local or close interactions, which are less expensive in terms of energy and resources.

Scaling can be complex when the discovery system is based on local diffusion technologies such as service location protocols (SLP) or UPnP [HOU 07] with UDP diffusion. In this case, ambient space controllers must be implemented to make information available to other ambient spaces [VEV 08].

5.3.3. *Mobility*

Mobility is an important facet of ubiquitous computing. Users are mobile in the physical environment; they carry and use mobile devices which are constrained by their energy autonomy and communication discontinuities. Thus we can not longer consider that devices are always available during the application running. In addition, autonomous and mobile robots have emerged and will be increasingly present in the future. The services they offer are also mobile in relation to their users and applications. We have already studied the consequences of this variability. Nevertheless, dynamic adaptation of applications depending on software and material entities available is not the only means of modifying their behavior. Code migration is another complementary and non-exclusive solution [COS 08].

Applications could migrate from one device to another, making their data and services permanently available while the user moves around [COS 08]. Migration can help reduce communication costs and avoid unannounced disconnections. It is triggered by an explicit action by the user or by detecting a change in context. There are at least three types of migration: task, code or data migration.

Task migration has been illustrated by the Aura Project [SOU 02]. The aim is to allow the user to continue to use an application while they change their interaction device. The application that they were using, such as, for example, a word processor, has its state protected before being stopped on the previous device and is restarted with the same parameters on a different device. The application can be different, for example, moving from a simple text editor to a rich text editor but the active line and the file's content remain identical as far as possible.

Code migration requires an important prerequisite: devices must be totally controlled by the system. However, as is often the case in ubiquitous computing, devices suffer, typically when the environment consists of commercial devices. A virtual machine or any other portable code deployment system must be executed on the device so that it can execute some code provided by the middleware. Furthermore, the middleware must not consider distribution transparently but also monitor it to decide on which node to deploy the code.

Data migration is, in part, used by task migration but the latter can also entail data-caching mechanisms in an ambient space; for example, in anticipation of disconnection with a server. LIME [PIC 99] is an example of this kind of mobile access system with distributed tuple based data. Used in disconnected mode when necessary, data is synchronized when connections become available again.

5.3.4. *Variability, unpredictability, extensibility, and spontaneous interactions*

The environment in an ambient space is characterized by high variability [PAS 08]. This variability can be expressed around three axes:

– a variability axis that concerns variations in the set of available devices in the system's software infrastructure. Ubiquitous computing applications rely on a software infrastructure, which can include a multitude of disparate heterogeneous devices. These can be mobile and thus enter or leave this infrastructure at anytime. They can also be subject to failure or become unavailable. They may therefore appear of disappear dynamically in this infrastructure. As a result, the application that will be constructed above it must vary according to the opportunities offered:

– a variability axis that concerns the high variability of the physical environment around an application. By its very nature, the physical environment is constantly changing; it is a continuous space in which physical phenomena intervene and evolve. Accounting for these changes is done through environmental observations (context perception). Variations are expressed in the form of changes in states' values associated with physical or software models. In order to measure and reason on these phenomena, the system must have these models [GEI 09];

– a variability axis that focuses on this set of adaptations for various concerns that must be implemented. Depending on the two previous variability axes, that is, depending on its environment and software infrastructure, an application may take various configurations. The mechanism of adaptation is the tool that allows it to pass from one configuration to another. Several adaptations can be described for various concerns and can be combined when a new situation requires it.

This last axis is strongly dependent on the other two since it is a reaction to their variation. Indeed, the set of configurations possible for an application will depend, in part, on the ability of the system to manage variations in its environment and infrastructure. The better the system can manage the two previous variability axes, the more likely it is to be able to manage numerous configurations in the application. The set of adaptations that can be implemented to change from one configuration to another can quickly become consequential and, as such, can result in a large increase in the number of combinations of adaptations.

All these variable elements and the way they are managed cannot necessarily be known *a priori*, raising the notion of unpredictability in addition to variability. Moreover, since we cannot know at the design stage all the entities that will compose the software infrastructure and interact together, it is necessary to include them in the system at runtime; this is referred to as dynamic extendibility. This requires discovering the set of entities that change over the time and are found in the environment at any given moment. Extendibility can be manifested as spontaneous interactions between newly discovered entities [COS 08]. In this case, these applications will be dynamically adapted to provide unforeseen features or a means of creating unforeseen features on the basis of entities whose availability had not been anticipated at the design stage.

Uncoupling between entities, also known as weak coupling or entity autonomy, is a significant factor that allows them to interoperate spontaneously and provide extensibility as well as give applications a dynamic adaptation capacity. This uncoupling occurs at several levels, mostly in terms of autonomy during execution, which tends not to express implicit dependency and requires the execution of specific entities, and in terms of interactions between these entities. In mobile or ubiquitous computing, interactions are generally based on events or other asynchronous communications [COS 08, TIG 09b]. These interactions are not as closely coupled as protocols such as method invocation, which are generally predicted during design and take place directly in the application's code. Event channels are more flexible such as, for example, in the case of a publish/subscribe pattern [EUG 03], where subscriptions to sources of information can be dynamically and unpredictably created.

Since the frequency of environmental variations may be high, it is not possible to stop the application to configure it each time this is necessary. Adaptation must therefore be dynamic, which modifies the application's behavior while it continues to operate [FOX 09].

5.3.5. *Dynamic adaptation*

Adaptation resulting from variability must be dynamic in ubiquitous computing. Applications' functions must be modified during execution without interrupting the interaction with the user. Dynamic adaptation entails a number of techniques and relies on different application design patterns [FOX 09]. However, two types of adaptations can occur, as identified by McKinley *et al.* [MCK 04]: parameter adaptation and compositional adaptation.

Parameter adaptation involves modifying variables, which determine the application's behavior. Parameters' values can be modified at runtime and result in the use of a new, predefined strategy in the application. It is therefore not possible to integrate new strategies after the design stage.

Compositional adaptation, however, results in an exchange of algorithmic or structural parts in the application with new information, which improves the application's adaptation to its current environment. This type of adaptation is widely used in ubiquitous computing because it allows situations to be controlled by dynamic contextual information and information specific to the application, which cannot be known at the design stage [BOU 10]. Applications based on model adaptation mean the application has to be regenerated [BEU 09] or redesigned [FER 09] and are therefore assimilated with compositional adaptations.

A third type of adaptation can be constructed from the two others, based on intercepting messages [FOX 09]. In this case, interceptors are placed between the different entities of the application and are configured to adapt the application. For example, interception will modify the format of an image or will forbid some information being transmitted on a secure communication channel. We can see that in some application design models, for example, fractal components [BRU 02] provide interceptors on the entry and exit components and this type of adaptation can therefore be easily implemented.

Adaptation, in addition to being triggered by variations in the software structure, is caused by modifications relating to the physical environment. Context awareness relates to this problem.

5.3.6. *Context awareness*

As we have seen, applications in ubiquitous computing environments must take into account the dynamics of their environment. Context is any information that may affect an application's behavior (whether or not they are within a software infrastructure), the user, or more generally the user's physical environment. Middleware in ubiquitous computing provides applications with the capability to collect, manage, and process contextual data as well as the ability to reason on processed data and adapt as a result (Figure 5.3).

Typically, contextual information is obtained from heterogeneous and remote sources. Collecting or sensing information requires other functionalities from the middleware such as discovery and interoperability. Information sources are often software services executed over sensors or mobile devices fitted with sensors and/or software entities providing purely software-based information such as an agenda or, more recently, Twitter [ROM 10]. Discovering sources of contextual information and their integration into the context management system can raise the same problems of extendibility and spontaneous interaction as found with the middleware.

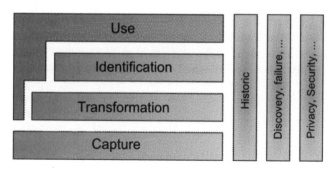

Figure 5.3. *Pyramid of context [COU 05]: processes necessary for accounting for context*

Gathering contextual information can be either centralized or distributed. Distributed systems have the advantage of not having a single failure point, but require a more significant number of communications to ensure coherent aggregation of necessary information [DEV 10].

The treatment of collected information can also take two main forms [BOU 10]: treatment based on mathematical operations such as inequalities or numerical functions and ontology-based treatment. Other related treatments focus on the quality of the information provided such as, for example, the use of an audit trail to extrapolate the nearest or missing values, the use of filters to smooth out values and not react to irregular contexts [STR 04]. The treatment of contextual information provides higher level information due to reasoning, to supply, for example, an address from a geographic coordinate [EJI 07].

A decision must be made, given the processed and identified context, on the adaptation to be carried out. The decision may combine several adaptations before applying them in real life in order to minimize the time of inactivity or reconfiguration of the application [FER 09] (section 5.3.8).

5.3.7. *Security*

The growing number of interactions between entities in ubiquitous computing, which are increasingly close to the user, means that we need to reconsider the security of personal data. Users transmit data to identify themselves on numerous systems, often via unsecured communication channels. And, since the applications or services offered are tailored to the user, transmitted data is increasingly more sensitive than before in the sense that it reveals information about the users' private lives. The protection of private life (privacy) is therefore the main security problem or, in any case, the most important for the public in ubiquitous computing [CAR 07]. Even if a single piece of information does not represent a genuine threat to private life, the accumulation of several pieces of information can be one. There is, however, no obvious solution to the problem of privacy as there is with other more traditional security issues (confidentiality, authenticity, integrity) [HOU 10].

Confidentiality must be taken into account in research mechanisms and decentralized discovery based on the transmission of messages that we find in ubiquitous computing [TRA 06], with, for example, the WS-Security protocol [NAD 04] applied to WS-Discovery [SCH 05]. Of course, such precautions must be taken for messages exchanged between entities after the discovery phase. The most evident answer for the issue of confidentiality seems to be the suppression of all unencrypted messages for encrypted ones, although this does not solve all problems: encrypted messages, even completely so using IPSEC, may still provide an inventory of existing devices in weak dynamic locations, such as a house. Indeed, based on the size and timing of messages, one can determine the type of devices from which they originate [ELL 02]. The distribution of encryption keys should be carried out only on trusted entities (devices and clients), which means they must be authenticated.

Authentication verifies that the entities in the infrastructure of ubiquitous computing systems are authentic and that they can be trusted to be used in applications. Access control must be implemented in order to limit the activity of entities on devices and applications to only authorized, and therefore authenticated, entities. As is the case for entities in the application, we cannot escape the principle that a centralized certification authority will not be available for the entire lifetime of an application [HOU 10]. In 2012, users are increasingly aware of the presence of the devices around them or they at least know how to identify them when necessary. Authentication is therefore simple. When devices are integrated into buildings or are multiplied, it is necessary to provide mechanisms such as remote webs of trust to authenticate devices or invisible software entities [LUO 02].

The integrity of messages verifies their authenticity, i.e. they are received as they were sent. Wireless communications generate more errors than wired ones and received information is frequently not intact or authentic when received in application layers. *Man-in-the-middle*-type attacks modify messages to obtain unauthorized information and the control of integrity prevents this. Integrity in ubiquitous computing does not affect the mechanisms specific to these environments.

5.3.8. *Adapted and controlled response times*

The frequency at which an adaptation mechanism can create adaptations is a major point of interest in ubiquitous computing. The constraints previously examined have resulted in complex systems. The relevance of adaptation must not only be logical but also temporal [FER 09]. Let us suppose that the adaptable applications are always in one of the three states shown in Figure 5.4. State 1 is that of normal execution in the application where it is relevant in relation to its environment, i.e. that it is behaving as desired for this environment. When a change occurs in the environment, the application before being adapted is in state 2 where it is no longer consistent with the environment. Once adaptation has started, it is in an unstable state (3) and can be partially or completely unavailable. It is also no longer consistent with its environment. While the application is in state 2, several new changes in the environment may happen. If one of these changes happens while the application is in state 3, then it switches back to state 2.

The time between states 2 and 3 must be restricted so that it corresponds as far as possible to the evolving dynamics of the environment and the application. If the time required to adapt the application is too close to the average time between changes in context, the application will more frequently be in the unstable state 3 than in the usable state 1 or even in the usable state with old data (2). In addition, if the application is in state 2 for too long and therefore the detection time for a change in context or reaction to this change is too significant, the application will run for a considerable amount of time using stale data. Depending on the resulting effect of using this data, the user may face a lack of reliability in the application or latency, which may indicate the system to be unreliable [MAC 93].

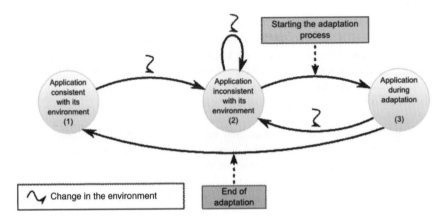

Figure 5.4. *The three states of an adaptable application*

The response time of a change in context must therefore be minimized throughout the entire context processing change. Using reactive and asynchronous communication protocols such as events [EUG 03] does not require any time to detect value changes in sensors. Simple considerations of context in relation to change provide a low response time although they are of a lesser quality. A recent sphere of interest has been using simple processes to rapidly react to easily detectable changes in context [TIG 09a] and more complex mechanisms based on ontologies to react to a different dynamic to more complex changes in context [BOU 10].

In this chapter, we have examined the specific characteristics of environments in ubiquitous computing and the properties they provide in middleware. In Chapter 6, we will focus on the systems specific to each of the fields examined: web services for devices such as infrastructure that discover and communicate with software entities by providing interoperability: the SLCA composition model for these services based on assembling dynamic components enables variability and extensibility to be managed and the compositional adaptation model called "Aspects of Assembly" (AA), which provides the dynamic adaptation required for extendibility and for accounting for context.

5.4. Bibliography

[ATH 08] ATHANASOPOULOS D., ZARRAS A., ISSARNY V., PITOURA E., VASSILIADIS P., "CoWSAMI: interface-aware context gathering in ambient intelligence environments", *Journal on Pervasive and Mobile Computing*, vol. 4, no. 3, pp. 360–389, 2008.

[BEL 03] BELLAVISTA P., CORRADI A., MONTANARI R., STEFANELLI C., "Context-aware middleware for resource management in the wireless Internet", *IEEE Transactions on Software Engineering*, vol. 29, no. 12, pp. 1086–1099, 2003.

[BEU 09] BEUGNARD A., CHABRIDON S., CONAN D., TACONET C., DAGNAT F., KABORE E., "Towards context-aware components", *Proceedings of the First International ESEC/FSE Workshop on Context-Aware Software Technology and Applications*, Amsterdam, Netherlands, pp. 1–4, August 2009.

[BOT 07] BOTTARO A., GERODOLLE A., LALANDA P., "Pervasive service composition in the home network", *Proceedings of Advanced Information Networking and Applications*, AINA'07, pp. 596–603, 2007.

[BOU 10] BOUZEGHOUB A., TACONET C., JARRAYA A., DO N., CONAN D., "Complementarity of process-oriented and ontology-based context managers to identify situations", *Proceedings of International Workshop on Context Modeling and Management for Smart Environments (CMMSE)*, July 2010.

[BRU 02] BRUNETON E., COUPAYE T., STEFANI J.B., "Recursive and dynamic software composition with sharing", *Proceedings of the Workshop on Component-Oriented Programming (WCOP) at ECOOP'02*, June 2002.

[CAP 03] CAPRA L., EMMERICH W., MASCOLO C., "CARISMA: context-aware reflective middleware system for mobile applications", *IEEE Transactions on Software Engineering*, vol. 29, no. 10, pp. 929–945, 2003.

[CAR 07] CARDOSO R.S., ISSARNY V., "Architecting pervasive computing systems for privacy: a survey", *Proceedings of the Sixth Working IEEE/IFIP Conference on Software Architecture*, IEEE Computer Society, Washington, DC, USA, pp. 26, 2007.

[CHA 03] CHAN A., CHUANG S., "MobiPADS: a reflective middleware for context-aware mobile computing", *IEEE Transactions on Software Engineering*, vol. 29, no. 12, pp. 1072–1085, 2003.

[COS 08] DA COSTA C., YAMIN A., GEYER C., "Toward a general software infrastructure for ubiquitous computing", *IEEE Pervasive Computing*, IEEE Computer Society, vol. 7, no. 1, pp. 64–73, 2008.

[COU 05] COUTAZ J., CROWLEY J.L., DOBSON S., GARLAN D., "Context is key", *Communications of ACM*, ACM, vol. 48, no. 3, pp. 49–53, 2005.

[DAV 06] DAVID P., LEDOUX T., "An aspect-oriented approach for developing self-adaptive fractal components", *Lecture Notes in Computer Science*, Springer, vol. 4089, pp. 82, 2006.

[DEV 10] DEVLIC A., "SIP-based context distribution: does aggregation pay off?", *ACM SIGCOMM Computer Communication Review*, ACM, vol. 40, no. 5, pp. 35–46, 2010.

[EJI 07] EJIGU D., SCUTURICI M., BRUNIE L., "CoCA: a collaborative context-aware service platform for pervasive computing", *Proceedings of Fourth International Conference on Information Technology*, ITNG'07, pp. 297–302, 2007.

[ELL 02] ELLISON C.M., "Home network security", *Intel Technology Journal*, vol. 06, no. 04, pp. 37–48, 2002.

[EUG 03] EUGSTER P., FELBER P., GUERRAOUI R., KERMARREC A., "The many faces of publish/subscribe", *ACM Computing Surveys*, vol. 35, no. 2, pp. 114–131, 2003.

[FER 09] FERRY N., HOURDIN V., LAVIROTTE S., REY G., TIGLI J.Y., RIVEILL M., "Models at runtime: service for device composition and adaptation", *Proceedings of 4th International Workshop Models@Run.Time at Models 2009 (MRT'09)*, October 2009.

[FOX 09] FOX J., CLARKE S., "Exploring approaches to dynamic adaptation", *Proceedings of the 3rd International DiscCoTec Workshop on Middleware-Application Interaction*, ACM, p. 19–24, 2009.

[GEI 09] GEIHS K., REICHLE R., WAGNER M., KHAN M.U., "Modeling of context-aware self-adaptive applications in ubiquitous and service-oriented environments", in CHENG B.H., LEMOS R., GIESE H., INVERARDI P., MAGEE J. (eds), *Software Engineering for Self-Adaptive Systems*, Springer-Verlag, Berlin, Heidelberg, pp. 146–163, 2009.

[GEL 85] GELERNTER D., "Generative communication in Linda", *ACM Transactions on Programming Languages and Systems (TOPLAS)*, ACM, vol. 7, no. 1, pp. 80–112, 1985.

[GU 05] GU T., PUNG H., ZHANG D., "A service-oriented middleware for building context aware services", *Journal of Network and Computer Applications*, vol. 28, no. 1, pp. 1–18, 2005.

[GUT 99] GUTTMAN E., "Service location protocol: automatic discovery of IP network services", *IEEE Internet Computing*, vol. 3, pp. 71–80, 1999.

[HON 02] HONG J., "The context fabric: an infrastructure for context-aware computing", *Proceedings of CHI, Conference on Human Factors in Computing Systems*, 2002.

[HOU 07] HOURDIN V., LAVIROTTE S., TIGLI J.Y., "UPnP services for autonomous devices", *Techniques de l'Ingénieur*, vol. H5002, February 2007.

[HOU 10] HOURDIN V., Context and security in Ubiquitous Computing Middlewares, PhD thesis, University of Nice Sophia Antipolis, France, July 2010.

[HU 08] HU P., INDULSKA J., ROBINSON R., "An autonomic context management ystem for pervasive computing", *PERCOM '08: Proceedings of the 2008 Sixth Annual IEEE International Conference on Pervasive Computing and Communications*, IEEE Computer Society, Washington, DC, USA, pp. 213–223, 2008.

[ISS 07] ISSARNY V., CAPORUSCIO M., GEORGANTAS N., "A perspective on the future of middleware-based software", *Proceedings of Engineering, International Conference on Software Engineering*, IEEE Computer Society, Washington, DC, USA, pp. 244–258, 2007.

[LEE 07] LEE J., HUANG C., LEE L., LEI C., "Design and implementation of secure communication channels over UPnP networks", *Proceedings of the 2007 International Conference on Multimedia and Ubiquitous Engineering*, IEEE Computer Society, pp. 307–312, 2007.

[LUO 02] LUO H., LU S., "Ubiquitous and robust authentication services for ad hoc wireless networks", *Proceedings of 7th IEEE Symposium on Computers and Communications (ISCC'02)*, 2002.

[MAC 93] MAC KENZIE I., WAR E. C., "Lag as a determinant of human performance in interactive systems", *Proceedings of the INTERACT'93 and CHI'93 Conference on Human Factors in Computing Systems*, ACM, pp. 488–493, 1993.

[MAS 02] MASCOLO C., CAPRA L., EMMERICH W., "Middleware for mobile computing (a survey)", *Networking 2002 Tutorial Papers*, vol. 2497, pp. 20–58, 2002.

[MCK 04] MC KINLEY P., SADJADI S., KASTEN E., CHENG B., A taxonomy of compositional adaptation, Report MSU-CSE-04-17, Michigan State University, 2004.

[MUR 01] MURPHY A., PICCO G., ROMAN G., "Lime: a middleware for physical and logical mobility", *Proceedings of 21st International Conference on Distributed Computing Systems*, IEEE Computer Society, Washington DC, pp. 524–533, 2001.

[NAD 04] NADALIN A. *et al.*, Web Services Security (WS-Security), OASIS joint specification by IBM, Microsoft, VeriSign, Sun Microsystems, and many others, March 2004.

[NIE 04] NIEMELA E., LATVAKOSKI J., "Survey of requirements and solutions for ubiquitous software", *MUM '04: Proceedings of the 3rd International Conference on Mobile and Ubiquitous Multimedia*, ACM, New York, NY, pp. 71–78, 2004.

[PAS 08] PASPALLIS N., ROUVOY R., BARON E.P., PAPADOPOULOS G., ELIASSEN F., MAMELLI A., "A pluggable and reconfigurable architecture for a context-aware enabling middleware system", *On the Move to Meaningful Internet Systems: OTM 2008*, vol. 5331, Lecture Notes in Computer Science, Springer, pp. 553–570, 2008.

[PIC 99] PICCO G., MURPHY A., ROMAN G., "LIME: linda meets mobility", *Proceedings of the 21st International Conference on Software Engineering*, IEEE Computer Society Press, Washington DC, pp. 368–377, 1999.

[REY 05] REY G., Context in man machine interaction: the contextor, Ph. D thesis, Joseph Fourier University Grenoble, 2005.

[ROM 02] ROMAN M., HESS C.K., CERQUEIRA R., RANGANATHAN A., CAMPBEL R.H., NAHRSTEDT K., "Gaia: a middleware infrastructure to enable active spaces", *IEEE Pervasive Computing*, pp. 74–83, December 2002.

[ROM 10] ROMERO D., ROUVOY R., SEINTURIER L., LOIRET F., "Integration of heterogeneous context resources in ubiquitous environments", *Proceedings of 36th EUROMICRO International Conference on Software Engineering and Advanced Applications*, 2010.

[SAL 99] SALBER D., DEY A., ABOWD G., "The context toolkit: aiding the development of context-enabled applications", *Proceedings of the SIGCHI Conference on Human Factors in Computing Systems: the CHI is the Limit*, ACM, pp. 434–441, 1999.

[SAT 96] SATYANARAYANAN M., "Fundamental challenges in mobile computing", *Proceedings of Fifteenth ACM Symposium on Principles of Distributed Computing*, May 1996.

[SAT 01] SATYANARAYANAN M., "Pervasive computing: vision and challenges", *IEEE Personal Communications*, vol. 8, no. 4, p. 10–17, 2001.

[SCH 05] SCHLIMMER J. *et al.*, "Web services dynamic discovery (WS-discovery)", *OASIS Joint Specification by Microsoft, BEA Systems, Intel, Canon and Web Methods*, April 2005.

[SOU 02] SOUSA J., GARLAN D., "Aura: an architectural framework for user mobility in ubiquitous computing environments", *Proceedings of the 3rd Working IEEE/IFIP Conference on Software Architecture (WICSA3)*, Kluwer Academic Publishers, p. 29, August 2002.

[SRI 95] SRINIVASAN R., RPC: remote procedure call protocol specification version 2, RFC 1831, Network Working Group Request for Comments: 1831, 1995.

[STR 04] STRANG T., LINNHOFF-POPIEN C., "A context modeling survey", *Proceedings of the Workshop on Advanced Context Modeling, Reasoning and Management as Part of UbiComp*, 2004.

[TIG 09a] TIGLI J.Y., LAVIROTTE S., REY G., HOURDIN V., RIVEILL M., "Context-aware authorization in highly dynamic environments", *International Journal of Computer Science Issues (IJCSI)*, vol. 4, September 2009.

[TIG 09b] TIGLI J.Y., LAVIROTTE S., REY G., HOURDIN V., CHEUNG-FOO-WO D., CALLEGARI E., RIVEILL M., "WComp middleware for ubiquitous computing: aspects and composite event-based web services", *Annals of Telecommunications (AoT)*, vol. 64, no. 3–4, pp. 197–214, April 2009.

[TRA 06] TRABELSI S., PAZZAGLIA J., ROUDIER Y., "Secure web service discovery: overcoming challenges of ubiquitous computing", *Proceedings of the European Conference on Web Services*, IEEE Computer Society, pp. 35–43, 2006.

[VAL 05] VALLEE M., RAMPARANY F., VERCOUTER L., "Flexible composition of smart device services", *Proceedings of the International Conference on Pervasive Systems and Computing (PSC-05)*, June 2005.

[VEV 08] VEVERIDIS C., POLYZOS G., "Service discovery for mobile Ad Hoc networks: a survey of issues and techniques", *IEEE Communications Surveys and Tutorials*, vol. 10, no.3, 2008.

[WAN 01] WANG N., SCHMIDT D., O'RYAN C., "Overview of the CORBA component model", *Component-Based Software Engineering*, Addison-Wesley Longman, pp. 557–571, 2001.

[YAU 02] YAU S., KARIM F., WANG Y., WANG B., GUPTA S., "Reconfigurable context sensitive middleware for pervasive computing", *IEEE Pervasive Computing*, vol. 1, no. 3, pp. 33–40, 2002.

Chapter 6

WComp, Middleware for Ubiquitous Computing and System Focused Adaptation

This chapter examines three solutions to issues of middleware in ubiquitous computing. Firstly, we need a dynamic software infrastructure to have access to the heterogeneous software entities used by the application or to sense context. Secondly, we need to be able to adapt the application dynamically and create applications on the basis of its current context and the availability of software entities. Thirdly, dynamic adaptation must have a mechanism which is controlled by the user or the context.

6.1. Service infrastructure in devices

In order to interact with the entities in a software infrastructure, these entities must provide a software part which can be used by other entities. As for distributed middleware, approaches for defining these software parts have evolved. The first were procedural, as in the case of RPCs, which did not allow asynchronous communications between entities in the infrastructure. In addition, their code was also difficult to maintain. Subsequent message-oriented approaches have enabled asynchronous communication although they have not provided better ease of maintenance. This is because, in these procedural approaches, the code of the various functions remains complex and is, as a result, difficult to maintain. This led the way for object-oriented approaches, which removed the need for procedural calls

Chapter written by Nicolas FERRY, Vincent HOURDIN, Stéphane LAVIROTTE, Gaëtan REY and Jean-Yves TIGLI.

but replaced them with object references. The abstraction entailed in these object structures has improved modularity and reusability in the applicative code. In addition, with the use of virtual machines, these approaches offer good hardware interoperability. However, this interoperability is not sufficient because it requires the virtual machine to be present in all the infrastructure's entities. In addition, it is necessary to provide interoperability at the communication protocol level. It has subsequently been widely accepted that service-oriented approaches offer such possibilities.

Service-oriented architectures (SOA) are a paradigm for organizing and using distribution capabilities, which may be subject to different, sometimes, non-modifiable controls. They provide a uniform means of providing, discovering, interacting, and using capabilities to produce desired effects compatible with measurable preconditions and expectations [MAC 06]. They were originally used to enable the easy design and deployment of distributed applications. They are used to create dynamic applications from a basic set of entities called "service". A service is defined as the means for unifying the needs of consumers and provider capabilities.

SOAs are one means of reorganizing a set of compartmentalized software applications and supporting the infrastructure in a set of interconnected services, each being accessed via standardized interfaces and standardized protocols. They define the interaction between software entities as an exchange of messages between service consumers (clients) and service providers (servers) [PAP 03].

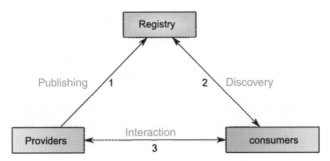

Figure 6.1. *Service-oriented architecture*

There is a third entity, the register, which affects the service discovery phase. It informs the system of available service providers and therefore allows consumers to find them (Figure 6.1) [CHA 02]. It generally retains service contracts rather than only references to providers. Services provide important properties with respect to the separation of concerns and the way they are used. Their main characteristics

[BRE 07, MAC 06] and features shared with ubiquitous computing, which have led to the use of SOAs to define the software infrastructure, are as follows:

Encapsulation: every feature can be encapsulated in a service and therefore forms part of the services available to create applications. All the entities in the system represented by a service of the same type will be accessible by the same infrastructure. SOAs therefore provide logical homogeneity. Devices also provide a range of features that can be encapsulated in services at a functional level;

Loose coupling and autonomy: there is no direct dependency between services. The absence of a service does not prevent others from carrying out their functions. They are independent, control their internal logic, and are executed without exterior intervention. Devices also have this property. A lamp, for example, does not need storage to operate;

Contracts and abstraction: services describe the features they offer in contracts. Services must conform to these contracts because they are the only means by which other entities obtain information on their functions as well as on a service's non-functional parts and metadata. Services are black boxes for which only their contract is known. The way they are implemented is unknown in advance and cannot be modified, which also corresponds to the functioning of the devices. The reuse of services is aided by the fact that service providers are not designed with consumers in mind. When a service is initiated, service providers publish their contract at a register to make an entity available to the system;

Dynamic discovery: services are discovered using specific criteria and can be replaced during runtime. Service consumers make a request to the registry to locate providers corresponding to their criteria. They then obtain a provider contract as well as a contact reference such as a URL;

Composability: services can be coordinated and assembled to create new applications or composite services. This composition does not occur within services but is organized by an external entity, such as, for instance, a composite service. The content of the composite service can be modified during runtime and black box abstraction is no longer possible. This is therefore referred to as a gray box.

All these properties shared by the services and devices, and their adoption in other research [BOT 07, CHA 05, VAL 05], have meant that SOAs have been considered for use as an infrastructure in ubiquitous computing. In this case, devices and software systems are represented by services.

Applications are therefore compositions of these services in constant relation with the infrastructure in order to observe and react, if necessary, to any infrastructural changes (i.e. (dis)appearance of a service) (Figure 6.2).

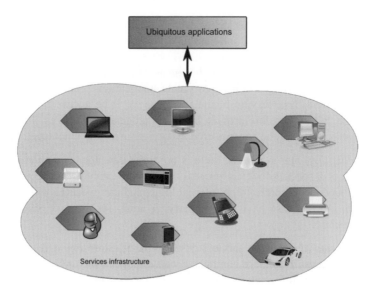

Figure 6.2. *The use of SOAs to represent the infrastructure of ambient computing*

To validate the use of services as an infrastructure for ubiquitous computing, it is necessary to examine whether the properties described in the introduction can be addressed; for example, heterogeneity, reactivity, and frequent disconnection due to user and devices mobility. Since their creation for distributed computing, SOAs have evolved in several directions, for the web, for information systems, and mobile and ubiquitous computing. Despite these different directions, a new type of service bringing together all these advances has emerged, web service-oriented architecture for devices (WSOADs).

6.1.1. *Interoperability*

With the SOAs that we now consider as standard, the choice of programming language, data representation format, or communication protocol should be made so as to be compatible with the consumers and providers of the system. Distributed applications are generally designed by a single working group, which in part resolves this problem. Two types of interoperability can therefore be guaranteed. First, interoperability in platforms where all the entities provide a service, as with JINI [ARN 99] that relies on Java, must use a virtual machine. The second type of interoperability is located in the communication protocols with, for example, CORBA or web services. With web services [CHA 02], the designers do not know how they will be used and will probably employ different hardware resources or languages from those of future consumers.

From the perspective of use for an infrastructure of devices, web service standards have a great benefit for heterogeneity which remains a major problem in mobile or ubiquitous computing. We can cite, for example, more than 600 different mobile phone platforms. More generally, mobile devices or smart objects use a wide diversity of communication and data representation protocols and programming languages. Interoperability as provided by web services is therefore essential.

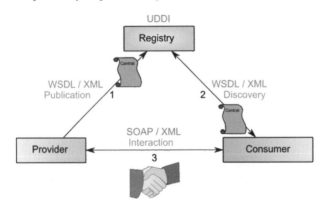

Figure 6.3. *A web-service-oriented architecture*

Web technologies have given SOAs several levels of interoperability (Figure 6.3). These WSOAs allow the creation of applications from services executed with heterogeneous programming languages and architectures of different hardware resources. This evolution of services is necessary while using SOAs as an infrastructure in ubiquitous computing due to the large heterogeneity of devices and applications found within it.

6.1.2. *Event communication*

Applications using mobile devices are reactive by nature since frequent disconnections must be rapidly accounted for. Battery operation forces programs to be efficient and use events rather than polling[1]. Human–machine interaction must also be rapid.

The processing capabilities of mobile devices are limited in terms of calculation speed, amount of memory, and duration of use due to battery power. Programs must therefore be as efficient and pertinent as possible. The implementation of queue systems or complex publication/subscription architectures

---

1 Also called "active waiting", this relates to regularly monitoring a condition

[EUG 03], such as message-oriented middleware (MOM), is rarely possible. It is for this reason that more simplified systems are used to connect an event transmitter with several receivers ($1 \rightarrow N$), with messages being immediately distributed.

Services for devices [HOU 06], provider entities in S*ervice-oriented architecture for devices* (SOADs), are lightweight services using event communications. Event communications enable device-based applications to effectively use hardware interruptions and provide loose coupling. Let us take the example of a smart interrupter: when activated, a material interruption occurs. Using events, a notification will be immediately sent to the consumers (Figure 6.4). Dynamicity and efficacy are maximal. Without using events, the interrupter would have to maintain an update variable expecting that consumers are asking for its value. Since these invocations occur periodically, there is a risk of missing a change in state if it is shorter than the client-invocation period.

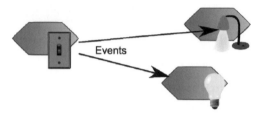

Figure 6.4. *Event communication in devices*

Event communications provide the dynamicity required for interactions between devices in ubiquitous computing applications. They also provide a dynamicity to these interactions by allowing the entities involved to reconfigure them at any point.

6.1.3. *Appearance and disappearance*

As we have seen, the infrastructure of an application in ubiquitous computing is highly variable due to the high mobility of its entities. User mobility, and therefore the devices in their personal networks, causes frequent disconnections and network changes. Network topology is also unknown in advance. In mobile networks, we cannot know the registry addresses nor even know if they exist. To construct applications on the basis of these entities, middleware must know the entities in this infrastructure. SOADs therefore represent an improvement on SOAs.

Service providers transmit announcements throughout the network when they enter (after addressing) or are leaving. This appearance or disappearance via announcements is asynchronic and gives this software infrastructure dynamicity.

However, when a consumer enters the infrastructure, it is their responsibility to initiate this (dis)appearance, otherwise providers will be unable to locate them quickly. In addition, if providers are suddenly disconnected or subject to a programming error, the disappearance announcement will not be sent. To overcome these problems, providers use a leasing mechanism which regularly confirms that they are still working.

Through these announcement mechanisms, the network's entities know the entities dynamically located within their network and can see them appear and disappear. The benefit of this mechanism is evident when coupled with decentralized dynamic discovery.

6.1.4. *Decentralized dynamic discovery*

Another evolution in the SOAs adopted from SOADs is the modification of discovery to account for networks, providers, and previously unknown consumers. The entities available to create an application are not known in advance and must be discovered dynamically.

When a registry is used, consumers make a request according to certain criteria (type of service, more complex names, or expressions [HOU 06]). Some types of architecture propose a second type of interaction between the registry and consumers. Consumers can subscribe on the registry to a type of service or other information and, when a provider corresponding to this criterion subscribes in the registry, the consumer is notified [BUS 02]. When consumer has obtained a reference to a provider (generally as an URL), it sends it a request to get the service contract of the provider. It can then interact with the provider at a functional level. This contract describes the service's technical specificities and its interpretation allows its discovery.

Decentralized research mechanisms have therefore emerged in industrial standards (SLP [GUT 99]), Jini [ARN 99], Bluetooth SDP[2], Salutation[3], Bonjour[4]) and various research projects [CHE 00, HUA 02, PRE 06, SED 03, ZHU 05]. They allow consumers to discover providers without going through a centralized registry. The research mechanism is, in fact, reduced in providers and consumers, which directly communicate with them. The discovery phase therefore uses appearance/ disappearance mechanisms.

---

2 Bluetooth Service Discovery Protocol, Specification of the Bluetooth System Core, version 1.1, 2001.
3 The "Salutation Consortium" no longer exists.
4 Bonjour is used in Mac OS X to locate printers and share data.

This mode is consumer oriented. As with registry architectures, consumers can make a research request, but using broadcasting. In Figure 6.5, the dashed lines represent broadcasting while those in a solid line represent point-to-point communication.

Nevertheless, for increased efficacy or security, some protocols (SLP and Jini) use broadcasting to discover a service registry. In mobile environments, wireless communications are often costly in terms of energy. The registry therefore allows consumers to have a single interlocutor and carry out point-to-point requests. This registry constructs its database using provider announcement messages.

Discovery is the first stage in creating applications from a service infrastructure. In ubiquitous computing, this is even more applicable because the environments in which they are created are not known *a priori*. Decentralized dynamic discovery, coupled with appearance/disappearance mechanisms, discovers services without knowing them previously and without being based on a static entity.

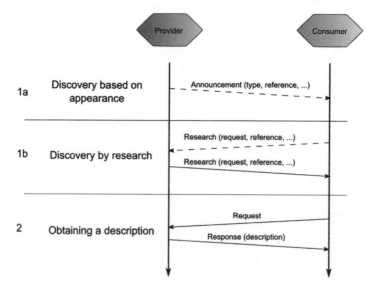

Figure 6.5. *Decentralized dynamic discovery: research and discovery protocols*

6.1.5. *WSOAD*

We have examined four main evolutions of classical SOA. In WSOAs, the use of web technologies has resulted in greater service interoperability (section 6.1.1). In SOADs, decentralized discovery (section 6.1.4) and announcement mechanisms for appearance/disappearance (section 6.1.3) allow services to be discovered in previously unknown mobile environments. Finally, event-based communications (section 6.1.2) improve dynamicity in interactions between providers and consumers and decouple them.

WSOADs have been born out of the accumulation of these evolutions. They retain all the benefits of SOADs and borrow the interoperability provided by WSOAs. These architectures' services must be connected to IP networks although they have embedded targets using few resources and varied communication methods. The current trend shows that an increasing number of devices are connected to Ethernet or Wi-Fi networks, therefore using the IP protocol. For devices that use proprietary or have short-range wireless communication protocols, programs bridging these device protocols to web services for devices will emerge, as proposed in the Amigo project [BRO 05]. Currently, there are two types of technology in this family of WSOADs: UPnP and DPWS.

WSOADs provide the properties required for a software infrastructure in ubiquitous computing. The codes of these entities cannot be modified and the application's creation in ubiquitous computing is therefore a composition of these various services. Two main types of service compositions exist: orchestration and choreography [SIN 05]. Orchestration relies on a centralized entity that manages all interactions between an application's services, like method calls or relaying of messages. The choreography proposes a decentralized approach, which partly breaks the black box property of services. Indeed, choreography supposes that services are capable of organizing themselves independently to communicate with each other. It is more complex to implement, however, since the services must be aware of each other and potential adaptations in their organization must be embedded in each service.

Orchestration therefore seems to be the most suitable approach for ubiquitous computing since frequent changes in the infrastructure would be complex to manage in all services [CAR 07]. The orchestration of services is generally described by defining *workflows* or abstract processes such as BPELs (*Business Process Execution Languages*). In the following section, we will examine how to create these compositions within the context of ubiquitous computing.

6.2. Dynamic service composition

In ubiquitous computing, applications rely on a range of non-modifiable web services for devices, which interact with each other. Applications and, as a result, compositions of services, must be modifiable at execution. While services respond well to problems of interoperability and reusability, components provide better dynamicity.

Components are more easily manipulated than services. They are created in containers by component manufacturers. The containers give the components non-functional properties. The component manufacturers define the type of component. Components are therefore executed in a totally controlled execution environment and can be instantiated and manipulated by the programmer whatever services and device available. Services may be deployed at the controlled nodes in a network, but do not provide the same advantages in terms of dynamicity, due to connections requiring service interface matching and the fact that they do not have an internal or instance state. To respond to this need for dynamicity, the proposed architecture must therefore be based on two essential paradigms:

Events: events are involved in the model, in services; for example, with Web services for devices, as well as in components. They have a double advantage in that they increase system reactivity and decoupling between entities and therefore applications' dynamicity;

Lightweight component assemblies: composite web services are created using a dynamic assembly of black box components executed in a local container, which does not provide mandatory technical services. Application's dynamicity is therefore provided and reusability is improved.

LCA (*Lightweight Component Architecture*) [HOU 09] therefore defines an event-based compositional architecture model to design assemblies of lightweight components and increment the services' and applications' cooperation graph. The environment is composed of mobile users interacting with the world or other users with carried or mobile devices. They are seen as many services available momentarily in the infrastructure and the assemblies of components allow the orchestration of these services.

6.2.1. *Composition of services for devices: LCA*

The model for LCA components is a slightly modified Beans model [ENG 97] adapted to other programming languages with concepts of input ports (provided interface), output ports (required interface) and properties.

These components are said to be "lightweight" for several reasons. The first is that they are executed in the same addressing and processing space [CLA 01]. Their interactions can be reduced to the simplest and most efficient, the function call. The second, less important reason is that they do not embed the non-functional code or technical services that are useless in the local environment. Their memory imprint is limited and they may be instantiated and be quickly destroyed [TIG 09]. The granularity of lightweight components is therefore smaller than that of standard components. A container is not limited to a type of component, but can contain all the components in an application. To conclude, they do not contain references between them during the design phase and respect black box concepts as well as late binding. An asynchronous interaction pattern with spatial decoupling [EUG 03] is used for the binding between lightweight components, which improves decoupling and reactivity.

The management of events and properties are the only non-functional codes that must be present in the component code. The container does not provide a technical service facilitating the work of programmers, but results in components that can correspond to various demands, such as, for example, mixed components that must access the hardware and therefore low-level functions. The addition of non-functional properties, such as security, logging or persistent messages, can be carried out by adding components into the collection which guarantees the model's evolutivity.

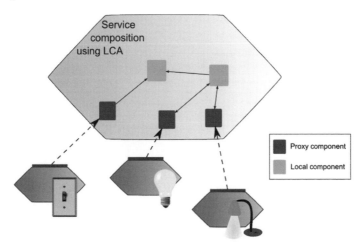

Figure 6.6. *Composition of Web services for devices with assemblies of event-based lightweight LCA components*

As described in the LCA model (Figures 6.6 and 6.7), the components have an interface that is defined by the type of the component. This interface is a set of input ports (methods) and output ports (events), each being defined by its parameters with a unique identifier. The interactions between components are bindings. They link the output port of a component with one or several components' input ports. Since the ports are explicit, no code needs to be generated or studied by introspection to know where to modify the components to change its binding target during execution. When the event is sent by the component at the source of the binding, the control flow passes through the destination components in an indeterminate order, but which can be fixed by sequence execution components. When limited to unique bindings and the use sequence components for multiple bindings, the application's control flow is completely determinist. Not having indirections related to technical services of the platform gives total control to the components over the control flow and facilitates debugging.

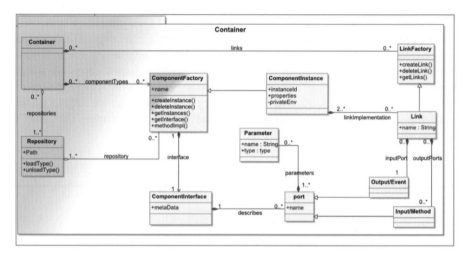

Figure 6.7. *Meta-model of lightweight LCA components*

When a service representing a device is discovered, a specific component called a "proxy" component can be generated from the service's description, fitted in the container and instantiated to be part of the component assembly. "Proxy" components play the role of service interface between services in the infrastructure and the components in assemblies.

Service for device composition with lightweight LCA component allows us to create new dynamic applications from the services in the infrastructure. However, the new functions are only available locally and create a particular application. It is therefore necessary to add a reusability dimension to the model and export the functions created by the assembly of components to the service infrastructure.

6.2.2. Distributed composition: SLCA

There are multi-paradigm approaches combining both event and component services, such as SCAs (*Service Component Architectures*) [CHA 07] or even iPOJO [ESC 07].

SCA allows the implementation of component-based architectures to create service orchestrations that can themselves be encapsulated in composite services. SLCA (*Service Lightweight Component Architectures*) [HOU 09], which is an architecture model for composing services based on assemblies of lightweight components, also follows the SCA-based principle. Nevertheless, SLCA relies on a software and material execution environment that evolves dynamically. This environment is defined as a set of resources, which are also software/physical entities whose appearance and disappearance are not controlled but generally experienced by the application. SLCA is based on an infrastructure of services using events and which can be remotely discovered dynamically. They represent the devices used in ubiquitous computing applications as well as composite services created by SLCA.

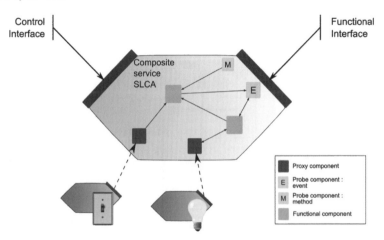

Figure 6.8. *Event-based composite Web service*

Applications are designed by a composition of services by assembling components. A composite service is an LCA container fitted in a service for a device containing an assembly of components. "Proxy" components of remote web services are therefore instantiated in the composite service and create applications on the basis of services already available in the environment. A composite service can create an application that communicates with another composite service. It can therefore be seen as a gray box; that is, its assembly can be modified and some of the component assembly's functions can be accessed.

A composite service provides two service interfaces (Figure 6.8). The dynamic functional interface allows us to publish or access new functions provided by the composite Web service. The control interface enables the dynamic modification of the internal SLCA component assembly, which provides these new functions.

6.2.2.1. *The functional interface*

The functional interface allows us to export a locally created application by assembling components to the service infrastructure. The composite services will therefore participate in the infrastructure's service cooperation graph (Figure 6.9). The interface is dynamic and exports events and methods of the internal assembly using probe components. Adding or removing a probe component is dynamically reflected in the functional interface and the contract of the related composite service. Adapting to changes in the environment is therefore possible during runtime.

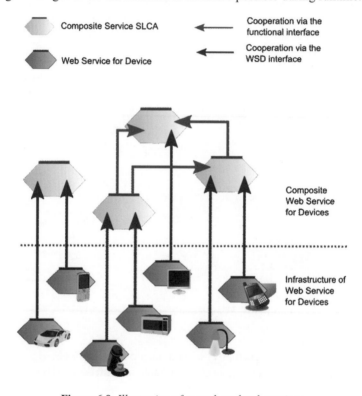

Figure 6.9. *Illustration of event-based web services*

There are two types of probe component (Figure 6.10). First, sinks that give method to the composite service's interface and have only one output port in the component's internal assembly. The invocation of a method on the composite service therefore transmits an event in the component's internal assembly. The second type of probe component is the source that adds an event to the composite service interface and has only one input port. The invocation of a method in the component assembly will transmit a web service event.

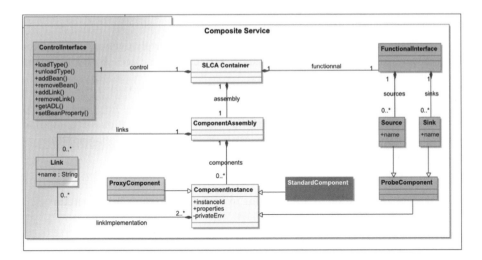

Figure 6.10. *SLCA meta-model: composite service interfaces*

6.2.2.2. *The control interface*

The control interface is used to dynamically modify the service's internal assembly. It provides the means of adding or removing components and bindings as well as collecting information on the type of components and on the assembly. As such, another client, which can be a composite service using a *proxy* component for the service, can act on the structure of a composite service. The adaptation of composite services is therefore possible. The control interface also provides events that notify the subscribed entities about structural changes in the container's internal assembly. As a result, adaptations can be reactive. We can therefore envisage all sorts of adaptation mechanisms and tools for creating applications, also known as designers.

Designers are service consumers for which the control interface of composite services is required. They allow us to visualize or adapt assemblies of composite service using various formalisms and representations. There are three designers that are most commonly used as an aid for designing ubiquitous computing applications, the visual assembly designer, the web services for the device's designer called the *UPnPProxyDesigner*, and the aspects of the assembly designer.

The aspects of assembly designer provide a mechanism for composite service adaptation. The composite service's control interface is used to manage a set of adaptation rules triggered by a modification in the component assembly. We will examine this adaptation mechanism in the next section.

6.2.2.3. *Overview of the SLCA model*

Composite SLCA services allow the creation of completely dynamic applications from a service infrastructure, particularly services for devices based on event communication.

The reactivity is both available in created applications, in the functions exported to the software infrastructure and in the control and adaptation of composite services. Various tools allow us to consider different issues in adapting applications such as the availability of entities in the infrastructure or user needs.

6.3. Dynamic adaptation of applications to variations in their infrastructure

We have seen that an application in ubiquitous computing, over the course of its lifetime, must be able to evolve in many different environments that the developer cannot statistically forecast at the design stage. The system therefore needs to be able to adapt to these changes at execution. Reflexivity is a mechanism that offers this possibility, which in turn relies on two other mechanisms: (1) intercession, the ability of a system to modify itself and (2) introspection, the ability of a system to observe itself.

In ubiquitous computing, system adaptations must not occur too frequently and must last until the next adaptation. These must therefore be structural and persistent, and not rely on the application's execution flow, as is the case with interception mechanisms. The carrying out of structural adaptations entails a certain level of data modularity and abstraction in the source code of the adapted application. Object-oriented programming therefore strongly facilitates the use of reflexivity by introducing such modularity using data representation and their connection (hierarchy, etc.). Run-time objects are reified as modifiable meta-objects (a representation of the given object) and meta-object protocols (MOPs) [KIC 99] manage the connections and the coherence between objects and meta-objects. Middleware such as CARISMA [CAP 03] or even OpenCOM [BLA 04] rely on such mechanisms. However, coupling between objects is strong and the use of MOPs remains complex.

Reflexivity, used to make structural adaptations in the component assembly, therefore consists of adding or removing components and their dependencies. Structural modifications in the component assembly must respect the components' black box properties. Approaches to achieve structural adaptations in assemblies of components cannot be based on modifications in the components' source code. Indeed, as we have seen previously, in ubiquitous computing a system relies on a material infrastructure that provides a software infrastructure. This software infrastructure is composed of a set of WSOADs, which cannot be modified by the system. Structural adaptations therefore cannot consist of code injections as with reflexive components in which we can, for example, inject references between components [BLA 04]. For this reason, it is necessary to externalize the dependencies that cannot be controlled by business layers. However this may be possible when an assembly of adaptable components can be encapsulated in a composite component. This kind of component can be seen from two perspectives: as a white or black box.

If simple reflexivity allows us to make such adaptations, it requires a transparent mechanism for the application that is difficult to evolve and is complex to implement. As shown, not all adaptations can be foreseen in advance. It is therefore apparent that the application is often better placed than middleware to determine the relevance of its adaptations [GRA 09]. It is therefore necessary to externalize the adaptation rules; the first approaches of this kind of response are script (*policy based*)-type approaches [GRA 09]. These entail implementing a set of rules such as ECAs (event-condition-action) [JUN 07] to describe the adaptations to be carried out. However, these approaches often result in a centralization and static writing of these rules to guarantee coherence [GRA 09]. Lastly, AOP is a less-static approach that allows structural adaptations with a high level of abstraction.

6.3.1. *The principles of AOPs*

Aspect-oriented programming (AOP) was first proposed by Kiczales *et al.* in 1997 [KIC 97]. It is a paradigm that allows us to define software abstractions that will be superimposed on an initial application. Aspect programming is in essence part of the following statement: despite all efforts made in this direction, there is still a strong relationship between an application's business code and that of transverse concerns (security, monitoring, etc.). The idea of aspect programming is to separately represent these concerns in aspects. This entails injecting code into the main source code. This injection is carried out through a weaver aspect.

An aspect is divided into pointcut and advice. The first identifies "where" the code must be woven while the second describes "how;" that is, how the code is injected (Figure 6.11). The set of bonds on which aspects can be woven are called joinpoints. Depending on the paradigms that aspect programming uses, this set can change in nature (objects, components, code, etc.) but AOP still provides good separation between transverse concerns and good transverse modularity [CHA 04]. The pointcuts allow us to choose a sub-set of joinpoints where a behavior can be added. The genericity of pointcuts allows an aspect to be woven in several places of the application; aspect programming therefore minimizes the code's dispersion by grouping it into reusable entities. Advice languages typically provide mechanisms to add behavior to the pointcut using "after", "before" and "around" operators. As a result, the "before" advice will be executed before the execution of the joinpoint verifying the pointcut associated with the advice and, conversely, with an "after" advice. An "around" advice allows us to replace the pointcut or execute the code before and after the pointcut.

```
public aspect Aspect_Name {
    pointcut Method_Name() : // code
    // Advice
    before( ) : Method_Name(){ // Code}
}
```

Figure 6.11. *Model of an aspect in AspectJ*

The weaver is the mechanism that takes these aspects and an application as its input and produces an improved application. The first weaving mechanisms such as AspectJ [KIC 01] are static and occur at compile time. The code described in the advices is woven into the application's code to generate a new source file such as java or bytecode with AspectJ. As such, the separation of concerns introduced by aspects has no place at runtime. Aspects are not always independent of each other and interaction problems can therefore arise between them. In conventional approaches, no method has been introduced to resolve these interactions, which remains a task in hand for developers. Weaving mechanisms have therefore evolved to respond to these problems. EAOP (Event based AOP), for example [DOU 02], proposes dynamic weaving where the trigger is based on the observation of events relating to the execution of the initial application. This research has also proposed mechanisms for solving interactions between aspects. An initial approach consists of composing advices intervening at the same joinpoint explicitly. The second approach consists of encapsulating aspects within aspects. The weaver in this research is designed to evaluate events and execute the corresponding advices. Lastly, other research has focused on the application of aspects to components, such as SAFRAN [DAV 06], CAM/ DAOP [PIN 05] or services, such as AO4BPEL [CHA 04]. These approaches therefore provide the modularity necessary for software adaptation, but also the needs of adaptations building on non-modifiable software bricks, as is the case in ubiquitous computing. SAFRAN introduces a new type of aspect trigger for the adaptation of these endogenous (i.e. within the system) and exogenous (from outside the system) events, the composition of adaptations is therefore external. CAM/DAOP, on the other hand, offers mechanisms to verify the non-competition between aspects and an external composition. In this approach, aspects are components and the pointcuts are separated from the advices to improve reusability. AO4BPEL proposes using aspects to extend BPEL (Business Process

Execution Language) to add modularity and render it dynamically adaptable, therefore not taking into account evolutions in the application's software infrastructure.

In the following sections, we will examine an example of a persistent structural adaptation mechanism based on the aspects triggered in modifications of the infrastructure that are fused during interactions. This approach allows auto-adaptation to take place modularly and declaratively and the complete construction of the application.

6.3.2. Transverse adaptation

Aspect of assemblies (AAs) are an original concept based on AOP (section 6.3.1), which define reconfigurations in an application's structure and are triggered in reaction to events of the software infrastructure, such as the appearance or disappearance of entities and components. These rules are woven and composed according to the logic defined in case of interference. AAs are dynamically applied to the applications represented by the assemblies of components, which are not necessarily known when the AA is written. The adaptation description language and the composition rules are modular, as required by the applications involved. AAs can therefore be used to adapt applications based on component models interacting via events [CHE 09].

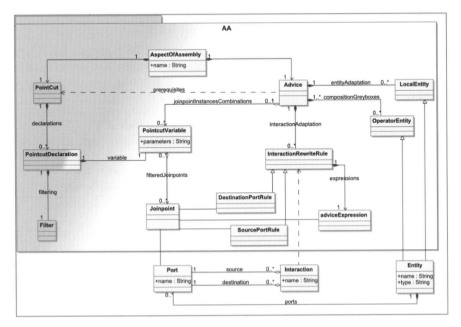

Figure 6.12. *Meta-model of the expression of aspect assemblies*

AAs differ from traditional aspects [BOU 01] in terms of how they respect the encapsulation of the components in the assemblies to be adapted, also known as a black box property.

We will examine the main concepts in AA: joinpoints (section 6.3.2.1), pointcuts (section 6.3.2.2), advices (section 6.3.2.3), and weavers (6.3.2.4).

6.3.2.1. *Joinpoints*

Joinpoints are all the assembly entities representing the applications; that is, the components and their ports that allow related messages to be targeted.

Since the modifications expressed by AAs are structural, it is only possible to weave adaptations on the known interfaces of black boxes, represented here by ports, changing the application's assembly.

6.3.2.2. *Pointcuts*

Pointcuts are a series of filters, applied to the list of joinpoints in the assembly where they are applied. Each filter constructs a list of joinpoints which it verifies. They allow to search and spelect the joinpoints where modifications described in the advices will take place in the assembly. This list is associated with a variable designed to create a link between the assembly of components representing the application and an abstract configuration described in its advice. The elements composing all these lists can be associated according to various combinations such that a combination contains a joinpoint of each filter. The aspect advice will therefore be duplicated as many times as there are combinations. An AA is duplicated when it can be applied in several places in the assembly. An AA can be duplicated when several joinpoints verify the same pointcut rule. Its advice is therefore instantiated several times.

A single AA can adapt in several places in a single application. The pointcuts are the means of describing several reconfigurations in an application with a high level of abstraction. This abstraction allows us to apply reconfigurations on assemblies of components, which are not known in advance. They interface each AA with a real application being executed, which modifies the generic adaptation of advices for a real and dynamic application.

Considerations other than syntactic correspondences are also studied. For example, an AA defining an adaptation relating to a switch instead of carrying out a switch* type recognition; recognition based on the semantic of entities or their ports would be more appropriate. This is because one of the ideals that we want to preserve in ubiquitous computing is the separation of functions offered by devices in more basic functions. A mobile phone, for example, is designed to call or send messages but can play the role of display, switch, etc. The ANR Continuum project is working on such an extension of AA.

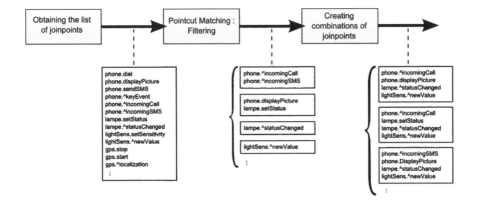

Figure 6.13. *Example of the identification process for pointcuts*

Pointcuts are evaluated when AAs are selected (Figure 6.19). When all the pointcuts have identified at least one joinpoint, the combination of joinpoints is constructed and the AA changes to the applicable state. The series of these processes is shown in Figure 6.13. It can therefore be woven into the application's assembly.

The pointcuts define the prerequisites for AA weaving. Even if they are selected by users to adapt to an application, AAs can only be woven if the application's assembly is in a state that is compatible with the pointcuts; that is, if they contain the entities and ports necessary for adaptation.

6.3.2.3. Advices

The advices in the aspect of assemblies do not describe pieces of code that must be injected into an application's code. Rather, they define the set of components and bindings that must be woven in a component assembly. These reconfigurations are based on the joinpoints obtained using pointcuts. Pieces of advice are composed of a set of abstract rules based on the pointcut variables. These rules define which components and bindings must be instantiated. The AA weaver produces pieces of advice by substituting the variables of advice rules by joinpoints. The set of instances of advices from the different AAs deployed in the weaver are then composed with each other.

The suppression of entities and interactions also occurs when an AA is unwoven from an assembly. Every modification must be seen as a transformation of one assembly to a new one (Figure 6.17).

A specific language is also used to express advices. In standard aspects, advices often take the form of the code written in the same language as the target application. On the one hand, in AAs, the entities are added and their programming is not based on the expression of advices. On the other, it is necessary to describe the interaction of these new entities in the existing assembly. The specific language of AA advices is not fixed by the model and aspect designers can define it according to the type of adaptation sought. The various keywords or language operators define how advices will be composed, as we will see with the weaver. We will also study the ISL4WComp language, which has been used in previous research in to ubiquitous computing. This describes advices based on event flows and can be used as a basis for operator sets in a new language.

6.3.2.3.1. Components used by advices

Advices describe the modifications in the assembly of components, which are additions of entities or additions of modifications in interactions. The added entities must be defined and available in the component assembly management system during AA weaving. There are two types of AA instantiable entities: black box and gray box components, which we will examine in further detail.

Black box components encapsulate the functions that can only be accessed via their ports [SZY 99]. Only the call order between these functions can be controlled. The entities explicitly added to provide a function in the adaptation described by a graph are black box components. This is known as external weaving between black box advices (Figure 6.14). The entities explicitly added by graphs are also called local entities, as in the AA meta-model (Figure 6.12).

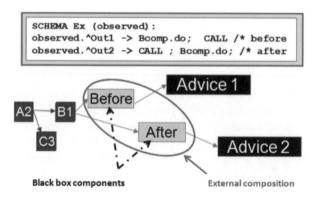

Figure 6.14. *Black box advices*

For example, an adaptation designed to filter every other message in an interaction will add a component that has this feature. This is a black box component whose only interface is known by the weaver. It will replace the old interaction and two new interactions will be created to connect it with the initial interaction ports.

The gray box components partially expose their semantics, either by description or reflexivity or it is, at least in part, known by the weaver. On the basis of this knowledge, it is possible to manually or automatically compose and we therefore speak of composing or fusing [CHE 09] gray box advices (Figure 6.15). This introduces the possibility of managing potential conflicts between instances of advices with several AAs. These entities are created by the weaver when advice language expression operators appear or when a composition is required between several definitions of interactions.

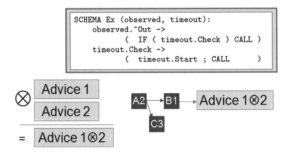

```
SCHEMA Ex (observed, timeout):
    observed.^Out ->
                ( IF ( timeout.Check ) CALL )
    timeout.Check ->
                ( timeout.Start ; CALL     )
```

Figure 6.15. *Gray box advices*

A composition rule of advice instances, for example, can specify that when two interactions in the same entity are created by adaptations, a sequence type gray box component must be introduced to put in place a priority between interactions.

6.3.2.3.2. Example of advice expression language: ISL4WComp

The ISL4WComp advice expression language is based on the ISL interaction specification language, which describes the independent interactions between objects [BER 01]. ISL4WComp adapts these specifications to adapt them to message-based interactions or events between components in aspect assemblies.

This language is specific in that it is composable: several instances of advices can be composed and fused into a single assembly combining their respective behaviors. The symmetry property [CHE 06b] in this composition is therefore exploited; that is, the order of the aspect application does not influence the result of their composition. This allows us to address the unknown nature of the ambient space since at each change in the space, the application of AAs is recalculated without requiring a list of previous weavings [FER 09].

The expression of ISL4WComp advices is based on three types of rule: adding black box components, rewriting bindings between components of the assembly, and creating new bindings. Rewriting target component ports, that is, the redirection of an entry port or the redirection of the transmission of a message (output port). These rules are identified by two key symbols: ":" for creating instances and "->" to rewrite and create bindings. The right part of the modification rules is subject to variation. A new behavior with the operators is defined by its language (Table 6.1).

	Keyword/Operator	Description
Types of port	*comp. port*	"." separates an instance of a component from the name of a port. This symbol indicates a provided port (method)
	comp.^ port	"^" at the start of the port name indicates a required port (event)
Rules defining structural modifications	*comp : type*	Expresses the creation of a local black box component
	comp : type (prop = val, ...)	Expresses the initialization of the properties of the created component
	port_required --> (port_provided)	Creation of a connection between the two ports. The keyword --> is the separator between the right and left parts
	port_required --> (port_provided)	Rewriting the existing connection by changing the destination port
Operators (symmetry properties, resolution of conflicts)	. . . ; . . .	Expresses a sequence
	. . . | | . . .	Expresses an indifferent order (parallelism)
	`if (condition) {...]` `{else}`	Expresses a condition evaluated by a black box component
	`nop`	Does not do anything (used for one "if" where one of the two actions is not used)
	`call`	Reuses the right part in the connection rewriting rule
	`delegate`	Specifies a unit on an interaction where there are conflicts

Table 6.1. *Operations and keywords in ISL4WCompt advice language*

An advice describes a set of adaptation rules relying on variable components defined in the pointcuts. Some language operators such as `call` and `delegate` allow us to control how the assembly schemas will be composed. These keywords, associated with sequence or parallelism operators, are similar to keywords such as *before, around,* and *after* of the pointcuts in the standard AOP.

6.3.2.3.3. Example of an advice expressed using the ISL4WComp language

To illustrate the concepts presented above, we will study an example of an advice written with the ISL4WComp language. It defines an independent adaptation for a domestic application, linking all kinds of interrupter to a lamp. The two devices are represented by components in the existing assembly and provide functions via their ports. The advice below (Figure 6.16) proposes adapting this function by accounting for a light sensor only turning on the lamp when light levels are low to avoid over use of energy. In addition, the new assembly sends a message indicating that there is too much light preventing the light being turned on, if not working properly.

```
advice lumin_light (light,lumen,switch) :
    transmitter : 'BasicBeans.PrimitiveValueEmitter'
    theshold: 'BasicBeans.Threshold' (threshold=10)
    t1,t2 : 'System.Windows.Forms.TextBox'
    light.SetState -> (
        if (threshold.IsReached){
            transmitter.FireValueEvent
        } else {
            call
        }
    )
    transmitter.^EmitStringValue -> (t1.set_Text)
    lumen.^Value_Evented_NewValue -> (
        threshold.set_Value ;
        t2.set_Text
    )
```

Figure 6.16. *Example of ISL4Wcomp advice*

The advice is called `lumen_light`. The two identifiers, `light` and `lumin`, between brackets in the first line represent the variable components provided by the calculation of pointcuts. They are replaced by joinpoints indentified by pointcut matching during weaving.

As an example, we can identify three kinds of rule. In lines 3, 4 and 5, black box components are added by the AA. For the `threshold` component, a property is explicitly initialized. A property is a public variable in a component that can be accessed by its interface. In line 7, rewriting of the bindings with an input port (method) is described. In lines 12 and 16, rewriting of the bindings with the output port (event) are described.

Among the operators in this example, the most complex is the `call` operator in line 9. The `if` block dictates that if the light threshold is reached, then an error message is set. In the opposite case, the `call` is replaced by the right part, therefore by the original method's call. This signifies that when this adaptation is woven into the basic application, if a binding exists with the provided port `lumiere.SetState`, it will not be modified.

The expression language for ISL4WComp advices often requires the expression of reactive adaptations to create ubiquitous computing applications. Its operators define behaviors, which are more complex than structural reconfigurations while guaranteeing that the result of weaving several of these components is idempotent, associative, and communicative.

6.3.2.4. *The weaver*

The weaver is the program responsible for weaving aspects. Since AAs describe component adaptations, the weaver must calculate the structural modifications to be applied to an assembly and compose them. It systematically constructs a single assembly from the assembly of components in the basic application and assemblies instantiated from aspect assembly advices. The base assembly of an application is the assembly of components in the application so that no AA is woven. The weaver also coordinates all the operations required in adaptation weaving (Figure 6.17), including those already described for pointcuts and advices. We will study these operations in the following sub-sections in further detail.

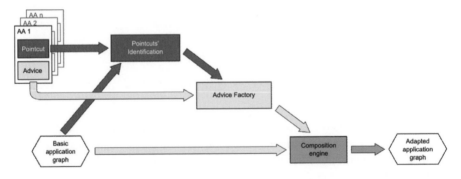

Figure 6.17. *Operations carried out during AA weaving: a weaving cycle*

6.3.2.4.1. Evaluation of pointcuts and instantiation of advices

The weaver possesses a list of aspects of assembly which have been selected by users to adapt an application. Their weaving in the targeted assembly depends on the evaluation of pointcut. When the joinpoints have been identified for each pointcut in an AA, it becomes applicable (Figure 6.19). Advice instances are created, corresponding to the implementation of generic adaptations in a real application.

Pieces of advice are created by replacing the variable components representing the pointcuts in the expression of advices by joinpoints. Several strategies are possible when several joinpoints are found (Figure 6.13). We will now use an example to illustrate the different options. If we take an application comprising two interrupters and two lamps, the first strategy creates two combinations. The first combination consisted of the first interrupter and the first lamp, and the second the second interrupter and the second lamp. An "all combinations" strategy creates combinations of all couples and lamps. The choice of strategy is left to the adaptation designer in the weaver configuration.

6.3.2.4.2. Detection of interference

Two instances of advice are in interference when they have a shared joinpoint. While pieces of advice and the base assembly are being composed, interference can occur. They must be detected and addressed by the weaver. Some language expression operators can dictate how interferences are managed. For example, in the ISL4WComp, the `call` and `delegate` operators are replaced by other conflicting rules but do not define order or priority when there are more than two in conflict.

6.3.2.4.3. Composition of instances of advices

Several aspects of assemblies can be applied to the same application. Since the result in any case must be a single assembly of components, it is necessary to compose the basic assembly, that of the existing application, with those of advice instances.

In the ISL4WComp advice expression language (section 6.3.2.3.2), operators are governed by a set of logical rules that allows the weaver to obtain a property of symmetry in the operation of composition of advice instances. This property can be split into three sub-properties: associativity, communicativity, and idempotence. The logical rules are grouped in an operator composition matrix validating the three sub-properties. The AA compositions correspond to the implementation of formal research into the composition of logical rules [CHE 06a]. The weaver therefore makes decisions on the composition to be made when it detects interference.

6.3.2.4.4. Triggering weaving

In the same way as cycles of automata, which consist of successive phases of data acquisition, execution, and production of output, we speak of weaving cycles. In this cycle, the AA weaver takes an assembly of components as its input that we will term the initial assembly and a set of aspect assemblies. It produces a final assembly, an adapted assembly. A weaving cycle can be triggered in two ways:

– dictated by the user, by the selection/deselection of a given AA as input at the execution of the weaver. If an AA is applied, its removal will result in a new weaving cycle. If a new AA is selected and can be applied, this also leads to a new weaving cycle;

– dictated by context. The second means of triggering a weaving cycle is the addition/removal of components in the given assembly as the weaver's input. When a new component appears or disappears, for example, new devices enter into the application's infrastructure, a new weaving cycle begins and only the AAs that can be applied to this new assembly will be woven. AAs based on SLCA benefit from a dynamicity of the architecture and can be triggered by the appearance of proxy components in containers since the container notifies the weaver when a new component is instantiated in the assembly.

An essential point for the reactivity of this mechanism is that it does not require information relating to the software infrastructure, but a dynamic specific to the infrastructure imposes its rhythm via this type of trigger. However, during a weaving cycle, the system does not tolerate new delays that terminate its cycle before making new evolutions (Figure 6.18).

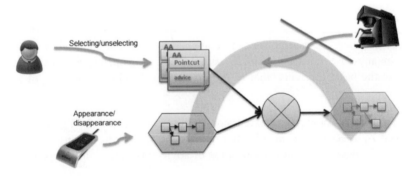

Figure 6.18. *Different types of trigger in aspect assemblies*

AAs can therefore take on different states (Figure 6.19). At the basis of an AA is a deselected state; that is, one that the user does not want to apply. In this case, the pointcuts are not even evaluated. When an AA is selected, these pointcuts are evaluated and will be again for each modification in the base assembly that the AA will carry out. If joinpoints verify the pointcuts, the AA changes to an applicable state before being woven. AAs that were not applicable can become so if a new entity appears in the application's assembly. Equally, those which could be woven can become inapplicable but remain selected if an entity identified in their pointcuts disappears.

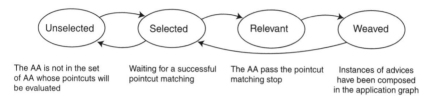

The AA is not in the set of AA whose pointcuts will be evaluated   Waiting for a successful pointcut matching   The AA pass the pointcut matching stop   Instances of advices have been composed in the application graph

Figure 6.19. *Different states of the aspect assembly*

6.3.3. *Summary*

AAs are a model of a compositional adaptation mechanism triggered by events in the software infrastructure. The model is fairly generic so that it can be used in various fields for a variety of uses. Depending on the language used to represent AAs, adaptations can be woven according to different policies and composed properly using symmetry properties and in respect of the black box model of the compositional adaptation.

6.4. Bibliography

[ARN 99] ARNOLD K., SCHEIFLER R., WALDO J., O'SULLIVAN B., WOLLRAT H.A., *Jini Specification*, Addison-Wesley Longman, Boston, 1999.

[BER 01] BERGER L., Mise en œuvre des interactions en environnements distribués, compilés et fortement typés : le modèle MICADO, PhD. thesis, University of Nice Sophia Antipolis, October 2001.

[BLA 04] BLAIR G., COULSON G., UEYAMA J., LEE K., JOOLIA A., "Opencom v2: a component model for building systems software", *IASTED Software Engineering and Applications (SEA.04)*, Cambridge, MA, USA, 2004.

[BOT 07] BOTTARO A., GÉRODOLLE A., LALANDA P., "Pervasive service composition in the home network", *Proceedings of AINA'07, 21st International Conference on Advanced Information Networking and Applications*, Niagara Falls, Canada, pp. 596–603, May 2007.

[BOU 01] BOURAQUADI-SAÂDANI M.N., LEDOUX T., "Le point sur la programmation par aspects", *Technique et science informatiques*, vol. 20, no. 4, pp. 289–512, 2001.

[BRE 07] BREIVOLD H., LARSSON M., "Component-based and service-oriented software engineering: key concepts and principles", *Proceedings of 33rd EUROMICRO Conference on Software Engineering and Advanced Applications*, pp. 13–20, 2007.

[BRO 05] BROMBERG Y., ISSARNY V., "INDISS: interoperable discovery system for networked services", *Proceedings of Middleware'05*, Lecture Notes in Computer Science, vol. 3790, pp. 164–183, 2005.

[BUS 02] BUSTAMANTE F., WIDENER P., SCHWAN K., "Scalable directory services using proactivity", *Proceedings of Supercomputing*, Los Alamitos, CA, USA, 2002.

[CAP 03] CAPRA L., EMMERICH W., MASCOLO C., "CARISMA: context-aware reflective middleware system for mobile applications", *IEEE Transactions on Software Engineering*, vol. 29, no. 10, pp. 929–945, 2003.

[CAR 07] CARDOSO R.S., ISSARNY V., "Architecting pervasive computing systems for privacy: a survey", *Proceedings of the Sixth Working IEEE/IFIP Conference on Software Architecture*, IEEE Computer Society, p. 26, 2007.

[CHA 05] CHAKRABORTY D., JOSHI A., FININ T., YESHA Y., "Service composition for mobile environments", *Mobile Networks and Applications*, vol. 10, no. 4, pp. 435–451, 2005.

[CHA 07] CHAPPELL D., Introducing SCA, July 2007. http:// www.davidchappell.com/articles/ Introducing-SCA.pdf.

[CHA 04] CHARFI A., MEZINI M., "Aspect-oriented web service composition with AO4BPEL", *Lecture Notes in Computer Science*, vol. 3250, pp. 168–182, 2004.

[CHA 02] CHAMPION M., FERRIS C., NEWCOMER E., ORCHARD D., Web services architecture, W3C working draft, http://www.w3.org/TR/2002/WD-ws-arch-20021114/, November 2002.

[CHE 00] CHEN H., CHAKRABORTY D., XU L., JOSHI A., FININ T., "Service discovery in the future electronic market", *Proceedings of the Workshop on Knowledge Based Electronic Markets*, AAAI, Austin, USA, 2000.

[CHE 06a] CHEUNG-FOO-WO D., BLAY-FORNARINO M., TIGLI J.Y., DERY A.M., EMSELLEM D., RIVEILL M., "Langage d'aspect pour la composition dynamique de composants embarqués", *RTSI L'Objet*, vol. 12, no. 2–3, pp. 89–111, 2006.

[CHE 06b] CHEUNG-FOO-WO D., BLAY-FORNARINO M., TIGLI J.Y., LAVIROTTE S., RIVEILL M., "Adaptation dynamique d'assemblages de dispositifs dirigée par des modèles", *Actes des 2es journées sur l'Ingénierie Dirigée par les Modèles (IDM)*, Lille, France, 2006.

[CHE 09] CHEUNG-FOO-WO D., Adaptation dynamique par tissage d'aspects d'assemblage, thesis, University of Nice Sophia Antipolis, March 2009.

[CLA 01] CLARKE M., BLAIR G., COULSON G., PARLAVANTZAS N., "An efficient component model for the construction of adaptive middleware", *Proceedings of the IFIP/ACM International Conference on Distributed Systems Platforms*, Heidelberg, Springer-Verlag, pp. 160–178, 2001.

[DAV 06] DAVID P., LEDOUX T., "An aspect-oriented approach for developing self-adaptive fractal components", *Lecture Notes in Computer Science*, vol. 4089, p. 82, 2006.

[DOU 02] DOUENCE R., SUDHOLT M., A model and a tool for event-based aspect-oriented programming (EAOP), Research Report, no. 02/11/INFO, Ecole des Mines de Nantes, 2002.

[ENG 97] ENGLANDER R., *Developing Java Beans*, O'Reilly & Associates, Sebastopol, 1997.

[ESC 07] ESCOFFIER C., HALL R., "Dynamically adaptable applications with iPOJO service components", *Lecture Notes in Computer Science*, Springer, vol. 4829, p. 113, 2007.

[EUG 03] EUGSTER P., FELBER P., GUERRAOUI R., KERMARREC A., "The many faces of publish/subscribe", *ACM computing Surveys*, vol. 35, no.2, pp. 114–131, 2003.

[FER 09] FERRY N., LAVIROTTE S., TIGLI J.Y., REY G., RIVEILL M., "Context adaptative systems based on horizontal architecture for ubiquitous computing", *Proceedings of International Conference on Mobile Technology, Applications and Systems (Mobility)*, September 2009.

[GRA 09] GRACE P., "Dynamic adaptation", in GARBINATO B. (ed.), *Middleware for Network Eccentric and Mobile Applications*, Springer, Berlin, pp. 285–304, 2009.

[GUT 99] GUTTMAN E., "Service location protocol: automatic discovery of IP network services", *IEEE Internet Computing*, vol. 3, pp. 71–80, 1999.

[HOU 06] HOURDIN V., LAVIROTTE S., TIGLI J.Y., Comparaison des systèmes de services pour dispositifs, Research Report, no. I3S/RR-2006-25-FR, Laboratoire I3S, Sophia Antipolis, August 2006.

[HOU 09] HOURDIN V., TIGLI J.Y., LAVIROTTE S., REY G., RIVEILL M., "Context sensitive authorization in interaction patterns", *Proceedings of Mobility '09: Proceedings of the 6th International Conference on Mobile Technology*, ACM, pp. 1–8, 2009.

[HUA 02] HUANG P., LENDERS V., MINNIG P., WIDMER M., "Mini: a minimal platform comparable to Jini for ubiquitous computing", *Proceedings of the International Symposium on Distributed Objects and Applications (DOA)*, Irvine, USA, 2002.

[JUN 07] JUNG J., PARK J., HAN S., LEE K., "An ECA-based framework for decentralized coordination of ubiquitous web services", *Information and Software Technology*, vol. 49, no. 11–12, pp. 1141–1161, 2007.

[KIC 97] KICZALES G., LAMPING J., MENDHEKAR A., MAEDA C., LOPES C., LOINGTIER J.M., IRWIN J., "Aspect-oriented programming", *Proceedings of ECOOP'07*, Springer Verlag, 1997.

[KIC 99] KICZALES G., BOBROW D., DES RIVIERES J., *The Art of the Metaobject Protocol*, MIT Press, Cambridge, 1999.

[KIC 01] KICZALES G., HILSDALE E., HUGUNIN J., KERSTEN M., PALM J., GRISWOLD W., "An overview of AspectJ", *Proceedings of ECOOP'01*, Object-Oriented Programming, Springer, vol. 2072, pp. 327–354, 2001.

[MAC 06] MAC KENZIE M., LASKEY K., MCCABE F., BROWN P., METZ R., Reference model for service oriented architecture 1.0, Report, no. wd-soa-rm-cd1, OASIS, February 2006.

[PAP 03] PAPAZOGLOU M., "Service-oriented computing: concepts, characteristics and directions, WISE'03", *Proceedings of the Fourth International Conference on Web Information Systems Engineering*, pp. 3–12, 2003.

[PIN 05] PINTO M., FUENTES L., TROYA J., "A dynamic component and aspect-oriented platform", *Computer Journal*, vol. 48, no. 4, pp. 401–420, 2005.

[PRE 06] PREUSS S., "JESA service discovery protocol: efficient service discovery in ad hoc networks", *Mobile and Wireless Communications*, Lecture Notes in Computer Science, vol. 2345, pp. 1196–1201, January 2006.

[SED 03] SEDOV I., PREUSS S., CAP C., HAASE M., TIMMERMANN D., "Time and energy efficient service discovery in Bluetooth", *Proceedings of the 57th IEEE Semiannual Vehicular Technology Conference*, Jeju, South Korea, pp. 418–422, April 2003.

[SIN 05] SINGH M., HUHNS M., *Service-Oriented Computing: Semantics, Processes, Agents*, John Wiley & Sons, Chichester, 2005.

[SZY 99] SZYPERSKI C., BOSCH J., WECK W., "Component oriented programming", *Lecture Notes in Computer Science*, Springer, vol. 1743, pp. 184–184, 1999.

[TIG 09] TIGLI J.Y., LAVIROTTE S., REY G., HOURDIN V., RIVEILL M., "Lightweight service oriented architecture for pervasive computing", *International Journal of Computer Science Issues (IJCSI)*, vol. 4, pp. 1-9, September 2009.

[VAL 05] VALLÉE M., RAMPARANY F., VERCOUTER L., "Flexible composition of smart device services", *Proceedings of the International Conference on Pervasive Systems and Computing (PSC'05)*, Las Vegas, NV, USA, June 2005.

[ZHU 05] ZHU F., MUTKA M., NI L., "Service discovery in pervasive computing environments ", *IEEE Pervasive Computing*, vol. 4, no. 4, pp. 81–90, 2005.

Chapter 7

Data Access and Ambient Computing

7.1. Introduction

Recent years have been marked by a significant development in mobile devices (e.g. laptop computers, mobile phones, satellite navigation assistants, sensors, etc.). While still restricted, these devices have seen a rapid evolution and perform increasingly better and are well equipped (memory capacity, touch screens, positioning systems, accelerometers, for example). The different existing mobile devices are therefore able to communicate with other fixed or mobile terminals using wireless networks. Different kinds of wireless network offering varying rates and ranges can be used for this purpose (such as IEEE 802.11, Bluetooth, 3G, etc.).

Today, a vast number of users employ these devices in their everyday lives to access different kinds of data. The importance of data access from mobile devices will become even more significant in coming years. ABI Research, for instance, estimates that by 2014 the amount of data exchanged every month from mobile devices will significantly surpass that transferred throughout the whole of 2008[1]. Research into the management of mobile data began at the start of the 1990s with several articles studying the issues raised by these new environments [BAR 99, IMI 93, IMI 96, PIT 98]. The emergence of mobile devices and wireless networks has had a particularly significant impact on query evaluation solutions [IMI 02, VAR 10].

Chapter written by Thierry Delot and Marie Thilliez.
1 For further information, refer to: www.abiresearch.com/press/1466-In+2014+Monthly+ Mobile+Data+Traffic+Will+Exceed+2008+Total.

The proliferation of all kinds of mobile devices has enabled the continuous development of new applications in numerous fields (automation, distribution, health, transport, etc.). We are entering today an era of pervasive, or ambient, computing to provide data access to users based on their devices that are available in any place at any time [WEI 99]. Information is not exempt from this evolution. It is stored everywhere, in different forms on different kinds of devices, more or less mobile and which are interconnected using wireless networks. Numerous issues must be considered in these kinds of environments, notably related to the limited resources of the devices used and the mobility they require.

In this chapter, we will focus on the problem of data access within an ambient computing context. This context is made particularly dynamic by user (consumers of data) mobility and data sources, which may appear or disappear at any moment. In addition, some mobile devices such as sensors do not store data but continually produce it. The mobility has a significant impact on data management techniques. The standard techniques used for data accces in the context of distributed databases or traditional peer-to-peer systems, for example, are therefore completely unadapted. Due to the mobility of data sources and potential disconnections, a data placement schema describing the location of data sources cannot be established and used in the query evaluation process.

The notion of query result is therefore in itself completely different in our context. In a database management system (DBMS), even when distributed, the result of a query consists of all tuples verifying the restrictions imposed by the user in this query. In the case of a distributed DBMS, if all the sites storing data send a positive response to the sub-query sent to them, then the user will be able to access all of the result and obtain a complete response. In the context of ambient computing, the notion of a complete result does not generally exist. It is in effect impossible to guarantee that all terminals with data relevant to the query will be contacted. Rather, the aim is to propose a result to the user using the data sources available and accessible at the query's execution.

In this chapter, our aim is to demonstrate how data access techniques have been revisited to face the problems introduced by mobile devices and to highlight some of the challenges that need to be addressed to provide adequate access to data in the context of ambient computing.

We will subsequently introduce the different types of queries used in ambient environments and then examine some of the different evaluation models.

7.2. General context

Whether we term it ambient, pervasive or mobile computing, recent developments in mobile technologies (such as wireless networks, mobile devices, etc.) have had a highly significant impact on data access. Before examining solutions to this, we will briefly examine the constraints imposed by these new environments on data management and will explain why the techniques used in standard information systems are no longer appropriate.

7.2.1. *Devices*

While they do not exclude the use of standard machines (such as fixed or portable computers, for example), ambient environments involve a number of mobile devices (sensors, smartphones, tablets, etc.). These devices provide relatively limited storage capacities even if these capabilities are increasingly significant. These devices propose different inputs and outputs to standard computers (e.g. screen size, keyboard, touch screen, etc.). As a result, applications must be able to consider these features. In addition, these devices rely on batteries that impose restrictions in terms of their independence. These constraints entail the use of optimized applications to limit energy consumption.

7.2.2. *Communication*

The mobile devices used in ambient environments communicate using different wireless networks (such as Zigbee, Wi-Fi, ULB, UMTS, etc.). These different modes of communication enable direct transfer between mobile devices (such as exchanging a message between two sensors) or provide access to a fixed infrastructure for mobile telephone networks. Using these wireless networks, information can be exchanged even in situations where devices are mobile. Data transfer carried out over such networks therefore generally suffers from limited flow and frequent disconnections.

7.2.3. *Mobility*

Using the mobile devices described above and examined more generally throughout this book, consumers of data, as with all data sources, must be mobile. The constraints may be more or less significant depending on whether the devices are designed for pedestrians or vehicles. The mobility of sources and/or consumers of data evidently raises issues of location. To determine the geographic location, there are currently a number of solutions available, both for outside and indoor environments. Outside, they rely mainly on using signals transmitted by satellites. The American Global Positioning System (GPS) is the most commonly used. Other systems are also available, or are soon to become so, such as the Russian GLONASS or the European GALILEO iniative, which is still under development. Inside buildings, satellite systems cannot operate if their signals are not amplified. A number of alternative solutions have therefore been proposed to locate mobile objects. Different technologies designed for this purpose have been investigated, such as sensors (e.g. pressure sensors with, for example, smartfloors), using the signal strength of wireless networks with systems such as Wireless Positioning Systems (WPS) [WAN 03], or even cameras [DEL 09].

In this way, the mobility of consumers and/or data services impacts on the relevance of information and can mean it is out of date. As such, when a driver searches for all the parking locations or service stations within a mile radius, all the results satisfying this query will depend on its location and change according to her/his movement.

To summarize, the use of mobile devices has a significant impact on query processing techniques. Mobile devices can appear or disappear at any moment, and thus their stored data can also appear and disappear. This results in a particularly dynamic distributed environment where standard techniques for accessing data, notably those proposed in the context of distributed databases, are no better suited. These techniques rely on using a data placement schema, which describes the location of different fragments of data stored at different sites. The placement schema is therefore at the heart of query evaluation processes in distributed databases. In addition, it enables us to identify all the data sources consulted to provide a result and thereby ensure transparency of location. Such a placement schema is nevertheless completely impossible to maintain in an environment with mobile data sources due to the well-known problem of potentially frequent disconnections.

In a mobile context, it is also impossible to guarantee that a device will reconnect and therefore that its stored data will also be accessible. The notion of a query result is therefore completely different in our context. In even a distributed DBMS, the result of a query consists of all the tuples verifying the restrictions expressed by the user. If all the sites with the data in question respond well to the received sub-query, then the user has access to all the results sought. In an "ambient" context, the notion of a complete result does not exist. This is because it is effectively impossible to guarantee that all terminals with relevant data in relation to the query considered can be contacted. The aim is rather to provide to the user a result depending on the data sources available in the user's vicinity when the query is executed.

In the rest of this chapter, we will examine the different types of queries that have emerged in mobile technologies to allow users to express her/his needs.

7.3. Types of queries

The use of mobile devices as producers and consumers of data requires the consideration of different types of queries to allow users to obtain relevant data. In the rest of this section we will examine the main types of queries used with mobile devices.

7.3.1. *Location queries*

Using existing positioning techniques, it is possible to locate mobile devices in the query evaluation process to treat location queries such as "what is the nearest bus stop to me?". The need to personalize a service to the user based on her/his geographic location existed well before the development of mobile devices. Within the context of the internet, user location is used by some search engines to sort results [BUY 99]. When a user searches for Italian restaurants, for example, the list of results given to them can be sorted according to their proximity to these restaurants. The development of mobility in recent years has considerably increased the interest in location queries.

A location query relates to the location of a user and/or that of other entities. For example, queries such as "where is Paul Jones?" or "where is the nearest cinema to me?" are location queries. In [SEY 01], the authors distinguish between two types of location queries:

– queries relating to location, also known as Location Aware Queries (LAQs), which are location queries whose filter is not based on the user's location. The query "where is the nearest Greek restaurant to the cinema?" is the example of an LAQ;

– location-Dependent Queries (or LDQs) are queries that are restricted by the client's location. The query "which is the nearest Greek restaurant to me?" is the example of an LDQ. LDQs mean that the user's position has to be known (i.e. the location of her/his mobile device) when s/he transmits the request.

To express these location-related restrictions, research has been carried out in recent years into spatial (such as contain, intersect) and new operators (e.g. close, closest to distance, straight ahead), which express relationships of proximity or direction [SEY 01, SEY 02, THI 05].

7.3.2. *Continuous queries*

One of the characteristics of some mobile devices such as sensors is that they produce a continuous flow of data. Access to the data produced by such devices requires continuous evaluation of queries. In contrast to one-shot queries, which are generally used in the world of databases and which produce a result from the data available at the point the query is executed, continuous queries allow us to follow the evolution of the result over time. The result of a continuous query is therefore not calculated once for all but periodically updated. Elements that have become obsolete are therefore rendered invalid and suppressed from the result given to the user. New valid elements are then added.

The use of continuous queries is particularly interesting when the data sought are produced or stored by mobile devices. This is because they allow us to effectively withstand frequent changes in the query results. These changes are not exclusively related to the production of a continuous flow of data by sensors. They may also be related to consumer mobility and/or the producers of data.

Continous queries were explicitly introduced in 1992 in the Tapestry system with TQL, a language based on SQL [TER 92]. More recently, the CQL (Continuous Query Language) was introduced for querying continuous data flows or relations within DSMS (Data Streams Management Systems) Frameworks [ARA 06].

If the location and continuous queries are those most commonly used within an ambient computing context, other types of query are also particularly useful. Notable examples include nearest neighbor queries or K-NNs, which express queries as information relative to k neighbors nearest to a mobile node. Sliding windows are particularly popular in sensor networks and are designed to monitor the evolution of a given spatio-temporal zone.

7.4. Data access models

Depending on the mobile device being considered, the networks available, or even the location of data, different access models can be used in ambient environments to provide the users with the data s/he needs.

In the rest of this chapter, we will examine the different possible models for accessing data via mobile devices.

7.4.1. *The Pull model*

Mobile telephone networks (such as 3G, for example) now allow users to connect to various data sources such as remote databases, Internet sites, or even web services. In recent years, research has also focused on evaluating queries relating to mobile web services (i.e. those deployed on mobile devices) [ADA 06].

To provide users with access to the data s/he needs, research has used the Pull model that consists of sending a query over remote nodes to extract the useful data from it. Using mobile telephone networks, one or several remote data sources (such as web services) can be sollicited (i.e. receive a query) to communicate with a mobile device using their stored data.

The basic idea here consists of transmitting queries to relevant data sources. This Pull model is not only used with client–server type architectures. It can also be applied to decentralized environments such as hybrid peer-to-peer contexts [THI 05] or pure peer-to-peer [AND 04], where no central server can process mobile users' queries. Their queries can therefore be transmitted directly or using multi-jump techniques [BIS 05] toward relevant data sources. Each node can then calculate a response relevant to the user and transmit the corresponding data toward the user who formulated the query.

The main advantage of this Pull model is that it saves the client's resources (e.g. network, batteries) since this only transmits relevant data. It therefore allows exploiting at a limited cost huge collections of data managed by specific servers.

7.4.2. *The Push model*

In contrast to the Pull model described in section 7.4.1, the Push model involves transmitting data over an *ad hoc* network to potentially interested mobile devices. Mobile devices therefore no longer need to send a query to a server to obtain data. They continuously receive a flow of data that they can then use. This Push model compensates for an important limitation of the Pull model. This is because, if transmission of a query to data sources is still possible, routing the partial results calculated by them toward their destination cannot be simple where no fixed infrastucture is available and/or when the target node is very mobile. Even if it has been demonstrated that this routing is possible in certain conditions [DEL 11a], the use of the Push model is generally preferred. The use of this model is, for example, frequently used in vehicle networks [OLA 09]. A communicating vehicle can, according to this principle, receive information produced or relayed by neighboring vehicles concerning, for instance, an emergency stop, a traffic jam, or an available stopping point. Continuous queries can then be evaluated on the mobile device (such as a smartphone fitted in the vehicle) on the flow of data to communicate the five parking spaces nearest to the driver [XU 04].

The difficulty here is not a question of evaluating queries since these are executed locally on the data received by the mobile device. The challenge, rather, consists of steering the data toward potential consumers (i.e. mobile devices interested by this data) as quickly as possible while avoiding network overload or loss of data. Different protocols have been proposed to address this problem [CEN 11].

As a result, once received and stored on a mobile device, it is essential to evaluate the data's relevance. Let us re-examine our example of vehicles receiving informaton about the location of potential parking spaces or traffic jams from their neighbors. In *ad hoc* networks such as vehicle networks where connections change as vehicles move around, not every mobile node in the network is guaranteed to receive an invalidation message when a parking space is being used or the traffic jam clears. Relevance evaluation mechanisms integrating time and geographic location have therefore been introduced to replace the least important elements stored in the mobile device's memory cache.

In summary, the use of the Push model is highly useful for environments where data centralization (whether partial or total) is not desirable and where direct interactions between mobile nodes is preferable. If this model allows mobile objects to obtain information, it has relatively significant limitations. In addition, only the "popular" data (i.e. that relevant to a large number of users or mobile nodes) are transmitted *a priori*. This is because this kind of model does not allow any information to be transmitted to any user to conserve bandwidth or, more importantly, private information. These restrictions mean that the Push model is inappropriate for some applications, such as social vehicle networks [SMA 08] where information is sent to every driver.

To conclude, both the Push and Pull models have their own advantages. In addition, some recent research [CUE 08, DEL 11] has attempted to combine them to benefit from both data flows communicated by close terminals and data stored in remote sources such as web services.

7.5. Query optimization

In standard environments (such as DBMS, for example), the query evaluation process is generally divided into three distinct phases [KOS 00]. During the first phase, the query is analyzed and transformed into an execution plan (i.e. an internal representation). The second stage optimizes the query, i.e. chooses from the set of candidate plans, which minimizes the calculation time for the result. The third and last phase consists of carrying out the best execution plan identified during the previous stage.

In environments with mobile devices and resource limitations, query optimization techniques must account for new constraints and are slightly different from those used traditionally, such as with databases, for example [DEL 11]. First, one of the difficulties is related to the absence of a data placement schema to identify the different potential data sources. On the other hand, the query optimization process must take into account the restricted resources of the mobile devices involved (e.g. autonomy, bandwidth, etc.). Standard query optimization techniques define an execution plan from the query, which is only focused on minimizing the execution time, i.e. reducing the time a user must wait for a result.

When mobile devices are used, the query execution time cannot be the only criterion considered, even if it remains the most significant. Reducing the execution time for a query as much as possible can rapidly use all the mobile device's resources (such as available energy, for example). It is therefore important to minimize the use of the device's battery during query evaluation. This generally involves limiting communications across wireless networks, which are particularly costly in terms of the energy consumption of the mobile devices used.

Figure 7.1 shows the different formulae for calculating query evaluation costs according to three different dimensions: execution time, financial cost, and energy consumed. The cost in time consists of the time required to transmit the remote query, the time required for the remote node(s) to receive the query and process it and, lastly, the time required to send the results to the mobile node producing the query. The financial cost is obtained by calculating the total costs incurred to send the query over the network or download the result(s) as well as the costs incurred to use the remote charging services. In line with the information given in [FEE 01], the cost of energy (in Joules) to evaluate a query can be estimated by the product of the number of bytes transferred for the calculation of the result by a constant $k = 44 \times 10^{-6}$.

Finally, the overall cost for a query is calculated using the total of the different costs cited previously. The weight of each of these dimensions can be fixed by the user according to her/his preferences. They can also be dynamically adapted according to the parameters observed (e.g. increasing the significance attributed to energy cost to maintain the mobile device's autonomy when this becomes weak).

$$C_{Time}(Q) = C_{QueryDelivery}^{Time}(Q) + C_{Processing}^{Time}(Q) + C_{ResultDelivery}^{Time}(Q)$$

$$C_{Money}(Q) = C_{QueryDelivery}^{Money}(Q) + C_{Processing}^{Money}(Q) + C_{ResultDelivery}^{Money}(Q)$$

$$C_{Energy}(Q) = K \times n$$

$$C(Q) = \sum_{i=Time, Money, Energy} w_i \times C_i$$

Figure 7.1. *Calculation of costs related to a query evaluation*

Beyond the costs related to executing a query that must be adapted to the user's preferences as well as her/his device's resources, the optimization process can have an unavoidable effect on the quality of the result. In addition to costs, the query optimizer must account for this parameter to select the least costly source if this only delivers better quality results. This is, however, significant because the statistics available on the data that can be used in ambient environments (such as the volume of data to be transferred, response time, etc.) are far fewer and lower than in standard DBMS.

7.6. Sensitivity to context

In ambient environments, data access takes place in a highly distributed and dynamic context. Due to users' mobility and the use of wireless networks, a large number of parameters do not change over time (such as geographic location, bandwidth, type of connection, autonomy, etc.). As a result, a query evaluator deployed in this kind of environment must be context aware to consider the changes that it might encounter. A single mobile device (such as a smartphone, for example) and therefore the query evaluator can be found in very different situations. The user may use their device to access data in a shopping center, a scenario in which the Pull model introduced in section 7.4.1 is particularly well adapted to find different providers of required information (e.g. "In which stores can I find women's sports shoes?"). A few moments later, this same user can get into her/his car and ask this same device for information for help with driving (e.g. "Are there normal driving conditions on my way home?"). In this case, with direct interactions between drivers' devices relaying traffic information, the Push model described in section 7.4.2 is the best option to provide the user with her/his desired data. In another context, the query evaluator can rely on the GPS receiver fitted in the mobile device to evaluate the user's location queries. Nevertheless, the user is not guaranteed to receive the location information anywhere and, if s/he is in a blind spot or inside a building, it is necessary to use an appropriate positioning service (such as Wi-Fi positioning, for example). If unsuccessful, it is also necessary to convert the provided location (e.g. with a symbolic representation in the form of an address) in the appropriate model (for example a physical representation with GPS coordinates) using the Google Maps web service, for instance.

Throughout these examples, we have tried to illustrate how access techniques must be adapted to different contextual parameters external to the query evaluator. With the current situation, the notion of context is generally defined as "any information which characterizes an entity's situation or which could influence an application's behavior" [DEY 99]. It is, of course, very difficult to produce an exhaustive list of contextual parameters, but time, geographic location, or user activity are examples of contextual elements. Different contextual models have been recently introduced. For example, the authors of [CAR 06] distinguish three distinct categories of context. The first includes characteristics of the execution environment. This corresponds to the device's material capacities (such as remaining autonomy, type of available connection, usable bandwidth, etc.). A second category includes the application's needs. In the context of the data access considered here, this category includes the elements configuring the query processor to respond to the application's needs (such as, for instance, the type of query to be evaluated, location dependent, continuous, etc.). Lastly, the final category includes the elements of context such as user-imposed constraints (e.g. maximum time allocated for searching for a result).

Being able to monitor contextual elements allows us to react to changes in the environment to parameterize the query processor and as such provides users with the best quality service possible. Query processor adaptation can be static, i.e. the evaluator can be configured in relation to the environment in which it is deployed. Adaptation must be dynamic to react to the changes in the environment. As such, "low battery", "limited" or "non-existent" connectivity, or "significant change in speed" are examples of elements that can impact on data access techniques. In this case, it is necessary to be able to react on demand and modify the query processor's behavior to maintain service quality. Adaptation can, for example, concern the query optimization process and consist of a change in importance relative to the different criteria considered (such as time, energy, financial cost).

To carry out contextual adaptation in the query processor, two components are essential. The first consists of observing the real-time development of contextual parameters to detect any significant changes requiring the implementation of defined adaptation policies. The second is adaptation management [GRI 05], which modifies the evaluator's behavior to optimize the service offered to the user. This adaptation may require a substitution of algorithm (e.g. join) according to a context change.

7.7. Conclusion

In this chapter, we have examined the challenges related to data access in ambient environments concentrating on the basic mechanisms that provide users with the information s/he needs. Other research has focused on data security and confidentiality. The following chapter will therefore focus on the impact of ambient systems on data access control models.

7.8. Bibliography

[ADA 06] ADACAL M., BENER A., "Mobile web services: a new agent-based framework", *IEEE Internet Computing*, vol. 10, no. 3, pp. 58–65, 2006.

[AND 04] ANDROUTSELLIS-THEOTOKIS S., SPINELLIS D., "A survey of peer-to-peer content distribution technologies", *ACM Computing Surveys*, vol. 36, no. 4, pp. 335–371, 2004.

[ARA 06] ARASU A., BABUR S., WIDOM J., "The CQL continuous query language: semantic foundations and query execution", *The VLDB Journal*, vol. 15, no. 2, pp. 121–142, 2006.

[BAR 99] BARBARÁ B., "Mobile computing and databases – a survey", *IEEE Transactions on Knowledge and Data Engineering*, vol. 11, no. 1, pp. 108–117, 1999.

[BIS 05] BISWAS B., MORRIS R., "ExOR: opportunistic multi-hop routing for wireless networks", *ACM SIGCOMM Computer Communication Review*, vol. 35, no. 4, pp. 133–144, 2005.

[BUY 99] BUYUKKOKTEN O., CHO J., GARCIA MOLINA H., GRAVANO L., SHIVAKUMAR N., "Exploiting geographical location information of web pages", *Proceedings of the International ACM SIGMOD Workshop on the Web and Databases (WebDB)*, Philadelphia, Pennsylvania, 1999.

[CAR 06] CARON O., CARRE B., GRANSART C., LE PALLEC X., LECOMTE S., MARVIE R., NEBUT M., SERIAI D., "Propositions pour la modélisation d'applications ubiquitaires", *Actes des 3es journées francophones Mobilité & ubiquité (Ubimob'06)*, ACM International Conference Proceeding Series, Paris, France, 2006.

[CEN 11] CENERARIO N., DELOT T., ILARRI S., "A content-based dissemination protocol for VANETs: exploiting the encounter probability", *IEEE Transactions on Intelligent Transportation Systems*, IEEE Computer Society, vol. 12, no. 3, pp. 771–782, 2011.

[CUE 08] CUEVAS-VICENTTIN V., "Towards multi-scale query processing", *IEEE 24th International Conference on Data Engineering (ICDE'08) Workshops*, IEEE Computer Society, pp. 137–144, 2008.

[DEL 09] DELOT T., "Interopérabilité & Hybridation adaptées aux besoins des utilisateurs", *Géopositionnement et mobilités (GPS, EGNOS et Galileo...)*, Maison du livre de Franche-Comté, 2009.

[DEL 11a] DELOT T., ILARRI S., THILLIEZ M., VARGAS-SOLAR G., LECOMTE S., "Multi-scale query processing in mobile environments", *Journal of Ambient Intelligence and Humanized Computing (JAIHC)*, Springer, vol. 2, no. 3, pp. 213–226, 2011.

[DEL 11b] DELOT T., MITTON N., ILARRI S., HIEN T., "Decentralized information gathering in vehicular networks using GeoVanet", *International Conference on Mobile Data Management (MDM)*, IEEE, Luleå, Sweden, pp. 174–183, June 2011.

[DEY 99] DEY A.K., ABOWD G.D., "Towards a better understanding of context and context-awareness", *Proceedings of the 1st International Symposium on Handheld and Ubiquitous Computing (HUC'99)*, Springer-Verlag, pp. 304–307, 1999.

[FEE 01] FEENEY L.M., NILSSON M., "Investigating the energy consumption of a wireless network interface in an ad hoc networking environment", *International Conference on Computer Communications (INFOCOM'01)*, IEEE Computer Society, 2001.

[GRI 05] GRINE H., DELOT T., LECOMTE S., "Adaptive query processing in mobile environment", *Third International Middleware Workshop on Middleware for Pervasive and Ad-hoc Computing*, New York, USA, 2005.

[IMI 93] IMIELINSKI T., BADRINATH B.R, "Data management for mobile computing", *SIGMOD Record*, vol. 22, no. 1, pp. 34–39, 1993.

[IMI 96] IMIELINSKI T., *Mobile Computing*, Kluwer, Boston, MA, 1996.

[IMI 02] IMIELINSKI T., NATH B., "Wireless graffiti: data, data everywhere", *International Conference on Very Large Data Bases (VLDB'02)*, VLDB Endowment, pp. 9–19, 2002.

[KOS 00] KOSSMANN D., "The state of the art in distributed query processing", *ACM Computing Surveys*, vol. 32, no. 4, pp. 422–469, 2000.

[OLA 09] OLARIU S., WEIGLE M.C. (eds), *Vehicular Networks: From Theory to Practice*, Chapman & Hall/CRC, Boca Raton, 2009.

[PIT 98] PITOURA E., SAMARAS G., *Data Management for Mobile Computing*, Kluwer, Boston, MA, 1998.

[SEY 01] SEYDIM A., DUNHAM M., KUMAR V., "Location dependent query processing", *Proceedings of the 2nd ACM International Workshop on Data Engineering for Wireless and Mobile Access (MobiDE'01)*, ACM SIGMOD, pp. 47–53, 2001.

[SMA 08] SMALDONE S., HAN L., SHANKAR P., IFTODE L., "RoadSpeak: enabling voice chat on roadways using vehicular social networks", *First Workshop on Social Network Systems (SocialNets'08)*, ACM, 2008.

[TER 92] TERRY D.B., GOLDBERG D., NICHOLS D., OKI B.M., "Continuous queries over append-only databases", *Proceedings of the 1992 ACM SIGMOD International Conference on Management of Data*, ACM, New York, USA, pp. 321–330, June 1992.

[THI 03] THILLIEZ M., DELOT T., LECOMTE S., "Hybrid peer-to-peer model in proximity applications", *Proceedings of the 17th International Conference on Advanced Information Networking and Applications (AINA'03)*, IEEE Computer Society, pp. 306–311, 2003.

[THI 05] THILLIEZ M., DELOT T., LECOMTE S., "Requêtes dépendantes de la localisation: évaluation distribuée et optimisation", *Ingénierie des Systèmes d'Information*, vol. 10, no. 5, pp. 39–58, 2005.

[VAR 10] VARGAS-SOLAR G., IBRAHIM N., COLLET C., ADIBA M., PETIT J.M., DELOT T., "Querying issues in pervasive environments", *Pervasive Computing and Communications Design and Deployment: Technologies, Trends, and Applications*, IGI Global Publications, Hershey, pp. 1–23, 2010.

[WAN 03] WANG Y., JIA X., LEE H.K., LI G.Y., "An indoor wireless positioning system based on wireless local area network infrastructure", *6th International Symposium on Satellite Navigation Technology Including Mobile Positioning & Location Services (SatNav)*, Melbourne, Australia, 2003.

[WEI 99] WEISER M., "The computer for the 21st century", *ACM SIGMOBILE Mobile Computing and Communications Review*, vol. 3, no. 3, pp. 3–11, 1999.

[XU 04] XU B., OUKSEL A., WOLFSON O., "Opportunistic resource exchange in inter-vehicle ad-hoc networks", *Fifth International Conference on Mobile Data Management (MDM'04)*, IEEE Computer Society, pp. 4–12, 2004.

Chapter 8

Security and Ambient Systems: A Study on the Evolution of Access Management in Pervasive Information Systems

8.1. Introduction

The evolution of information systems is linked to the development of telecommunications, connectivity, hardware and software. These systems aim to create seamless and interoperable environments to share information between different (sub-)systems with varying levels of confidentiality.

With the technological development and the integration of new technologies in daily-life applications, connectivity has improved accessibility to resources. This evolution has given the user a lot more freedom to interact and has allowed them to access information sources at anywhere, anytime, and anyhow. This is how systems have become pervasive or ubiquitous [PAR 04].

The concept of ubiquity was first proposed by Weiser [WEI 91], who predicted the future of information systems in the 21st Century, where computing elements would "disappear" while functioning homogeneously in total transparence.

Increasingly, transparency has become essential to ensure better accessibility to resources at all levels of a system or a business. However, this transparency risks making resources vulnerable to security threats and attacks.

Chapter written by Dana AL KUKHUN and Florence SÈDES.

Considering the problem of access management to information sources in Pervasive Information Systems (PIS), we are faced with the challenge of finding the right balance between ensuring data protection and providing transparent access to information sources that exist in open environments and may be managed by different parties. The evolution of PIS has thus posed a new challenge linked to managing data access for mobile users. These systems must simultaneously facilitate and implement wide-ranging accessibility, but also protect the system by applying access policies that ensure its security and protect it from being vulnerable to intruder attacks. The objective also involves respecting "private" data and keeping it confidential.

To meet the challenges of information management, many forms of access control have been proposed. These include DAC (Discretionary Access Control), MAC (Mandatory Access Control), and RBAC (Role-Based Access Control). However, technological evolution has introduced new challenges linked to decision-making while considering the user's contextual constraints (time, location, etc.). There are also challenges linked to the multi-distributive nature of information sources and the access control policies responsible for managing these sources.

With the development of service-oriented architectures and taking into consideration the quasi-systematic distribution of resources, control efforts are more geared toward decision-making based on several access policies that have been distributed and managed by various services and are sometimes generated in real time. Ensuring a quality of service in this context has been achieved by guaranteeing the efficiency of making access decisions. Different standards have been proposed, such as XML-Signature [SIG 02], XML Encryption [ENC 02], and XACML [XAC 03, XAC 05]. The latter aims to make access decisions by basing itself on the attributes and access policies that are represented in XML. The power of XACML lies in its ability to take into account the contextual constraints that come from a pervasive environment.

Many pieces of research have extended the basic access control models to add context awareness, but this research has taken into consideration neither the importance of system usability nor the improvement of access possibilities – the impossibility of responding to a user's request usually leads to an access denial that is often linked to the dynamicity of their context or the existence of changing or contradicting access policies.

To ensure usability during critical situations, we have introduced PS–RBAC (Pervasive Situation-aware RBAC Model), an access control model that extends the RBAC model by adding to its context and situation awareness [ALK 09]. In anticipation of this proposition, we have analyzed various benchmarks, methods, norms, and good practices that deal with the security of information systems (for example, EBIOS, MEHARI, CMMI, COBIT, ITIL, ISO 27001, ISO 27002, etc.) to have a broad vision of these policies and their assessments. The proposed model has implemented mechanisms that aim to react, in the case of an access denial, by using adaptive decision-making that allows us to propose a list of similar, equivalent, "palliative", or degraded resources that differ from those requested by the user and that are authorized. The originality of our approach lies in its capability in avoiding access denials by reformulating the denied access requests when possible, and in avoiding the "deadlock" that faces the user and that helps in managing the user's needs during urgent situations.

The PS–RBAC model aims to improve access possibilities through an XACML query rewriting process that identifies, through the initiator's contextual constraints, the access control policies that can be applied and the resources that they can access. The model reacts, in the case of an access denial, to see if there are similar resources that contain the requested information to offer them as an alternative solution.

8.2. Managing access in pervasive information systems

An access management process, in the PIS era, is carried out in three main steps: the first includes establishing access, rights to which is carried out by adopting a generic model that responds to the needs of administrators, users, and to the nature of the capability distribution. The second step involves choosing a service-oriented mechanism that can carry out decentralized access management to ensure decision-making with access privileges distributed. Finally, the third step consists of adapting decision-making according to the user's contextual constraints. In fact, with the evolution of PIS, an access control model is often extended to manage the user's contextual constraints while granting a permission.

In this chapter, we will cite a representative part of the research works that has contributed to the improvement of access management in these three steps. We will start by looking at the evolution of the basic access models, then some mechanisms and service-oriented access standards, and finally we will explore the works that deal with the adaptation of decision-making to respond to the dynamics of the pervasive context and to the importance of the situation in which the user requests access to the system.

8.2.1. *Basic access control models*

8.2.1.1. *The DAC model*

The Discretionary Access Control (DAC) model has been defined by the Trusted Computer System Evaluation Criteria (TCSEC) as: "a means of restricting access to objects based on the identity of subjects and/or groups to which they belong. The controls are discretionary in the sense that a subject is capable of passing that permission on to other subjects" [NCS 87].

The DAC model represents access control policies by using a triplet <user, object, action>, which states that the user can perform a certain operation that is identified by the action (for example, read) to be performed on the specified object. The three values together form an authorization rule.

In some systems, access is granted only by explicitly specifying a set of authorization rules. In other words, if no authorization rule is defined for a user, access will be denied. This type of policy is known as a closed policy [SAM 00]. Conversely, in systems which have an open policy, access to an object will only be denied if there are (negative) authorization rules, i.e. the user can gain access to all the system's objects unless if there is an authorization rule that has been explicitly defined forbidding them access to the objects.

8.2.1.2. *The MAC model*

To solve the problem of information leakage within the DAC models, the Mandatory Access Control (MAC) model establishes unbreakable rules that are designed to ensure respect for access control demands. The MAC model thus gives subjects and objects several levels that cannot be changed by the user, and consequently limits their power to manage access to their data.

The DAC model does not distinguish users from subjects. Consequently, this lack of distinction leads to problems of information leakage. The MAC model deals with this problem by differentiating between users and subjects. Users are passive entities that can connect to the system while subjects are processes executed on behalf of users. A user connecting to the system with a given access class generates a subject of this access class. According to the security level (trust) attributed to the user, different subjects can be generated.

Although the MAC model resolves the problem of information leakage that the DAC model has, it remains a very rigid model. It does not allow the user to manage exceptions between different security levels.

8.2.1.3. *The RBAC model*

The main motivation behind proposing Role-Based Access Control (RBAC) model was to make it easier to administer access privileges for a large number of users demanding access to distributed resources. The solution presented by [FER 92] is to group users together into roles that reflect the organizational structure of the business and then to grant permissions to roles instead of repeating permission assignment on an individual basis.

The role is placed at the heart of the RBAC model, where it acts as an intermediary between users and permissions. A role groups a set of privileges and hands them out, and then does so to users according to their function in the organization.

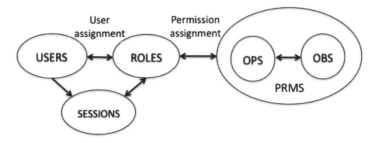

Figure 8.1. *Roles and permission assignment in RBAC*

As shown in Figure 8.1, the assignment of roles to users follows a mutual relationship in the RBAC model, where a user (person, computer process, machine, etc.) can play several roles in a single session and a role can be attributed to several users.

UA $\subseteq$ Users $\times$ Roles

Attributing a role to a user grants them several permissions (PRMS) and at the same time a permission can be attributed to several roles.

PA $\subseteq$ Roles $\times$ PRMS

The nature of a permission describes the type of operations (OPS) (for example reading, writing, updating, etc.) that can be performed on system objects (OBS) (data sources: documents, computer process, machines, etc.).

The relationship between these objects and the attributed operations is mutual as well; an operation can be performed on several objects and many permissions can be attributed to an object.

PRM $\subseteq$ OPS $\times$ OBS

To respond to the changing needs of access management within organizations, the RBAC model has been extended to various profiles to fill in the gaps and to perform better through different principles, such as: the hierarchy of roles in RBAC-1 model [SAN 96], where a user can inherit another user's access rights; the inclusion of constraints on role attribution as presented in RBAC-2; and the separation of distinct tasks between the various stakeholders on a mission in RBAC-3 [KUH 97].

8.2.2. *Managing service-oriented access: the XACML standard*

The RBAC model has succeeded in solving the problem of administering distributed data sources by managing them in a centralized or semi-centralized way. However, with the evolution of service-oriented architectures and web services, the problem of managing access has become more complex because of the distribution of access policies and because of their real-time evolution.

XACML (eXtensible Access Control Markup Language) [OAS 03] is an XML-based standard that describes access control policies that allow privileges entitled to users to be defined on the different resources of a computing system. This standard allows authenticated and secure access for systems to be made by taking into account various elements linked to the user context.

The fact that XACML is based on XML language has given it many qualities such as interoperability, without needing to specify a formal language, which has facilitated its use in web services.

The XACML specification has supplied an architecture that describes the process of managing access during an access request (see Figure 8.2). During an access request to a capability, a Policy Enforcement Point (PEP) checks to see whether access is authorized or not. To verify the validity of the access request, the system must verify if there is a security policy that corresponds to this request. The verification is carried out by the PEP, which creates a request containing the user's attributes and sends them to the Policy Decision Point, which makes the decision by consulting the list of access policies located in the Policy Administration Point (PAP). By using the relevant security policy (chosen by the PDP), the PEP responds to the client appropriately, ensures that this decision is respected, and that the client can access only authorized resources.

XACML is considered as an efficient standard because of its ability to manage access rights in a distributed manner taking into account the context of the user or service. An XACML RBAC profile was introduced by [OAS 05], thus encouraging the portability of the standard toward large-scale services.

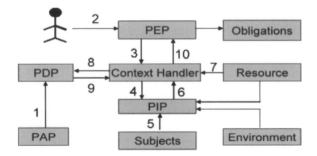

Figure 8.2. *Simplified XACML access management flow chart*

8.3. The evolution of context-aware RBAC models

With the evolution of PIS, attributing a permission to a user has become more complex and context dependent. This is why many new access models have been proposed, to take into account the evolution of the definition of the context (time, location, system characteristics, network connection, user device, etc.).

8.3.1. *Examples of context-aware models*

The evolution of contextual access models started with the recognition of the temporal aspect within the RBAC model. The works of [BER 01] has extended the RBAC model to a TRBAC model (Temporal RBAC), which considers time as a constraint that can determine the activation and the deactivation of a role. The integration of this temporal aspect has given more flexibility to create exceptions for individuals and to specify time-based dependencies between the actions carried out by a user.

The user's mobility and the constant evolution of mobile devices have encouraged the integration of the user's location in an authorization. This was the aim of many research works such as [HAN 03], who proposed a Spatial RBAC model where the attribution of a role depends on the spatial position of the user.

The dynamism of the context has also been dealt with by [ZHA 03] who proposed an extension of the RBAC model toward a Dynamic-RBAC model. The model adapts the attribution of roles and permission by taking into account the change in contextual information. The dynamism of the model has been carried out through the use of automatons.

The works of [BER 05] offer a geographical RBAC (Geo-RBAC) model, which determines the location of the user, either by their exact physical position (with the help of a GPS), or by their logical position, calculated implicitly (in the area in which they are moving; this area can be defined using various levels of granularity).

With the evolution of ubiquitous systems, various context-aware models have been proposed, such as the uT-RBAC [CHA 06], which uses an automaton to describe and take into account the changes in context represented by the time and the location of the user. These elements are considered to be important for the activation and the deactivation of a role.

The use of artificial intelligence mechanisms was introduced by [LIM 07], who proposed employing neural networks to allow more flexibility during access decision-making in ubiquitous contexts.

Other research works have presented a context-aware RBAC model for pervasive systems [EMA 07] and have underlined the fact that contextual attributes are very dynamic, which can disturb authorizations. As a consequence, the authors distinguished two types of contextual elements: (1) long-term elements – supposed to attribute roles and (2) short-term elements – supposed to attribute permissions. These elements can be linked either to the user or to the environment.

Another extension has been proposed to supply an RBAC model adapted to the needs of pervasive systems by [KUL 08]. This model distinguishes context management and access control to make decision-making easier in the event of an authorization related to several contextual constraints. The authors supply a service dedicated to the management of pervasive information sources. A decision to grant access to a capability is made by taking into account all the contextual constraints.

The fact that the user context represents real-life situations means that the precision and the reliability of the context are important and are evaluated by quality indicators. The research works from [FIL 08] has proposed an access control model that is interested in ensuring a better quality of context during an access request.

8.3.2. *Summary*

This analytical study of the various extensions of the RBAC model gives us the opportunity to emphasize the importance of taking into account the user's context during access decision-making. The aim is to make applications more adapted to the real-time constraints and the dynamics of pervasive systems.

Contextual constraints		Time	Location	Date	Others
Model	**Reference**				
T-RBAC	Bertino *et al.* 2001	x			
Spatial RBAC	Hansen *et al.* 2003	x	x		
Dynamic RBAC	Zhang *et al.* 2003	x	x	x	
Geo-RBAC	Bertino *et al.* 2005	x	x		
uT-RBAC	Chae *et al.* 2006	x	x		Logical
Context-Aware Access Control Model for Pervasive Computing Environments	Emami *et al.* 2007	x	x	x	
Intelligent Access Control Mechanism for Ubiquitous Applications	Lim *et al.* 2007	x	x		Neural networks
Context-aware RBAC in pervasive computing systems	Kulkarni *et al.* 2008	x	x	x	
Quality-Aware Context-Based Access Control model for ubiquitous applications	Filho *et al.* 2008	x	x	x	context quality

Table 8.1. *The evolution of context-aware access models*

8.4. Conclusion

Accessibility to data sources is a critical factor within pervasive information systems, particularly when considering real-time consultations or critical situations. Controlling access, therefore, forms an essential basic building block in managing this accessibility. This chapter draws a synthetic state of the art about the evolution of access control modeling to respond to the needs of PIS. These systems are characterized by the distribution of their resources, in terms of data, the dynamics of the context, and the distribution of access policies managing these resources. This distribution has to be taken into consideration when the policies are defined; for example, when protection levels of databases and other resources vary to the point that they are incompatible. One of the paths that is explored is related to the recognition of granularity levels when describing resources whether they are initially digital or not (for example, Open Data, Linked Data), via the modeling of variable structuring levels.

8.5. Bibliography

[ALK 09] AL KUKHUN D., SÈDES F., "La mise en œuvre d'un modèle de contrôle d'accès adapté aux systèmes pervasifs, Application aux équipes mobiles gériatriques", *Document numérique*, Hermès, vol. 12, no. 3, pp. 59–78, December 2009.

[BER 01] BERTINO E., BONATTI P., FERRARI E., "TRBAC: a temporal role-based access control model", *ACM Transactions on Information and System Security*, vol. 4, no. 3, pp. 191–233, 2001.

[BER 05] BERTINO E., CATANIA B., DAMIANI M.L., PERLASCA P., "GEO-RBAC: a spatially aware RBAC", *Proceeding of the Tenth ACM Symposium on Access Control Models and Technologies (SACMAT 2005)*, pp. 29–37, Stockholm, Sweden, 2005.

[CHA 06] CHAE S.H., KIM W., KIM D.K., "uT-RBAC: ubiquitous role-based access control mode", *IEICE Transactions*, vol. 89, no. 1, pp. 238–239, 2006.

[EMA 07] EMAMI S.S., AMINI M., ZOKAEI S., "A context-aware access control model for pervasive computing environments", *Proceedings of the International Conference on Intelligent Pervasive Computing*, IPC, IEEE Computer Society, pp. 51–56, Jeju, South Korea, 11–13 October 2007.

[ENC 02] ENCRYPTION, W3C, XML Encryption Syntax and Processing, W3C Candidate Recommendation 04 March 2002, www.w3.org/TR/2002/CR-xmlenc-core-20020304.

[FER 92] FERRAIOLO D.F., KUHN D.R., "Role-based access controls", *Proceedings of the 15th National Computer Security Conference*, Baltimore MD, pp. 554–563, 1992.

[FIL 08] FILHO J.B., MARTIN H., "A quality-aware context-based access control model for ubiquitous applications", *ICDIM 2008*, Aracaju, SE, Brazil, pp. 113–118, 2008.

[HAN 03] HANSEN F., OLESHCHUK V., "SRBAC: a spatial role-based access control model for mobile systems", *Proceedings of the 7th Nordic Workshop on Secure IT Systems*, Gjvik, Norway, 2003.

[KUH 97] KUHN D.R., "Mutual exclusion of roles as a means of implementing separation of duty in role-based access control systems", *2nd ACM Workshop Role-Based Access Control*, Fairfax, VA, USA, pp. 23–30, 1997.

[KUL 08] KULKARNI D., TRIPATHI A., "Context-aware role-based access control in pervasive computing systems", *SACMAT 2008*, Estes Park, CO, USA, pp. 113–122, 2008.

[LIM 07] LIM T., SHIN S., "Intelligent access control mechanism for ubiquitous applications", *ICIS 2007*, Montreal, Quebec, Canada, pp. 955–960, 11–13 July 2007.

[NCS 87] NATIONAL COMPUTER SECURITY CENTER, *A Guide to Understanding Discretionary Access Control in Trusted systems*, National Computer Security Center, 1987.

[OAS 03] OASIS, A Brief Introduction to XACML, 14 March 2003, www.oasis-open. org/committees/download.php/2713/Brief_Introduction_to_XACML.html.

[OAS 05] OASIS, Core and hierarchical role based access control (RBAC) profile of XACML v2.0, Standard, February 2005.

[PAR 04] PARK I., KIM W., PARK Y., "A Ubiquitous streaming framework for multimedia broadcasting service with QoS based mobility Support", *Information Networking. Networking Technologies for Broadband and Mobile Networks*, LNCS, vol. 3090, pp. 65–74, June 2004.

[SAM 00] SAMARATI P., VIMERCATI S.C., "Access control: policies, models, and mechanisms", *Foundations of Security Analysis and Design FOSAD*, 2000.

[SAN 96] SANDHU R., COYNE E.J., FEINSTEIN H.L., YOUMAN C.E., "Role-based access control models", *IEEE Computer*, vol. 29, no. 2, pp. 38–47, 1996.

[SIG 02] W3C, XML-Signature Syntax and Processing, W3C Recommendation, 12 February 2002, www.w3.org/TR/2002/REC-xmldsig-core-20020212.

[WEI 91] WEISER M., "The computer for the twenty-first century", *Scientific American*, pp. 94–10, September 1991.

[XAC 03] OASIS, A Brief Introduction to XACML, 14 March 2003, www.oasis-open.org/committees/download.php/2713/Brief_Introduction_to_XACML.html.

[XAC 05] OASIS, XACML Version 2.0, OASIS Standard, 1st February 2005, http://docs.oasis-open.org/xacml/2.0/access_control-xacml-2.0-core-spec-os.pdf.

[ZHA 03] ZHANG G., PARASHAR M., "Dynamic context-aware access control for grid applications", *Proceedings of the 4th International Workshop on Grid Computing*, International Conference on Grid Computing, IEEE Computer Society, Phoenix, AZ, USA, pp. 101–108, 17 November 2003.

Chapter 9

Interactive Systems and User-Centered Adaptation: The Plasticity of User Interfaces

9.1. Introduction

An interactive system is a digital system that interacts with human beings. It comprises two main classes of functions: a set of domain-dependent services (called the functional core of the system), and a set of hardware and software components that act as intermediaries between the functional core and human beings (called the user interface (UI) of the system). The hardware elements of this UI such as screens and keyboards, which users can perceive and manipulate, play the role of interaction resources. Human–Computer Interaction (HCI), as a field of study, is of primary importance in the appropriate development of high-quality interactive systems.

HCI is concerned with the elaboration of theories, concepts, models, methods, and technical solutions for the design and implementation of useful, usable, and appealing interactive systems, i.e. value-added systems for the target users. Benefits can be measured in terms of the functional conformity of the functional core of the system with the services that the target user expects. For example, a heating system must allow users to save money and energy if that is what they want. For other users (or even for the same user but in different circumstances), savings will not be important, but comfort will. Usability can be measured in terms of the conformity of the UI with the cognitive and sensory-motor abilities of the user. In our example, the heating system of the first user must ensure that the savings are made visible while for the second user, the temperature must be made visible. In both cases, this

Chapter written by Joëlle COUTAZ, Gaëlle CALVARY, Alexandre DEMEURE and Lionel BALME.

information will have to be presented in an understandable way adapted to the situation. The hedonic quality of an interactive system is more difficult to evaluate. It is the object of active research, particularly with the work on affective computing as carried out by Rosalind Picard [PIC 97].

The example of the heating system shows that the functional needs of the user, as well as their cognitive, sensory-motor, and interaction capabilities are neither fixed nor totally predictable. If we establish as a principle that the requirements of functional and interactional conformity must be met under all circumstances, we should then look at the question of adaptation of interactive systems. In this regard, research in HCI is being organized into two complementary branches. One trend is centered on inventing new interaction techniques to solve particular interaction micro-issues for precise usage situations; for example pointing in a 2D graphic scene [BLA 11]. This is "HCI on a small scale". The second trend observes a holistic approach according to which the system is envisioned as a whole for uses in the real world with its diversity and hazards. This is "systemic HCI", or "HCI on a large scale". Design methods, software architectures for interactive systems, toolboxes, and UI generators are part of this second trend. The problem of adaptation can crop up with the use of two branches of research. We shall illustrate this with the example of selecting a value among N possibilities.

The concurrent availability of mice and bit-mapped screens has made it possible to implement linear menus that were invented to serve as an extension of the short-term memory. It is easier for humans to recognize a value among N than to find it *ex nihilo* [NOR 79]. Fitts' law (explained and used in [CAR 83]) has motivated pie menus to reduce time selection, provided that the menu has at the most eight items. In turn, smartphones introduced new constraints. But then, motion sensors provided new opportunities for innovation: the Wavelet menu displays hierarchical lists on a small surface [FRA 10] or a linear menu changes into 3D sheets when the user tilts the telephone forward (see Figure 9.1). On multi-point interactive tables, each finger of the user's hand can be used as an entry point for the MTM menu [BAI 08], such as the chords that are formed with the piano keyboard [BAU 10]. Information projection can also take place on a wall where the shadow of a finger, rather than the finger itself, is used to select a target that is out of range [SHO 07], or even a pico projector can be used to move the target on the wall at a convenient place for manipulation [CAO 06].

These examples show how "HCI on a small scale" research has been able to evolve the concept of menu as new interaction resources are made available. It did not however consider the integration of these various form of menus into actual interactive systems. In a complementary manner, "HCI on a large scale" such as research in UI adaptation, would aim to produce interactive systems that are able to choose the menu type that is most appropriate to the situation so that users can reach their objectives (in our example, choosing a value among N) in the best possible conditions.

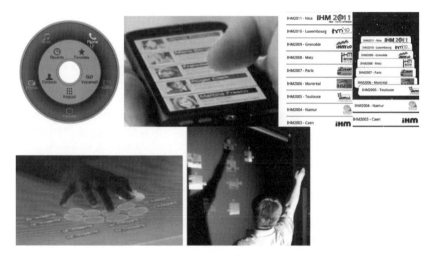

Figure 9.1. *Various versions of a menu. From left to right and from top to bottom: the Wavelet menu on a cell phone [FRA 10], polymorphic 2D/3D menu, MTM (Menu MultiTouch) for an interactive multi-point table [BAI 08], shadow reaching: selecting a target with one's shadow [SHO 07]*

UI adaptation is therefore a problem that simultaneously demands deep knowledge not only of HCI but also of computing systems, software engineering, and distributed systems notably. Although they deal with software adaptation, software engineering and distributed systems often ignore the human factor. This is why, in 1999, we introduced the concept of UI plasticity to qualify user-centered adaptation [THE 99]. This is the object of this chapter that we will structure in two sections: one to define precisely the concept of UI plasticity and its problem space (section 9.2), the other, in two installments, dedicated to technical implementation: the reference framework (sections 9.3 and 9.4) and our recommendations on how to implement it (section 9.5). We will conclude this chapter on the gains and the problems found.

9.2. The problem space of UI plasticity

DEFINITION.– The plasticity of the UI of an interactive system denotes the capacity of this interface to adapt to the context of use to preserve system utility and usability [THE 99] and, by extension, its value [CAL 07] all the while providing the user with the adequate means of control [COU 06].

Before going into detail about the key elements of our definition (adaptation in section 9.2.2, context of use in section 9.2.3, user control in section 9.2.4, and utility, usability, and value in section 9.2.5), we should stop for a moment to look at a related property, elasticity (in section 9.2.1).

9.2.1. *Plasticity and elasticity*

The field of cloud computing uses the term "elasticity" to denote the capacity of the cloud to supply changing services in such a way as to respond in an adjusted way to, for example, loading requests[1]. In economic science, elasticity is the know-how of adapting an economic phenomenon to outside influences. In statistics, it is the degree to which a dependant variable (such as expenditure) changes in response to a change in an associated independent variable (such as income). This concept is also studied in physics, biology and other fields.

In material resistance, an elastic solid body becomes deformed under the effect of a charge but, after discharge, integrally it regains its initial form [FRA 92]. The application of a higher charge at the elasticity limit of the solid causes a brutal rupture with barely any prior deformation (as in the case of fragile materials) or a permanent deformation, a so-called plastic deformation (as in the case of ductile materials) that prolongs the integrity of the material. The nervous system of mammals, which is said to be plastic, is able to change its network of synaptic connections to overcome injury.

This brief analysis of the terminology formalized in established disciplines such as physics has made us choose the term "UI plasticity", which broadens it beyond the limits of elasticity, even including the ability to self-repair.

9.2.2. *Adaptation capacity and its problem space*

Software adaptation has been the object of active research in every specialty of computer science. To clarify our position, we propose to characterize the adaptation capacity of a UI in a multi-dimensional space as seen in Figure 9.2. Other frameworks are also completely acceptable [CAL 07, CAL 10]. The problem space here includes seven orthogonal axes, each of which raises a set of questions that should be asked while designing or analyzing a plastic UI.

---

1 NIST's definition of elasticity: "capabilities can be rapidly and elastically provisioned, in some cases automatically, to quickly scale out and rapidly released to scale in. To the consumer, the capabilities available for provisioning often appear to be unlimited and can be purchased in any quantity at any time" (http://csrc.nist.gov/groups/SNS/cloud-computing/).

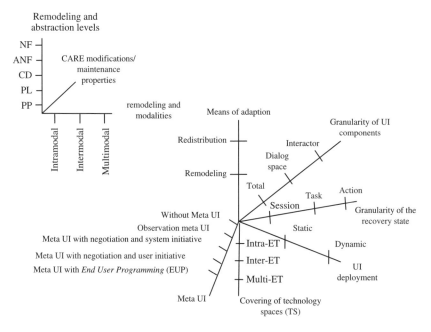

Figure 9.2. *A problem space for UI plasticity*

9.2.2.1. *Adaptation means*

Is the UI of the interactive system adapted by remolding (i.e. by changing its shape or appearance that the user can perceive), or is it adapted by redistribution (i.e. by migration/re-allocation to different interaction resources), or does adaptation apply a combination of the two?

The example of the plastic version of the Sedan–Bouillon site, which promotes the French regions of Sedan and Bouillon, illustrates the concurrent use of remolding and redistribution. Figure 9.3 shows the homepage when visualized on a PC workstation. It includes a title, a navigation bar, and content. The user, exploring the site from a PC, also connects to the site via a Personal Digital Assistant (PDA). The platform now includes two nodes: the PC and the PDA. UI redistribution is offered to the user (Figure 9.4(a)): the user chooses to have the title and the content on the PC and wishes to place the title and the navigation bar on the PDA. Figure 9.4(b) shows the results. We can notice that the navigation bar, which has migrated from the PC to the PDA, is also subject to a remolding that takes into account the screen size of the PDA. In addition, the title displayed on the PDA includes an essential piece of information: the name of the site. In contrast, the slogan "*Entrez dans la legende des pays de Sedan et Bouillon*", which contains only secondary information, has disappeared.

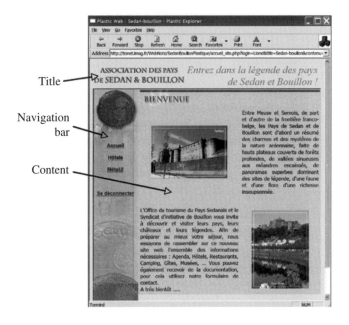

Figure 9.3. *The website of the French region of Sedan–Bouillon when explored using a PC*

It is perhaps useful to define the nature of remolding first. For that, we propose the three-dimensional sub-space drawn in Figure 9.2. The first dimension of the remolding space concerns the software abstraction levels that are susceptible to being affected by remolding. This aspect characterizes the impact of adaptation ranging from cosmetic surface adjustments to the deep reorganization of the interactive system. For that, we use the five abstraction levels of the Arch architecture model [ARC 92]: in ascending order, the Physical Presentation Component (PPC), the Logical Presentation Component (LPC), the Dialog Component (DC), the Functional Core Adaptor (FCA), and the Functional Core (FC)[2]:

---

2 As a reminder: FC implements the domain-dependent services of the interactive system. At the other extreme, PPC is implemented with the widgets (also called interactors) of the toolboxes available on the platform (for example, AWT, SWING). The DC is in charge of task sequencing and therefore of the calls made to the services of the FC (for example, the DC of a document editor states that a user has to open a document before editing it). FCA and LPC serve as corrective intermediaries to minimize all sorts of dependencies between, on the one hand, the pure FC world and the pure UI world, and on the other hand between the DC (oriented toward goals and services) and the PPC world made concrete. Thanks to the LPC level, a graphic UI can be replaced by a vocal UI without modifying the DC.

– Remolding of the Physical Presentation (PPC) level. Remolding consists of changing the appearance and/or the layout of the interactors, but keeps the classes of interactors. This can be seen in the example of Sedan–Bouillon or the 2D/3D polymorph menu from Figure 9.1.

– Remolding of the Logical Presentation Component level (LPC). Remolding at this level consists of replacing interactors with others that are functionally equivalent. For example, in a graphic UI, replacing a graphic menu with an input field is a remolding at the LPC level. These two interactors are functionally equivalent (they both allow the specification of a value), but they do not have the same interactional properties, both from the cognitive and the articulatory points of view: above we saw that, for the user, generating is more costly than recognizing, and generally inputting causes more errors than selecting.

– Remolding the Dialog Component (DC). Here, it is a question of reorganizing the sequence of tasks. For example, for the task of buying a train ticket, sub-tasks that could be performed in an interleaved manner when the purchase is made at home, become sequential to improve guidance when this purchase is made from a train station terminal, a context that is well-known for being stressful.

– Remolding of the functional core adaptor level or of the functional core level. This remolding manifests itself by adding or subtracting business services. For example, for managing heating, it may not have been considered wise to program one's home from a long distance on a smartphone, whereas this possibility might have been considered indispensable from a PC or from a dedicated home-based device. As a result, access to program commands would not be possible on the smartphone. Alternatively, an initial study might have identified that programming should be accessible under all circumstances, but that this need would be uncommon from smartphones. In this case, programming functions would also be accessible from a telephone, but not in an obvious way as on a PC or on a dedicated device. In this case, we would have to resort to remold at the DC level. Figure 9.5 shows an example of remolding at the FCA of the UI of a weather service accessible from a PC and a Nabaztag.

Generally, we should note that remolding at any given level of abstraction has an impact on the lower level of abstraction. In other words, remolding the FC or FCA level causes a DC-level remolding and, by extension, a remolding of the LPC and PPC levels.

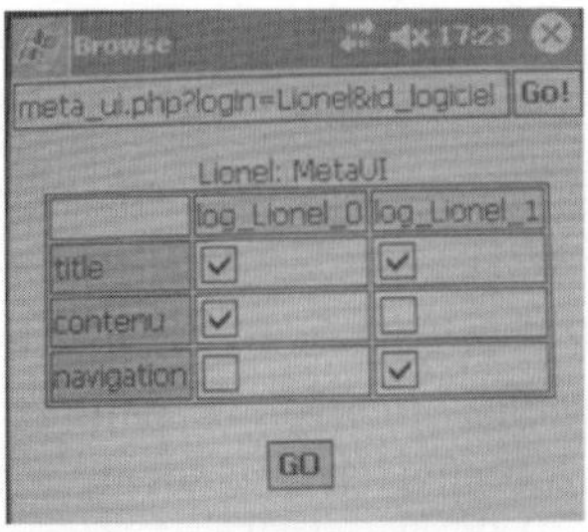

Figure 9.4. *The Sedan–Bouillon site in a version distributed between the interaction resources of the PC and the PDA. The control panel shown in a) uses a negotiation meta–UI that allows users to express their wishes about how to redistribute the Sedan–Bouillon's UI. The resulting redistribution for the request shown in a) is presented in b)*

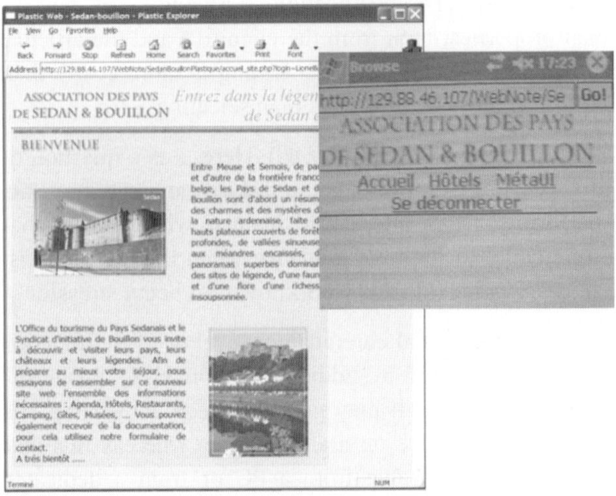

While the dimension "abstraction level" of the remolding space measures the impact of remolding on software, the second dimension, interaction modalities[3], characterizes the impact of the remolding that the user can perceive:

– Remolding is intra-modal (for example graphics to graphics) when the human sensory modality is preserved (i.e. the interaction resource is preserved, but the representation language changes).

---

3 An interaction modality for input or for output is defined as the couple "representation language, interaction resource", [NIG 94, NIG 96]. For example, "NL, microphone" and "NL, keyboard" define two input modalities using the natural language defined by the grammar NL. In the case of the first modality, NL sentences are produced via a microphone while for the second, sentences are entered using a keyboard.

– Remolding is intermodal (also known as transmodal) when a modality is substituted for another (the language of representation and the interaction resource change as in the replacement of graphic interactors by vocal interactors).

– Remolding is multi-modal when the combination of modalities as expressed by the CARE properties (Complementarity, Assignation, Redundancy, and Equivalence) properties [COU 95] change. A remolding can either maintain or change these properties. For example, because of the lack of computing power, a synergistic complementarity can become an alternate complementarity. Typically, the vocal pronouncement "put that there" accompanied simultaneously by deictic gestures to designate the "that" and the "there" is synergistic and multi-modal (gesture and words are produced at the same time). Remolding becomes alternate multi-modal when the user must use the modalities in sequence (i.e. the vocal pronouncement "put that" followed by the gesture to designate the "that" then the vocal pronouncement "there" followed by the gesture to designate the "there"). It should be noted that a monomodal system can become multi-modal and vice versa. That is the case of the weather forecast service in Figure 9.5: we go from a graphic monomodal UI on the PC to a graphic multi-modal UI + sound on the Nabaztag. Moreover, multi-modality on Nabaztag is redundant for output for the expression of time (LED graphic + vocal pronouncement – three flickering yellow LEDs + vocal "sun!") while it is complementary for the expression of temperature (vocal statement only of the value of the temperature).

Weather UI with PC   Weather UI on a Nabazatag

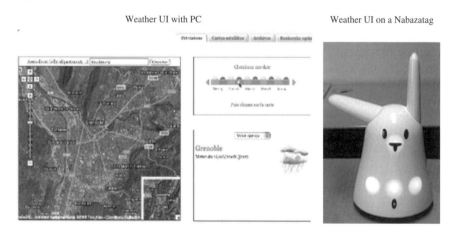

Figure 9.5. *Remolding of the Functional Core Adaptor (FCA) of the UI of the weather forecast service. While the PC version offers many functions, the Nabaztag only gives information on the weather in a given place (previously chosen by the user via PC). This information is expressed in the form of three LEDs whose color and flickering rhythm translate the weather (for example, three nicely flickering yellow LEDs mean sunny weather). The graphic rendering is completed by a vocal expression of the temperature such as "today, sunny, 20C!" announced at times previously chosen by the user via their PC*

9.2.2.2. *UI components' granularity*

Do the means of adaptation (remolding and redistribution) apply to the whole UI, taken then as a software unit, or is the unit of adaptation a sub-set of this UI ranging from a dialog space (for example, a window or a canvas) to a simple interactor (for example, a menu)? A dialog space (also called workspace) is a logical grouping of information that is needed and enough to complete a task. A task can consist of sub-tasks, and a dialog space can consist of dialog sub-spaces. The whole set of dialog spaces of an interactive system and their coordination constitute the Abstract UI. We will come back to this concept in section 9.3.

This typical scenario from the Aura Project illustrates an adaptation whose UI granularity is total [SOU 03, SOU 05]: the user edits a text at home with Word. They then go to the office, leaving their work in the construction site. When they arrive at the office (automatically detected by the system), Aura offers to continue their task from the edition of the document with the facilities available in this new environment (Unix and Emacs). From the user's point of view, the UI of the text editor has migrated from the personal computer at home to the professional work station and has been completely remolded to adapt to the new platform. It is as if, at this level of granularity, the interactive system is manipulated as an indivisible entity, and redistribution is only possible in the form of a platform migrating completely toward another.

In the example of Sedan–Bouillon, the granularity of adaptation (by migration and remolding) is that of the dialog space: the navigation bar, the title, the request form, and the results constitute dialog spaces. At the finest granularity, adaptation is carried out at the scale of an interactor. For example, in FlexClock, which responds to human goals to determine time and date [GRO 02] when the surface of the available screen is no longer big enough to display the time in the form of a dial, the dial interactor is replaced by an interactor that is capable of displaying the time in text. If there is not enough space to display the time and date, the "date" dialog space, which corresponds to a task that is judged not to be a priority, is deleted.

9.2.2.3. *State recovery granularity*

That adaptation is done by remolding and/or redistribution, and whatever the granularity of the UI components affected by this adaptation, what is, from the user's point of view, the granularity of the state recovery? In other words, the granularity of state recovery characterizes the effort users must apply to carry on their activity after adaptation has occurred. State recovery can be performed at the session, task, and physical action levels.

Does the user find themselves right at the start of the session? In websites, it can happen that a request to change language takes us back to the homepage. We therefore go back to a new session. Does the user have to start again, not from the start of the session, but only from the start of the task that was interrupted by the adaptation process, or do they have to continue their task from the point they left it before adaptation (restarting the new action)? In the Sedan–Bouillon case, the restart took place at the new task: if the user is in the middle of filling a text field (for example a hotel address) that they might not have validated before adaptation, they must retype this field once adaptation has been carried out. In Aura, the user finds their document opened in the state they left it in (including the current insertion point). The granularity of the state recovery is then that of the physical action.

9.2.2.4. *UI deployment*

When does adaptation take place? At design time or at installation of the system (static deployment)? At run time (dynamic deployment)? The static level concerns adaptations carried out while the interactive system is not in use. This groups together the "adaptation during the development" and "adaptation at installation" taxonomy levels of [THE 01] as well as the levels that are "before the first use" and "between sessions" of [DIE 93].

The dynamic level characterizes interactive systems capable of adaptation at the moment of their execution, during interaction with the user. We can refine this aspect by distinguishing pre-computed dynamic adaptation at design time and the adaptation that is computed dynamically. The first class of dynamic adaptation allows an interactive system to be adapted at run time for a whole set of contexts of use that are identified at design time. The second class of dynamic adaptation is that of systems capable of adapting to contexts of use that have not been predicted by designers. For example, websites tend to offer an "office" version and a "mobile" version[4]: this is an illustration of adaptation for a whole set of contexts predicted at design time. Conversely, systems like SUPPLE [GAJ 04] or Arnauld [GAJ 05, GAJ 08] allow UIs to be generated according to screen dimensions and usage. This is an illustration of adaptation to contexts that are not explicitly predicted at design time.

9.2.2.5. *Coverage of technological spaces*

What degree of technological diversity is the UI capable of supporting? A technological space is a "working context with a set of associated concepts, body of knowledge, tools, required skills, and possibilities" [KUR 02]. For example, the worlds of Java and C# are two distinct technological spaces. Most UIs are implemented within a single technological space such as Tcl/Tk, Swing, or HTML. This homogeneity no longer applies to plastic UIs whose simultaneous distribution on various devices can require technological spaces to be crossed.

---

4 By way of illustration, the French newspaper *Le Monde* has a dedicated workstation site for workstations (www.lemonde.fr) and another for cell-phones (http://mobile.lemonde.fr/).

From there, the possibilities are the following: intra-space technological adaptation for example Java to Java), inter-space technological adaptation (e.g. Java to WML), or multi-space technological adaptation, (for example combining Java and HTML before or after adaptation has occurred). In Sedan–Bouillon, adaptation is technologically intra space (from HTML to HTML). PhotoBrowser, a plastic digital photo album, illustrates the case of multi-technological space adaptation (see Figure 9.6).

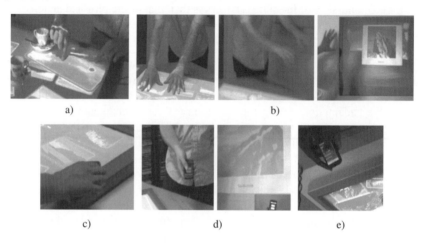

Figure 9.6. *Example of multi-technological space plasticity. PhotoBrowser's UI is a dynamic combination of multiple technological spaces, including Java, HTML, and Tcl/Tk. a) Alone, the table is present: a centralized UI; mono-technological Tcl/Tk space; a single or multi-user sorting task of photos. b) Meta-UI for commanding UI redistribution through a sweep gesture of the hands from the table toward the wall. Table and PC present: a distributed UI on the table and wall; multi-technological space with Tcl/Tk, and HTML; photo sorting task and public sharing of the photo that is currently selected on the table. c) Meta-UI to connect the gPhone to the platform by laying down the phone on the table. d) Table, PC, and gPhone present: the UI is distributed across the table, the wall, and the phone; multi-technological space with Tcl/Tk, HTML, and Java; photo- sorting task, public sharing of the photo at the main point of interest, changing the main point of interest by using the table but also by using the "next" and "previous" buttons displayed on the gPhone. e) The gPhone as a way of remotely controlling current photo selection from a list of names. It should be noted that in the version presented above, gesture recognition is carried out by a wizard of Oz*

PhotoBrowser allows a photo album to be browsed centrally or in a distributive way, according to the interaction resources present and the physical and social environment (a public place or at home). Possible interaction resources include a Diamond Touch multi-point interactive surface, a wall managed by a PC on which is projected the photo that is currently selected on the table, and an Android smartphone. PhotoBrowser's UI is a (dynamic) multi-technological space composition that includes a Tcl/Tk component that can be executed on the table, a web browser (HTML) to scroll through images one by one on the wall, and, on the gPhone, two Java components: on the one hand, the menu of the names of all the album's pictures, on the other hand the "next" and "previous" buttons to scroll through the photos in a sequence. In the two cases, the gPhone plays the role of a remote control. The appearance and disappearance of interaction resources are controlled by the user through a meta-UI (this concept is presented in section 9.2.4).

The two last key concepts of UI plasticity, context of use and meta-UI, are presented in the two following sub-sections.

9.2.3. *Context of use*

The importance of the context of use has long been recognized in the design of interactive systems. Beyer and Holzblatt's contextual design is a typical example of it [BEY 98]. The Situated Action model [SUC 87], the Activity Theory [BAR 97], Distributed Cognition [HAL 94], or even scenario-based design [CAR 00] aim to go beyond the strict breaking down of GOMS [CAR 83] into tasks and sub-tasks by considering context as a directive element.

If context is a notion that has long been included in the design of interactive systems, in practice it is only used in the earliest stages of the development process. All that comes from context progressively becomes diluted during the development process, and the classic triangle in UI design ("user-task-machine") works only for a static context predicted in advance. With the emergence of ambient intelligence, context is rediscovered and placed at the heart of debates without making it the object of a consensual, clear and definitive definition.

However, analysis of the state of the art leads to the following observation: 1) there is no context without a context [BRÉ 02]. In other words, context does not exist in and of itself. It emerges, or defines itself, for a precise finality. 2) Context is a whole set of structured, shared, and evolving information used for interpretation [WIN 01]. The nature of information, as well as the interpretation that is derived from it, depends on the finality (or goal). The finality that concerns us here is the software adaptation of ambient systems. Among the numerous ontologies that deal with context for software adaptation (see AMIGO [EUZ 08] and many others [DEY 01]), that of Crowley *et al.* [CRO 02, REY 05] represents, according to us, work that is sufficiently generic. We will present it below in further detail. We will then see how it can be applied to the model context of use.

9.2.3.1. *Ontology for the concept of context according to Crowley et al.*

A context is defined against a set of entities E, a set of roles Ro that certain E entities are capable of ensuring, and a set of relationships Rel between the E entities. The entities, roles, and relationships are modeled by expressions of observables. An observable is a piece of information that is captured and/or computed by the system. For example, if we consider a meeting, E denotes the participants, Ro includes the roles of orator and audience, and Rel may include spatial relationships such as "the e1 entity (which plays the role of orator) and its opposite e2 (which plays the role of audience)".

A context is a network of situations where each node represents a situation and where the arcs denote the transition conditions between situations. The passage conditions between two situations are the following:

– Modification of E's cardinality. In the example of the meeting room, two people enter the room late and are recognized by the system as participants (their observables correspond to the characteristics and to the behavior of a participant). The situation is changed. The system responds to that, for example, by supplying them with a rundown of exchanges since the start of the meeting.

– Changing the "role-entity" association. In our case, the orator cedes their role to the advantage of another participant. In response to this change of situation, the system turns the meeting's recording camera toward the new orator and "plugs" the phone of the new speaker to the only video projector in the room. The system knows that each participant has their presentation on their personal laptop.

– Changing the relationship between the entities. For example, participant e, who was in front of e', is now behind e'. Against this change of situation, the system allows e to visualize the slides projected in public onto their own computer. The system now knows that e is too far away to see the slides of the working group well.

These definitions of context and the conditions for situation changes imply that all situations from the same context share the same set of E, Ro, and Rel. It is now enough that one of the following conditions is satisfied to cause a context change:

– E is replaced, wholly or partially, by another set of entities. For example, E, the set of participants of the meeting where the concept of "participant" is characterized by a set of observables, is now the set of family members where "family member" is characterized by another set of observables, the intersection between these two sets not necessarily being empty.

– Ro is replaced, wholly or partially, by another set of roles. In the example of the meeting room, if the role of the orator is no longer filled, the context is changed (to informal discussions, for example).

– Rel is replaced, wholly or partially, by another set of relationships. For the meeting room, as well as spatial relationships, relationships of time can now become relevant.

To summarize, context is modeled at two levels of refinement: a graph of contexts where each node denotes a context – each context being defined by a unique triplet of three sets (E, Ro, Rel) and whose arcs correspond to a condition of context change. In turn, each node of the context graph is refined into a network of situations where each node denotes a situation – each situation being defined by instances on E, Ro, and Rel, and of which each arc denotes a condition of situation change. Figure 9.7 illustrates this definition.

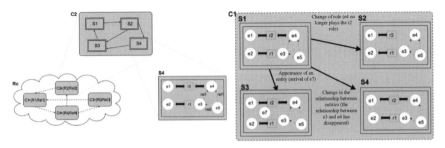

Figure 9.7. *Context model (according to [REY 05]). On the left: context as a context graph (Rc for "Context networks", here including four contexts, C1, C2, C3, C4). Each Ci is a graph of situations. The situations of a given context share the same set of entities, relationships, and roles. On the right, the conditions of situation changes within a context*

The ontology we have just presented in no way imposes the nature of entities, roles, relationships and observables. These are abstract classes that must be specialized to address a particular finality. How can we apply this abstract model to the context of use?

9.2.3.2. *Context of use as a specialization of Crowley et al.'s ontology*

The entities of the context of use when seen as a specialization of Crowley *et al.*'s model are organized into three classes: the user, the platform, and the social and physical environments.

The user is represented by attributes (i.e. observables) and functions (i.e. roles) that describe the archetypal person who is supposed to use the system and/or the person who is currently using the system. This information ranges from the typical profile (business and computing competences, age, size, sensor-motor capacities, etc.) to the preferences and habits inferred by the system, and even the activity and the current task within this activity. For example, in SUPPLE [GAJ 04, GAJ 08], the user is modeled by their performances in terms of Fitts' law and by traces of their prior use of the interactive system.

The environment is represented by attributes (i.e. observables) and functions (roles) that describe the target spatio-temporal space where the system will be used and/or is currently being used. As for the user model, the number of relevant dimensions is large. That can include an observable corresponding to a symbolic digital spatial location (at home, at the train station, in the street, on a train, in a car, in Rome, or in Second Life!) or even in a region rather than at a point in a spatial representation system ("between Grenoble and Nice"). It can also do so for an observable corresponding to a digital or symbolic temporal location ("it is 2 pm, February 2, 2011" or even "at the start of the afternoon"), as well as a period of time ("between midday and 4 pm"). The environment model can include social rules in use in this environment as well as physical conditions like the lighting conditions, the temperature, the air quality, and many others, those also being expressed digitally or symbolically.

The platform describes the communication, interaction, and computing resources as well as the basic software resources that link the physical environment to the digital world. By "basic software", we mean the operating system, its drivers, and more generally the run time environment (libraries, interpreters, middleware, etc.). In the conventional interactive world, the platform is basic: it groups together into a whole that is quasi-unchanging containing "computation resources, communication resources, interaction resources and basic software". With ambient intelligence, users become their own constructors of ecosystems (see the examples in Chapter 1 of this book). More generally, any everyday object can play the role of an interaction resource (including skin surface as in Skinput [HAR 10]) and dynamically be a part or be pulled from the platform. While research on UI plasticity has concentrated on adaptation to the platform, to our knowledge, there is no platform model rich enough to include diverse dynamic clusters. In the examples cited above (Sedan–Bouillon, CamNote, PhotoBrowser), the platform model is implicit, i.e. is diluted in the application code.

We have just given examples of observables and roles for the three classes of entities considered to be key for the context of use: the user, the platform, and the physical/social environment. The observables and the roles must be completed by the set of relevant relationships that the system is supposed to ensure. For example, "the user is here", "this device is used by such and such user" or "is near the door", "it is time to leave", etc.

If the interactive system is supposed to adapt to the context of use changes, the user sometimes has their word. In this case, what? As a response, we offer the concept of meta-UI.

9.2.4. *Meta-UI and user control*

A meta-UI is a special kind of end-user development environment whose set of functions is necessary and sufficient to control and evaluate the state of an interactive ambient space [COU 06]. This set is *meta-* because it serves as an umbrella *beyond* the domain-dependent services that support human activities in this space. It is UI oriented because its role is to allow users to control and evaluate the state of the ambient interactive space. By analogy, a meta-UI is to ambient computing what desktops and shells are to conventional workstations.

As Figure 9.8 shows, we can distinguish meta-UIs for observation, meta-UIs for negotiation (with the initiative coming from the system or from the user), and meta-UIs as end-user programming/end-user development tools.

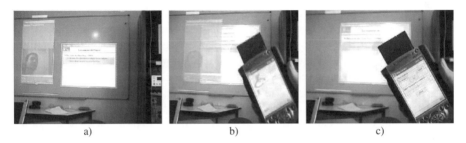

a)   b)   c)

Figure 9.8. *CamNote, a slide viewer [DEM 05]. Example of an observation meta-UI that makes the control panel migration between the PC and PDA explicit. a) Centralized UI on a PC before the arrival of the PDA. b) Observation meta-UI. The control panel visible on the wall now moves toward the slide to fade into it progressively c) The control panel has disappeared from the wall. It reappears on the PDA after being remolded in the form of large buttons to facilitate selection in a mobility situation*

9.2.4.1. *Observation meta-UI*

An observation meta-UI makes the state of the adaptation process observable but the user cannot intervene in this process except, in the best case scenario, to suspend it to eventually go back to it later. For example, the 2D/3D polymorphic menu of Figure 9.1 progressively changes form, in a tightly coupled interaction[5] while tilting the smartphone, supporting a continuous back and forth (but which can be interrupted and is therefore reversible) between the two stable 2D and 3D forms of

---

5 An interaction is tightly coupled on a given time interval when human and artificial systems are engaged in a continuous manner in accomplishing physical actions that are mutually observable and dependent on this interval. Moving a graphic object with a mouse is an example of a tightly coupled interaction.

the menu. Animation, which deports the evaluation of the state change of the UI to the human visual processor [ROB 91], is now part of the basic apparatus in toolboxes for developing centralized UIs. The question is open when it comes to express the migration of UI components within the physical space. In the example of the CamNote slide viewer, the migration of the control panel from the wall to the PDA is expressed as a movement toward the slide displayed on the wall followed by some progressive fading before reappearing on the PDA (by intra-modal remolding) (Figure 9.8).

9.2.4.2. *Meta-UI with negotiation*

A meta-UI with negotiation, whether it is at the initiative of the system or of the user, allows the user to stay in the loop to control the adaptation process. For example, the meta-UI of Sedan–Bouillon shows the available interaction resources, as well as the dialog spaces that can migrate, in the form of a control panel (Figure 9.4). It allows on-the-fly allocation of the system's dialog spaces to the set of the interaction resources (in this case, that of the PC and the PDA). As for PhotoBrowser, the sweeping gesture of Figure 9.6 allows migration onto the wall of the photo that is currently selected on the table. The gPhone's position on the edge of the table expresses the desire to use the gPhone as an additional device of the platform. These gestures constitute the meta-UI of PhotoBrowser. In Sedan–Bouillon, the system takes the initiative in adaptation (caused by the detection of the arrival of the PDA): it offers redistribution possibilities and the user has them available. In the case of PhotoBrowser, the user has the initiative of adaptation. Concerning the rendering onto the gPhone used as a remote control, the choice between the sequential navigation buttons and the list of photo names can be left to the user (via a negotiation meta-UI) or may be decided by the system according to the situation (absence of meta-UI). But, for PhotoBrowser, for Sedan–Bouillon as well as for Arnault [GAJ 05], these negotiation meta-UIs have been planned at design time and therefore pre-programmed by developers.

The next step, which poses many challenges, consists of giving full power to the end user by giving them an effective development environment. This is what we call end-user programming/end-user development (EUP/EUD).

9.2.4.3. *End-user programming/end-user development*

The objective of EUP/EUD is to democratize computing by allowing non-specialists in computing to construct and shape their own interactive systems, to update them, to reuse them, and to maintain them; all that without competence in software engineering (SE) or the motivation to learn the "good practices" of SE. The challenge posed by EUP/EUD (which is valid for all software development tools) is to establish the right compromise between the power of expression of the tools and the learning cost. According to psychologists, the conditions that favor learning rely on the right balance between the challenge posed by learning and the level of expertise of the learner [REP 04]. As Figure 9.9 shows, if the challenge is too high with regard to the learner's expertise, anxiety and rejection may happen. Conversely, the absence of a challenge may cause boredom.

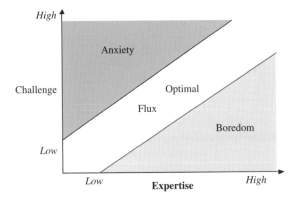

Figure 9.9. *Optimal learning flow seen as the relationship between the challenge posed and the learner's expertise (according to [REP 04])*

If we refer to Norman's theory of action [NOR 86], the challenge/expertise relationship can only be optimal if the distances of execution and evaluation that the user must cross in interacting with a system conform to their competences and motivations. Spreadsheets offer a good example: adding a set of numbers is obtained by applying the SUM operator to the set. This technique, which functions by making an analogy with the competence acquired from elementary school, is easy to assimilate: cognitive distances are optimal. By contrast, in imperative language like C, the equivalent algorithm is far from the common forms of thought:

```
sum = 0 ;
for (i=0 ; i<numItems ; i++) {
        sum += items [i] ;
}
return sum ;
```

However, as humans we want to make progress. By the repeated use of an EUP/EUD, we are led to explore new possibilities provided that we do not encounter insurmountable barriers for our level of expertise. Hence, the ideal profile of EUP/EUD with a gentle slope, as illustrated by Figure 9.10.

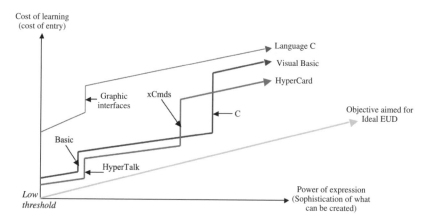

Figure 9.10. *Learning in relation to the power of expression of a EUP/EUD*
(according to [MYE 00])

In contrast to an EUP/EUD that shows a gentle and regular slope profile:

–the curve corresponding to the C language shows that the entry cost is high, and that, to program graphic UIs, the user comes up against a wall as represented by MFC (Microsoft Foundation Classes);

– with Visual Basic, the curve starts lower. Initial contact is less sharp. But the curve shows two vertical rises: when the user has to learn Basic, and then when it comes to learn C;

– hypercard is simple to access but poses two barriers: learning HyperTalk, and then the xCmds language;

– the softly sloping curve models the ideal system for EUP/EUD: a learning cost and a power of expression that regularly progress in relation to the optimal learning flow. The entry cost has a low threshold with, eventually, the capacity to produce high ceiling documents/programs.

To sum up, the use of a meta-UI of the EUP/EUD type must be seen as a learning experience. The consequence for the design of such meta-UIs is that the user must be able to produce simple programs for simple objectives without making any error, then, once trust has been gained, the tool must allow the users to progressively discover the most powerful functions to reach complex objectives[6].

---

6 This is also what Carroll advocates with the "training wheels" principle, an analogy with the stabilizers installed on children's bikes [CAR 84]. Stabilizers allow children to familiarize themselves with driving in total safety before moving on to a more challenging style without wheels.

Spreadsheets constitute the most successful example of EUP/EUD. Mashups such as Pipes and Yahoo! illustrate this trend with services and data from the Web, but still address highly motivated users. In the field of EUP/EUD for ambient intelligence, efforts up until now have concentrated on the syntax of authoring languages: syntax in pseudo-natural language like CAMP [TRU 04], the iconic graphic language of JigSaw [ROD 04], and programming by example and by demonstration etc. With Jigsaw, the user programs their space by assembling puzzle pieces where each piece represents an environment object (Figure 9.11). Media Cubes are part of the same principle of moving closer to the physical world where a word or an icon is presented on each face of the physical cube [BLA 01]. The user composes a phrase by correctly building and orienting cubes (Figure 9.12). Finally, Façade [STU 06] allows users to rebuild the UI of their application according to their needs by copying and pasting interactors, even by substituting interactors for other ones.

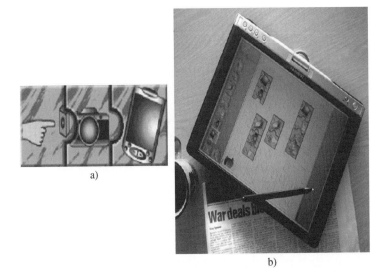

Figure 9.11. *JigSaw [ROD 04]: an example of iconic programming language based on the puzzle metaphor. Pieces denote the alarm bell, the camera, and the PDA respectively. The program shown in a) means that: "when someone knocks on the door, take a photo and send the photo to my PDA". In b), an overview of the editor*

Until now, we have presented three of the four components of UI plasticity: adaptation capacity (section 9.2.2), context of use (section 9.2.3), and meta-UI (section 9.2.4). What remains is for us to consider the quality of adaptation in terms of utility, usability and value.

Figure 9.12. *Two concrete syntaxes to build sentences in pseudo-natural language. In a), the poetic CAMP magnets [TRU 04], in b) the physical Media Cubes of AutoHan that carry the vocabulary elements [BLA 01]*

9.2.5. *Utility, usability and value*

Utility (functional conformity) and usability (interactional conformity) are presented in the introduction of this chapter. These two properties, until now, have served as two reference criteria to characterize the value of a system. Today, they are also considered as elements of value to more subtle concepts like pleasure (caused by esthetics particularly), esteem, affection or attachment, but also of conformity to the principles of life, culture, morality and ethics. Let us develop this last point before coming back to the fundamentals of human-centered development.

Respecting ethical values means that the ambient system must be able to model moral and legal values to take or help take the "good" decisions in case of conflict. Currently, we do not know how to specify moral behavior. The simplistic approach would be to consider ethical values as additional constraints that the system must satisfy, as it does for any constraint. Constraints still have to be identified. They can be very specific (e.g. reduce energy consumption) or very abstract (e.g. never hurt another human being). They can be very personal, but also come from legislator or regulator mechanisms that are cultural or social in origin. Should we still dream of ethical machines, as Allen suggests? [ALL 06] We are not going to answer this question: utility and usability present, already by themselves, a whole host of difficulties.

As for utility, numerous methods of analyzing functional needs have addressed this issue, both in HCI and in software engineering with more or less successful attempts at bringing them together or integrating them. These methods and support tools, however, are based on the assumption that an application is a closed system. And yet, the emergence of service-oriented software solutions in conjunction with the rise of social participation allowed by technologies [SHN 11] has opened the way to the construction, by the end user, of their own functional core. Consequently, the utility of a system can no longer be totally decided *a priori* by designers. In other words, user-centered design is currently moving away from professionals, which, ultimately, is rather good news. It remains a fact that this phenomenon forces to reconsider the way systems are developed: it should be possible to break them down into small units that can be re-assembled according to the user's needs. Clearly, this requirement is supported by the service-oriented paradigm. However, the additional challenge here is no longer limited to the composition of functional cores, but includes UI composition as well.

As for usability, a large number of reference frameworks have been developed, some of which are standardized (for example ISO/IEC 9126), others are general [ABO 92, BAS 93, BRA 03, CON 99, DIX 93, IFI 96, PRE 94, SHA 91, SHN 11, STE 09, VAN 99]), while others are specific (typically, [MON 04, NOG 08] for the web, or [LOP 04] for adaptation). For example, observability[7] is a general criterion. Examples of criteria that are specific to UI plasticity include inter-usability[8] [KAR 05], also called horizontal usability [SEF 04], or interaction continuity [TRE 03]. Interaction continuity can be evaluated, for example, as the granularity of state recovery that measures adaptation cost in terms of the number of actions on input devices the user has to perform to carry on the work. We do not recommend any particular reference framework, but we recommend that developers specify a set of criteria that are relevant for the case at hand. This set must serve as a systematic referential to judge the plastic quality of the system in question [GAR 11]. In section 9.7.1, we will find a refinement of this issue.

9.2.6. *Summary*

How can the concept of plasticity as outlined in section 9.2 be summarized in a few words? UI plasticity is a complex multi-dimensional property.

---

7 Observability: "the capacity of the system to make perceptible, at any time, the necessary and sufficient the business-dependent concepts and functions so that the user can evaluate the current state of the system and/or so that they can accomplish any possible tasks without making errors" [IFI 96].
8 Inter-usability: "the ability with which users transfer and adapt what they have learned during prior use of a service when they access it with new support" [KAR 05].

UI plasticity means the ability to adapt, not to simple changes, but to the context of use for which there is no reference technical solution. This adaptation:

– requires more than service continuity (a property that software engineering has been studying for a decade): utility, usability, and, by extension, value must be guaranteed. And yet, these quality requirements, from the user's point of view, depend on the context of use. In other words, they cannot be decided *a priori*, but they must be modeled explicitly so that the system can evaluate them during the adaptation process;

– must be controllable, at a sensible level, by the user (while research into distributive and robotic systems aims to exclude the user!). Therefore, meta-UIs and their integration into the adaptation process should be studied more carefully;

– is supported by the remolding and/or the redistribution of all or a part of the UI of the system, with state recovery ranging from session level to physical actions; UI, whether it be adaptive or adaptable, may be deployed statically or dynamically, and may include several technological spaces. Remolding can go from cosmetic changes of the surface (i.e. limited to the physical presentation) to deep redesign of the functional core. Remolding can also exploit multi-modality, an aspect that has been so far rarely used for UI plasticity [DUA 06, PAT 08, SER 09].

We have just presented in detail the dimensions of UI plasticity along with their quality requirements. We now consider the technical implementation of UI plasticity with the description of the CAMELEON reference framework(s) (sections 9.3 and 9.4) and our recommendations for implementation (section 9.5).

9.3. The CAMELEON reference framework for rational development of plastic UI

The CAMELEON reference framework (Figure 9.13) clarifies and formalizes the various issues related to the development of plastic UIs in terms of models and relationships between these models[9]. In that, it is compliant with the Model-Driven Engineering principles as developed in software engineering. We will go into detail on these two points – models and relationships in sections 9.3.1 and 9.3.2, respectively – then, in section 9.3.3, we will show how to use the models for rational development.

---

9 This reference framework gets its name from the European IST-2000-30104 CAMELEON project (Context Aware Modeling for Enabling and Leveraging Effective interactiON), 2001–2004, http://giove.isti.cnr.it/projects/cameleon.html during which it was designed. In truth [CAL 01] is the first publication relating to this reference framework which, at that time, had no name.

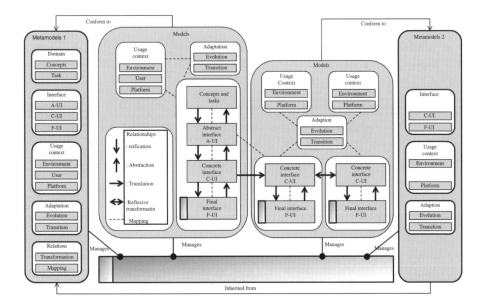

Figure 9.13. *The CAMELEON Reference framework* (*adapted from* [*CAL 03*])

As a reminder, a model of an entity is a representation of this entity designed for a given purpose. In our case, the entities are UIs (or UI elements) and the purpose is the operational production of plastic UIa. As Figure 9.13 shows, the models recommended by the CAMELEON reference framework are the following: task model and domain-dependent concepts model, abstract UI, concrete UI, final UI, context-of-use model, and the adaptation model:

– The task model (TM) and the domain-dependent concepts model, respectively, describe the procedures for reaching the goals and sub-goals that the user wants to achieve with the system, and the domain-dependent entities that are manipulated while these tasks are carried out. Figure 9.14(a) is an example of the task model corresponding to the management of the comfort of the home.

– The abstract UI (A-UI) describes the structure of UI in terms of workspaces (also called dialog spaces) and of navigation between these spaces, as independently as possible from the target platform. In other words, at this level of representation of an UI, the look and feel of the UI is not determined. Figure 9.14 shows a graphic representation of several possible A-UIs (a, b, c) that correspond to the task model for comfort management.

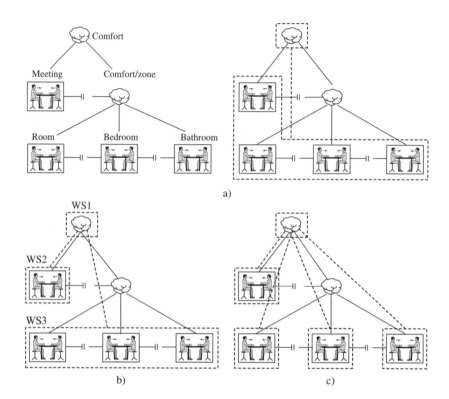

Figure 9.14. *Three possible A-UI for the same task tree: "Programming your comfort" (example taken from [THE 01]). This task consists of defining one's life rhythm (LR) and programming the comfort by zone. Three zones (i.e. three domain-dependent concepts) are identified: the living-room, the bedroom, and the bathroom. In a), the four task leaves are grouped in the same elementary workspace (WS for workspace). In b), editing life rhythm is isolated in a dedicated elementary workspace (WS2) while the three other tasks are grouped together in WS3. In c), an elementary workspace is assigned to each leaf of the task model. In the three cases, the elementary workspaces are accessible from the workspace that corresponds to the root task (WS1)*

– The concrete UI (C-UI) represents the UI in terms of interactors (for example, buttons, menus, images, etc.). Here, the look and feel are specified. Figure 9.15 shows the C-UI corresponding to the A-UI and to the task model of Figure 9.14.

– The final UI (F-UI) corresponds to the UI as perceived and manipulated by the user at run time. Although the C-UI and the F-UI are conceptually close, experience shows that the same source code (Java or HTML, for example) does not behave in the same way depending on the JVM and browsers used at run time.

– The context of use includes the user model, the platform model, and the physical and social environment model (see section 9.2.3).

– The adaptation model includes the evolution model, which specifies the nature of adaptation in response to context change, and the transition model that expresses the nature of the transition UI that accompanies adaptation in such a way that the user can evaluate and control the state of this process. We should note that these two models – the evolution model and the UI transition model, are observable, controllable, and even programmable, via a meta-UI (see section 9.2.4).

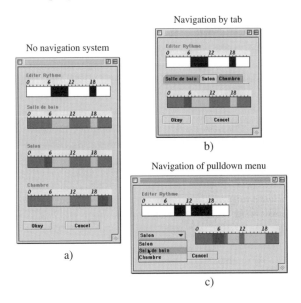

Figure 9.15. *Examples of C-UI produced from the A-UI of Figure 9.14 (example taken from [THE 01]). a) C-UI produced from A-UI (a) where all the leaf tasks are transformed into a single workspace. This C-UI could also have been produced from A-UI (c) in which all the elementary workspaces are simultaneously visible in the parent workspace. b) and c), respectively, correspond to the C-UI on a mobile telephone and PDA. Only the navigation interactors between the workspaces change. These two C-UI can be produced from A-UI (b) and (c) from Figure 9.14 where the workspace that corresponds to the management of life rhythm is always visible*

9.3.1. *Relationships between models*

All models of the CAMELEON reference framework have two classes of relationships that Figure 9.13 shows: conformity, transformation and mapping.

9.3.1.1. *Conformity relationship*

All models are supposed to be compliant with a meta-model. A meta-model defines a language that allows the production of (instances of) models that are compliant with it. For example, the task model of Figure 9.14 is compliant with the CTT meta-model [PAT 03a]. The ontology presented for context in section 9.2.3.1 is a meta-model for describing contexts.

9.3.1.2. *Transformation and mapping*

A transformation is the production of a set of target models from a set of source models. This transformation is defined by a set of rules that specify how the source set is transformed into the target set. In turn, a set of transformation rules is a model that is compliant with a transformation meta-model. QVT (Query/View/Transformation), an OMG standard, and ATL (A Transformation Language) [BÉZ 03], developed above Eclipse, are two examples of meta-models for model transformations. Figure 9.16 shows an example of ATL rules that transform every task of the task model into a workspace along with the navigation links between these workspaces that reflect the operators between the source tasks. Figure 9.16 illustrates the principle of the transformations of MT operators into links between workspaces.

```
module M2TaskToM2Workspace {
  from M1Task : M2Task
  to  M1Workspace : M2Workspace
          -- One workspace per task
  rule TaskToSpace {
   from t : M2Task !Task
   to w : M2Workspace !Space (
    name <- t.name )
   }

-- OrOperator to SequenceOperators
  rule OrOperatorToSequence{
    from o : M2Task !BinaryOperator (
     o.name = "or"
    )
    to motherToLeft : M2Workspace !Sequence (
    origin<- [Tas*£kToSpace.w]o.motherTask,
    destination<-[Tas*£kToSpace.w]o.leftTask )
```

Figure 9.16. *Example of ATL transformation of an M1Task model (compliant with a M2Task meta-model) into the A-UI M1Workspace (compliant with the M2Workspace meta-model (example taken from [SOT 08]). The TaskToSpace rule creates a workspace w for each source task t where w takes the name of t. t and w are elements of M1Task and M1Workspace model, respectively. The OrOperatorToSequence rule transforms all OR operators o between two tasks (o.leftTask and o.rightTask) into a sequence operator between the parent workspace and its siblings (from o.motherTask to o.leftTask, and from o.motherTask to o.rightTask)*

There are several sorts of transformation:

– reification top-down transformations lower the level of abstraction between the source models and the target model (for example, from the task model to the C-UI). Typically, an A-UI is obtained by a reification transformation of a task model and domain-dependent concepts model (and if relevant, using other models such as the context model). The A-UIs shown in Figure 9.14 result from the transformation of the task model represented at the top left of Figure 9.14 by applying different transformation rules;

– abstraction bottom-up transformations raise the level of abstraction between the source and target model (for example, from a C-UI to an A-UI);

– translation transformations keep the level of abstraction level between the source and target models (for example, going from an A-UI designed for a given context to an A-UI applicable in another context);

– reflexive transformations replace a given model with a new instantiation of itself [BOU 02];

– mappings support traceability by making the correspondence between elements of the source and target models explicit. For example, the correspondence between a source task (and concepts) and its target workspace, window, and widgets, is maintained as a mapping function.

In practice, how can these models and their relationships be organized in the development process of interactive systems?

9.3.2. *Development process*

In HCI, it is recommended to produce the final UI of an interactive system by applying a sequence of reifications starting from the task and domain-dependent concepts models. This approach relies on the assumption that designers/developers know how to produce a task model, which, in practice, is far from being the case. In addition, the current requirement is largely centered on reverse engineering final-UIs so that they are simultaneously available on workstations and smartphones. In other words, there is no unique development process but a rational approach to be adapted on a case-per-case basis.

The CAMELEON reference framework responds to this demand for flexibility with the concept of entry point and of transformation composition. For example, a C-UI designed for a given context of use is transformed by abstraction, possibly in a single step, into a task model that corresponds to this context. In turn, this task model is translated into a task model that fits a different context of use, and then a new C-UI is produced by a sequence of reifications. Figure 9.17 illustrates a sub-set of possibilities.

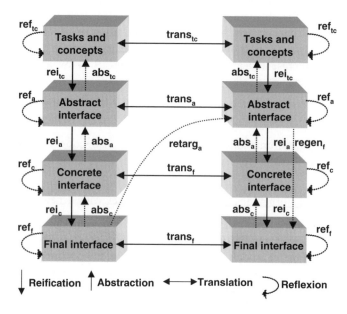

Figure 9.17. *Design process by of the way of transformation composition (according to [LIM 04])*

All or part of the models that we have just looked at are produced during the design phase of interactive systems to feed the run time phase *in fine*. By definition, the run-time phase requires a run-time infrastructure that is technologically distinct from interactive systems.

9.4. The CAMELEON-RT run time infrastructure

The original CAMELEON reference framework does not say much about the run-time infrastructure, only that it includes "SCE" mechanisms that are distributed between the final UI of the interactive system and the run time infrastructure. An "SCE" mechanism can be broken down like this:

– S (for sensing) denotes the functions that cover situation and context recognition as well as detection of situation/context changes;

– C (for compute) is the computation of the reaction to situation/context changes, i.e. computation of the system adaptation to be applied;

– E (for execute) refers to the execution of the reaction.

The cross-cutting nature of adaptation justifies the distribution of the SCE mechanisms between the final UI and the run time infrastructure. This is the "Slinky"[10] effect, introduced in software architecture modeling of interactive systems [ARC 92].

This section describes CAMELEON-RT (for CAMELEON Run Time) [BAL 04], the execution infrastructure, which we have proposed as a complement of the original CAMELEON framework.

9.4.1. *Functional decomposition of CAMELEON-RT*

Figure 9.18 shows the functional decomposition of CAMELEON-RT. Above the CAMELEON-RT, interactive plastic UI systems are executed. Below, there are native system use and material layers (basic software).

The "hardware" layer represents the set of elementary platforms that make up the user's platform (their personal cloud). These elementary platforms are characterized by the power and their type of microprocessor, the bandwidth offered by network technology, the sensors and actuators they control, and their interaction resources. Note that these characteristics are observables that represent the platform in the context of use.

The "operating system" layer relies on the "hardware" layer. Here, the concept of the operating system (OS) is to be considered in a broader sense including legacy OS, virtual machines, for example JVM or .Net, modality interpreters or toolboxes for implementing user interfaces (for example Swing[11], OpenGL[12], Direct-Sound[13], and ALSA[14]).

---

10 This concept was introduced with the Arch architecture model to "emphasize that functionalities can shift from components to components in an architecture depending upon the goals of the developers" [ARC 92]. The term has been chosen by analogy with the Slinky toy. Once put into movement, this toy, which is in the form of a spring, sees its mass move dynamically. See www.poof-slinky.com/Slinky-Museum/Slinky-History/.

11 http://java.sun.com/javase/6/docs/technotes/guides/swing/index.html.

12 www.opengl.org.

13 www.microsoft.com.

14 www.alsa-project.org.

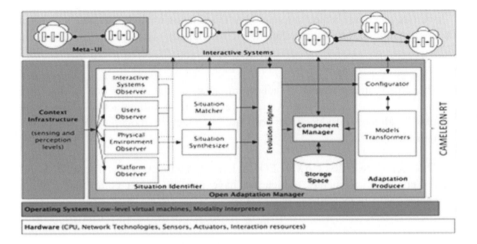

Figure 9.18. *CAMELEON-RT. Canonical functional decomposition of a run time infrastructure for plastic UIs (according to [BAL 04]). In this layered model, the top edges of the boxes offer an API to higher layers. Solid line arrows denote the orientation of information exchanges. Dotted arrows indicate functions made accessible by API to higher layers. The flower-shape symbol represents software components. Solid lines ending in little black disks symbolize links between components*

CAMELEON-RT runs on top of the "hardware" and "operating system" layers. It is the middleware that supports plasticity. It includes:

– a context infrastructure that builds and maintains a model of the context of use (data acquisition and data transformation at the appropriate level of abstraction) [COU 05, REY 05]. This infrastructure informs the adaptation manager;

– the adaptation manager is in charge of the SCE functions: the situation identifier provides the evolution engine with information about situation/context changes. In turn, the evolution engine builds an adaptation plan with the help of the component manager. This plan is transferred to the adaptation producer in charge of executing the plan.

We will go into more detail about the adaptation manager in the following sections.

9.4.2. *Situation identifier*

The situation identifier includes two classes of function: observers and synthesizers, and situation comparators.

The observers are in charge of filtering and combining symbolic observables from the context infrastructure to provide the situation synthesizer with information at the appropriate level of abstraction. There are four classes of observer: observers of the currently active interactive systems and of the meta-UI (for example, what is the current task? What are its components?), the platform observers, the observers of the user, and the observers of the physical and social environments, thus covering the set of symbolic observables that are characteristic of the three dimensions of the context of use (see section 9.2.3).

The observables produced by the four classes of observer are interpreted in the form of a situation by the situation synthesizer. This situation models the current state of the context in which the interaction takes place. The situation synthesizer is in charge of detecting situation/context changes (see section 9.2.3). The model of the current situation is then transmitted to the evolution engine on the one hand and to the situation comparator on the other hand. The role of the situation comparator is to check whether there is a correspondence with a known interaction situation (planned in the design phase or met before).

9.4.3. *Evolution engine*

If the new situation is known, the evolution engine can execute either the adaptation rules defined by the developers or by the user through a meta-UI, or those that have been inferred by the system from previous execution. If the situation comparator is unable to establish a correspondence with a known interaction situation, the evolution engine uses other types of mechanisms to build an adaptation plan, or even asks the user for help through the meta-UI. In all cases, the evolution engine calls the component manager to build the adaptation plan.

9.4.4. *Component manager*

The component manager is the interface between the repository of software components and its clients (i.e. the evolution engine, the adaptation producer, and the interactive systems). Its function corresponds to that of service repositories as used in service-oriented approaches: it supports the registration and dynamic discovery of components. In order for clients to be able to formulate search requests, components are meta-described (which means that there is a component meta-model). The clients of the component manager formulate requests that refer to the functional and extra-functional properties of the type of the components that are searched for. For example, the evolution engine looks for a component that supports such or such a user task (functional property), that can be integrated into an interactive system designed according to a particular software architecture and runtime environment (extra-functional property) and that uses a particular interaction modality (extra-functional property).

9.4.5. *Adaptation producer*

The adaptation plan supplied by the evolution engine refers to the components that have been selected as well as to the description of the links that should be established or destroyed. Depending on the state of these components (inert or instantiated) and depending on their type (executable or transformable), the adaptation producer applies the appropriate component transformations, instantiations, or suppressions, followed by the suppression and creation of links.

An inert component is in the component data base. It is not yet installed (instantiated) in memory. An executable component exists in the form of code (compiled or interpretable). A transformable component (for example, a component that encapsulates a task model) must be transformed to become executable. Thus, an inert executable component requires a loading step to become instantiated executable. An inert transformable component must be loaded in memory (it becomes instantiated transformable), then once transformed enters the instantiated executable state. It should be noted that the nature of the plan depends on the software of the interactive system that is to be adapted.

The software of interactive systems can be divided into two classes. The "traditional" class includes developed interactive systems that follow a classic design process where design models are progressively reified to obtain an executable program. The second class, which is MDE oriented, groups together interactive systems that have been developed according to the model-driven approach. In this approach, high-level abstraction models are not "consumed" by the reification process but, on the contrary, are semantically linked to each other and then maintained by the final executable program with a view to being used at run time. To cover the adaptation of these two classes of interactive systems, the function adaptation producer is broken down into two sub-functions: the model transformer, dedicated to model transformation, and the configurator for the adaptation per se through APIs (Application Programming Interface). The API is offered by the interactive system and the configurator must be designed according to this API. It is therefore an *ad hoc* solution. Or the API is offered by the infrastructure and the design of interactive systems must take the API. It is then a standardized generic solution.

To summarize, the original CAMELEON framework and its complement, CAMELEON-RT, serve as a canonical model that can be used both for designing and executing plastic UIs. Numerous implementation tools refer to this framework and apply it in a variety of manners. See section 9.7.2 for a synthesis of these.

9.5. Our principles for implementing plasticity

We advocate the application of the following principles for the technical development of plastic UI interactive systems, or of tools that allow such systems to be implemented.

1) Choose a problem space (like that of Figure 9.2) in such a way as to formulate the requirement of the solution space precisely. In addition, choose a reference system to measure the ergonomic quality of the target system (for example, the Bastien–Scapin framework [BAS 93]).

2) Use the CAMELEON and CAMELEON-RT reference framework as a basic solution space: models that conform to meta-models as well as the functional decomposition of the run-time infrastructure are the canonical units that should be referred to.

3) Select from the CAMELEON and CAMELEON-RT reference framework the units that are necessary and sufficient to satisfy the requirements of the solution space. For example, eliminate the task model if UI adaptation will be concerned by surface remolding only (Physical Presentation Component level). It should be noted that: (1) transformations and quality must be models. This will allow transformations to be controlled finely in relation to the required ergonomic quality; (2) Any UI component in the components data base must be meta-described according to a component meta-model [BOU 07]. This will support dynamic retrieval and reuse. These components are not always executable directly (section 9.4). Typically, task models and A-UIs are transformable.

4) Blur the distinction between the design phase and the run time phase[16]. More precisely: every productive model specified by a designer (i.e. a model that can be interpreted by a computing machine, every model that results from transformations as well as mappings between models and elements of models, must be accessible at run time. As a consequence, as Figure 9.19 shows, an executable interactive system is not only a code but also a graph of models in which each model describes a particular aspect of the system. Typically, the existence of task models and domain-dependent concepts allow semantically rich dynamic adaptations [BLU 10]. Without that, adaptation would *de facto* be limited to surface modifications (PP and LP levels).

5) Decide how to allocate (the slinky effect) SCE functions between the interactive systems and the run time infrastructure (as a reminder: S = identification and detection of situation/context changes, C = computation of the adaptation plan,

and E = execution of the plan). This decision depends heavily on the SCE coverage of the implementation tools. For example, in the case of a system implementation with COMET [DEM 07, DEM 08], the SCE functions are all moved to the interactive system. At the other extreme, in the case of PhotoBrowser, the SCE functions are entirely supported by the Ethylene run time structure [BAL 08].

6) UI transition should not be neglected. There again, we rely on implementation tools. For example, the NOMAD toolbox offers the possibility of specifying a morphing behavior at the widget level (Figure 9.20).

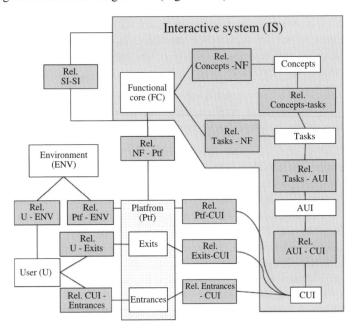

Figure 9.19. *An interactive system is a graph of models*

9.6. Conclusion: lessons learned and open challenges

UI plasticity is a complex, multi-dimensional problem that we have been trying to resolve for a decade or more. Some results are sound, but multiple challenges are still open. Among the results, we must include definitions, the problem space, and the CAMELEON reference framework. Whereas concepts are quite well shared among the UI community, technical solutions are diverse and piecemeal. However, the MDE approach, which brings with it automation and rigor, has its fervent supporters. MDE has demonstrated clear advantages for design phase (making the developer's task easier, therefore reducing development costs). However, given the current state of the art, the full-MDE approach has not solved everything.

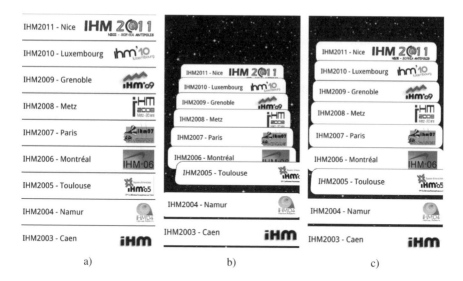

Figure 9.20. *Transition b) from a 2D menu a) to a 3D menu c)*

We can see many limitations of the full-MDE approach:

– MDE, as a development methodology, has favored the dichotomy between the design phase and the run time phase. And yet, the CAMELEON reference framework shows that an interactive system is a graph of models and therefore an interactive system is not only made from executable code. As a consequence, design and execution phases are part of the same struggle;

– absence of a norm concerning meta-models, even if UsiXML [GAR 11] aims at this objective. The profusion of initiatives on the development of user interface description languages is symptomatic of the difficulty of defining a set of meta-models that is coherent, unambiguous, easy to understand, and complete (i.e. capable of covering the problem space of plastic UI). In other words, we have the right models, but we do not have the models right;

– from our point of view, three meta-models are key to the success of MDE for UI plasticity: meta-models for transformation, for quality, and for C-UIs.

Transformations and their composition constitute a generic and elegant theoretical tool that opens the way to all forms of development processes and technical integration. However, transformations are difficult to understand: languages (meta-models) like ATL or QVT are only accessible to knowledgeable and motivated programmers. But also, what is essential for us in the UI community is that these languages do not support the expression of usability rules [GAR 11, SOT 07]. More fundamental is the impossibility of automatically deducing, from the specification of a transformation, its inverse transformation. There, we see a major flaw that can lead to inconsistent models as the result of reifications and abstractions that are applied in an iterative way during the life cycle of an interactive system.

At the C-UI level, current meta-models, not only lag behind innovation, but also bridles creativity. Languages to express C-UI follow technology instead of opening new avenues. While the CARE [COU 95] properties were introduced more than 15 years ago and the famous "put that there" [BOL 80] paradigm is more than 30 years old, C-UI level description languages still find it difficult to describe multi-modal UIs. Certainly, we are able to generate simplistic multi-modal UI (for example, with XHTML + VoiceXML), but with very limited micro-dialogs for interaction repair. Actually, we still have not been able to define the language that will describe direct-manipulation graphical UIs appropriately. Meanwhile:

– new forms of "constructible" computers like the siftables from MIT and the toy blocks from CMU have arrived on the market;

– novel interaction techniques proliferate from everywhere whether it be for supporting mobility (for example, SixthSense [MAE 09, MIS 09]), for 3D interaction (where 3D gestures and 3D screens are becoming predominant), or even for graphical tabletops and multi-surface interaction [BAL 09];

– new quality requirements are emerging: design is switching from the development of useful and usable systems for people with precise goals in a precise context of use, to engaging and inspired interaction spaces where the user moves from the status of a consumer to that of an inventor.

In summary, meta-models at the C-UI level should capture the expression of unlimited convergence between the digital and the physical. Maybe, meta-modeling is in essence the wrong approach for C-UI: a model, which represents one thing, is necessarily a simplification, and so a reduction of this real thing. From there, the subtle aspects of interaction, which make a great difference between an inspired design and an ordinary design, are probably best expressed by directly using executable code rather than an abstraction of this code. From there, this code must present itself as a service in such a way as to allow dynamic recruitment. But also, the following has to be taken into account: designers excel in translating into drawings interaction solutions, but they have some difficulty in expressing the dynamic behavior of these drawings, which leads them to express themselves in natural language [MYE 08]. A promising avenue to reconcile designers' practice and code is to revive the work *à la* Peridot [MYE 90], like SketchiXML [COY 04, KIE 10] where drawings are retro-engineering into machine-computable C-UI. As for inferring behavior from examples, the promising "Watch What I Do" paradigm initiated in the late 1970s (see Dave Smith's PYGMALION system [SMI 93]) remains an open question.

A final problem that has not been explicitly dealt with in this chapter is the dynamic (re)composition of the functional core, which implies the (re)composition of its UI. This aspect has still barely been outlined for web technologies [CAN 09, PIE 09, YU 07]. It will be the focus of Chapter 10.

9.7. Appendices

9.7.1. *There is plasticity and there is plasticity!*

Let us remember our definition:

"The plasticity of the user interface of an interactive system denotes the capacity of this interface to adapt to the context of use to preserve system utility and usability [THE 99] and, by extension, its value [CAL 07] all the while providing the user with the adequate means of control".

In the following, we reformulate the property of being plastic in more precise terms:

"A user interface is said to be plastic for a value V on a set of contexts of use C if it is capable of adapting to all changes of the contexts of use over C while respecting V".

This definition for plasticity gives rise to different qualifications and quantifications by playing on V and on C. From a qualitative point of view, we can make distinctions according to the variations of V and C. Plasticity is said to be [CAL 07]:

– maximal in value (versus minimal) if it does not exist any property p not considered in V, such that the UI is plastic for $V \cup \{p\}$ over C;

– maximal in context of use (versus minimal) if it does not exist any context of use c not considered in C, such that the UI is plastic for V over $C \cup \{c\}$;

– maximal (versus minimal) if the plasticity is maximal in both value and context of use. If, over a period of time, V or C increases (say from machine-learning), plasticity is said to be incremental. If V or C decreases, plasticity is said to be decremental. If V or C varies, the UI is said to be elastic. If V or C does not change, plasticity is said to be rigid.

From a quantitative point of view, the domain of plasticity is only one possible measure of plasticity [CAL 01]. For a given value V, we call "plasticity island" a set of contexts of use C such that the UI is maximally plastic in context of use for

V over C. The domain of plasticity of a UI for value V is the union of the plasticity islands of this UI for V. Figure 9.13 shows three plasticity islands. The domain of plasticity is the union of these islands.

9.7.2. *Implementation tools*

The analysis of the state of the art on UI plasticity reveals great diversity in approaches, each of those conveying important progress without any of them covering all the aspects of the problem space. Nevertheless, we observe the existence of two complementary approaches: one, model driven, is inspired by MDE; the other, centered on the development of reusable software components, is primarily code oriented as is the case of window managers, toolboxes, and middleware. Although these two main branches of approaches have been adopted by research communities that ignore each other, fundamentally they can be reconciled.

9.7.2.1. *Model-driven approaches*

Model-driven approaches are suitable for business domains for which the capitalization of knowhow in UI design is effective. This capitalization is expressed in terms of patterns implemented as assemblies of WIMP (Window Icons Menus Pointers) interactors. Post-WIMP toolboxes are emerging, but their integration into generative approaches has not been performed yet. As Table 9.1 shows, a large number of description languages take A-UI as an entry point. We have excluded from the table all C-UI description languages such as XUL, MXML, EMMA, inkML, VRML, VoiceXML, and many more. Very few models deviate from the task model. All of these tools are concerned with remolding, but none of them deals with redistribution or quality (except UsiXML in its future versions [GAR 11]). To the best of our knowledge, the tools that use these models to generate concrete and final UI lose the mapping with the source models. As a result, run time UI regeneration implies static deployment and session-level state recovery. In other words, a code-oriented approach is unavoidable.

9.7.2.2. *Code-oriented approach*

As for the "code" approach, we can note the absence of interaction resource management for ambient computing (the virtualization of interactive resources would be very welcome here). Toolboxes like Ubit [LEC 99] or ETk [GRO 07] are attempts at compensating for this lack of virtualization, but within a single technological space. COMET is an exception [DEM 07]. Table 9.2 provides a summary of the state of the art related to window managers and toolboxes. If window managers and UI toolboxes were coupled with the language-based generation tools of Table 9.2, the gain in interactional richness would be significant.

MDE-centered approaches	Remarks	Coverage of the CAMELEON models/Problem space
Languages		
XIML [PUE 01], DISL [SCH 06], GIML [KOS 04], MDML [JOH 03], PlasticML [ROU 03], SunML [PIC 03]	DISL: support for multi-modality, an UIML extension [ABR 04, HEL 08]; SunML: Widget composition operations	Total remolding of the entire UI. Context of use covered: elementary platform. Models covered: A-UI with dialog (behavior). Generation of F-UI by reification for a single technological space, but a choice between several target technological spaces (for example, DHTML, WML, VoiceXML, Java, C++, Perl)
ISML [CRO 04], TeresaXML [PAT 03b], MariaXML [PAT 09], XIML [EIS 00]	MariaXML (Maria tool is the successor of Teresa): support for multi-modality with complementarity and redundancy	Total remolding of the entire UI. Context of use covered: elementary platform. Models covered: task models, domain-dependent concepts model. Generation of F-UI by reification for a single technological space (most often Java and ML from the web – WML, XHTML, VoiceXML)
SeescoaXML [LUY 04]	SeescoaXML (Seescoa tool): generation at run time for several elementary target platforms. Dygimes [CON 03], an extension of Seescoa [LUY 04] part of a CTT task model then translated in A-UI	Total remolding of the entire UI. Context of use covered: elementary platform. Models covered: A-UI. Generation of F-UI for several technologically simultaneous spaces (for example, HTML, Java AWT, Java Swing), first by translating A-UI, then for each A-UI, by reification with XSLT

Table 9.1. *Examples of UI description languages. Concrete UI description languages are not mentioned*

MDE-centered approaches	Remarks	Coverage of the CAMELEON models/Problem space
UsiXML [LIM 04] aims to cover all models and principles of the original CAMELON reference framework and from there, serve as a norm	Existence of interoperable tools and run time infrastructure compatible with UsiXML	Complete coverage of CAMELEON models. The entire space problem is potentially covered provided that the MDE limitations are lifted (see section 9.6) and that appropriate run time tools and infrastructures are developed
Damask [LIN 08] aims to cover the first steps of the design phase	Damask allows sketches to be manipulated and takes into account the design of vocal interfaces	Coverage of the concrete interface level. Damask allows the designer to assemble patterns

Table 9.1. (*Continued*) *Examples of UI description languages. Concrete UI description languages are not mentioned*

Code-centered approaches (1/2)	Theories	Coverage of the problem space
Window administrator		
FAÇADE [STU 06]. UI for legacy applications reconstructed by drag & drop by the user (in a mashup style)	Legacy UI developed with toolboxes that support introspection. Requires the Métisse renderer running on top of X Window	EUD meta-UIUI, remolding at the interactor level, dynamic deployment with state recovery at the action level. Graphic intra-modal remolding at the LP and PP levels, context of use = elementary or static composite platform running Métisse
Toolboxes		
Ubit [LEC 99]. Multiple rendering of the same widget (scene graph and condition nodes)	It is up to the programmer to predict all forms of rendering	Basic mechanisms for graphic intra-modal dynamic remolding of interactors with state recovery at the physical action level. Context of use= elementary platform or static composite

Table 9.2. *Examples of toolboxes for plastic UI*

Code-centered approaches (1/2)	Theories	Coverage of the problem space
Multi-modal Widget [CRE 00]. Multiple rendering of a widget using several modalities according to interaction resources. For example, a graphic button, when a mouse visits it, can simultaneously repaint itself in yellow and emit a sound if a sound generator is available	It is up to the programmer to predict all forms of rendering	Basic mechanisms for graphic intra-modal dynamic remolding of interactors with state recovery at physical level. Context of use = elementary platform equipped with a dynamic set of interaction resources
		Meta-UI to control the proportion of desired modalities (for example, 100% graphic and 30% sound)
ETk [GRO 07]. Usual Tk widgets but which can also be cut and replaced, recomposed, and migrated	Existence of a single technological space hides the diversity of platforms that can be dynamically composed: Mozart [VAN 04]	Covers almost all the problem space but for just one technological space: the Mozart system, its Oz language, and Tk, whose properties it uses for redistribution and remolding
COMET [DEM 07]. Tree structure of widgets (COMET) isomorphic to the task model. Some COMET play the role of task operators, others each cover a sub-task, with several A-UI where each A-UI may have several C- and F-UIs implemented in distinct technological spaces	It is up to the programmer to predict all forms of rendering by the way of style sheets relying on the COMET polymorphism	Basic mechanisms for intra- and inter-modal dynamic remolding with using style sheets. Redistribution of UI via HTML or "B207 implementation". Context of use = elementary platform or dynamic composite

Table 9.2. *(Continued) Examples of toolboxes for plastic UI*

We find two classes of infrastructure as long as the class of problems dealt with concerns redistribution (BEACH [TAN 01], Aura [SOU 05]), remolding (ICrafter [PON 01], Eloquence [ROU 06]), and UI aggregation – a particular case of remolding whose importance is growing (Huddle [NIC 06]). As Table 9.3 shows, none of these solutions, with the exception of Ethylene [BAL 08], covers both remolding and redistribution. The reason is essentially because of the application domains, which *de facto* define the outline of the solution: BEACH, ICrafter and Huddle deal with confined fields that are relatively stable and controllable; Aura has introduced a new concept (that of information space that follows the user everywhere), but which relies on traditional legacy applications. Ethylene tackles the general problem of plasticity by applying CAMELEON-RT.

Code-centered approaches (2/2)	Theories/Target	Coverage of the space problem
Infrastructures and UI redistribution		
Beach [TAN 01]. One of the first middlewares for collaborative "RoomWare" (Project i-LAND [STR 99])	Workstations of the composite platform are PCs with homogeneous interaction resources. For example, the Dynawall = several *SmartBoard* screens of identical resolution and size	Absence of redistribution UI remolding at the interactor level (even at the pixel level), with state recovery at the physical action level and dynamic redeployment. Context of use: absence of adaptation to the user, but to a homogeneous dynamic composite platform. A single technological space (that of Beach) and a meta-UI with negotiation to command UI redistribution
Aura [SOU 03, SOU 05]. Computational Halo attached to the user in all circumstances: aims at service continuity as the user moves between places. For example, the user starts editing a document with MS Word then puts it into a new place where MS Word is unavailable; MS Word is replaced by another editor with the document open at the right insertion point. Aura dynamically chooses the services that are best adapted to the user's preferences, preferences specified by a meta-UI (Aura does not learn a user's model)	Open legacy applications. They must offer "the right inspection API" so as to model the state of these applications to ensure service continuity	"Total" redistribution (migration unit corresponds to one, even several, applications). UI redistribution, remolding or multi-modality is not supported by Aura. If any of them, they are provided but by the native applications. Recovery state level depends on the inspection (API) that is allowed by applications (at minima: task level). Context of use: platform (but for software services only) user (in terms of expression of preferences) and physical environment. Aura is clearly a technological inter space, but at a high level of granularity. Elementary Meta-UI

Table 9.3. *Examples of infrastructures for plastic UI*

Code-centered approaches (2/2)	Theories/Target	Coverage of the space problem
Infrastructures and UI remolding		
Eloquence [ROU 06]. Set of tools to design, generate, and execute output multi-modal F-UIs capable of remolding at run time. The choice of output modality depends on the (dynamic) availability of modality renderers	Adaptation rules specified by the UI designer. For example, if the unit of information is a telephone call and if the battery is low, exclude photo modality from the caller and the vibrator. Elementary platform	Absence of redistribution. Multi-modal remolding with support for the CARE properties at the interactor level (but output only), with state recovery at the physical action level. Dynamic adaptation to the interaction resources of the (elementary) platform. Uncertainty about other aspects of the context of use. Absence of meta-UI (adaptation rules precoded by the designer). Probably support for inter-technological space (at best)
Huddle [NIC 06] Configuration of personal multimedia devices. Data flow model constructed by the user via a meta-UI. For example, connecting the image flux from the TV antenna to the TV screen and linking the antenna's audio flux to the loudspeakers of the Hi-Fi. Generation of aggregated UI	Target platform limited to personal multimedia apparatus. Control UI generation for PDA. Multimedia devices must by meta-described in a dedicated (XML) language	Absence of redistribution. Conventional graphic intra-modal remolding, at a total level with state recovery at the session level, but the UI is dynamically regenerated. Context of use: adaptation to the platform that includes the multimedia devices and a PDA for rendering the generated Ui. The covered technological space is intra-TS (that of Huddle). EUP meta-UI to construct the data flow between the multimedia devices

Table 9.3. *(Continued) Examples of infrastructures for plastic UI*

Code-centered approaches (2/2)	Theories/Target	Coverage of the space problem
Infrastructures and UI remolding		
ICrafter [PON 01]. Interactive rooms, deployment of new services, and aggregation of services where a service designate an application (a web navigator, MS PowerPoint) or physical utility devices (lamps, video projector). Data flow model. A meta-UI allows the user to choose the services they want. ICrafter gives them back an aggregated UI (conventional graphics), a union of the UI of the chosen services	Services that include their own UI (like MS Word) cannot be remolded. The context model is expressed in a dedicated XML language: description of the target platform (languages and interpreters like html and web browser), configuration of the interactive room (spatial relationships between utilitarian devices)	Remolding, by UI generation, for services and composition of services that do not have a UI. The granularity of the recovery state is that of the session level, but UI deployment is dynamically commanded under the user's control, thanks to a negotiation generated meta-UI in the same way as other UI (remoldable meta-UI) with adaptation to the physical environment and to the target elementary platform. ICrafter supports inter-TS: as the elementary platforms of one ICrafter room may be able to offer different technological spaces, UIs generated via ICrafter can be expressed in different technological spaces
Ethylene [BAL 08]. Hybrid MDE and service-oriented approach. Infrastructure compliant with CAMELEON-RT. Used for implementing PhotoBrowser (Figure 9.6). Applies the principles described in section 9.6	Each elementary platform must be capable of executing Ethylene. Relies on the existence of a context manager (capture) and of a component repository. Components must be meta-described with EthyleneXML	All of the problem space is potentially covered provided that all CAMELEON-RT functions are implemented

Table 9.3. *(Continued) Examples of infrastructures for plastic UI*

9.8. Bibliography

[ABO 92] ABOWD G.D., COUTAZ J., NIGAY L., "Structuring the space of interactive system properties", in LARSON J., UNGER C. (eds.), *Engineering for Human-Computer Interaction*, Elsevier Science Publishers, Amsterdam, pp. 113–126, 1992.

[ALL 06] ALLEN C., WALLACH W., SMITH I., "Why machine ethics?", *IEEE Intelligent Systems*, vol. 21, no. 4, pp. 12–17, 2006.

[ARC 92] ARCH, "A meta-model for the runtime architecture of an interactive system, The UIMS", *Developers Workshop, SIGCHI Bulletin*, vol. 24, no. 1, ACM, 1992.

[BAI 08] BAILLY G., DEMEURE A., NIGAY L., LECOLINET E., "MultiTouch Menu", *IHM 2008, 20e conférence francophone sur l'interaction homme-machine*, ACM Press, Metz, France, 2008.

[BAL 09] BALAKRISHNAN R., BAUDISCH P., "Special issue on ubiquitous multi-display environments", *Human-Computer Interaction*, vol. 24, pp. 1–2, 2009.

[BAL 04] BALME L., DEMEURE A., BARRALON N., COUTAZ J., CALVARY G., "CAMELEON-RT: a software architecture reference model for distributed, migratable, and plastic user interfaces", in MARKOPOULOS P., EGGEN B., AARTS E. *et al.* (eds), *Ambient intelligence: Second European Symposium, Lecture Notes in Computer Science*, vol. 3295, EUSAI 2004, Netherlands, Springer-Verlag, Heidelberg, Eindhoven, pp. 291–302, 8–11 November 2004.

[BAL 08] BALME L., Interfaces homme-machine Plastiques: une approche par composants dynamiques, Thesis Joseph Fourier University, Grenoble I, 2008.

[BAR 97] BARDRAM J.E., "Plans as situated action: an activity theory approach to workflow systems", *Proceedings of ECSCW'97 Conference*, Lancaster, UK, September 1997.

[BAS 93] BASTIEN J.M.C., SCAPIN D., Ergonomic criteria for the evaluation of human-computer interfaces, INRIA technical report, no. 156, 1993.

[BAU 10] BAU O., Interaction streams: helping users learn, execute and remember expressive interaction grammars, PhD thesis, Paris-Sud University, 2010.

[BÉR 09] BÉRARD F., Vision par ordinateur pour l'interaction homme-machine fortement couplée, Thesis Joseph Fourier University, Grenoble, France, 2009.

[BEY 98] BEYER H., HOLTZBLATT K., *Contextual Design: Defining Customer-centered Systems*, Morgan Kaufman, San Fransisco, 1998.

[BÉZ 03] BÉZIVIN J., DUPÉ G., JOUAULT F., PITETTE G., ROUGUI J., "First experiments with the ATL transformation language: transforming XSLT into Xquery", *OOPSLA Workshop*, Anaheim, California, 2003.

[BLA 01] BLACKWELL A.F., HAGUE R., "AutoHAN: an architecture for programming the home", *Proceedings of the IEEE Symposium on Human-Centric Computing Languages and Environments*, Stresa, Italy, pp. 150–157, 2001.

[BLA 11] BLANCH R., ORTEGA M., "Benchmarking pointing techniques with distractors: adding a density factor to Fitts' pointing paradigm", *CHI 2011: Proceedings of the Twenty-Ninth Annual SIGCHI Conference on Human Factors in Computing Systems*, Vancouver, Canada, 2011.

[BLU 10] BLUMENDORF M., LEHMANN G, ALBAYRAK S., "Bridging models and systems at runtime to build adaptive user interfaces", *Proceedings of the 2010 ACM SIGCHI Symposium on Engineering Interactive Computing Systems, EICS 2010*, Berlin, Germany, pp. 9–18, 2010.

[BOL 80] BOLT R., "Put that there: voice and gesture at the graphics interface", *Proceedings of the 7th International Conference on Computer Graphics and Interactive Techniques*, pp. 262–270, ACM, New York, NY, 1980.

[BOU 02] BOUILLON L., VANDERDONCKT J., "Retargeting web pages to other computing platforms", *Proceedings of IEEE 9th Working Conference on Reverse Engineering WCRE'2002*, IEEE Computer Society Press, Richmond, pp. 339–348, 29 October–1 November 2002.

[BOU 07] BOURGUIN G., LEWANDOWSKI A., TARBY J.C., "Defining task oriented component", *Proceedings of TAMODIA 2007, Lecture Notes in Computer Science*, Springer, Toulouse, France, vol. 4849, pp. 170–183, 2007.

[BRA 03] BRANGIER E., BARCENILLA J., *Concevoir un produit facile à utiliser*, Editions d'Organisation, Paris, 2003.

[BRÉ 02] BRÉZILLON P., "Expliciter le contexte dans les objets communicants", in KINTZIG C. *et al.* Chapter 21, *Les objets communicants*, Hermès-Lavoisier, Paris, pp. 295–303, 2002.

[CAL 01] CALVARY G., COUTAZ J., THÉVENIN T., "A unifying reference framework for the development of plastic user interfaces", *IFIP WG2.7 (13.2) Working Conference, Engineering Human Computer Interaction (EHCI01)*, LNCS 2254, Toronto, Canada, pp. 173–192, 2001.

[CAL 02] CALVARY G., COUTAZ J., BOUILLON L., FLORINS M., LIMBOURG Q., MARUCCI L., PATERNÒ F., SANTORO C., SOUCHON N., THEVENIN D., VANDERDONCKT J., The CAMELEON Reference Framework, deliverable D1.1, IST FP5 CAMELON project, http://giove.isti.cnr.it/projects/cameleon/deliverable1_1.html.

[CAL 03] CALVARY G., COUTAZ J., THEVENIN D., LIMBOURG Q., SOUCHON N., BOUILLON L., VANDERDONCKT J., "A unifying reference framework for multi-target user interfaces", *Interacting with Computers*, vol. 15, no. 3, pp. 289–308, 2003.

[CAL 07] CALVARY G., Plasticité des interfaces homme-machine, Habilitation à Diriger des Recherches, Joseph Fourier University, Grenoble 1, November 2007.

[CAL 10] CALVARY G., SERNA A., KOLSKI C., COUTAZ J., "Les transports: un terrain fertile pour la plasticité des interfaces homme-machine", in KOLSKI C. (ed.), *Interaction homme-machine dans les transports – information voyageur, personnalisation et assistance*, Hermès-Lavoisier, Paris, pp. 287–312, 2010.

[CAN 09] CANFORA G., DI PENTA M., LOMBARDI P., VILLANI M.L., "Dynamic composition of web applications in human centered processes", *IEEE PESOS'09*, Vancouver, Canada, 18–19 May 2009.

[CAO 06] CAO X., BALAKRISHNAN R., "Interacting with dynamically defined information spaces using a handheld projector and a pen", *Proceedings of UIST 2006, ACM Symposium on User Interface Software and Technology*, ACM Press, Montreux, Switzerland, pp. 225–234, 2006.

[CAR 83] CARD S.K., MORAN T.P., NEWELL A., *The Psychology of Human-Computer Interaction*, Lawrence Erelbaum Associates, Hillsdale, 1983.

[CAR 84] CARROLL J.M., CARRITHERS C., "Training wheels in a user interface", *Communication of the ACM*, vol. 27, no. 8, pp. 800–806, ACM, 1984.

[CAR 00] CARROLL J.M., *Making Use, Scenario-Based Design of Human-Computer Interactions*, MIT Press, Cambridge, MA, 2000.

[CON 99] CONSTANTINE L.L., LOCKWOOD L.A.D., *Software for Use: A Practical Guide to the Models and Methods of Usage-Centred Design*, Addison-Wesley, New York, 1999.

[CON 03] CONINX K., LUYTEN K., VANDERVELPEN C., VAN DEN BERGH J., CREEMERS B., "Dygimes: dynamically generating interfaces for mobile computing devices and embedded Systems", *Proceedings Mobile HCI 2003*, Udine, Italy, pp. 256–270, 2003.

[COU 95] COUTAZ J., NIGAY L., SALBER D., BLANDFORD A., MAY J., YOUNG R., "Four easy pieces for assessing the usability of multimodal interaction: the CARE properties", *Proceedings of the INTERACT'95*, Lillehammer, Norway, pp. 115–120, 1995.

[COU 05] COUTAZ J., CROWLEY J., DOBSON S., GARLAN D., "Context is key", *Communications of the ACM*, vol. 48, no. 3, pp. 49–53, 2005.

[COU 06] COUTAZ J., "Meta-user interfaces for ambient spaces", *Proceedings of TAMODIA 2006*, LNCS 4385, Hasselt, Belgium, pp. 1–15, October 2006.

[COY 04] COYETTE A., FAULKNER S., KOLP M., LIMBOURG Q., VANDERDONCKT J., "SketchiXML: towards a multi-agent design tool for sketching user interfaces based on USIXML", *Proceedings of the 3rd Annual Conference on Task Models and Diagrams, TAMODIA 2004*, Prague, Czech Republic, 2004.

[CRE 00] CREASE M., GRAY P., BREWSTER S., "A toolkit of mechanism and context independent widgets", *Proc. Interactive Systems: Design, Specification, and Verification, 7th International Workshop DSV-IS*, Limerick, Ireland, June 5–6, 2000, pp. 121–133. Lecture Notes in Computer Science 2000, Springer, 2000.

[CRO 02] CROWLEY J.L., COUTAZ J., REY G., REIGNIER P., "Perceptual components for context aware computing", *Proceedings of International Conference on Ubiquitous Computing (UbiComp 2002)*, Gothenberg, Sweden, Lecture Notes in Computer Science 2498, Springer FRA 10, Rome, Italy, ACM Press, pp. 117–134, 2002.

[CRO 04] CROWLE S., HOLE L., "ISML: an interface specification meta-language", in VAN LEEUWEN J., HARTMANIS J., GOOS G. (eds), *Proceedings of Interactive Systems, Design, Specification, and Verification 2004 (DSV-IS 2004)*, Springer, Berlin, Heidelberg, pp. 362–376, 2004.

[DEM 05] DEMEURE A., BALME L., CALVARY G., "CamNote: a plastic slides viewer", *Proceedings of Plastic Services for Mobile Devices (PSMD) Workshop Held in Conjunction with INTERACT'05*, Rome, Italy, 2005.

[DEM 07] DEMEURE A., Modèles et outils pour la conception et l'exécution d'interfaces homme-machine Plastiques, Thesis Joseph Fourier University, Grenoble I, October 2007.

[DEM 08] DEMEURE A., CALVARY G., CONINX K., "A software architecture style and an interactors toolkit for plastic user interfaces", *Proceeding of the 15th International Workshop DSV-IS 2008*, LNCS, Kingston, Ontario, Canada, pp. 225–237, 2008.

[DEY 01] DEY A.K., "Understanding and using context", *Journal of Personal and Ubiquitous Computing*, vol. 5, pp. 4–7, 2001.

[DIE 93] DIETERICH H., MALINOWSKI U., KÜHME T., SCHNEIDER-HUFSCHMIDT M., "State of the art in adaptive user interfaces", *Adaptive User Interfaces, Principle and Practice, Human Factors in Information Technology series*, vol. 10, pp. 13–48, 1993.

[DIX 93] DIX A., FINLAY J., ABOWD G., BEALE R., *Human-Computer Interaction*, Prentice-Hall, Upper Saddle River, 1993.

[DUA 06] DUARTE C., CARRIÇO L., "A conceptual framework for developing adaptive multimodal applications", *Proceedings of the 11th International Conference on Intelligent User Interfaces, IUI'06*, ACM, Sydney, Australia, pp. 132–139, 2006.

[EIS 00] EISENSTEIN J., VANDERDONCKT J., PUERTA A., "Adapting to mobile contexts with user-interface modeling", *Proceedings of 3rd IEEE Workshop on Mobile Computing Systems and Applications WMCSA'2000*, IEEE Press, Monterey, CA, USA, pp. 83–92, 7–8 December 2000.

[EUZ 03] EUZÉNAT J., PIERSON J., RAMPARANY F., "Dynamic context management for pervasive applications", *Knowledge Engineering Review*, vol. 23, no. 1, pp. 21–49, 2003.

[FER 09] FERRY N., HOURDIN G., LAVIROTTE S., REY G., TIGLI J.Y., RIVEILL M., "Models at runtime: service for device composition and adaptation", *4th International Workshop Models@run.time, Models 2009 (MRT'09)*, Denver, CO, USA, 2009.

[FRA 92] FRANÇOIS D., PINEAU A., ZAOUI A., *Elasticité et Plasticité*, Hermès, Paris, 1992.

[FRA 10] FRANCONE J., BAILLY G., MANDRAN N., NIGAY L., "Wavelet menus on handheld devices: stacking metaphor for novice mode and eyes-free selection for expert mode", *Proceeding of the Conference on Advanced Visual Interfaces (AVI)*, 2010.

[GAJ 04] GAJOS K., WELD D., "SUPPLE: automatically generating user interfaces", *Proceedings of ACM International Conferene on Intelligent User Interfaces*, IUI, Funchal, Madeira, Portugal, pp. 93–100, 2004.

[GAJ 05] GAJOS K., WELD D., "Preference elicitation for interface optimization", *UIST '05: Proceedings of the 18th Annual ACM Symposium on User Interface Software and Technology*, ACM Press, Seattle, USA, pp. 173–182, 2005.

[GAJ 08] GAJOS K., WOBBROCK J., WELD D., "Improving the performance of motor-impaired users with automatically-generated, ability-based interfaces", *CHI '08: Proceeding of the Twenty-Sixth Annual SIGCHI Conference on Human Factors in Computing Systems*, pp. 1257–1266, ACM, Florence, Italy, 2008.

[GAR 11] GARCÍA FREY A., CÉRET E., DUPUY-CHESSA S., CALVARY G., "QUIMERA: a quality meta-model to improve design rationale", *Proceedings of the Third ACM SIGCHI Symposium on Engineering Interactive Computing Systems (EICS 2011)*, Pisa, Italy, ACM New York, 2011.

[GRO 02] GROLAUX D., VAN ROY P., VANDERDONCKT J., "FlexClock, a plastic clock written in Oz with the QTk toolkit", *Proceedings of the 1st International Workshop on Task Models and Diagrams for User Interface Design (TAMODIA 2002)*, Bucharest, Romania, INFOREC Publishing House Bucharest, pp. 135–142, 2002.

[GRO 07] GROLAUX D., Transparent migration and adaptation in graphical user interface toolkit, PhD Thesis, Faculté des sciences appliquées, Université Catholique de Louvain, September 2007.

[HAL 94] HALVERSON C.A., Distributed cognition as a theoretical framework for HCI: don't throw the Baby out with the bathwater – the importance of the cursor in Air Traffic Control, Technical Report, no. 94–03, Department of Cognitive Science, University of California, San Diego, 1994.

[HAR 10] HARRISON C., DESNEY T., MORRIS D., "Skinput: appropriating the body as an input surface", *Proceedings of CHI'10, the 28th International Conference on Human Factors in Computing Systems*, ACM, Atlanta, USA, pp. 453–462, 2010.

[HEL 08] HELMS J., SCHAEFER R., LUYTEN K., VANDERDONCKT J., VERMEULEN J., ABRAMS M., UIML Version 4.0: Committee Draft. Available at http://www.oasis-open. org/committees/download.php/28457/uiml-4.0-cd01.pdf, 2008.

[IFI 96] IFIP, *Design Principles for Interactive Software*, in GRAM C., COCKTON G., (eds), produit par l'IFIP WG 2.7 (13.4), Chapman & Hall, London, 1996.

[JOH 03] JOHNSON P.D., PAREKH, J., Multiple device markup language a rule approach, SE MS Project & Thesis (SE690), DePaul University, Chicago, 2003.

[KAR 05] KARSENTY L., BOTHEREL V., "Analyse empirique de l'inter-utilisabilité d'un service multisupport Web et téléphone", *Actes des Deuxièmes Journées Francophones sur l'Ubiquité et la Mobilité (UbiMob'05)*, ACM Press, Grenoble, France, 31 May–3 June 2005.

[KIE 10] KIEFFER S., COYETTE A., VANDERDONCKT J., "User interface design by sketching: a complexity analysis of widget representations", *Proceedings of the 2010 ACM SIGCHI Symposium on Engineering Interactive Computing Systems*, ACM, Berlin, Germany, pp. 57–66, 2010.

[KOS 04] Kost S., Dynamically generated multi-modal application interfaces, Thesis, Technical University of Dresden and Leipzig University of Applied Science, 2004.

[KUR 02] Kurtev I., Bézivin J., Aksit M., "Technological spaces: an initial appraisal", *CoopIS, DOA'2002 Federated Conferences*, Industrial Track, Irvine, 2002.

[LEC 99] Lecolinet E., "A brick construction game model for creating graphical user interfaces: the ubit toolkit", *Proceedings of the 7th IFIP TC13 International Conference on Human-Computer Interaction, INTERACT 1999*, Edinburgh, UK, September 1999.

[LIM 04] Limbourg Q., Vanderdonckt J., Michotte B., Bouillon L., Lopez-Jaquero V., "UsiXML: a language supporting multi-path development of user interfaces", *Proceedings of 9th IFIP Working Conference on Engineering for Human-Computer Interaction Jointly with 11th International Workshop on Design, Specification, and Verification of Interactive Systems, EHCI-DSVIS'2004*, Hamburg, Germany, 11–13 July 2004.

[LIN 08] Lin J., Landay J.A., "Employing patterns and layers for early-stage design and prototyping of cross-device user interfaces", *Proceedings of the Twenty-Sixth Annual SIGCHI Conference on Human Factors in Computing Systems (CHI '08)*, ACM, Florence, Italy, pp. 1313–1322, 2008.

[LOP 04] Lopez-Jaquero V., Montero F., Molina J.P., Gonzalez P., "A seamless development process of adaptive user interfaces explicitly based on usability properties", *Proceedings of the EHCI04*, Hamburg, Germany, 11–13 July 2004.

[LUY 04] Luyten K., Abrams M., Vanderdonckt J., Limbourg Q., "Developing user interfaces with XML: advances on user interface description languages", *Satellite Workshop of Advanced Visual Interfaces*, Gallipoli, Italy, ACM Press, 2004.

[MAE 09] Maes P., Mistry P., Unveiling the 'Sixth Sense', game-changing wearable tech, TED 2009, Long Beach, CA, USA, 2009.

[MIS 09] Mistry P., Maes, P., "SixthSense – A wearable gestural interface", *Proceedings of SIGGRAPH Asia 2009*, Emerging Technologies, Yokohama, Japan, 2009.

[MON 04] Montero F., Vanderdonckt J., Lozano M., "Quality models for automated evaluation of web sites usability and accessibility", *Proceedings of the International Conference on Web Engineering, ICWE'2004*, Munich, Germany, 28–30 July 2004.

[MYE 90] Myers B., "Creating user interfaces using programming by example, visual programming, and constraints", *ACM Transaction on Programming Languages and Systems (TOPLAS)*, vol. 12, no. 2, pp. 143–177, 1990.

[MYE 00] Myers B., Hudson S.E, Pausch R., "Past, present, and future of user interface software tools", *ACM Transactions on Computer-Human Interaction (TOCHI)*, vol. 7, no. 1, pp. 3–28, 2000.

[MYE 08] MYERS B., PARK S.Y., NAKANO Y., MUELLER G., KO A., "How designers design and program interactive behaviors", *Proceedings of the IEEE Symposium on Visual Languages and Human Centric Computing (VL/HCC)*, Herrsching am Ammersee, Germany, IEEE publ., pp. 177–184, 2008.

[NIC 06] NICHOLS J., ROTHROCK B., CHAU D.H., MYERS B.A., "Huddle: automatically generating interfaces for systems of multiple connected appliances", *Proceedings of the 19th Annual ACM Symposium on User interface Software and Technology, UIST 2006*, Montreux, Switzerland, pp. 279–288.

[NIE 94] NIELSEN J., "Heuristic evaluation", in NIELSEN J., MACK R.L. (eds), *Usability Inspection Methods*, John Wiley & Sons, New York, 1994.

[NIG 94] NIGAY L., Conception et modélisation logicielles des systèmes interactifs : applications aux interfaces mutlimodales, Thesis Joseph Fourier University, Grenoble I, 1994.

[NIG 96] NIGAY L., COUTAZ J., "Espaces conceptuels pour l'interaction multimédia et multimodale", *Technique et Science Informatique (TSI)*, vol. 15, no. 9, spécial Multimédia et Collecticiel, Hermès, 1996.

[NOG 08] NOGIER J.F., *Ergonomie du logiciel et design web – Le manuel des interfaces utilisateur*, 4th edition, Dunod, Paris, 2008.

[NOR 79] NORMAN D.A., BOBROW D.G., "Descriptions: an intermediate stage in memory retrieval", *Cognitive Psychology*, vol. 11, pp. 107–123, 1979.

[NOR 86] NORMAN D.A., DRAPER S.W., *User Centered System Design: New Perspectives on Human-Computer Interaction*, Lawrence Erlbaum Associates, Hillsdale, 1986.

[PAT 03a] PATERNÒ F., "Concur task trees: an engineered notation for task models", Chapter 24 in DIAPER D., STANTON N. (eds), *The Handbook of Task Analysis for Human-Computer Interaction*, Lawrence Erlbaum Associates, Hillsdale, pp. 483–503, 2003.

[PAT 03b] PATERNÒ F., SANTORO A., "Unified method for designing interactive systems adaptable to mobile and stationary platforms", *Interacting with Computers*, vol. 15, pp. 349–366, Elsevier, 2003.

[PAT 08] PATERNÒ F., SANTORO C., MANTYJARVI J., MORI G., SANSONE S., "Authoring pervasive multimodal user interfaces", *International Journal of Web Engineering and Technology*, vol. 4, no. 2, pp. 235–261, 2008.

[PAT 09] PATERNÒ F., SANTORO C., SPANO L.D., "MARIA: a universal, declarative, multiple abstraction-level language for service-oriented applications in ubiquitous environments", *ACM Transactions on Computer-Human Interaction (TOCHI)*, vol. 16, no. 4, ACM, 2009.

[PIC 97] PICARD R.W., *Affective Computing*, MIT Press, Cambridge, MA, 1997.

[PIC 03] PICARD E., FIERSTONE J., PINNA-DERY A.M., RIVEILL M., Atelier de composition d'IHM et évaluation du modèle de composants, Livrable 13, RNTL ASPECT, Laboratoire I3S, 2003.

[PIE 09] PIETSCHMANN S., VOIGT M., MEIBNER K., "Dynamic composition of service-oriented web user interfaces", *Proceedings of the 4th International Conference on Internet and Web Applications and Services, ICIW 2009*, IEEE CPS, Venice, Italy, 2009.

[PON 01] PONNEKANTI S., LEE B., FOX A., HANRAHAN P., WINOGRAD T., "Icrafter: A service framework for ubiquitous computing environments", in ABOWD G., BRUMITT B., SHAFER S. (eds), *Proceedings Ubicomp 2001*, LNCS 2201, Atlanta, USA, pp. 57–75, 2001.

[PRE 94] PREECE J., ROGERS Y., SHARP H., BENYON D., HOLLAND S., CAREY T., *Human-Computer Interaction*, Addison Wesley Publication, Wokingham, 1994.

[PUE 01] PUERTA A., EISENSTEIN J., "XIML: a common representation for interaction data", *Proceedings IUI01*, ACM, Santa Fe, USA, pp. 214–215, 2001.

[REI 07] REIGNIER P., BRDICZKA O., VAUFREYDAZ D., CROWLEY J.L., MAISONNASSE J., "Context aware environments: from specification to implementation", *Expert Systems: The Journal of Knowledge Engineering*, vol. 5, no. 24, pp. 304–320, 2007.

[REP 04] REPENNING A., IOANNIDOU A., "Agent-based end-user development", *Communications of the ACM*, vol. 47, no. 9, pp. 43–46, 2004.

[REY 05] REY G., Le Contexte en interaction homme-machine: le contexteur, Thesis, Joseph Fourier University, Grenoble I, 2005.

[ROB 91] ROBERTSON G.G., MACKINLAY J.D., CARD S.K., "Cone trees: animated 3D visualizations of hierarchical information", *Proceedings of the ACM CHI 91 Human Factors in Computing Systems Conference*, New Orleans, USA, pp. 189–194, 1991.

[ROD 04] RODDEN T., CRABTREE A., HEUINGS T., KOLEVA B., HUMBLE J., AKESSON K.P., HANSSON P., "Configuring the ubiquitous home", *Proceedings of the 2004 ACM Symposium on Designing Interactive Systems (DIS 2004)*, Cambridge, MA, USA, 2004.

[ROU 03] ROUILLARD J., "Plastic ML and its Toolkit", *Proceeding of the HCI International*, Heraklion, Crete, Greece, 2003.

[ROU 06] ROUSSEAU C., BELLIK Y., VERNIER F., "A conceptual model for multimodal and contextual presentation of information", *French Human-Computer Interaction Journal, RIHM*, vol. 7, 2006.

[SCH 06] SCHAEFER R., BLEUL S., "Towards object oriented, uiml-based interface descriptions for mobile devices, In Computer-Aided Design of User Interfaces V", *Proceedings of 6th International Conference on Computer-Aided Design of User Interfaces CADUI'2006*, Bucharest, Romania, 6–8 June 2006.

[SEF 04] SEFFAH A., JAVAHERY H., *Multiple User Interfaces, Cross-Platform Applications and Context-Aware Interfaces*, Wiley & Sons, New York, 2004.

[SER 09] SERRANO M., NIGAY L., "Temporal aspects of CARE-based multimodal fusion: from a fusion mechanism to composition components and WoZ components", *Proceedings of the 11th International Conference on Multimodal Interfaces (IMCI '09)*, Cambridge, MA, USA, pp. 177–184, 2009.

[SHA 91] SHACKEL B., *Usability-Context, Framework, Design and Evaluation*, Human Factors for Informatics Usability, Cambridge University Press, Cambridge, pp. 21–38, 1991.

[SHN 11] SHNEIDERMAN B., "Technology-mediated social participation: the next 25 years of HCI challenges", *Human Computer Interaction. Design and Development Approaches*, Lecture Notes in Computer Sciences, Springer, HCI International, vol. 6761, pp. 3–14, 2011.

[SHO 07] SHOEMAKER G., TANG A., BOOTH K., "Shadow reaching: a new perspective on interaction for large displays", *Proceedings of the User Interface Software and Technology 2007 (UIST 2007)*, ACM Press, Newport, Rhode Island, USA, 2007.

[SMI 93] SMITH D.C., "Pygmalion: an executable electronic blackboard", Chapter 1 in CYPHER A. (ed.), *Watch What I Do*, The MIT Press, Cambridge, MA, 1993.

[SOT 07] SOTTET J.S., CALVARY G., COUTAZ J., FAVRE J.M., "A model-driven engineering approach for the usability of user interfaces", in GULLIKSEN J. *et al.* (eds), *Proceedings of the Engineering Interactive Systems (EIS2007)*, LNCS 4940, Salamanca, Spain, pp. 140–157, 2007.

[SOT 08] SOTTET J.S., Méga-IHM : Malléabilité des interfaces homme-machine dirigées par les modèles, Thesis Joseph Fourier University, Grenoble I, 2008.

[SOU 03] SOUSA J.P., GARLAN D., The Aura Software architecture: an infrastructure for ubiquitous computing, Carnegie Mellon Technical Report, CMU-CS-03-183, 2003.

[SOU 05] SOUSA J.P., Scaling task management in space and time: reducing user overhead in ubiquitous-computing environments, PhD Thesis, Carnegie Mellon University, CMU Technical Report CMU-CS-05-123, 2005.

[STE 09] STEPHANIDIS C., *The Universal Access Handbook*, CRC Press, Boca Raton, 2009.

[STR 99] STREITZ N., GEIBLER J., HOLMER T., KONOMI S., MÜLLER-TOMFELDE C., REISCHL W., REXROTH P., SEITZ P., STEINMETZ R., "i-LAND: an interactive landscape for creativity and innovation", *Proceedings of the ACM Conference On Human Factors in Computer Human Interaction (CHI99)*, ACM, Pittsburgh, USA, pp. 120–127, 1999.

[STU 06] STUERZLINGER W., CHAPUIS O., PHILLIPS D., ROUSSEL N., "User interface façades: towards fully adaptable user interfaces", *Proceedings of the 19th Annual ACM Symposium on User Interface Software and Technology, UIST 2006*, Montreux, Switzerland, pp. 309–318, 2006.

[SUC 87] SUCHMAN L., *Plans and Situated Actions*, Cambridge University Press, Cambridge, 1987.

[TAN 01] TANDLER P., "Software infrastructure for ubiquitous computing environments: supporting synchronous collaboration with heterogeneous devices", *Proceedings of UBICOMP 2001*, LNCS 2201, Atlanta, USA, pp. 96–115, 2001.

[THE 99] THEVENIN D., COUTAZ J., "Plasticity of user interfaces: framework and research agenda", in SASSE A., JOHNSON C. (eds), *Proceedings Interact99*, Edinburgh, IFIP IOS Press Publication, pp. 110–117, 1999.

[THE 01] THEVENIN D., L'adaptation en interaction homme-machine: le cas de la plasticité, Thesis Joseph Fourier University, Grenoble I, 2001.

[TRE 03] TREVISAN D., VANDERDONCKT J., MACQ B., "Continuity as a usability property", *HCI 2003 – 10th International Conference on Human-Computer Interaction*, vol. I, Heraklion, Greece, pp. 1268–1272, 22–27 June 2003.

[TRU 04] TRUONG K.N., HUANG E.M, ABOWD G., "CAMP: a magnetic poetry interface for end-user programming of capture applications for the home", *Proceedings of the 6th International Conference on Ubiquitous Computing (Ubicomp'04)*, Nottingham, UK, Lecture Notes in Computer Science, vol. 3205, Springer, pp. 143–160, 2004.

[VAN 04] VAN ROY P., HARIDI S., *Concepts, Techniques, and Models of Computer Programming*, MIT Press, 2004.

[VAN 99] VAN WELIE M., VAN DER VEER G.C., ELIËNS A., "Usability properties in dialog models", *6th International Eurographics Workshop on Design Specification and Verification of Interactive Systems DSV-IS99*, Braga, Portugal, pp. 238–253, 2–4 June 1999.

[WIN 01] WINOGRAD T., "Architectures for context", *Human-Computer Interaction – Special Issue on Context-Aware Computing*, Lawrence Erlbaum Associates, vol. 16, no. 2–4, pp. 401–420, 2001.

[YU 07] YU J., BENATALLAH B., SAINT-PAUL R., CASATI F., DANIEL F.M. MATERA M., "A framework for rapid integration of presentation components", *WWW'07 Proceedings of the 16th International Conference on World Wide Web*, Banff, Alberta, Canada, pp. 923–932, 2007.

Chapter 10

Composition of User Interfaces

10.1. Problem

In ambient intelligence, humans are imagined as evolving in an ecosystem, symbiotic with the physical and digital worlds. Their roles are dynamic: the human, for example, like all physical entities of the ecosystem [MAE 09], can play the role of the display surface [ANT 02] from the moment that it is perceived by a camera and present in a video-projector's area of action (Figure 10.1). Of course, this same entity can play several roles. In [TAY 09], it is the gesture that defines the function. So, a bar of soap, according to how it is held, is sometimes a telephone or sometimes a screen: when held to somebody's ear, it is used as a telephone, when held to their face, it becomes a screen. If this dynamic appeals from a usage point of view, it poses serious challenges in the field of Human Computer Interaction (HCI) engineering.

At a large degree of granularity, two sources of variability can be distinguished, from the point of view of HCI:

– the Functional Core (FC), i.e. the set of available services. This group and how relevant it is evolve dynamically, typically according to the user's location. For example, when the user arrives at the train station of another town, it could be a good idea to tell them where they can rent a car. This would be unnecessary in their own town;

Chapter written by Gaëlle CALVARY, Anne-Marie DERY-PINNA, Audrey OCCELLO, Philippe RENEVIER and Yoann GABILLON.

– the context of use in its three dimensions (user, platform, environment) [CAL 03]. The user evolves at the same time during interaction both at the levels of their state (how tired the users are, what they are learning, etc.) and their intentions: new objectives can in fact emerge, either induced by its state (for example, having flu that needs to be treated by a doctor) or by the context (being able to spot an older person makes the user think of their parents and makes the user want to call them). The platform refers to the physical (PC, telephones, tables, camera, video-projectors, objects from the physical world, etc.) and software (middleware, toolboxes, etc.) that support interaction. This infrastructure evolves dynamically: for example, when the user passes by an augmented wall, the platform temporarily extends with this new surface. The *environment* denotes the physical (light, noise, heat, etc.) and social (presence of people in the room) aspects of the space in which the user is evolving. Even there, the environment is changing, evolving at least as fast as the user's movements.

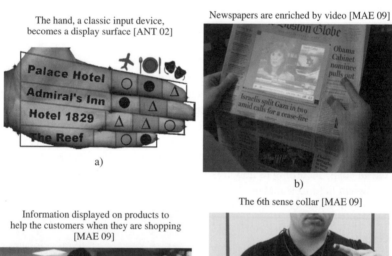

Figure 10.1. *In ambient intelligence, all objects become display surfaces and take part in interaction*

The functional variability of the FC and the context of use call for a re-configuration of the User Interface (UI): Re-configuration can consist of re-modeling (for example, by integrating a localization service) or re-distribution (for example, migration of a localization service to the telephone to aid mobility). In these two cases, the resulting UI can be obtained by the *composition* of the existing UIs. The reason for doing this is twofold:

- at design time, existing components can be re-used;

- at run time, it ensures a certain stability by preserving the state of components.

The following section illustrates UI composition with a case study (section 10.2). The difficulties in that are then analyzed (section 10.3) and then the state of the art is presented (section 10.4). Two approaches are developed (section 10.5) and then perspectives are formulated (section 10.6), which show the whole potential of the subject.

10.2. Case study

Let us place ourselves in the field of health and consider an emergency medical assistance service. John Peter Doe suddenly feels ill at the office. A colleague calls the emergency services and gives them the necessary information for them to take care of John (his symptoms, his social security number, etc.). The emergency services immediately launch an emergency medical assistance system. This system is built from four elementary services: a social security information service, a business information service, a route calculation service (for example, Google Maps or viamichelin.com), and a service to assist the emergency services. New applications can be built from web services by orchestrating these services. For example, a service that helps to guide the emergency services to the place where they need to go, at home or at work, can be created by a composition of these services.

10.2.1. *Description of the available services*

S1, the social security information service (Figure 10.2)

In input, this service takes the social security identifier of the person concerned ("Insurance Card Id") and at output supplies, among other things, the first and last name of the insured person, their social security number, references from the doctor treating them ("Social Insurance Account"), a postal address ("Administrative Information"), and information pertaining to children ("Children").

Insurance Card Id : 123456   show insurance information

Social Insurance Account				
Last Name	Doe		**First Name**	John Peter
Birthday	1975-12-24		**Birthplace**	PARIS
			Country	FRANCE
Number	1751275056266		**Key**	56
Medical Referent	Dr. Mabuse			

Administrative Information				
Family Status	married		**on the**	2009-05-09
Address	**Street** 2010 promenade des Anglais			
	Zip Code 75000 PARIS			
	Country FRANCE			

Children				
Last Name	**First Name**	**Sex**	**Birthday and Birthplace**	**Handicap**
Doe	MARIANA	female	2006-01-30, LAMBRES LEZ DOUAI	0 %
Doe	CHARLES	male	2008-07-28, NICE	0 %

Figure 10.2. *Social security information service*

S2, the business information service (Figure 10.3)

In input, this service has the employee's name and supplies, in output, the professional address(es), the office numbers, and the employee's telephone number as well as their work email.

Figure 10.3. *Business information service*

S3, the route calculation service

In input, this service takes the departure and destination addresses and supplies, in output, the itinerary is planned out as well as a road map (Figure 10.4).

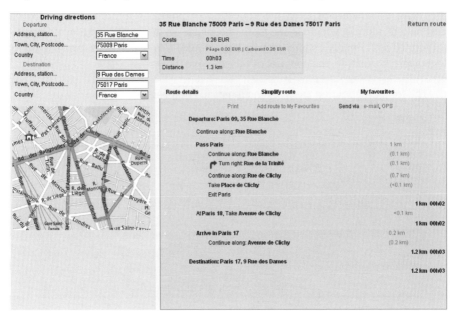

Figure 10.4. *The route calculation service*

S4, the emergency assistance service to the emergency services (Figure 10.5)

In input, this service takes information about the patient: name, telephone information (person who alerted to the problem), the place where it happened, and a description of the symptoms. It supplies, in output, the list of people involved who should be called and material to bring.

10.2.2. *Examples of services built by composition*

Enriching the business information service (S2) with the employee's personal information (S1) would make medical treatment easier within the company. This is an argument in favor of composing S1 and S2 when the incident occurs in the enterprise building. Improving the emergency services' assistance service (S4) and the localization service (S3) would help the emergency services to prepare their assistance and get to the place where the incident occurs more quickly. This is an argument for composing S3 and S4 when the emergency services do not know the area very well.

This example can be increased by multiple orders. In these two cases, the resulting UI clearly cannot be a simple juxtaposition of the original UIs. Juxtaposing the services would lead to information becoming redundant (for example, the name in S1 and S2), the visualization of information that is not useful (the doctor providing treatment), or even the collection of pointless information (in S3, the destination address which is *de facto* the place of the incident known from S4 (Figure 10.5)). Finally, some information would also gain from being grouped together (for example, the contacts of the employee).

The following section analyzes the issues in composition.

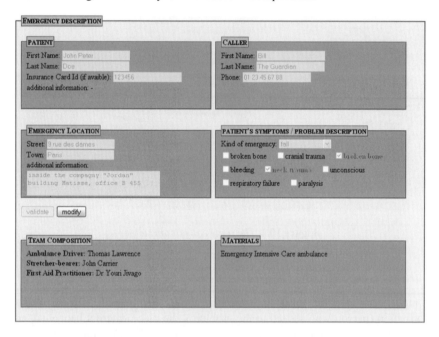

Figure 10.5. *Assistance service to the emergency services*

10.3. Issues

UI composition can be envisaged at design time and at run time. In the two cases, general issues crop up, linked to the combinatory explosion, which requires us to reason about the properties to be satisfied so that to select the best option for the user:

– from the point of view of time, composition can be achieved in conjunction of the source UIs: they are then displayed simultaneously rather than sequentially;

– from a spatial point of view, source UIs can be co-located or not.

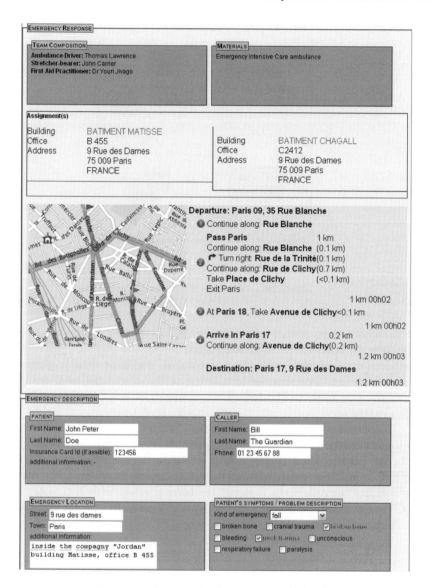

Figure 10.6. *An example of composition of S3 and S4*

The combination of these two dimensions supplies a structuring problem space with (Figure 10.7), of course, a wide range of degrees of slackness: "different spaces", for example, can be interpreted in terms of different pixels, canvases, windows, or even screens. It is the same for the time, the breakdown of which can be expressed in different units (from seconds to hours, for example).

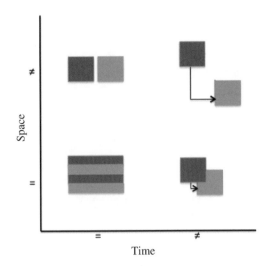

Figure 10.7. *Taxonomy of UI composition*

It is ergonomic properties that allow, in this set of what is possible, the best composition for the user to be chosen. For example, for a global perception of interaction, UI concomitance should be encouraged. It is these same properties that are sometimes an argument for duplicates to be eliminated and pre-treated semantically (the name of the patient for example) or re-grouped to reduce the workload of the user.

If the combination and relevance of ergonomic properties to give nuance to the variants are general, valid at design time as well as at run time, other issues are specific to run time: those relating to the composition process that must be observable and controllable by humans. The corresponding UI is said to be "meta-UI" [COU 06]. This meta-UI must itself consist of source UIs: the problem space is thus applied recursively, which shows how complex the problem is. The following section presents the state of the art.

10.4. State of the art in UI composition

This section goes through research that is useful to UI composition. It covers general research in composition as well as specific works in UI composition. Then, it presents key knowledge in HCI engineering that may serve to UI composition: development processes, generation of UIs at design time, and adaptation of UIs at run time.

10.4.1. *Composition: a shared concern*

According to A. Filkenstein of UCL (*University College London*), S. Krakoviac, or even J. Sifakis from Grenoble, composition is one of the grand challenges that must be met in the years to come. A theory of composition is necessary. Properties are today identified for reasoning. For example:

– composability: when properties of each component are preserved in the composed system, i.e. the invariant of the component is preserved;

– compositionality: when properties of the composed system are deduced from those of the components and the assembly rules.

To our knowledge, this research remains general, and has still not been applied to HCI. At first glance, the exercise is far from being easy. For example, let us consider the composability and examine the criterion of homogeneity consistency. Clearly, the composition of two consistent UIs gives rise to an inconsistent UI if the styles of the two UIs are not consistent. As another example, let us consider the workload criterion. If two UIs are well designed with regard to this criterion, their composition can be unsatisfactory from this point of view, since it induces articulatory tasks such as navigation within tabs, for example.

10.4.2. *UIs composition*

The functional decomposition FC–UI provides a framework, at large granularity, for classifying the state of the art [GAB 11a]. AMUSING [PIN 03] composed, for example, UIs from the FC. It draws from the models of pre-existing components to infer a user task and assemble the corresponding components. The context of use is therefore implicit. Composition is carried out at design time. Mashups [FUJ 04, LIN 09] support a composition driven by data. Composition is pre-computed at design time and placed under the control of the end user for data selection and services on the fly. ComposiXML [LEP 06] supports UI composition by the designer. The UI is graphic. The designer can make a union of it, a union without a duplicate, intersection, etc. The context of use is implicit there again. The UIs are graphic and centralized on a single platform.

Other works investigate the context of use and the distribution of the UIs on a set of platforms [NIC 08, STÜ 06]. De/re-composition and tailoring [WUL 08] of UIs allow the user to manually control distribution of their UIs on a set of windows and platforms. The user manually selects the parts of the UI to move. Selection can be made by the system [PAT 08] to adapt to the modifications of the context of use.

10.4.3. *The development process of UIs*

The development process of UIs is organized around four levels of abstraction [CAL 03] (Figure 10.8). The task model (or task tree [PAT 97]) describes the user task in terms of its objective and procedure. The procedure breaks down the objective recursively into sub-objectives. The sub-objectives are linked among themselves by logical or time-based relationships. For example, the task "Get medical assistance" is broken down into three sequential sub-tasks: "Choose the city", "Choose the doctor", and then "Contact the doctor". Each (sub)task is linked to the domain concepts that it manipulates (for example, the concept of the pharmacy).

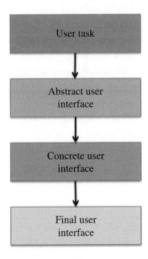

Figure 10.8. *The spine of the CAMELEON reference framework [CAL 03]: four fundamental levels of abstraction in UI design*

A structuration of the UI, which can be deducted from the task model, is called "workspaces". The spaces group together the entities necessary for the user to accomplish their sub-objectives. The description obtained is called "abstract user interface" (AUI). For example, the task "Get medical assistance" can structure its sub-tasks "Choose the city", "Choose the doctor", and then "Contact the doctor" in three different workspaces. The workspaces make the domain concepts that are manipulated in the tasks observable and, if needed, modifiable.

In this top-down approach, workspaces and their content are then made concrete in interactors (windows, text-field, pictures, radio buttons, check boxes, sound, etc.). A UI like this is called a "concrete user interface" (CUI), which is a UI description. It has not yet been implemented into a programming language. The sketches are typically concrete UIs.

When the CUI is then implemented in a programming language, it gives rise to a "final user interface" (FUI).

A great deal of research has covered the generation of AUI, CUI and FUI from a task model. This is at the heart of the following section.

10.4.4. *Generation of UIs*

Since the 1990s [MOR 02], model transformations have been "hard-wired" into the code of the generators. They were neither modifiable nor extensible [JOH 93], as a consequence resulting in poor-quality UIs, generally graphic, single-screen, and a long way from modern UIs (so-called "post-WIMP"), leaving no place at all for creativity.

A leap was made in 2004 with the development of model-driven engineering (MDE): model transformations became models. From there, transformations could be capitalized on and traced during evolutions, at design time as well as at run time. New possibilities were then opened up to design process models [MYE 00]. The following section explores their interest for the adaptation of UIs at run time.

10.4.5. *Plasticity of UIs*

In HCI, plasticity [CAL 07] denotes the adaptation capacity of an UI to its context of use with respect to user-centered properties. A plastic UI, for example, has the capacity to migrate toward another platform when its battery runs down. It knows how to re-model itself to accommodate the characteristics of this new platform in such a way that the user can continue their task with comfort, efficiency, and security.

As the set of the evolutions of the context of use is not predictable at design time, [SOT 07] proposes to keep the design models alive at run time. The models cover the FC, the UI, and the context of use. They are linked among each other by mappings and form a graph in this way of models, which correspond to the design decisions. They are motivated by ergonomic properties that have to be satisfied. [DEM 08] invents a toolbox of plastic interactors. A plastic interactor is an interactor defined at the task level (for example, the "choose" interactor) and includes several manifestations (for example, the radio buttons, a linear, circular menu, etc.) that offer it, consequently, adaptation potential. The interactors are called COMET, and in fact trigger a micrograph of models (see Chapter 9 on plasticity).

Generally, even in plasticity, a strong hypothesis is made: that of a task model known at design time. This hypothesis strongly limits ambient intelligence by not supporting, *de facto*, opportunistic tasks. As a result, [GAB 11a] has studied the dynamic generation of a task model from a given user objective and a set of fragments of available task models in a zoo of models. The Compose software almost becomes a personal assistant. As it was originally imagined for end users, there is no reason why it cannot be used by designers and, in that, become a tool for rapid prototyping.

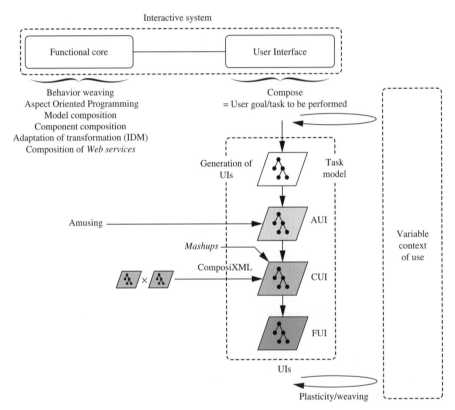

Figure 10.9. *Summary of the state of the art that is useful to UI composition [GAB 11b]*

10.4.6. *Summary of the state of the art in UI composition*

Figure 10.9 proposes a summary of the state of the art that is useful to UI composition [GAB 11b]. We retain from it two large classes of approach: those that create the UI from the FC and make, as a consequence, the impasse on the task model (for example, AMUSING); and those which, on the contrary, emphasize UI design with, in particular, consideration of the four levels of abstraction but which, on the other hand, neglect the FC. This second class of approaches can be nuanced according to the level of abstraction that is considered. Compose, for example, works at the task level while ComposiXML works at the CUI level.

The following section exemplifies each class of approaches.

10.5. Two examples of approaches

This section illustrates the two classes of approach (i.e. composition driven by the UI versus that driven by the FC) by two emblematic examples: Compose and Alias.

10.5.1. *Composition driven by the UI and the context of use: Compose*

Compose adopts an approach that is based on planning [GHA 04]. The principle is to build a UI whose function is to take the user from their current situation to a situation in which their needs are satisfied. In a more formal way, the current situation is the initial s_0 state of an exploration space. This state is represented by a set of logical propositions (Figure 10.10). In the same way, the user's needs, i.e. their goals, are represented by a set of g propositions. The states containing g are called "s_g targeted states" (Figure 10.10).

$$s_0 = \begin{cases} \text{has (Victor, Smartphone)} \\ \text{internet (Smartphone)} \\ \text{at (Victor, Philadelphia)} \\ \ldots \end{cases}$$

$$s_g = \begin{cases} \text{found(Victor, medical\_assistance)} \\ \ldots \end{cases}$$

Figure 10.10. *Initial s_0 state of the planning algorithm*

The exploration space is a graph of the changes of states whose nodes are states and the arcs are actions that the user can carry out using the UI (Figure 10.11).

a actions are defined by the triplets (*precond(a), add(a), del(a)*) where *precond(a)* is a set of logical propositions, which represent conditions that trigger the action: an action is applicable if and only if the state under consideration contains *precond(a)*. *add(a)* and *del(a)*, respectively, are the effects that are added and taken away from the current state. If an *a* action is applicable, the following state can be calculated by:

$$\gamma(s_i, a) = (s_i - \text{del}(a)) \cup \text{add}(a) = s_{i+1}$$

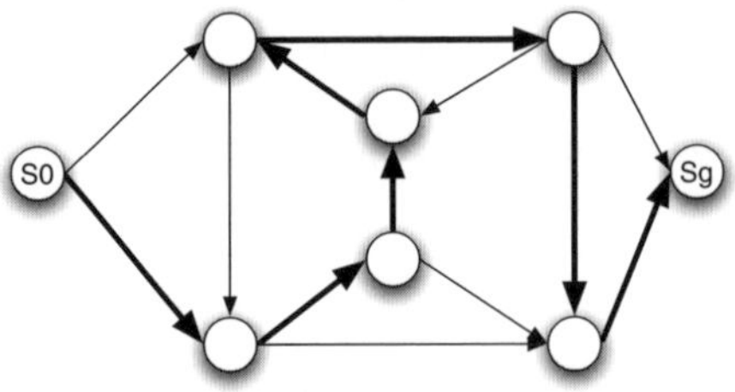

Figure 10.11. *State-change graphs*

The problem therefore lies in constructing a UI in such a way that, whatever the actions of the user are, the UI takes him from the initial state to the state that is aimed for (Figure 10.11). That is to say π is a list that is the length of k of these actions and s is the current state; the state that is obtained is defined by:

$$\gamma(s, \pi) = \begin{cases} s & \text{if } k = 0 \\ \gamma(\gamma(s, a_1), [a_2, \ldots, a_k]) & \text{if } k > 0 \text{ and } a_1 \text{ is applicable to } s \end{cases}$$

In practice, how the composition system functions is presented in Figure 10.12. The user expresses their needs. These are translated into a set of logical *g* propositions. The system perceives the context of use and represents it in the form of a set of s_0 logical propositions. The planning algorithm knows the actions that the user can carry out via the UI. The actions are expressed in "intention" in the form of operators and methods.

An *o* operator is in the form of *(precond(o), add(o), del(o))*. It is defined by its preconditions, what has been added, and what has been taken away, which are sets of logical predicates of the first order. For example, in the "*Call_the_office(?u, ?p)*" operator, the preconditions contain the predicates "*has(?u, ?p)*" and "*internet(?p)*" ; the user *?u* and the platform *?p* are variables linked to domains, i.e. to sets of constants. Thus, the "*Call_the_office(?u, ?p)*" operator represents the "*Call_the_office(Victor, Smartphone)*", "*Call_the_office (Victor, Wall)*" actions, etc.

An *m* method is in the form of *(type(m), precond(m), subAct(m))*, where *precond(m)* defines its preconditions and *subAct (m)* breaks down the method in operators or methods to be accomplished to carry out *m*. The type of breakdown expressed in *type(m)* is either a sequence or a parallelism. In a sequence, the *subAct(m)* methods or operators are ordered completely. In a parallelism, the *subAct(m)* elements can be carried out in any order. For example, the method of *"Get_medical_assistance"* corresponds to the sequence of *"Choose_the_city"*, *"Choose_the_doctor"*, and then *"Contact_the_ doctor"*. On the other hand, the method of *"Contact_the_doctor"* corresponds to the parallelism of *"Call_the_office"* and *"Find_route_information"*.

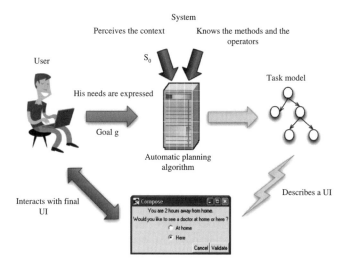

Figure 10.12. *How UI composition works in compose*

From the initial state s_0, from the goal of g and from a set of methods and operators, the planning algorithm calculates a task model that allows the user to accomplish their goal. This task model is a tree. Each node corresponds to an existing UI. For example, the task *"Contact_the_doctor"* corresponds to a window. Once calculated, the task tree makes it possible to know which UIs the window will contain. For example, here it will contain the UIs that correspond to the sub-tasks *"Call_the_office"* and *"Find_route_ information"*.

The task tree contains two types of node: the internal nodes are completely instantiated methods (all variables are linked to constants) of type sequence (">") or parallelism ("II"); the leaves are actions, i.e. completely instantiated operators (Figure 10.13a). We call *projection* $\wp$ of the task tree the set of partially ordered actions that come from it (Figure 10.13b). The ordering relationship "$C > D$" expresses that the C action has to precede the D action. 0 and ∞ are formal actions that represent the beginning and the end of interactions. Linearization of $\wp$ is a set consisting of the same actions completely ordered by the relationship of precedence. An example of this is given in Figure 10.13c.

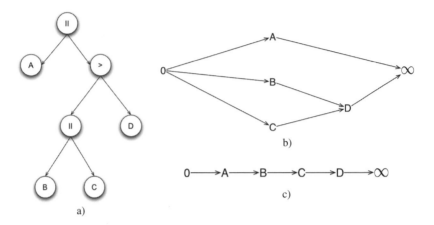

Figure 10.13. *(a) Task tree obtained by the planner;*
(b) ℘ projection of the task tree; and (c) linearization

$L(\wp)$ is the set of linearizations of $\wp$. The composition issue is simply formalized from there: $P = (s_0, g, A)$ a planning problem where s_0 is the initial state, g the goal, and A the set of possible actions (in practice, expressed in the form of methods and operators). Solving the problem means finding a $\wp$ set (in practice, a task model) such as:

$$\forall \pi \in L(\wp), \ g \subseteq \gamma(s_0, \pi)$$

In the case where no task model is found, the problem has no solution and no UI can be composed. In the case where π exists, planning algorithms do not guarantee that the corresponding task model is the "best", but it allows the user to carry out their objective in the context of use considered here.

A prototype has been developed and implemented in Java. It generates a task model that is then concretized in UI in the form of COMET.

10.5.2. *A resolution driven by the functional core: Alias*

The aim of the Alias approach [JOF 11] is to avoid entirely re-developing the UI when developers create a new interactive system through the composition of the existing services. Instead of that, the developer concentrates on the business composition (i.e. of the FC). Then, the UI of a σ interactive system built by composition are deducted from:

– the interaction links between each re-used service and the UIs that are associated with it;

– the way in which the re-used services are composed to form the FC.

This approach is all the more important for the dynamic composition of systems since services appear and disappear at will. The designers cannot envisage all possible compositions in advance, so it is interesting to take advantage of the way in which the services are composed to obtain an adapted UI.

The only requirement for using the Alias approach is the separation of concerns between the different elements that make up an interactive system: the UI and the FC must be clearly identified, as well as the interaction links between the two (setting off a given operation on a user action is an example of an interaction between the UI and the FC).

The FC and UI are represented in the form of components with data and event ports at input and output. The ports represent the interaction links between the FC and UI, but also the composition of several services. The interactive system is seen then as an assembly of FC and UI components. The semantics differs from a category of components at the other end. The data ports of an FC component represent the input or output parameters of a service operation while they correspond to the data access by the user, represented respectively to the user, according to whether it is a question of input or output port. The event ports of an FC component correspond to service operations whereas they correspond to trigger service operations on a UI components.

The input data ports of a UI component are linked to the input data ports of an FC component. Thus, information entered by a user transmitted to operations as input parameters. The output data ports of an FC component are linked to the output data ports of a UI component. Thus, the result of the execution of an operation is displayed to the user. When event ports are linked together, it makes it possible to know which operation to trigger on which user action.

The Alias composition engine produces a first UI of the composed service. The composition properties allow:

– elements of UIs of the services that can be re-used to be identified;

– *workflow* to be analyzed to reproduce it in the sequencing of the UI;

– to reveal any conflict on the choice of the UI element that should be used.

Conflicts arise when two UI elements can represent the same information. Functional composition can solve conflicts in two cases: when the output of a service is linked to the input of another and when the composed service does not select data. In certain cases, the motor does not find the information that the UI element needs for selection in functional composition. This is the case when input or output ports are linked by functional composition and the two associated representations are potentially eligible. By default, the engine chooses the representation that is associated with the first service. An interrogation mode lets the developer choose the representation between the two.

Once the UI components have been obtained, there is still work to be done on the disposition of different elements of the resulting UI as well as the ergonomic properties. This aspect cannot be directly achieved on representation in the form of Alias components. It is necessary to reason on the real UI of the interactive system. This comes out of the scope of Alias. Interoperability with different tools, UsiXML for example, is to be studied here.

10.6. Key statements and propositions

The intrinsic complexity of designing interactive systems has today been increased by technological advances and new usage, which run from that. Space-time diversity and variability require a lot of agility in design and adaptation to always guarantee perfect quality in use.

Existing approaches essentially follow two paths. In the first path, the interactive system is completely or partially modeled by the designer: the functional core, a part of the UI, etc. Modeling is carried out at one or several levels of abstraction and can include variable aspects to take adaptation into account. These approaches generally constrain the designer by making them focus on a given point of view and the UI is generated as a consequence. This approach is not in keeping with practice in a company where models are not used very much, in particular, for UIs that designers often sketch directly. Moreover, there is no support for partial or total re-use of UI models. In the second path, a service-oriented approach promotes execution environments that modify the interactive system according to the availability of functional services that may appear and disappear opportunistically. These solutions do not take into account the models inherent to HCI (for example, the task model) and therefore do not ensure the ergonomic quality that is expected.

It now seems important for us to overcome these limitations to explore a new path that could exploit model composition at design time and at run time. For the interactive system as a whole and its adaptations to be considered, it will be necessary for the set of models to fully cover the functions to be supported (FC and UI) as well as the contexts of use (users, platforms, and environments) the interactive system may have to face. The idea is to reuse the existing models as much as possible and to avoid creating new ones. For that, it is important to survey all the models that exist for modeling the UI and/or the FC, to identify any shortcomings and redundancy to make clear how current models could co-operate to uniformly address the needs as a whole.

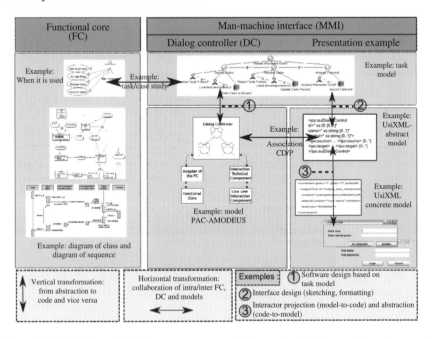

Figure 10.14. *Horizontal (i.e. between concerns with regard to the "separation of concerns" principle) and vertical (i.e. between levels of abstraction) collaborations between models*

To ensure appropriate adaptation that copes with the identified cases of variability, models will have to be alive at run time and will have to collaborate dynamically to preserve the system's consistency. Figure 10.14 [CAL 09] presents examples of horizontal (i.e. between concerns with regard to the "separation of concerns" principle) and vertical (i.e. between levels of abstraction) collaborations between models.

This approach is interesting because it unifies phases (of design, execution, and evaluation) as well as communities. Unification of communities is an opportunity to be grasped here. For that, research on ergonomic properties from an engineering point of view (formalization and composition) is needed in HCI, on the one hand, to take advantage of the advances made in other communities (for example, in software or system engineering) and, on the other hand, to indirectly contribute to these other communities through the definition of a difficult "playground" which is HCI. Beyond composition, establishing good properties is mandatory for the maturity of the domain.

10.7. Bibliography

[ANT 02] ANTONIAC P., PULLI P., KURODA T., BENDAS D., HICKEY S., SASAKI H., "Wireless user perspectives in Europe: handsmart mediaphone interface", *Wireless Personal Communications*, vol. 22, pp. 161–174, 2002.

[CAL 03] CALVARY G., COUTAZ J., THEVENIN D., LIMBOURG Q., BOUILLON L., VANDERDONCKT J., "A unifying reference framework for multi-target user interfaces", *Interacting with Computers*, vol. 15, no. 3, pp. 289–308, 2003.

[CAL 07] CALVARY G., Plasticité des interfaces homme-machine. Habilitation à Diriger des Recherches préparée au Laboratoire d'Informatique de Grenoble (LIG), Joseph Fourier University, 2007.

[CAL 10] CALVARY G., DERY-PINNA A.M., OCCELLO A., RENEVIER-GONIN P., "A la croisée de l'ingénierie de l'interaction homme-machine et de l'ingénierie dirigée par les modèles", in BLAY-FORNARINO M., DUCHIEN L. (eds), *Revue Technique et science informatiques-RSTI série TSI, Numéro spécial Ingénierie dirigée par les modèles*, vol. 29, no. 4–5, pp. 479–503, April–May 2010.

[COU 06] COUTAZ J., "Meta-user interfaces for ambient spaces", invited talk at *Tamodia'06*, Bucharest, Romania, 2006.

[DEM 08] DEMEURE A., CALVARY G., CONINX K., "COMET(s): a software architecture style and an interactors toolkit for plastic user interfaces", *DSVIS'08*, Springer-Verlag, pp. 225–237, 2008.

[FUJ 04] FUJIMA J., LUNZER A., HORNBÆK K., TANAKA Y., "Clip, connect, clone: combining application elements to build custom interfaces for information access", in FEINER S., LANDAY J.A. (eds), *UIST'04*, ACM Press, pp. 175–184, 2004.

[GAB 11a] GABILLON Y., Composition d'interfaces homme-machine par planification automatique, Thesis, University of Grenoble, 14 October 2011.

[GAB 11b] GABILLON Y., CALVARY G., FIORINO H., "Composition d'interfaces homme-machine par planification", *Revue TSI*, Numéro spécial Composition 10, vol. 30, December 2011.

[GHA 04] GHALLAB M., NAU D., TRAVERSO P., *Automated Planning: Theory & Practice*, Morgan Kaufmann, San Francisco, CA, USA, 2004.

[ISH 98] ISHII H., WISNESKI C., BRAVE S., DAHLEY S., GORBET M., ULLMER B., YARIN P., "Ambient room", *Video at the ACM CHI'98 Conference*, Florence, Italy, 1998.

[JOF 11] JOFFROY C., Composition d'applications dirigée par la composition fonctionnelle pour la réalisation de la composition d'interfaces homme-machine, Thesis, University of Nice Sophia Antipolis, 2011.

[JOH 93] JOHNSON P., WILSON S., MARKOPOULOS P., PYCOCK J., "ADEPT: advanced design environments for prototyping with task models", *Proceedings of the Conference on Human Factors in Computing Systems INTERCHI*, ACM Press, Amsterdam, Netherlands, pp. 56–57, 24–29 April 1993.

[LEP 06] LEPREUX S., VANDERDONCKT J., "Towards a support of user interface design by composition rules", in CALVARY G., PRIBEANU C., SANTUCCI G., VANDERDONCKT J. (eds), *CADUI'04*, Springer, Berlin, pp. 231–244, 2006.

[LIN 09] LIN J., WONG J., NICHOLS J., CYPHER A., LAU T.A., "End-user programming of mashups with vegemite", in CONATI C., BAUER M., OLIVER N., WELD D.S. (eds), *IUI'09*, IUI, ACM Press, pp. 97–106, 2009.

[MAE 09] MAES P., MISTRY P., "Unveiling the 'sixth sense', game-changing wearable tech", *TED 2009*, Long Beach, CA, USA, 2009.

[MOR 02] MORI G., PATERNÒ F., SANTORO C., "CTTE: support for developing and analyzing task models for interactive system design", *IEEE Transactions on Software Engineering*, vol. 28, no. 8, pp. 797–813, 2002.

[MYE 00] MYERS B., HUDSON S.E., PAUSCH R., "Past, present, and future of user interface software tools", *ACM Transaction on Computer-Human Interaction*, vol. 7, no. 1, pp. 3–28, 2000.

[NIC 08] NICHOLS J., HUA Z., BARTON J., "Highlight: a system for creating and deploying mobile web applications", in COUSINS S.B., BEAUDOUIN-LAFON M. (eds), *UIST'08*, ACM Press, pp. 249–258, 2008.

[PAT 97] PATERNÒ F., MANCINI C., MENICONI S., "ConcurTaskTrees: a diagrammatic notation for specifying task models", *Proceedings of the 13th International Conference on Human-Computer Interaction IFIP TC*, Chapman & Hall, Sydney, Australia, pp. 362–369, 14–18 July 1997.

[PAT 08] PATERNÒ F., SANTORO C., SCORCIA A., "Preserving rich user interface state in web applications across various platforms", in FORBRIG P., PATERNÒ F. (eds), *TAMODIA/ HCSE'08*, Lecture Notes in Computer Science, Springer, Berlin, vol. 5247, pp. 255–262, 2008.

[PIN 03] PINNA-DERY A.M., FIERSTONE J., PICARD E., "Component model and programming: a first step to manage human computer interaction adaptation", in CHITTARO L. (ed.), *Mobile HCI'03*, Lecture Notes in Computer Science, Springer, Berlin, vol. 2795, pp. 456–465, 2003.

[SOT 07] SOTTET J.S., GANNEAU V., CALVARY G., COUTAZ J., DEMEURE A., FAVRE J.M., DEMUMIEUX R., "Model-driven adaptation for plastic user interfaces", *Proceedings of the 11th International Conference on Human-Computer Interaction INTERACT'07*, Rio de Janeiro, Brazil, Springer, pp. 397–410, 10–14 September 2007.

[STÜ 06] STÜRZLINGER W., CHAPUIS O., PHILLIPS D., ROUSSEL N., "User interface facades: towards fully adaptable user interfaces", in WELLNER P., HINCKLEY K. (eds), *UIST'06*, ACM Press, pp. 309–318, 2006.

[TAY 09] TAYLOR B.T., BOVE V.M., "Graspables: grasp-recognition as a user interface", *Proceedings of the 27th International Conference on Human Factors in Computing Systems* (CHI'09), ACM Press, pp. 917–926, 2009.

[WUL 08] WULF V., PIPEK V., WON M., "Component-based tailorability: enabling highly flexible software applications", *International Journal of Human-Computer Studies*, vol. 66, no. 1, pp. 1–22, 2008.

Chapter 11

Smart Homes for People Suffering from Cognitive Disorders

11.1. Introduction

Who has never looked for their keys? Who has never forgotten about a casserole on the stove after a telephone call? Taken in isolation, these lapses of attention and memory have benign consequences. People suffering from cognitive deficits, on the other hand, have to confront this daily. People who have undergone a traumatic brain injury (TBI), schizophrenics, people with intellectual disabilities and people with Alzheimer's disease know how much such deficits can shatter somebody's life.

Because of the scarcity of human and material resources in healthcare, professional caregivers are overstretched. As a consequence, natural caregivers are often left to their own devices and become exhausted. However, in many cases, and given appropriate assistance, people affected would be able to live independently in their homes.

The DOMUS laboratory at the University of Sherbrooke integrates pervasive computing, ambient intelligence, tangible user interfaces, and cognitive modeling to develop innovative solutions for cognitive remediation to encourage people who suffer from cognitive deficits to live autonomously at home. Ultimately, DOMUS aims to transform the living space as a whole (residences, work environments, public places, etc.) into a real orthosis. The home, in particular, would become personalized, contextual, and an adaptive cognitive support capable of bridging the cognitive deficits of its occupant. It would help the occupant to manage time, carry

Chapter written by Sylvain GIROUX and Hélène PIGOT.

out daily activities, maintain social contacts, find things, take their medication, etc. However, restricting this assistance only to the home would be confining. Outside the home, other systems, either mobile or worn, could also assist the user in being ambulant – services that would help get around outside and within buildings, systems which would help individuals not to be late and remind the reason they went out. In a restaurant, social conventions will be made clear to them: that they should wait for a seat to be shown to them, and that they should leave a tip.

In their design and use, systems developed at DOMUS always consider how those receiving care and the caregiver go hand in hand; therefore, it is not a question of replacing the caregiver with machines, but rather of supporting them and improving how they help. Moreover, as a complement to cognitive assistance actions which are directly targeted at those they seek to help, other features have remote and medical monitoring short-term as well as long-term functions. In the long term, essential ecological data[1] are collected and analyzed to ensure better medical monitoring. In the short term, the caregiver is informed, for instance, when medication has been taken. Thus, natural and professional caregivers are better able to accompany people who have cognitive deficits.

Finally in DOMUS, we are convinced of the importance of the environment. Individuals suffering from cognitive deficits and their caregivers are involved from the start to identify their needs throughout the research process, move their solutions forward, and validate them. Moreover, prototypes and services undergo fire tests, and numerous experiments and usability studies have been carried out. This approach and these studies have proved on the one hand that widely accepted ideas should be treated skeptically and on the other hand that cognitive assistance, remote and medical monitoring using pervasive computing are doable, relevant and effective. They help the people suffering from cognitive deficits and relieve the burden on those who care for them.

This chapter looks at the work carried out at DOMUS during the last decade or so. This interdisciplinary work relies on ambient intelligence, mobile computing and tangible user interfaces. Firstly, we show the importance of the impact of cognitive disorders on society (section 11.2). Then we identify clients in terms of types of cognitive disorder and levels of cognitive deterioration who are good candidates for being able to live at home (section 11.3). From this, we can set precise research objectives (section 11.4). Ambient intelligence and mobile computing (section 11.5) form the backbone of an integrated and interdisciplinary approach (section 11.6) enabling us to foster aging at home of the targeted population. Finally, we will show how to transform a residence into a smart home (section 11.7), to perform research activities there regarding infrastructure, middleware, ambient applications, and evaluation (section 11.8).

---

1 By ecological data, we mean data gathered in the patient's living environment.

11.2. The impact of cognitive disorders on society

In daily conversation, the mention of cognitive disorders immediately evokes Alzheimer's disease, but cognitive disorders do not only affect older people and are not necessarily disorders that offer no hope of improvement. It is true that in degenerative processes, disturbances are very often irreversible and generally concern people in the later stages of life. However, in cases of schizophrenia, learning difficulties, or TBI, the person affected is generally young and will have to imagine, along with those around them, the rest of their life and the hazards linked to memory and attention difficulties, as well as executive function. In all cases, the impact on the whole of society still remains great (section 11.2.1). Fortunately, solutions are emerging, which will make aging in place easier and which will encourage the integration of people affected into society (section 11.2.2).

11.2.1. *Cognitive deficits have high human, social and economic costs*

People who have cognitive deficits represent a fairly significant proportion of the population, and caring for them incurs significant costs. Thus, "each year, 1,900 people suffer a TBI in a road accident, although three-quarters of these victims suffer only light trauma, readaptation costs can be indicated. TBI represent 6% of the clients of Quebec Automobile Insurance Corporation [SAAQ] but represent 28% of the costs" [LAB 98]. In 1997, SAAQ had links with 28 establishments that dealt with TBI. In 2003, the Estrie Readaptation Centre (ERC) alone billed SAAQ for 1.8 million Canadian dollars in readaptation costs following 250 road accidents. The report on mental illnesses in Canada [SAN 02] evaluates the economic impact of schizophrenia in 1996 in Canada in the following way: the direct cost is estimated at 2.35 billion Canadian dollars, i.e. 0.3% of Canadian GDP, and indirect costs represent another 2 billion dollars per year. On a worldwide scale, almost 3% of the total burden of human diseases is attributed to schizophrenia [MUR 96]. [TAS 03] reports that the frequency rate of intellectual disability, to which scientific literature habitually makes reference, varies between 1% and 3% of the population. In the United States in 2003, [HON 03] evaluated the average lifetime cost for a person with an intellectual disability at $1.014 million. All of that does not even take into account the alarming statistics linked to the costs of an aging population and the increase in cases of dementia or Alzheimer's disease. Among Quebeckers who are 65 and older, with regard to Alzheimer's disease alone there were "100,000 people affected in 2009, and this number will rise to 120,000 in 2015 and to 200,000 in 2030", [MSS 09]. Finally, "twenty per cent of Canadians will be personally affected by a mental illness during their lifetime" [SAN 02].

Natural caregivers and healthcare professionals are continually exhausted by the cumbersome nature of the task and the scarcity of resources [FRE 10, GIL 04, STO 10]. Moreover, currently there is a lack of cognitive assistance systems and supervision, and people suffering from cognitive deficits too often have to leave their homes to go and live in an institution.

11.2.2. *Cognitive assistance and remote monitoring: a source of hope*

Over the years, many assistance technologies have been developed for people suffering cognitive deficits as well as for their caregivers [LOP 04, PIG 08b]. These solutions offer functions which remind the user of their activities [WIL 01], procedural information for the completion of activities [CAR 05, GOR 03], support for managing time in daily life [LEV 04, SCH 04], and a capacity for communicating with caregivers [GIR 06a]. Several projects integrate technological devices and automatic systems in people's homes [PAT 02, STA 06]. For aging populations (dementia, Alzheimer's, stroke, etc.), these solutions encourage their independence and delay the moment when they will have to leave their homes to go and live in an institution [BOG 06, DIS 04, POL 05]. For younger populations (TBI, schizophrenia, intellectual disability, etc.), independence means the chance to live alone. Thus, they can leave the family home or hospital and live a full life [LAC 05].

The ability to carry out the activities of daily life (ADL) [KAT 63, LAW 69] is key to being able to stay at home. It is neither possible nor desirable to rely on a caregiver who is always available on-site, but technology can take over.

11.3. Cognitive disorders, relevant clients and research at DOMUS

Over the years, government policies have been fostering deinstitutionalization, ambulatory care, aging at home. They have created an auspicious context for technological solutions [MSS 98]. However, this is no small task. Moreover, to target efforts and carry out pertinent interventions, a better understanding of the clients is needed to identify their needs better.

This section first addresses the effects and manifestations of cognitive deficits on the people affected (section 11.3.1). Then we describe the directions taken by reasearch at DOMUS: cognitive remediation, i.e. cognitive remediation that is directly geared towards affected people (section 11.3.2) and remote and medical monitoring services that are more focused on the needs of the caregivers (section 11.3.3).

11.3.1. *Manifestations of cognitive difficulties in affected people*

Although there is a lot of variability based on pathology and severity, people suffering from cognitive disorders have the following characteristics in varying degrees:

– manifestations on a behavioral level:

  - social disinhibition,

  - behavioral changes (irritability/aggression),

  - lack of recognition of cognitive sequelae and their impact (safety);

– sequelae affecting ADL from being performed:

  - executive functions severely affected,

  - serious cognitive difficulties related to attention, memory, and learning;

– impact on the level of assistance needed from caregivers:

  - need for a great deal of care on a regular basis,

  - medical monitoring required punctually because it is an at-risk client;

– consequences on social life:

  - difficulty in finding paid employment,

  - vulnerability to exploitation.

Going from a needs analysis [PIG 05] and feedback from the interdisciplinary team, research from DOMUS emphasized carrying out ADL and assistance to caregivers.

11.3.2. *Fostering autonomy and aging in place*

Given the importance of ADL in enabling people to stay at home and the desire to not confine people to their homes, the services developed cover organization of daily life, assistance in carrying them out and assistance in moving (getting around, preventing wandering, etc.) More specifically, the research at DOMUS addresses remediation and assistance to compensate the damage to executive and cognitive functions, in particular deficits in memory, initiation, attention, and planning. The deterioration of executive functions affects how people want to do things (the ability to form intentions and express aims), planning (the ability to identify important elements and organize them in stages to carry out an intention) and effectively carrying out an intention (the ability to carry out a plan and evaluate its results).

The target clientele mainly includes older, fragile individuals who suffer from dementia or Alzheimer's disease, individuals with schizophrenia, and individuals with mental retardation. In terms of abilities, efforts are focused on people who can be kept at home. For example, in the case of Alzheimer's disease, they belong to levels 3, 4 and 5 on the Reisberg scale (Tables 11.1 and 11.2).

Level	Description	Symptoms
1	Absence of cognitive decline	No subjective or objective cognitive deficits
2	Very slight cognitive decline	Some subjective complaints, for example benign forgetfulness, no objective deficits
3	Slight cognitive decline	Slight working memory troubles (attention, concentration)
4	Moderate cognitive decline	Episodic memory troubles (memory of recent events). Slightly affected independence
5	Moderately severe cognitive decline	Declarative memory troubles (ability to carry out activities of daily life). Affected independence
6	Severe cognitive decline	Important memory troubles (which cause illusions). Highly reduced autonomy
7	Very severe cognitive decline	Loss of verbal activity. Complete loss of independence. Have to be taken care of completely

Table 11.1. *Global scale of the stages of deterioration of the primary cognitive functions of an individual suffering from degenerative dementia [REI 82]*

Level	Deficit	Incapacities linked to meal preparation	Degree of independence
1, 2	Normal		Independent
3	Slight	Converting quantities	Objective loss of independence
4	Moderate	Preparing supper for a guest	Assistance required in complex and new tasks
5	Moderately severe	Preparing two meals at the same time	Assistance required in general
6,7	Severe	Eating	Supervision

Table 11.2. *Meals. Some examples of the effects of the disorganization of daily activities according to the Reisberg deterioration scale*

11.3.3. *Accompanying caregivers*

Caregivers can be divided into professional caregivers and natural caregivers.

Among professional caregivers, we mainly include family and friends, specialized educators, recreational technicians, occupational therapists, and physiotherapists, social workers, and nurses. Their needs are generally very well-targeted. For example, occupational therapists are interested in very precise activities: has the person eaten? Have they washed? Have they taken their medication?

For their part, "natural caregivers are family members or friends who offer care and help to a person with physical, cognitive or mental difficulties. They do it by choice or necessity. In contrast to those who supply paid care, natural caregivers are not paid for their work. [...] Natural caregivers often face the challenge of reconciling their work, their own healthcare needs and their responsibilities as caregivers. Stress and exhaustion result from this, to the point where they themselves need care. Some of them choose to cut their work hours or quit their job to be able to provide care, thus undergoing economic (and non-economic) consequences in the short- and long-term" [DÉV 06]. Moreover, familial caregivers wish to be reassured on the ability of their loved ones to stay at home and continue their occupations.

As for the caregivers, DOMUS research is directed toward telemonitoring systems, and ecological medical assessment applications which allow:

– the tasks of caregivers to be relieved;

– cooperation between caregivers to be encouraged;

– a rest to be offered to the caregivers;

– emotional insecurity to be limited.

11.4. The objectives of the research program conducted at DOMUS

Since the context is favorable and the clientele and their needs have been identified, the moment has come to define the objectives of the research programmed led at DOMUS. This is in the area of:

– the benefits for society and individuals (section 11.4.1);

– significant scientific advances (section 11.4.2);

– innovation in research, valuation and transfer of results (section 11.4.3).

11.4.1. *Benefits for individuals and society*

In the long-term, our interdisciplinary collaboration on intelligent habitats aims to:

– give people who have physical and cognitive disabilities the means to develop their own life plan that encourages their independence among others through an adapted environment and personalized assistance systems;

– relieve exhausted human resources, whether they are natural or professional caregivers;

– compensate for the lack of professional resources in healthcare;

– relieve financial and organizational pressures on the healthcare system.

11.4.2. *Transforming the habitat of people with cognitive deficits*

To manage this, DOMUS is conducting interdisciplinary research activities into pervasive computing in intelligent habitats, allowing people to age in place thanks to cognitive remediation. This research studies the theoretical and practical basis of pervasive information systems to create intelligent habitats for people who have cognitive deficits. The first target is to design an intelligent residence for people who have cognitive deficits, to allow them the chance to carry out their daily activities in total safety at home as well as outside.

At the scientific level, the objectives are to develop:

– cognitive assistance systems in the home. The home becomes a cognitive orthosis capable of proving useful in combating problems of attention, memory, planning and initiation;

– mobile cognitive assistance systems that accompany individuals away from their homes so that their residences do not become like prisons for them;

– telemonitoring systems, which allow better medical and human monitoring over short (daily, weekly) and long periods (monthly, yearly) all the while relieving caregivers of these tasks;

– assistance systems that encourage social links and a social life;

– systems that ensure safety in the home and outside and which respect the private life of people suffering from cognitive deficits.

11.4.3. *Building bridges between research, practice and users*

Infrastructure and research activities which are taking place at the DOMUS laboratory also allow the following objectives to be reached:

– gather the disciplines in one place to continue interdisciplinary research;

– progressively experiment, validate, and transfer developed prototypes in real time;

– create a technological showcase to make research known and propagate it.

11.5. Pervasive computing and ambient intelligence

At home, we look to supply appropriate cues in the immediate environment to help people keep their independence and reduce risks to ensure that the affected person is capable of staying at home and takes fewer risks. To achieve that, our work calls for pervasive computing and tangible user interfaces. Objects from everyday life are used to interact with information systems. To ensure continuity of cognitive assistance outside the home, we are careful to include mobile information systems and geolocated services. To inform natural caregivers and the medical team of the changing state of health of the individual, telemonitoring systems and ecological medical assessment applications are constructed. Finally, since each person is unique with respect to cognitive abilities, ways of life, environment, history, medical profile, each system and intervention is personalized.

This is how DOMUS has, among others, developed functional cognitive assistance prototypes, supervision of activities of daily life, telemonitoring, and gathering ecological data [GIR 06b]. However, to carry out these ambient and mobile systems successfully, two prior elements have been necessary:

– tracing ethical guidelines and defining an adapted interdisciplinary approach, which is capable of integrating people suffering from cognitive deficits in the process (section 11.6);

– transforming residences into intelligent habitats where ambient systems can be deployed (section 11.7).

The following sections will present ambient and mobile systems that have been carried out in more detail.

11.6. An integrated and interdisciplinary approach to research

The approach to research we developed rely on three aspects: a line of ethical conduct and guidelines for system design (section 11.6.1), the implementation of an enlarged interdisciplinary team where everyone has their place (section 11.6.2), and systematic validation of our ideas and systems on the field (section 11.6.3). It is perfectly illustrated by the close collaboration between DOMUS and the Estrie Readaptation Center perfectly since 2003 (section 11.6.4).

11.6.1. *Guidelines and ethical lines that should not be crossed*

As regards ethics, especially when we are dealing with fragile people, ethical questions come to mind regularly and there is a gray area which is not always easy to identify. Moreover, to build systems that allow or prolong the ability to stay at home, we at DOMUS implemented our own guidelines for the design and implementation of assistive technology:

– sharing control and the initiative between the user and the system. The user can ask for help (to open lights, turn on the heating etc.) or the system can offer it, but the decision is down to the user;

– encouraging the independence and the use of cognitive capacities. It is not desirable that the system takes the place of the individuals, but rather that it reminds or advises them what they should do. The system intervenes as little as possible and does so gradually;

– to personalize; each situation is unique;

– encouraging the relationship between the caregivers and those they help. Ideally, a caregiver is always at the end of the system and a part of the functionalities of the system is dedicated to him;

– staying discrete. The home is modified as little as possible. Moreover, it is not necessary to know everything to be useful, and we do not intend to look over everything, nor to over-equip the apartment;

– beware of technological one-upmanship and also consider non-technological solutions. For example, to indicate quantities in recipes, measuring cups can be replaced by a set of cups of different color and size, avoiding the installation of a complex gesture or weith sensor system cups;

– work in the short term by using what is already commercially available while foreseeing long-term requirements;

– ensure the continuity of services between the home and outside. Assistance must be available anywhere anytime.

11.6.2. *Multidisciplinary solutions*

To provide assistance, telemonitoring and medical assessment raise complex problems at the computing level. Pervasive computing, mobile computing, ambient intelligence, context awareness, and tangible user interfaces are the research fields that have emerged recently and which will be at the heart of solutions that will be introduced. But computing alone is not enough. Currently, it is recognized that users (patients and caregivers) must be involved from the beginning in innovative design whether it is in participatory approaches or user-centered design [GIR 08]. Health sciences must also be involved as early as possible in the development process of new technologies. Thanks to knowledge of their clientele, doctors, psychiatrists, and geriatricians specify the capacities and specific needs of each pathology in different aspects of their daily life and management of their health. By following the recipients of this help daily, occupational therapists, psychoeducators, and social workers express concrete needs, offer evaluation methods of the technologies, and help in communication between researchers and recipients. The design helps to create adapted objects and interfaces, which will be integrated into the lives and social networks of individuals without stigmatizing them. Moreover, new technologies will have an impact on work practices that the field of healthcare administration will be able to analyze.

Therefore since the creation of DOMUS in 2002, we have tried to construct a network of researchers and practitioners who come from nine disciplines, having learned to work together and having the necessary expertise to lead this research program. We have also cultivated close links with the world of practice. Thus, DOMUS has grouped together an interdisciplinary team of researchers in computing, engineering, psychiatry, psychoeducation, ergotherapy, psychology, social service, industrial design, ergonomics and administration. In terms of research at DOMUS, these collaborators have worked on projects linking with cranial traumas, schizophrenia, dementia and Alzheimer's disease, intellectual disability, etc.

11.6.3. *Leaving the laboratory to evaluate, validate and transfer solutions*

However, if the solutions developed stay in the laboratory or are only validated there, it is unlikely that they will be transferred into the public sphere. The real world has to be integrated into research activities, more specifically the real world has to be conceived as being an integral part of a laboratory dedicated to research on intelligent habitats, in the mold of the *Living lab* concept [ECI 09, NII 06]. Moreover, our past experiences have shown us that we should sometimes be wary of conclusions established on the basis of simple interviews or on trials that are too short [BOI 09b]. We have to start from the ground and do this over long periods.

11.6.4. *A concrete example of the research approach applied at DOMUS*

The collaboration that has been supported for several years with the Estrie readaptation center (CRE) is a good example of the research approach applied at DOMUS. The observation, experience and expertise of CRE's clinical personnel, CRE's clients and their families have oriented research at DOMUS by identifying improvements necessary for prototypes as well as new needs [PIG 05]. Meetings with patients and discussions with them on how they use technology have also led to a better understanding of the needs of orthoses by the clientele with cognitive disorders. Then, several versions of prototypes are constructed. Experiments and validations are integrated into development with the cooperation of CRE personnel and participants targeted by CRE. These experiments can be carried out at the DOMUS laboratory itself, at the CRE, or in private residences [BOI 09b, GRO 10b, PAC 07]. The objective is to construct an integrated assistance system inside and outside the home for people with head traumas [GRO 10b].

Frequent meetings have been added between stakeholders (users, professionals and researchers). Short seminars have also taken place around therapists and directors. This is how meetings with patients, their families, and CRE professionals open avenues of research and conversely how research brings new practices and innovative solutions that were unexpected by caregivers and patients.

11.7. Transforming a residence into an intelligent habitat

The DOMUS laboratory, therefore, has available to it an apartment of 5 rooms (Figure 11.1). This apartment has been transformed into an intelligent habitat in two stages (Figure 11.2). Firstly, it has been equipped with heterogeneous networks (Ethernet, WiFi, Bluetooth, Zigbee, power lines, infrared, etc.), sensors and effectors (Ubisense, movement detectors, electromagnetic contacts, tactile carpets, debitmeters, microphones, loudspeakers, readers and RFID tags, etc.), kitchen appliances (cooker, dishwasher, etc.), apartment furniture (table, chairs, cabinets, bed, etc.) and communication objects (wireless screens, touch screens, PDA, cell phones, etc.). The server room, walls and ceiling of the apartment have been designed to facilitate re-organization and reconfiguration of sensors and effectors. Secondly, cognitive assistance systems, remote and medical monitoring systems have been used. During its implementation and use, it is clearly apparent that a large amount of information can be gathered in real environments, and that several sensors are already commercially available are reasonable costs, the other should be in place soon, so that a heterogeneous communication infrastructure is available, and information gathered from the sensors can be relayed by several types of complementary networks. In short, an infrastructure of flexible and addressable effectors should arrive soon on the market to be deployable at reasonable costs in conventional habitats.

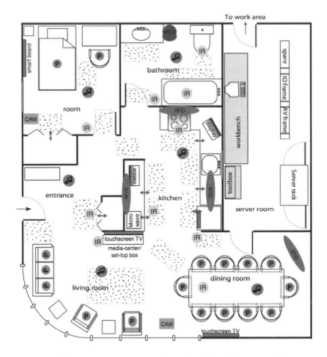

Figure 11.1. *The intelligent apartment at the DOMUS Laboratory. The apartment has, in particular, movement detectors (IR), electromagnetic contacts, tactile carpets and pressure captors (P), a camera (CAM), microphones and loudspeakers (♫), and RFID antennae (RFID)*

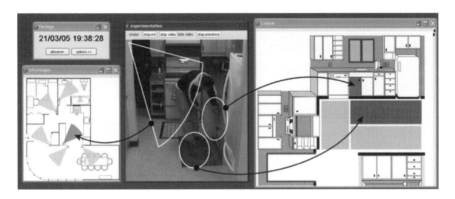

Figure 11.2. *Transforming the home into an intelligent habitat to provide intelligent care. As the photo shows, there is nothing special in the DOMUS apartment, which resembles any other. But discrete sensors can obtain a lot of information that reflects a person's actions: turning on a faucet, opening a door, etc.*

11.8. Research activities

This section presents past and current research activities in the DOMUS laboratory. It shows the richness and the complexity of the problems raised and how ambient intelligence, mobile computing and tangible user interfaces can help to solve these problems. These research activities are at the following levels:

– application:

- cognitive and remote monitoring orthoses (section 11.8.1),

- cognitive assistance in the home assistance (section 11.8.2) and outside (section 11.8.3),

- telemonitoring and organization of work between caregivers (section 11.8.4),

- the AMELIS interactive calendar: a portal towards an intelligent habitat (section 11.8.5),

- medical monitoring: gathering of ecological and psychological data (section 11.8.10),

- accompanying social networking (section 11.8.6),

- risk detection (section 11.8.7);

– artificial intelligence:

- ambient intelligence: ubiquity, activity recognition, and context awareness (section 11.8.8),

- advanced user interfaces (section 11.8.9),

- cognitive modeling and personalization (section 11.8.11);

– infrastructure and middleware:

- heterogeneous networks, distributed systems, and use in real life (section 11.8.12),

- identification, localization, simulation, and artificial intelligence (section 11.8.13),

- private life, security, and reliability (section 11.8.14);

– interdisciplinarity;

– design and ergonomics (section 11.8.15);

– research into health, usability studies, clinical research (section 11.8.16).

For each area of research identified, this section also talks about avenues of research that will be pursued in the next few years at DOMUS.

11.8.1. *Cognitive ortheses and remote monitoring*

Cognitive ortheses are apparatus and software that help people to compensate for their cognitive deficits, for example by reminding them of the task that have to be done [PIG 08]. Telemonitoring ensures the supervision at a distance of individuals suffering from cognitive deficits. To this end, a portable agenda has been developed to assist people in their daily life activities [GIR 08b]. Thanks to research into pervasive computing, mobile computing and ambient intelligence, this agenda is permanently available, both within the intelligent apartment as well as outside. As a cognitive assistance tool, the system helps the individual to manage their time and to prepare for appointments for example. As a telemonitoring system, the system helps professional caregivers to assure themselves from a distance that the user has really fulfilled certain tasks that were determined beforehand. Usability studies of this system were carried out for people with schizophrenia and adults with acquired cognitive disabilities [GIR 08].

11.8.2. *Cognitive assistance in the home*

A cognitive assistance system has been developed to assist the individual concerned in carrying out daily tasks at home [PIG 08b]. The home that has been transformed into an intelligent home can then compensate for deficits in memory, initiative, planning and attention. Control is shared between the resident and the cognitive assistant who can each set off interactions. Information is also transmitted to caregivers when it is pertinent, for example, to keep them informed on days when the patient appears more disoriented and thus allowing them to focus their efforts on patients who need their help most, or when it is necessary, for example, because they have to intervene with a patient who has not taken their medication. Caregivers can thus, always, ensure supervision as a complement to the assistance system, and if necessary, communicate with the individual, for example by a videoconference. A specialized version of this system has also been developed for assistance in meal preparation [BAU 09]. A usability and effectiveness study of this specialized version has been carried out with people who suffer from mental disabilities [BAU 09, LUS 07]. A simplified version of this system has been developed and validated with an individual who has semantic memory problems [BIE 11, GRO 10].

The next steps will consist of integrating into these systems the results of other research carried out at DOMUS to improve them and make them more intelligent: cognitive modeling to better understand and better intervene, generating erroneous plans according to diagnostic deficits and activity recognition to better anticipate errors and problematic situations, supervision, and assistance of several activities at the same time, assistances in multi-person contexts, choice and integration of more sophisticated and discrete sensors[2], definition of assistance strategies and dynamic changing of these strategies according to the evolution of the individual's cognitive profile over short or long periods of time.

11.8.3. *Cognitive assistance outside the home*

A cognitive assistance system that uses intelligent telephones and GPS has been developed [PIG 07]. Among other things, this system enables people to find their way lost, manage their bus journeys, and arrive at meetings on time. Contextual information (person, activity, time, place) is also used to give appropriate and personalized help. A usability study has been carried out in real life for people with cranial traumas [GIR 08].

Research has been carried out in collaboration with Ericsson and Rogers for the development and testing of a package of continuous and mobile remote and medical monitoring services, as well as assistances in milieu, some of which are confined to people suffering from cognitive disorders (schizophrenia, cranial trauma, Alzheimer's, etc.) and to professional and familial caregivers. These services are organized around the cell phone. They are tilted according to the infrastructure of the communication available. The currently available communication networks, as well as emerging communication networks are explored. Thus, the intelligence of services will derive from their capacity to adapt to the context. In fact, to be intelligent, these health services will take into account the context of their use, in particular the place (inside/outside, public/private), the user (patients/caregivers), the network (reliable, intermittent, costs, bandwidth, security etc.), the user apparatus (bracelet, PDA etc.), the available sources of information (sensor types (fixed, mobile, biometric), reliability, precision etc.), the possibilities of interaction with the user (screens, sounds, videos, etc.), telecommunication services (voice, SMS, MMS, IMS, etc.), the characteristics of the healthcare service offered (monitoring, remote monitoring, assistance, immediate action required, long-term analysis, etc.).

---

2 For example, in the context of a contract with France Telecom, we have studied the use and the reliability of a sensor capable of identifying openings and closure of electrical apparatus to be used for cognitive assistance when patients are placed in a context of cognitive surcharge. We are also trying to determine what complementary sensors would be necessary, the objective being of course to study and maintain as few sensors as possible.

11.8.4. *Remote monitoring and organization of work between caregivers*

Encouraging people with cognitive disorders to stay at home also supposes assisting formal and informal caregivers. Cognitive ortheses developed at the DOMUS laboratory allow the network of caregivers on the one hand to know if the individual needs assistance and to enable collaboration between caregivers. In particular, the laboratory carries out research to facilitate information sharing within the interdisciplinary team, whose different members cannot be present at the same location at the same time [CHA 06, CHA 09, CHA 09b]. In fact, preliminary research at the laboratory has shown the importance of understanding what a medical team that moves into the home is, in particular because its members rarely have the opportunity to meet. The home then becomes the location where convergence and filing of information about the person who has cognitive deficits takes place. The smart home can become an important source of information that has to be regulated, to give access to the resident and the caregiver and to avoid that not authorized people could read private information.

11.8.5. *The interactive AMELIS calendar: portal to an intelligent habitat*

For many years, pervasive computing has given rise to much hope and research to make our daily lives easier, but it is now coming up against a home environment whose habits are anchored in the use of familiar objects. Extending communicative capacities supposes rigorous research into the interactions the individual develops with them. More specifically, people who have cognitive deficits would benefit from objects whose aspects and/or functionalities change according to the context of use, for example the time of day or the way in which it is used. In particular, people whose declarative memory is disturbed conserve procedural memory longer, and therefore, the capacity to carry out activities thanks to the symbolism of the objects which surrounds them. They could be the first beneficiaries of a ubiquitous environment where assistance would come from common communicative objects, when they are no longer able to organize their daily life. For that reason, we propose to make a very common object smart -- the wall calendar [DES 09].

This research activity consists of designing AMELIS, an interactive calendar, to facilitate temporal orientation and break the isolation felt by people with cognitive deficits. An intelligent environment portal, AMELIS will assist the individual through visual and sound-based multimodal interactions. The individual will also have available telepresence functions with their families. The AMELIS approach is intrinsically interdisciplinary: a design to respect the familiarity of the object, neuropsychology to promote residual capacities of people with cognitive deficits, and computing to design the intelligent environment, the portal, and the telepresence.

11.8.6. *Accompanied social networking*

In several cases, people suffering from cognitive deficits cannot be independent in their own homes, because they place themselves in high-risk situations by poorly evaluating potential dangers, by behaving inappropriately in public or even feeling attracted to activities that are more or less socially acceptable. Thus, DOMUS is currently developing services adapted to behavioral difficulties. For example, the advanced communication system focuses the attention of the resident toward attractive activities, but not dangerous ones.

It is in this spirit that services have already been developed to stimulate the social relationships of people with cognitive deficits, to encourage the creation of social links, increase the amount of their interpersonal communications, and increase the amount of activities outside the home; in short, to help them manage their social network [MAR 09]. In the years to come, this base will be extended toward the creation of the micro (restricted, for example, to life in the housing structure) and macro (opening out further, but still under supervision) social network systems.

11.8.7. *Risk detection*

Risk detection is a very important area when the desire is to enable people to stay at home [BOU 09, CLE 99, GIB 04, GIL 04, GIL 07, HAR 95, HIL 02, LET 98, POU 06, SOR 06]. Research is concerned on immediate risk detection linked to cognitive deficits (for example, a lit stove, a lit cigarette, bath overflowing etc.) and accident detection (for example, physiological parameters, medical monitoring, falls, water damage). This research examines risk prevention and the way in which this can be overcome by the individual if it happens [LUS 07b].

Risks inside the home are categorized to establish the risks that exist and the danger perceived by the individual, the formal and unformal caregivers. These risks are classified in terms of importance according to how serious they are, how often they occur, and how dangerous they are perceived to be. DOMUS works specifically on an intelligent habitat that is sensitive to the context of a risk of fire via an intelligent stove which informs how well it is working and which can extinguish itself in case of emergency [DEC 11]. The first development at the laboratory has allowed a prototype which detects stove overheating to be developed. Sensors will be added to it to more precisely detect the elements involved, as well as fumes which are released from it. A fusion algorithm will allow the device's reliability to be increased. Finally, the prototype will be installed in a built-in system. Within five years, the assistance technology will cover all risks in the home, thus enabling people to stay in their homes in total safety.

11.8.8. *Ambient intelligence: ubiquity, activity recognition and context awareness*

Ambient intelligence implements four basic elements: ubiquity, context awareness, natural interaction, and artificial intelligence. To ensure the omnipresence of systems, the sensors and effectors have to be linked, with the help of heterogeneous networks. At DOMUS, we have been convinced, among other things, by our interactions with clinicians and studies of needs [PIG 05] that it is not necessary to know everything to be able to help and interact in a relevant way. Research seeks to determine what appropriate sensors in a given configuration are required in such a way as to not overequip the home. This objective is pursued, for example, through the study of the mechanisms that monitor activity and assistance to individuals with disabilities with the help of sensors linked to electrical consumption. We also explore the whole range of possible sensors, however, giving priority to sensors that are already commercially available at a low cost. Ontologies [ABD 10a, CHI 09] are also put in place to represent intelligent habitats and allow sophisticated reasoning of the context [ABD 10b].

To help individuals, it is essential to recognize certain activities [ROY 11]. Many activity-recognition systems, from the most simple [PAC 94] to the most complex [BOU 07, KAD 10, ROY 09] are developed with this end in mind. For example, these allow erroneous plans to be generated according to the types of cognitive deficit a person has. They also allow possible plans to be classified according to their probability.

Finally, it is also necessary to precisely know the context (medical profile, aim, place, time, objects available in the habitat) [ROY 08] according to the individuals present in an apartment [CAS 10]. Other research also explores if it is possible to obtain ambient intelligence without explicit representation of the context, for example, using the design adapted from the objects [GIR 09] or to obtain ambient intelligence with a local and minimal knowledge of the context [ABD 10b].

11.8.9. *Advanced user interfaces*

To interact with the user, the laboratory explores the use of traditional interfaces (screen, mouse and keyboard), but also communicating objects and tangible interfaces. The laboratory ensures first of all that the interfaces respond to the needs and expectations of the individuals they are aimed at [PIG 05]. The research about tangible interfaces [BOU 07b] will allow better-integrated and better-adapted assistance in the habitat to transform it into a real cognitive orthesis. Thus, the objects of daily life will offer new interactions adapted to individuals [VER 05]. The senses required will be sight, hearing, touch and smell. Already the various remediation modalities have been proposed according to the type of disorder:

initiation, attention, memory or planning. [BAU 06]. Automatic generation of user interfaces is also explored [GIR 03].

Having a interaction with a computer can become insurmountable at home, all the more for people with cognitive difficulties. The interfaces we offer are very simplified to offer easy access in the home as well as on mobile devices [BOI 09, IMB 10, PAC 07]. All the combinations are explored at DOMUS. In SemAssist, the user ineracts with a tactile screen [GRO 10]. In ARCHIPEL, the emphasis has been placed on assistance information available in the environment and not only on a screen [BAU 09]. We will further pursue research into tangible interfaces that the resident will be able to manipulate to obtain assistance, by exploring in particular the relationships which can exist between the object, space and functionalities.

Finally, on the one hand, we are studying the use of different mobile devices with distinct formats and characteristics to determine the usability of the interfaces, given the size of the screen and available interaction modalities. On the other hand, we are studying the complementary and collaborative use of several devices to determine if we can create a continuity vector that integrates unique characteristics, for example a wristwatch and a cell phone.

11.8.10. *Medical monitoring: gathering ecological data and physiological data*

To evaluate the evolution of the state of health of individuals and carry out medical monitoring, data has to be gathered and analyzed over a long period in order, for example, to detect trends, to identify low actimetry levels, to identify and recognize changes in behavioral patterns, for example disorganization of daily life. It is also necessary to be able to modulate these conclusions according to the context. For example, it is obviously normal in winter that the actimetry level goes down to a certain extent. This data on daily living can be gathered from sleep sensors, mobile sensors, for example a GPS, or worn sensors.

In several cases, medication can have important side effects (drowsiness, anxiety etc.). Therefore, it is necessary to be able to finely adjust the dosage but the information supplied by the individual during medical visits can be questionable. It then becomes essential to gather information on the physiological state during their life over a prolonged period (week, month), for example to evaluate the level of anxiety, drowsiness etc. The MOBUS orthesis contains a monitoring system, which allows subjective ecological information to be gathered [GIR 04]. This symptom information is entered by the individual himself onto the cell phone. Such data allow, among other things, for patients' medication to be adjusted. We are also developing tools to supply intelligible information and analysis to the resident and medical team about the data gathered. We have observed that such information allows the individual with cognitive deficits and their occupational therapist to document the previous week or month, for example "well done, this week you arrived on time to 85% of your meetings, but on the other hand you need to keep to your medication routine more".

We are currently working on developing methods to determine if a new learned routine (preparing a given recipe) can be integrated into daily life and to measure how fast learning and integration occur.

The following step consists of gathering physiological data (pulse, sweating etc.), combining this with subjective ecological data to, for example, determine the psychological state of a person with cognitive disorders. This type of inference could also be used in the short term to modulate the cognitive assistance offered. For example, when the individual's anxiety level rises because he does not understand the indications, we can give more detailed indications or suggest taking a break. In this context, we wish to develop and integrate, with our partners, physiological sensors on supports that are easily transportable by the individual.

11.8.11. *Cognitive modeling and personalization*

Several research works have centered around the personalization of assistance based on cognitive disorders and behaviors diagnosed by the environment. To do this, sophisticated models must be built to represent the cognition, the state of health and even the habitat. Fundamental studies on cognitive disorders specific to each clientele, computer cognitive models that refine assistance according to the disorders detected, models and classifications of errors will allow specifying appropriate assistance according to the disorders detected [DIO 07, SER 07]. Ontologies have been developed to characterize and reason on the habitat [ABD 10a, CHI 09].

Past and ongoing research explores how to use the disability creation process (DCP[3]) [FOU 98] or the measuring system of functional autonomy (SMAF[4])

---

3 DCP is a "model that explains the causes and consequences of diseases, trauma and other attacks on the integrity or development of the individual" [FOU 98].

4 SMAF is an "instrument to evaluate the independence developed from the functional design of the health and the international classification of disabilities, incapacities, and handicaps of the World Health Organziation. It evaluates 29 functions covering activities of daily life (ADL), mbility, communications, mental functions and activities of domestic life (AODL). For each of these items, an evaluation of the resources in place to compensate for incapacity allows us to rank the handicap" [HÉB 03].

[HÉB 01] to identify, select and install automatic assistance services according to the results obtained via these evaluation methods [CHA 06].

11.8.12. *Heterogeneous networks, distributed systems and use in real life*

The establishment of pervasive information systems raises a number of issues related to research, both on the level of networking the services, facilitating their collaboration, as well as their deployment. Firstly, the multiple intelligent components dispersed in the apartment must communicate among themselves through heterogeneous modes, for example, Ethernet, WiFi, Bluetooth, Zigbee, power line carriers (e.g. X10), GPRS, 3G, etc. Then, services must be able to be discovered dynamically to be able to collaborate among themselves. Finally, the resident should not call a technician every time a device does not work or when the devices enter or leave the habitat. This is why DOMUS is carrying out research on:

– the integration and continuity of service through hetereogeneous networks [BER 06];

– middleware and autonomous computing to create systems capable of autoconfiguration, of auto-optimization, auto-recovery, and autoprotection [GOU 08];

– spontaneous networking, peer-to-peer networks (P2P) [GON 08], multi-agent systems, and OSGI [ALV 09, OSG 11] to allow deployment and composition of services by many suppliers that share the same infrastructure [GOU 07];

– the quality of service and the use of public networks for medical applications.

On the whole, research activities at the level of infrastructures and middleware in the home and on the move can be articulated in three aspects. The first aspect consists of determining what can be done with current telecommunications infrastructures (Ethernet, WiFi, GPRS, 3G, etc.), the current fixed sensors and effectors (movement detectors, tactile screens, lighting systems, etc.), and current mobile devices (GPS, cell phones, wrist-watch etc.) The second aspect consists of determining what can be done with emerging telecommunications infrastructures (IMS, Zigbee etc.), emerging sensors and effectors (RFID, OLED on flexible support, UWB localization, sifteo, etc.), and emerging mobile devices (medical sensors permanently worn, wearable computing, body area networks etc.). The third aspect consists of studying how to provide healthcare services no matter which devices and networks are available. On the one hand, it is about taking into account more specifically the material context and the context of telecommunications (devices available in the environment, quality of service, the debit of available networks etc.), on the other hand it is a question of ensuring continuity of service (among the different versions of the same service that are available the most appropriate one will be selected according to the context), and finally enabling cooperation between several fixed and mobile devices to give the same health services.

More concretely, it is a question of:

– identifying relevant health services based on the needs expressed by users, i.e. the clientele affected by cognitive disorders, professional caregivers and familial caregivers;

– implementing various versions of these health services according to the telecommunications infrastructures and devices available in the user's environment;

– creating an integrated platform capable of delivering these services according to the human, environmental, and material contexts. This platform will allow, among the services available, those which are relevant to the user to be chosen, then the correct version of these services according to the context to be used;

– experimenting in real life with these services and the platform to validate and refine the different prototypes of the implemented health services;

– obtaining concrete measures on the costs of installation, deployment, and maintenance of the devices and service from the commercialization point of view.

Moreover, deployment, management and maintenance in an alternative residence for TCC, in Sherbrooke, of our assistance services will allow data and information to be gathered on the procedures to be put in place, and required costs and movements.

11.8.13. *Identification, localization, simulation and artificial intelligence*

As well as distributed techniques of artificial intelligence, ambient intelligence relies on identifying and locating people and objects. In fact it is important to know their position to, for example, analyze the behavior of an individual or to choose the communicating object that is most appropriate to interact with others. Trajectory recognition models have been developed for one [RAH 08] or several people [CAS 10]. These models will benefit from the infrastructure of the alternative residence to improve precision and validate the analysis of moves in real life. A platform that integrates localization solutions has been developed [CHA 10] and different identification and location systems have been tested at the DOMUS laboratory: *ultra-wide band*, RFID, etc. Moreover, to allow cognitive ortheses to be personalized according to a user's way of life, it is necessary to use automatic learning techniques in artificial intelligence. To make this learning easier, the DOMUS laboratory has developed a daily life activities simulator that can manage multiple data on the life habits of the occupants of a habitat [BUS 06].

11.8.14. *Private life, security and reliability*

Protecting a user's private life, security of information and of systems, and reliability and tolerance to faults are difficult and complex challenges that urgently need to be addressed to allow people with cognitive deficits to evolve in intelligent habitats. These challenges concern technical aspects as much as they do ethics and law. From its beginnings, ethical questions have been taken into account at DOMUS, for example when establishing collaboration with ethicists like Vincent Rialle and philosophers like Philippe Gagnon, by making projects get approval from the ethics committees concerned, by discussing legal aspects with law professors, etc. The technological alter ego of these aspects is also explored. In fact, one of the research aspects at DOMUS aims at constructing a catalog of approved customers to ensure the reliability and security of ubiquitous services, specifically in the context of intelligent home for people with cognitive deficits [BUS 09, BUS 10].

11.8.15. *Design and ergonomics*

Research in design and ergonomics has also been carried out in collaboration with the *Ecole de design industriel* of the University of Montreal and the UFR of psychology, clinical and social practices of the University of Paris 8, whether it is for carrying out user interfaces, common life objects or communication objects [GIR 09]. Since 2005, the DOMUS laboratory has been involved in supervising the projects of industrial design at the University of Montreal. This collaboration has offered a field of investigation on the objects in order that intelligent habitats are designed for intuitive uses and adapted for people with cognitive deficits [LEB 08].

11.8.16. *Clinical studies, usability studies*

To identify needs and validate the prototypes produced, meetings and studies have involved diverse clienteles with cognitive deficits and professional and familial caregivers and have been carried out regularly in Quebec and France.

On the one hand, a study of the needs [PIG 05] of TCC, older people, and professional and familial caregivers in Quebec and in France has been vital and has allowed the big aspects of research at DOMUS to be traced: clientele, types of service, staying at home.

Usability study and clinical studies	Clienteles					Place		Services		
	Older people, people with dementia, Alzheimer's	Schizophrenia	Cranial traumas	Intellectual retardation	Other sources of cognitive deficits	Residence	Mobility	Cognitive assistance	Remote monitoring	Medical monitoring
Usability study of the use of an electronic agenda for people with schizophrenia (section 11.8.16.1)		X					X	X	X	
Usability study of cognitive assistance systems and medical monitoring for adults with cognitive deficits (section 11.8.16.2)			X		X		X	X	X	X
Study on the impact of a cognitive assistance for meal preparation inside a smart habitat (section 11.8.16.3)				X	X	X		X		
Usability study of the use of an electronic agenda by people with schizophrenia (section 11. 8.16.4)		X					X	X	X	X
Randomized study into the use of an electronic agenda by people with schizophrenia (section 11. 8.16.5)		X					X	X	X	X
Multi-device usability study into cognitive assistance systems, medical monitoring for adults with cognitive deficits (section 11. 8.16.6)	X						X	X	X	X
Usability and relevance study of a cognitive assistance system and of medical monitoring for people with semantic memory deficits (section 11.8.16.7)					X	X		X		
Usability and relevance study of mobile cognitive assistance services, of remote monitoring and of medical monitoring for people with cognitive deficits (section 11.8.16.8)			X				X	X	X	X
Usability study and the relevance of AP@LZ (section 11.8.16.9)	X						X	X		
Usability study and the relevance of AMELIS (section 11.8.16.10)	X					X		X		
Study on the minimum configuration of evolved sensors for assistance of people placed in a situation of cognitive overload (section 11.8.16.11)	X					X		X		

Table 11.3. *Summary of usability studies and clinical studies carried out in fragile people or people with cognitive deficits*

On the other hand, usability studies and clinical studies in real life have been conducted in Quebec and France. The process of leading these studies is long. Firstly, it is necessary to prepare a detailed dossier describing the study, and then get it approved by the ethics committee(s) concerned. This is followed by recruitment of the people involved, the signing of consent forms, generally followed by a period of training for use of the prototype. Experimentation can then begin. During this period, meetings take place regularly with users. At the end of the study, an evaluation questionnaire is often filled out by the participants. The study ends with data collection and analysis. When video recording has been done, this step can also be quite long. Table 11.3 gives a brief description of the studies carried out. The following sections detail each of these studies.

11.8.16.1. *Usability study of the use of an electronic agenda by people with schizophrenia*

This usability study [SAB 07] firstly aims to evaluate the impact of using a wireless mobile organizer-type cognitive ortheses or PDA (Personal Digit Assistant) on the daily functioning of patients with schizophrenia in the course of rehabilitation. The mobile organizer functionalities evaluated were the ADL reminders and the remote supervision and communication by the caregiver. Then, the second objective of this study was to verify that the user interface of the PDA is easy to use for people with cognitive deficits. At that point, the study ensures that the services were functional and useful for the patients and their caregivers. Three patients with schizophrenia, according to the DSM-IV criteria, and their caregivers (occupational therapists and social workers) participated in this study. In one case, a person close to one of the patients was also enrolled. The study was carried out in 2006 in collaboration with the L.H. Lafontaine hospital and the Fernand-Séguin research center in Montréal. These experiments took place in the patients' homes (parent's or group spaces) and in the young adult clinic at the hospital.

11.8.16.2. *Usability study of the cognitive assistance systems, medical monitoring for adults with cognitive deficits*

The familial caregivers (cranial trauma, cerebro-vascular accidents, spina bifida) worry that people with cognitive deficits will forget to carry out basic activities or will become lost. The mobile assistant, Mobus, contains a simplified agenda and helps with journeys undertaken outside. These services are available on a cellphone. Contextual information, photos or text, are displayed when an individual goes to a place, to remind the person of the way to get there and the instructions that should be observed. The caregiver can manage the agenda by registering the activities and monitoring which have been carried out. The individual can communicate with the caregiver at all times thanks to an assistance button. He can also indicate specific symptoms. This serves for a better medical monitoring where data are registered when the symptom occurs, allowing the doctor to have access to more reliable data.

The study was carried out in 2006–2007 with five adults with cognitive disorders and of diverse origins, in collaboration with therapists from the CRE [MOR 06, PAC 07]. It took place at the CRE, at the individuals' home and near to the CRE.

11.8.16.3. *Study on the impact of a cognitive assistance in meal preparation inside a smart home*

Memory and planning deficits can significantly impair the cooking activities of people with intellectual retardation. The ARCHIPEL assistant, developed at DOMUS, automatically monitors the different steps of a recipe and indicates to the user the missing ingredients, where they are, the next step, etc. The aim of this study is to evaluate how people with an intellectual retardation interact with a technological assistant and whether this assistant makes them more independent in carrying out complex activities. The study was carried out with 12 adults with intellectual retardation in collaboration with therapists from the Notre Dame de l'enfant Center in Sherbrooke [BAU 09, LUS 07]. This experiment took place in the DOMUS apartment.

11.8.16.4. *Usability study of the use of an electronic agenda for people with schizophrenia*

The above usability study [SAB 07] has been repeated with a clientele with scizophrenia, living in France. Following the improvements made in the first study, the MOBUS cognitive orthesis has been modified, particularly to offer better connections thanks to usage of a cellphone. The objective remained the same. The study was carried out during Summer 2007 in collaboration with the Fernand Séguin research center and the Le Vinatier psychiatric hospital in Bron, France. It is a day hospital with a part-time therapeutic activity center. Five patients with schizophrenia who live at home participated in this study [SAB 09, SAB 10]. This experiment took place at the Le Vinatier hospital and at the subjects' homes.

11.8.16.5. *Randomized study of the use of an electronic agenda by people with schizophrenia*

This randomized study took place in January 2009. Seventy patients were divided randomly into two groups of 35 schizophrenics. The patients of one of the groups used MOBUS; the patients of the other group had mass consumer applications on their PDA. This study allowed health services developed in the MOBUS framework to be validated over a long time-period [SAB 10b].

11.8.16.6. *Multi-device usability study of cognitive assistance systems, medical monitoring for adults with cognitive deficits*

This usability study [BOI 09b] is aimed to recommend the most appropriate device among various mobile devices. The devices format is a device worn on the wrist in the style of a watch versus a cell phone. The collaborative use of several devices has also been studied. The MOBUS interfaces and services have been redesigned and adapted. New services have been developed. Among the questions explored are the following:

– Are the health services used in the experiments relevant?

– Can a continuity vector be created that integrates the unique characteristics of the Urgentys bracelet from Medical Intelligence and the PDA, so that one completes the other?

– How usable are the interfaces, given the screen size and the available interaction modalities?

11.8.16.7. *Study of usability and relevance of a cognitive assistance system and medical monitoring of people with semantic memory deficits*

This study proposes to evaluate the usability and relevance of SemAssist [BIE 11, GRO 10], a system that helps prepare meals and also gathers ecological data to allow researchers to analyze the use. The user essentially has a touch screen placed in the kitchen. SEMASSIST has semantic information on the objects involved in the recipe. Thanks to this screen, the user can follow a recipe and consult all semantic information linked to the recipe, from the list of utensils to the preparation steps.

11.8.16.8. *Study of usability and relevance of cognitive mobile assistance services, remote and medical monitoring for people with cognitive deficits*

In one of our research projects, we have developed a platform capable of selecting and deploying health services according to human, environmental, and material contexts. This study has been carried out in the context of participatory design, where the subjects are part of the process to diagnose needs and bring out solutions [GRO 10b].

The objectives are:

– to continuously supply medical and remote monitoring services, as well as cognitive assistance services that are adapted to human, environmental, and material contexts;

– design services that allow dependant individuals to increase their independence in their daily lives;

– evaluate the impact of these different services on the people suffering from cognitive disorders, as well as on their caregivers.

11.8.16.9. *Study of usability and relevance of AP@LZ*

A study has been carried out to evaluate AP@LZ [IMB 10], an electronic organizer available on a cell phone and made up of specific services for people with Alzheimer's. Ap@LZ is a version of MOBUS that is adapted to people with Alzheimer's, where in particular the short-term memory is rarely called-on and the individual has the opportunity to register their appointments themselves. The study consists first of testing if people with Alzheimer's are capable of learning how to use a simplified electronic organizer. Second, the study evaluates how the patients are capable of using it in their daily lives.

11.8.16.10. *Study of usability and relevance of AMELIS*

A study was conducted to evaluate AMELIS [DES 09], an interactive wall calendar that helps users to organize their daily lives by displaying appointments and important tasks interactively, and which makes person-to-person contact easier thanks to reminding users of past events that are accessible on the calendar. It is specifically designed for people with Alzheimer's. However, as it integrates perfectly into the home, it can suit anybody wishing to easily access information linked to the wall calendar.

11.8.16.11. *Study on the minimum configuration of sensors evolved for assistance to people placed in a situation of cognitive overload*

In a real-life situation, this study aims to evaluate the relevance and reliability of sophisticated and non-intrusive sensors for cognitive assistance. Four older people, with or without Alzheimer's, participated in the study which took place in the DOMUS apartment.

11.9. Conclusion

Nowdays, microprocessors are more present and invade everyday objects. Easily accessible networks, which are often wireless, interconnect smart objects. Thus, the explosive evolution of technology, combined with the lowering of material costs, has given the green light to the development of applications that have been inconceivable until recently. Many objects of daily life will allow innovative and new interactions. Our clothes will transport our profile to reconfigure our physical environment according to our preferences. Lamps will help us to find lost objects. Interactive portraits will reflect the health of our loved ones remotely. It becomes imperative to rethink the field of computer science and to rethink our habitats. Computing has become pervasive and is no longer just associated with the traditional computer. In our habitats, some objects will become meaningless and will be converted into museum pieces. But nobody can predict which ones!

To enable people with cognitive deficits to stay at home, the DOMUS laboratory has put in place an innovative infrastructure and an interdisciplinary team to develop numerous prototypes and innovative services. Among them, let us mention:

– a meal preparation assistant [BAU 09];

– activity recognition systems [BOU 07, ROY 09], using tangible interfaces [BOU 07b];

– an interactive calendar [DES 09];

– reminder services and those that monitor activities [MOR 06];

– services that gather medical data in the natural environment [GRO 10, SAB 10];

– navigation assistance services in the city [GIR 04];

– services for asynchronous collaborative work with caregivers [CHA 09];

– assistance services for a social life [MAR 09], etc.

Most of these assistance services, remote monitoring and medical monitoring services have already been validated in real life, over shorter or longer durations with people who have cognitive disorders. We hope, in the years to come, to be able to apply these results in non-palliative contexts. Aiming for the most difficult clientele helps to understand better the needs and uses of smart habitats for the entire population.

In the long term, it is a matter of transforming our habitat (homes, public buildings, cities) for people with cognitive disabilities in the same way we have transformed them for people with physical disabilities. Fortunately, today, it is not surprising to see access ramps for wheelchairs and sound indicators at traffic lights for the visually impaired – hopefully it will be the same for cognitive prostheses!

11.10. Bibliography

[ABD 10a] ABDULRAZAK B., CHIKHAOUI B., GOUIN-VALLERAND C., FRAIKIN B., "A standard ontology for smart spaces", *International Journal of Web and Grid Services*, vol. 6, no. 3, 2010.

[ABD 10b] ABDULRAZAK B., ROY P., ABDULRAZAK B., GOUIN-VALLERAND C., BELALA Y., GIROUX S., "Macro and micro context-awareness for autonomic pervasive computing", *The 12th International Conference on Information Integration and Web-based Applications & Services*, Paris, November 2010.

[ALV 09] ALVES A.C., *OSGi Application Frameworks*, 1st ed., Manning Publications, Greenwich, CT, 2009.

[BAU 06] BAUCHET J., VERGNES D., GIROUX S., PIGOT H., SAVARY J.P., "A pervasive cognitive assistant for smart homes", *ICADI 2006, International Conference on Aging, Disability, and Independence*, St. Petersburg, FL, USA, 1–5 February 2006.

[BAU 09a] BAUCHET J., PIGOT H., GIROUX S., LUSSIER-DESROCHERS D., LACHAPELLE Y., MOKHTARI M., "Designing judicious interactions for cognitive assistance: the acts of assistance approach", *Proceedings of the 11th International ACM SIGACCESS Conference on Computers and Accessibility*, Pittsburgh, PA, USA, 25–28 October 2009.

[BAU 09b] BAUCHET J., GIROUX S., PIGOT H., LUSSIER-DESROCHERS D., LACHAPELLE Y., "Pervasive assistance in smart homes for people with intellectual disabilities: a case study on meal preparation", *International Journal of Assistive Robotics and Mechatronics*, vol. 9, no. 4, pp. 53–65, 2009.

[BER 06] BERGEVIN L., Middleware pour les transmissions de messages dans les systèmes et réseaux hétérogènes, mémoire pour l'obtention du grade de Magister Scientiæ, University of Sherbrooke, 2006.

[BIE 11] BIER N., MACOIR J., JOUBERT S., BOTTARI C., CHAYER C., PIGOT H., GIROUX S., SEMASSIST TEAM, "Cooking 'Shrimp à la Créole': A pilot study of an ecological rehabilitation in semantic dementia", *Neuropsychological Rehabilitation*, vol. 21, no. 4, pp. 455–83, 2011.

[BOG 06] BOGER J., HOEY J., POUPART P., BOUTILIER C., FERNIE G.R., MIHAILIDIS A., "A planning system based on markov decision processes to guide people with dementia through activities of daily living", *IEEE Transactions on Information Technology in BioMedicine*, vol. 10, pp. 323–333, 2006.

[BOI 09a] BOISVERT A.A., PAQUETTE L., PIGOT H., GIROUX S., "Design challenges for mobile assistive technologies applied to people with cognitive impairments", *ICOST*, pp. 17–24, Tours, France, 1–3 July 2009.

[BOI 09b] BOISVERT A.A., Conception et évaluation des interfaces d'appareils mobiles pour favoriser l'autonomie des personnes avec troubles cognitifs, mémoire pour l'obtention du grade Magister Scientiæ, University of Sherbrooke, 2009.

[BOU 07a] BOUCHARD B., BOUZOUANE A., GIROUX S., "A keyhole plan recognition model for Alzheimer's patients: first results", *Journal of Applied Artificial Intelligence (AAI)*, vol. 22, no. 7, pp. 623–658, 2007.

[BOU 09] BOURGEOIS J., OCHS J., COUTURIER P., TYRRELL J., "Safety at home of people with dementia: contributions of an evaluation of risk situations in a geriatric consultation clinic", *19 IAGG World Congress of Gerontology and Geriatrics*, Paris, 5–9 July 2009.

[BOU 07b] BOUSSEMART B., GIROUX S., "Tangible user interfaces for cognitive assistance", *First International Workshop on Smart Homes for Tele-Health*, Niagara Falls, Canada, 21–23 May 2007.

[BUS 06] BUSNEL P., GHOURAF A., PIGOT H., "Validation process of an activity of daily living simulator", *Summer Computer Simulation Conference, SCSC 06*, pp. 356–363, Calgary, Canada, 1–3 August 2006.

[BUS 09] Busnel P., ElKhoury P., Giroux S., Li K., "An XACML-based security pattern to achieve socio-technical confidentiality in smart homes", *International Journal of Smart Home*, (IJSH), vol. 3, no. 1, pp. 17–26, 2009.

[BUS 10] Busnel P., Giroux S., "Security, privacy, and dependability in smart homes: a pattern catalogue approach", *ICOST 2010, 8th International Conference on Smart Homes and Health Telematics*, Séoul, South Korea, 22–24 June 2010.

[CAR 05] Carmien S., "End user programming and context responsiveness in handheld prompting systems for persons with cognitive disabilities and caregivers", *CHI '05 Extended Abstracts on Human Factors in Computing Systems*, Portland, Oregon, USA, pp. 1252–1255, 2–7 April 2005.

[CAS 10] Castebrunet M., Boissier O., Giroux S., Rialle V., "Organization nesting in a multi-agent application for ambient intelligence", *PAAMS 2010, 8th International Conference on Practical Applications of Agents and Multi-Agent Systems*, vol. 70/2010, pp. 259–268, Salamanca, Spain, 26–28 April 2010.

[CHA 06] Chamberland-Tremblay D., Bauchet J., Pigot H., Giroux S., "La médiation par l'espace intelligent: collaboration et communautés de soins à l'intérieur du domicile", RIC 2006, Nîmes, France, 22–24 May 2006, in Penalva J.M. (ed.), *Intelligence collective – Rencontres*, Presses de l'Ecole des Mines de Paris, 2006.

[CHA 09a] Chamberland-Tremblay D., Giroux S., Caron C., Berthiaume M., "Space-mediated learning at the locus of action in a heterogeneous team of mobile workers", *Mobile, Hybrid, and On-line Learning, ELML '09, International Conference on Publication*, Cancun, Mexico, pp. 35–40, 1–7 February 2009.

[CHA 09b] Chamberland-Tremblay D., Giroux S., Caron C., "Coopérer par l'espace: La microgéomatique dans l'espace intelligent", *Revue internationale de géomatique*, vol. 19, no. 2, pp. 231–243, April–June 2009.

[CHA 10] Chakroun O., Abdulrazak B., Chiazzaro M., Frikha M., "Indoor and outdoor localization architecture for pervasive environment", *8th International Conference on Smart Homes and Health Telematics (ICOST)*, Seoul, South Korea, pp. 242–245, June 2010.

[CHI 09] Chikhaoui B., Benazzouz Y., Abdulrazak B., "Towards a Universal Ontology for smart environments", *11th International Conference on Information Integration and Web-Based Applications & Services*, Kuala Lumpur, Malaysia, December 2009.

[CLE 99] Clemson L., Fitzgerald M.H., Heard R., "Content validity of an assessment tool to identify home fall hazards: the westmead home safety assessment", *British Journal of Occupational Therapy*, vol. 62, no. 4, pp. 171, 1999.

[DEC 11] de Champs T., Ouenzar M., Abdulrazak B., Frappier M., Pigot H., Fraikin B., "Pervasive safety application with model checking in smart houses: the INOVUS intelligent oven", *2011 IEEE International Conference on Pervasive Computing and Communications Workshops (PERCOM Workshops)*, SmartE 2011: Smart Environments to Enhance Health Care, Seattle, USA, pp. 630–635, 21–25 March 2011.

[DES 09] DESCHENEAUX C., PIGOT H., "Interactive and intuitive memory aids for elderly people and people with mild cognitive impairments", *International Conference on Smart Homes and Health Telematics (ICOST)*, Tours, France, July 2009.

[DÉV 06] DÉVELOPPEMENT SOCIAL CANADA, "Aidants naturels – Document d'information", 2006, http://iugm.asp.visard.ca/GEIDEFile/aidants_naturels.HTM?Archive=102320292050 &File=Aidants+naturels_HTM.

[DIO 07] DION A., PIGOT H., "Modeling cognitive errors in the realization of an activity of the everyday life", *Cognitio2007*, Montréal, Canada, 15–17, June 2007.

[DIS 04] DISHMAN E., "Inventing wellness systems for aging in place", *Computer*, vol. 37, no. 5, pp. 34–41, 2004.

[ECI 09] EUROPEAN COMMISSION INFORMATION SOCIETY AND MEDIA, Unit F4 New Infrastructure Paradigms and Experimental Facilities. Living Labs for user-driven open innovation. An overview of the Living Labs methodology, activities and achievements, Office for Official Publications of the European Communities, Luxembourg, January 2009.

[FOU 98] FOUGEYROLLAS P., CLOUTIER R., BERGERON H., CÔTÉ J., ST-MICHEL G., "Classification québécoise Processus de production du handicap", *Réseau international sur le Processus de production du handicap (RIPPH)/SCCIDIH*, Québec, Canada, 1998.

[FRE 10] FREDMAN L., CAULEY J.A., HOCHBERG M., ENSRUD K.E., DOROS G., "Mortality associated with caregiving, general stress, and caregiving-related stress in elderly women: results of caregiver-study of osteoporotic fractures", *Journal of the American Geriatrics Society*, vol. 58, no. 5, pp. 937–943, May 2010.

[GIB 04] GIBB C., LUCE A., CLARKE C., KEADY J., WILKINSON H., "Risk management and dilemmas in dementia care", *The Gerontologist*, vol. 44, no. 1, p. 111, 2004.

[GIL 07] GILLESPIE L.D., GILLESPIE W.J., ROBERTSON M.C., LAMB S.E., CUMMING R.G., ROWE B.H., "Interventions for preventing falls in elderly people", *The Cochrane Library*, no. 4, 2007, review.

[GIL 04] GILMOUR H., "Living alone with dementia: risk and the professional role", *Nursing Older People*, vol. 16, no. 9, 2004.

[GIR 03] GIROUX S., CARBONI D., PADDEU G., PIRAS A., SANNA S., "Delivery of services on any device: from Java code to user interface", in STEPHANIDIS C., JACKO J. (eds), *10th International Conference on Human-Computer Interaction 2003*, Crete, Greece, 22–27 June 2003, *Human-Computer Interaction*, vol. 1–2, 2003.

[GIR 04] GIROUX S., PIGOT H., "Computing and outdoors mobile computing for assisted cognition and telemonitoring", *9th International Conference on Computers Helping People with Special Needs*, pp. 953–960, Paris, 7–9 July 2004.

[GIR 06a] GIROUX S., PIGOT H., MOREAU J., SAVARY J., "Distributed mobile services and interfaces for people suffering from cognitive deficits", *Handbook of Research on Mobile Multimedia*, pp. 544–554, 2006.

[GIR 06b] GIROUX S., PIGOT H., MOREAU J.F., SAVARY J.P., "Distributed mobile services and interfaces for people suffering from cognitive deficits", in IBRAHIM I.K. (ed.), *Handbook of Research on Mobile Multimedia*, pp. 544–554, Idea Group Publishing, Vienna, 2006.

[GIR 08] GIROUX S., PIGOT H., PACCOUD B., PACHE D., STIP E., SABLIER J., "Enhancing a mobile cognitive orthotic: a user-centered design approach", *International Journal of Assistive Robotics and Mechatronics*, vol. 9, no. 1, pp. 36–47, 2008.

[GIR 09] GIROUX S., LEBLANC T., BOUZOUANE A., BOUCHARD B., PIGOT H., BAUCHET J., "The praxis of cognitive assistance", in GOTTFRIED B., AGHAJAN H. (eds), *Behaviour Monitoring and Interpretation (BMI)*, vol. 3, Ambient Intelligence and Smart Environments (AISE) Series, IOS publication, Amsterdam, pp. 183–211, 2009.

[GON 08] GONTHIER F.D., Etude de la conception d'un simulateur de réseaux P2P pour l'informatique diffuse, mémoire pour l'obtention du grade Magister Scientiæ, University of Sherbrooke, 2008.

[GOR 03] GORMAN P., DAYLE R., HOOD C., RIMRELL L., "Effectiveness of the ISAAC cognitive prosthetic system for improving rehabilitation outcomes with neurofunctional impairment", *NeuroRehabilitation*, vol. 18, pp. 57–67, 2003.

[GOU 07] GOUIN-VALLERAND C., GIROUX S., "Managing and deployment of applications with OSGi in the context of Smart Homes", *3rd IEEE International Conference on Wireless and Mobile Computing, Networking and Communications (Wimob)*, New York, NY, USA, October 2007.

[GOU 08] GOUIN-VALLERAND C., GIROUX S., ABDULRAZAK B., MOHKTARI M., "Toward a self-configuration middleware for smart spaces", *3rd International Symposium on Smart Home, SH 2008, part of IEEE 2008, Future Generation Communication and Networking Conference FGCN '08*, vol. 2, Hainan Island, China, pp. 463–468, 13–15 December 2008.

[GRO 10a] GROUSSARD P.Y., BIER N., GIROUX S., PIGOT H., MACOIR J., MILHAU J., DESCHENEAUX C., ROY P., ARAB F., CHIKHAOUI B., MEDINI S., KAMMOUN M.F., PARAKH Y., "SemAssist: assistance and assessment tools for semantic memory rehabilitation", *Gerontechnology*, vol. 9, no. 2, pp. 106–107, 2010.

[GRO 10b] GROUSSARD P.Y., PIGOT H., GIROUX S., KARA N., "User needs identification for a smart cognitive assistant based on participatory design", *ANT 2010, The International Conference on Ambient Systems, Networks and Technologies*, Paris, 8–10 November 2010.

[HAR 95] HARPER R.D., DICKSON W.A., "Reducing the burn risk to elderly persons living in residential care", *Burns*, vol. 21, no. 3, pp. 205–208, 1995.

[HÉB 01] HÉBERT R., GUILBEAULT J., DERROSIERS J., DUBUC N., "The functional autonomy measurement system (SMAF®): a clinical-based instrument for measuring disabilities and handicaps in older people", *Journal of Canadian Geriatrics Society*, no. 4, pp. 141–147, 2001.

[HÉB 03] HÉBERT R., DERSOSIERS J., DUBUC N., TOUSIGNANT M., GUILBEAULT J., PINSONNAULT E., "Le système de mesure de l'autonomie fonctionnelle (SMAF®)", *Revue de gériatrie*, vol. 28, no. 4, pp. 323–336, 2003.

[HIL 02] HILL A.J., GERMA F., BOYLE J.C., "Burns in older people – outcomes and risk factors", *Journal of the American Geriatrics Society*, vol. 50, 2002.

[HON 03] HONEYCUTT A., GROSSE S.D., DUNLAP L.J., SCHENDEL D.E., CHEN H., BRANN E., AL HOMSI G., "Economic costs of mental retardation, cerebral palsy, hearing loss, and vision impairment", in ALTMAN B.M., BARNARTT S.N., HENDERSHOT G., LARSON S. (eds), *Using Survey Data to Study Disability: Results from the National Health Interview Survey on Disability*, pp. 207–228, Elsevier Science, London, 2003.

[IMB 10] IMBEAULT H., BIER N., PIGOT H., GAGNON L., MARCOTTE N., FULOP T., GIROUX S., "Development of a personalized electronic organizer for persons with Alzheimer's disease: the AP@lz", *Gerontechnology*, vol. 9, no. 2, pp. 293, 2010.

[KAD 10] KADOUCHE R., PIGOT H., ABDULRAZAK B., GIROUX S., "Support vector machines for inhabitant identification in smart houses", *Seventh International Conference on Ubiquitous Intelligence and Computing*, Xi'an, China, October 2010.

[KAT 63] KATZ S., FORD A.B., MOSKOWITZ R.W., JACKSON B.A., JAFFE M.W., "Studies of illness in the aged. The index of ADL: A standardized measure of biological and psychological function", *JAMA: The Journal of the American Medical Association*, vol. 185, pp. 914–919, 1963.

[LAB 98] LABERGE-NADEAU C., MESSIER S., HUOT I., "Guide des services offerts aux blessés de la route, au Québec", Laboratoire sur la sécurité des transports du Centre de recherche sur les transports, University of Montréal, December 1998.

[LAC 05] LACHAPELLE Y., WEHMEYER M.L., HAELEWYCK M.C., COURBOIS Y., KEITH K.D., SCHALOCK R., VERDUGO M.A., WALSH P.N., "The relationship between quality of life and self-determination: an international study", *Journal of Intellectual Disability Research*, vol. 49, pp. 740–744, 2005.

[LAW 69] LAWTON M.P., BRODY E.M., "Assessment of older people: self-maintaining and instrumental activities of daily living", *Gerontologist*, vol. 9, pp. 179–186, 1969.

[LEB 08] LEBLANC T., GIROUX S., TEUWEN M., "Knowledge-building environments", *Human-Computer Interaction (HCI) Educators*, Rome, Italy, 2–4 April 2008.

[LET 98] LETTS L., SCOTT S., BURTNEY J., MARSHALL L., MCKEAN M., "The reliability and validity of the safety assessment of function and the environment for rehabilitation (SAFER tool)", *British Journal of Occupational Therapy*, vol. 61, no. 3, pp. 127, 1998.

[LEV 04] LEVINSON R., "A custom-fitting cognitive orthotic that provides automatic planning and cueing assistance", *CSUN Technology and Persons with Disabilities Conference*, California State University, Northridge, USA, 2004.

[LOP 04] LOPRESTI E.F., MIHAILIDIS A., KIRSCH N., "Assistive technology for cognitive rehabilitation: state of the art", *Neuropsychological Rehabilitation*, vol. 14, no. 5, 2004.

[LUS 07a] LUSSIER-DESROCHERS D., LACHAPELLE Y., PIGOT H., BAUCHET J., "Apartments for people with intellectual disability: promoting innovative community living services", *2nd International Conference on Intellectual Disabilities/Mental Retardation*, Bangkok, Thailand, 6–8 November 2007.

[LUS 07b] LUSSIER-DESROCHERS D., PIGOT H., LACHAPELLE Y., "Des appartements intelligents pour promouvoir l'inclusion sociale et l'autodétermination des personnes présentant une déficience intellectuelle", *Revue québécoise de psychologie*, 2007.

[MAR 09] MARCOTTE N., GIROUX S., KARA N., "Mobile contextual assistance for social life", *Context-Aware Mobile Media and Mobile Social Networks Workshop in MobileHCI 2009 Conference*, Bonn, Germany, 15 September 2009.

[MOR 06] MOREAU J.F., PIGOT H., GIROUX S., SAVARY J.P., "Assistance to cognitively impaired people and distance monitoring by caregivers: a study on the use of personal digital assistants", *ICADI 2006, International Conference on Aging, Disability and Independence*, St. Petersburg, FL, USA, 1–5 February 2006.

[MSS 98] MINISTÈRE DE LA SANTÉ ET DES SERVICES SOCIAUX, Direction générale de la planification et de l'évaluation, Le virage ambulatoire en santé physique: Enjeux et perspectives, Coll. Etudes et analyses, Québec, 1998.

[MSS 09] MINISTÈRE DE LA SANTÉ ET DES SERVICES SOCIAUX, Relever le défi de la maladie d'Alzheimer et des maladies apparentées Une vision centrée sur la personne, l'humanisme et l'excellence, rapport du Comité d'experts en vue de l'élaboration d'un plan d'action pour la maladie d'Alzheimer, Government of Québec, May 2009.

[MUR 96] MURRAY C.J.L., LOPEZ A.D. (eds), *The Global Burden of Disease*, Harvard School of Public Health, Cambridge, 1996.

[NII 06] NIITAMO V.P., KULKKI S., ERIKSSON M., HRIBERNIK K.A., "State-of-the-art and good practice in the field of living labs", *Proceedings of the 12th International Conference on Concurrent Enterprising: Innovative Products and Services through Collaborative Networks*, pp. 349–357, Milan, Italy, 2006.

[OSG 11] OSGI ALLIANCE, OSGI Service PlatformCore Specification, Release 4, Version 4.3, OSGI Alliance, April 2011.

[PAC 94] PACHET F., GIROUX S., PAQUETTE G., "Pluggable advisors as Epiphyte systems", *CALISCE '94, International Conference on Computer Aided Learning and Instruction in Science and Engineering*, pp. 167–174, Paris, 31 August– 2 September 1994.

[PAC 07] PACCOUD B., PACHE D., PIGOT H.,GIROUX S., "Report on the impact of a user-centered approach and usability studies for designing mobile and context-aware cognitive orthosis", *ICOST*, Nara, Japan, 21–23 June 2007.

[PAT 02] PATTERSON D.J., ETZIONI O., FOX D., KAUTZ H., "Intelligent ubiquitous computing to support alzheimer's patients: enabling the cognitively disabled", *Ubicomp, Adjunct Proceedings*, Gothenburg, Sweden, pp. 21–22, 29 September – 1 October 2002.

[PIG 05] PIGOT H., SAVARY J.P., METZGER J.L., ROCHON A., BEAULIEU M., "Advanced technology guidelines to fulfill the needs of the cognitively impaired population", *3rd International Conference on Smart Homes and Health Telematics, ICOST 2005*, Sherbrooke, Canada, pp. 25–32, 4–6 July 2005.

[PIG 07] PIGOT H., PACHE D., PACCOUD B., GIROUX S., SAVARY J.P., STIP E., SABLIER J., "Agenda d'aide aux déplacements", *The 2nd International Conference on Technology and Aging (ICTA)*, Toronto, Canada, 16–19 June 2007.

[PIG 08a] PIGOT H., GIROUX S., BAUCHET J., "Assistive devices for people with cognitive impairments", in HELAL A., MOKHTARI M., ABDULRAZAK B. (eds), *The Engineering Handbook on Smart Technology for Aging, Disability and Independence*, Computer Engineering Series, John Wiley & Sons, Hoboken, 2008.

[PIG 08b] PIGOT H., LUSSIER-DESROCHERS D., BAUCHET J., GIROUX S., LACHAPELLE Y., "A smart home to assist recipe completion", in MIHAILIDIS A., BOGER J., KAUTZ H., NORMIE L. (eds), *Technology and Aging, Selected Papers from the 2007 International Conference on Technology and Aging*, vol. 21, Assistive Technology Research Series, January 2008.

[POL 05] POLLACK M.E., "Intelligent technology for an aging population: the use of AI to assist elders with cognitive impairment", *AI Magazine*, vol. 26, pp. 9–24, 2005.

[POU 06] POULIN DE COURVAL L., GÉLINAS I., GAUTHIER S., GAYTON D., LIU L., ROSSIGNOL M., SAMPALIS J., DASTOOR D., "Reliability and validity of the safety assessment scale for people with dementia living at home", *The Canadian Journal of Occupational Therapy*, vol. 73, no. 2, pp. 67, 2006.

[RAH 08] RAHAL Y., PIGOT H., MABILLEAU P., "Location estimation in a smart home, system implementation and evaluation using experimental data", *International Journal of Telemedicine and Applications*, pp. 1–9, 2008.

[REI 82] REISBERG B., "Signs, symptoms and course of age-associated cognitive decline", in CORKIN S., *et al.* (eds), *Aging: Alzheimer's Disease: a Report of Progress. Signs, Symptoms and Course of Age-Associated Cognitive Decline*, Raven Press, New York, pp. 177–182, 1982.

[ROY 08] ROY P., ABDULRAZAK B., BELALA Y., "Approaching context-awareness for open intelligent", *Sixth International Conference on Advances in Mobile Computing & Multimedia*, Linz, Austria, pp. 430–435, 24–26 November 2008.

[ROY 09] ROY P., BOUCHARD B., BOUZOUANE A., GIROUX S., "A hybrid plan recognition model for Alzheimer's patients: interleaved-erroneous dilemma", *Web Intelligence and Agent Systems (WIAS)*, vol. 7, no. 4, pp. 375–397, 2009.

[ROY 11] ROY P., BOUCHARD B., BOUZOUANE A., GIROUX S., "Challenging issues of ambient activity recognition for cognitive assistance", *Handbook of Research on Ambient Intelligence and Smart Environments: Trends and Perspectives*, IGI Global, pp. 320–345, 2011.

[SAB 07] SABLIER J., STIP E., FRANCK N., GIROUX S., PIGOT H., MOREAU J.F., PACCOUD B., "Etude de convivialité de l'utilisation d'un agenda électronique par des personnes souffrant de schizophrénie", *Santé Mentale au Québec*, vol. 32, no. 2, pp. 209–224, 2007.

[SAB 09] SABLIER J., STIP E., GIROUX S., PIGOT H., JACQUET P., FRANCK N., "MOBUS, un assistant cognitif pour la schizophrénie: limites et promesses", *77ᵉ Congrès de l'Acfas*, Ottawa, Canada, 11–15 May 2009.

[SAB 10a] SABLIER J., STIP E., FRANCK N., MOBUS GROUP, "Mobus project – randomised study of an assistive technology for improving cognition and autonomy of patients with Schizophrenia: exploring preliminary data", *Schizophrenia Research*, vol. 117, no. 2, pp. 512–513, 2010.

[SAB 10b] SABLIER J., Développement d'assistants technologiques cognitifs pour la schizophrénie: favoriser l'autonomie et l'adhésion au traitement, thèse de doctorat, Ecole Doctorale Neurosciences et cognition, University of Lyon 2, 8 September 2010.

[SAN 02] SANTÉ CANADA, Rapport sur les maladies mentales au Canada, October 2002, www.cihi.ca/cihiweb/dispPage.jsp ?cw_page=reports_mental_illness_f

[SCH 04] SCHULZE H., "MEMOS: A mobile extensible memory aid system", *Telemedicine Journal and e-Health*, vol. 10, pp. 233–242, 2004.

[SER 07] SERNA A., PIGOT H., RIALLE V., "Modeling the progression of Alzheimer's disease for cognitive assistance and smart homes", *User Modeling and User-Adapted Interaction (UMUAI)*, vol. 17, pp. 415–438, 2007.

[SOR 06] SORCINELLI A., SHAW L., FREEMAN A., COOPER K., "Evaluating the safe living guide: a home hazard checklist for seniors", *La Revue canadienne du vieillissement*, 2006.

[STA 02] STANDFORD V., "Using pervasive computing to deliver elder care", *IEEE Pervasive Computing*, no. 1, pp. 10–13, 2002.

[STO 10] STOCKWELL-SMITH G., URSULA KELLETT U., MOYLE W., "Why carers of frail older people are not using available respite services: an Australian study", *Journal of Clinical Nursing*, vol. 19, no. 13–14, pp. 2057–2064, 2010.

[TAS 03] TASSÉ M.J., MORIN D., *La déficience intellectuelle*, Gaëtan Morin, Montréal, 2003.

[VER 05] VERGNÈS D., GIROUX S., CHAMBERLAND-TREMBLAY D., "Interactive assistant for activities of daily living", *3rd International Conference on Smart Homes and Health Telematics, ICOST 2005*, Sherbrooke, Canada, 4–6 July 2005.

[WIL 01] WILSON B.A., EMSLIE H.C., QUIRK K., EVANS J.J., "Reducing everyday memory and planning problems by means of a paging system: a randomised control crossover study", *Journal of Neurology, Neurosurgery & Psychiatry*, vol. 70, pp. 477–482, 2001.

Chapter 12

Pervasive Games and Critical Applications

12.1. Introduction

The field of pervasive applications is particularly rich, from the point of view of the approaches followed as well as regarding the technologies used to create new experiences. One particularly promising aspect is in the field of pervasive games. Improved by new immersion and communication technologies, but still anchored in the real world, the games aim to minimize the gap between the virtual and real worlds. In these environments, game play is improved by new types of immersion, particularly with sensors (affective computing) or even geolocation mechanisms. Today, games are no longer confined to the home. They are increasingly invading public spaces like parks and museums.

Mixing the virtual world and reality is an exciting idea from a commercial viewpoint. However, in research, pervasive games still pose technical challenges. It is a question of managing technical faults, of "debugging" embedded applications, of accommodating diversity at all network layers, all the while maintaining the game's aesthetic qualities. Moreover, the games are very demanding in terms of packaging and ease of use which makes designing and deploying a pervasive game particularly difficult.

Our objective is to explore several pervasive games developed over the past few years. Playing and learning have been intimately linked since the beginning of

Chapter written by Isabelle Astic, Coline Aunis, Jérome Dupire, Viviane Gal, Eric Gressier-Soudan, Christophe Pitrey, Matthieu Roy, Françoise Sailhan, Michel Simatic, Alexandre Topol and Emanuel Zaza.

mankind [KOS 04]. So our approach aims at providing vision instantiations of the pervasive game and detailing them. Although most of the considerations addressed are generally shared with the pervasive games, we do not cover all the aspects relating to these games. We want to keep things more general, and this is expressed by analyzing further and thus applying games to another application domain: critical applications. To be effective, pervasive games must offer the most welcome game environment possible [HÖF 07]: "the more positive the real environment is for the player, the more the in-game development benefits". Critical applications must be able to operate in a highly degraded environment (following accidents). By making good use of the nature of these two types of application that are *a priori* opposed, we invite the reader not only to witness a detailed examination of the essential elements that characterize a pervasive application, but also to share our experience in such a way that allows others to anticipate difficulties that are similar or that derive from this.

The rest of this chapter is organized in the following way. We will introduce the preliminary concepts of pervasive games by describing two variants of pervasive games. Taking technical applications as a starting point, we will address the main challenges relating to the design, development and evaluation of pervasive games (section 12.2). We will then talk about a new application field – critical applications – and then for the rest of the chapter about pervasive games (section 12.3). Finally, we conclude with a summary of the challenges and promising research directions (section 12.4).

12.2. Pervasive games

One day, whether it is a pervasive game or not, fun and motivation will be fundamental elements and *sine qua none* to the immersion of the player. This is actually related to the gamification process [ZIC 11].Without wishing to curb or limit the player's enjoyment, the game looks to challenge the player with rules all the while highlighting their competence, ability, and physical and mental capacities. This wise fusion between immersive elements and the skills of the player is taken into account by the game designer who, according to their vision, emphasizes one or the other. If there is one element that must not be neglected, it is the imagination or faculty of the player to project a mental image and therefore to immerse themselves in a world created for them by the game designer. This emphasis on imagination presupposes storytelling, characters, game conditions, and win and lose states in a game to make different game design patterns, ranging from adventure to simulation, competition, cooperation, puzzle and quiz games. In the rest of the chapter, we will describe two pervasive games that respond to these demands. Both take place in a public environment. In that, they follow the current trend which takes advantage of wireless technologies that offer a short-, medium- or long-distance connection via WWAN, WMAN, WLAN or WPAN (*Wireless Wide, Metropolitan, Local, Personal Area Network*) access networks. The use of on-board wireless technologies with regard to players allows spontaneous access to be offered in public areas, giving the games the ubiquitous character. These two games are also characterized by the fact that the environment dictates objectives and prefigures the game's design. For the former, the CNAM museum gives the "Plug: Secrets of the Museum" (PSM) game its educational dimension. While the "Sound Park" game takes place in a park and naturally brings much amusement. At this level, it is interesting to try to understand how the game itself influences the choice of technologies used and the organizational structure of adjacent material and software platforms. In the Plug project, the objective is both educational and fun. The idea can perhaps be summed up by the following quote: "play is a serious matter, it is an expression of creativity, and creativity is at the very root of our ability to learn". All the participants must implicitly take part in the game as investment in the game depends on learning. That means that there should be no passive spectators (players).

By taking place in a public park, the second game involves the potential presence of spectators. On the other hand, in a museum, spectators (i.e. non-players) must not have their visit, contemplation or attention disturbed by the players or the game. Two different strategies flow from this. The first consists of distributing the logic of the game with regard to the systems the players are equipped with. Information is transmitted here following a paradigm of sharing. The second strategy consists of structuring the game around middleware, which centralizes all information in such a way as to display the most recent events of the game on the screen. The public can thus be invited to watch the game. Here, we can find two complementary digital management organizations that are a result of these types of games' application context. Conversely, the material platforms of pervasive games, by being based on software and material systems like RFID-NFC (*Radio Frequency Identification/Near Field Communication*), geolocation mechanisms, and biomedical sensors, supply the level necessary for a transformation of the real world, a park, or a museum into a mixed reality world, or how these technologies transform the application context to come to the aid of our "lack of imagination". But to go further, let us come back to our two pervasive games. Firstly, we will describe in detail the challenges relating to their development, and secondly, we will focus our study onto biomedical sensors, a material platform from which our real world becomes virtual (section 12.2.1.2).

12.2.1. *"PSM: the game where you are the network"*

Developed in the context of the ANR Plug[1] project, the "PSM" pervasive game was tested at the *Musée des arts et métiers*[2] museum in Paris. The players were invited to participate in game sessions, attracted by Professor Wandermonde[3] or the following message: "six objects of the museum's collection were chosen. For each one, a virtual card of the object in question is carefully placed in a terminal next to it. But the night before, all the maps moved from terminal to terminal: what a mess today! Your mission: to survey the museum, use the secret passages, do so as quickly as possible and find the maps. By using a cellphone, in a team or individually, you can then confer with them and set them right, all the while discovering the secrets of the museum's objects. Are you curious? Do you like working with others? Civically minded? A cheater? A collector? It is up to you to develop your strategy according to your profile as a player. The winner of the game is the player who scores most points!"

Figure 12.1. *Screen of a Nokia mobile phone, artworks label*

The objective of the "PSM" game is to allow players to discover the *Musée des arts et métiers in* an original way, by testing scientific qualities. The players must win points by proving their abilities to:

– collect by gathering four maps of the same family on their telephones (by carrying out exchanges like "map stored in their telephone/map stored in an NFC tag" or even "map stored in the telephone/map stored in the telephone of another team");

---

1 http://cedric.cnam.fr/PLUG.

2 www.arts-et-metiers.net.

3 www.dailymotion.com/video/xalcd9_plug-les-secrets-du-musee-formation_creation.

– show civism by placing a virtual card in its associated terminal (via a "map stored in the telephone/map stored in an NFC tag" exchange);

– show generosity by exchanging one of their cards with that of another player. To do this, two players place their telephones a few centimeters away from each other. The exchange is then done by pair-to-pair NFC protocol;

– show curiosity by answering quizzes concerning objects represented on the virtual card.

Eight players are equipped with a cellphone[4] that can read/write tags. During the game, thanks to their telephone, players manipulate virtual cards that contain the photo of a specific object of the museum and its family (e.g. the family that hunts the ghosts of famous scientists who have objects featured in the museum). Moreover, passive NFC tags are used in the museum next to one of the real objects represented by a virtual card.

Once the game session is initialized, the player moves in the museum to interact with the various NFC tags. To do this, the player places their telephone on the NFC tag to read its content. The content displays the virtual card stored inside the tag, a Clue menu option and eventually a Quiz menu option:

– If the player chooses the Clue menu option, the telephone indicates the location of an NFC tag that contains an object of the family collected by the player and how old this information is. The player can then evaluate how fresh it is and decide if this information deserves to be taken into account;

– When the player chooses the Quiz menu option, the telephone asks a question about the object associated to the tag. If the player responds correctly (by drawing from their knowledge or even by observing the object's environment), they win points for their curiosity. If they make a mistake, the telephone displays an error message and shows the correct response.

Each time players complete a family on their telephone, they win collector points. At the end of a session, the telephone calculates the total collector, civism, generosity and curiosity points, and displays this score

In practice, the implementation of the game design of the "PSM" game takes into account the highly distributive and collaborative nature of this multiplayer game, which comes from the fact that players freely move in the museum and exchange virtual cards. One of the unique things about the "PSM" game comes from the

---

4 Nokia 6131 NFC mobile phones were used during this project.

architecture chosen, which is a distributed and shared memory. This approach is in total opposition to the classic centralized RFID/NFC architecture approach promoted in the context of GS1 EPC [ARM 07], and in which, an RFID/NFC reader reads the RFID/NFC identifier stored in each tag that equips a product and relays this information to a dedicated application. This application, by accessing a central database, is able to identify this product and the procedure to manipulate it. In contrast, the distributed approach of the Plug project allows it to branch out from a network connecting the RFID/NFC reader and the database. It takes advantage of the player's movements. In this sense, "PSM" becomes the game where you are the network. But without a network, how is it possible to indicate to a place the clue is related to the content on distant tags?

Each telephone and tag has its vision of the content of different tags (as well as how old this information is) [SIM 09]. It behaves like some kind of causal distributed shared memory [AHA 91]. When two entities of the system (two telephones or even one telephone and a tag) meet each other, they compare how old the different pieces of information they have on the system are, and only keep what is most recent. At the design level, this ubiquitous game is unique in the fact that it does not create a virtual world in which the player is immersed. On the contrary, by making reference to the museum's objects, the game is anchored in reality and pushes the player to observe and analyze its scientific qualities. On the other hand, in the Soundpark game that we will talk about soon, the objectives aimed at, and therefore the game design of the technical architecture, is completely different. While in one sense, viewing (observation) is valued in "PSM", "SoundPark" adds audio, and therefore something which is no longer science but art, that is music. By creating a virtual world based on sounds, this game emphasizes the player's imagination and artistic qualities, but is also highly scientific.

12.2.1.1. *The SoundPark game*

SoundPark which is a multiplayer ubiquitous game project is a joint venture between the on-board and mobile systems group for ambient intelligence of the CEDRIC Laboratory at CNAM Paris1 and the Shared Virtual Reality team of the Centre for Intelligent Machines of McGill University, completed by members of the University of Montreal specialized in PureData [WOZ 07]. The contributors to this project are R. Pellerin, N. Bouillot, T. Pietkiewicz, M. Wozniewski, Z. Settel, E. Gressier-Soudan, and J.R. Cooperstock. A detailed description of this work can be found in [PEL 09a] and [PEL 09b], as well as a video [SOU 10] that specifies the role of each contributor to the project.

The ubiquitous game naturally makes reference to leisure spaces in mixed realities: the real/concrete world in which the player moves and the virtual/digital world in which their avatar/digital double shares the adventure of the game. The ubiquitous game therefore produces two parallel and interdependent dynamics, which join each other at certain particular places where real and virtual space come together [YAN 07]. The game design allied to pervasive technology allows this concordance. It produces the magic that is immersion in the game. This immersion, crucial from the player's point of view, also allows them to overcome the occasional frustrations caused by the limitations of current technologies.

3D audio for a virtual world (musical instruments)

Figure 12.2. *Hunter and scout*

In practice, SoundPark is a game in a mixed reality which is played out in Jane Manson Park in Montreal. This mixed reality, based on 3D audio, is what makes it original: it allows both people who can see and the visually impaired to enjoy the experience. It also invites them to follow the progression of the game on a screen where all the instruments associated with the various sounds and all the avatars are represented in a regeneration of 3D images of Jane Manson Park. The players move inside a perimeter limited to searching for sounds coming from a musical instrument that they must collect and bring back to their base to assemble and create a musical instrument. The game is played in pairs. Each player has a particular role (Figure 12.2).

The scout looks for clues in the park which will allow the hunter to be informed about the location of sounds. The hunter is the only one who can collect sounds and bring them back to the base. They hear them but do not know their exact location. On the other hand, from the clues they have discovered, the scout knows the positions of sounds and notes them on a map. The first team to bring back all the sounds associated with the piece of music wins.

SoundPark is at the crossroads of three components:

– a technical substrate through pervasive computing technologies (wireless networks, on-board processors, middleware, treatment distribution, and RFID/NFC);

– an application core halfway between video game, game in the field, and game that takes place outside;

– the individual as much as from an interaction point of view that can be formed between individuals as much as the relationship they have with their avatar in the virtual dimension of the game.

The players have a lot of peripheral equipment available to them: a 3D headphone amplifier, an RFID reader, and a display mini-console figured out by a Nokia 6131 NFC enabled (for the scout) wiimote to gather sounds and the instrument associated to the 3D virtual sound space (for the hunter). The player, whatever his or her function, is equipped with an on-board processor called Gumstick, which serves as an audio stream multiplexor (game sounds, and dialog between players), datastreaming (RFID reading, GPS positions, actions on wii-mote[5], text messages to players, and a gameplan that constitutes intermediary representation between the YahooMap[6] and the GoogleMap[7] of Jane Manson Park) between the peripheral equipment and servers of the game's logic or sound. This peripheral equipment communicates via the Bluetooth protocol with the Gumstick. The rest of the network relies on the local Wifi network in infrastructure mode, which covers the space of the game. Communication is built on the protocols of the Internet family. Two servers compute the evolution of the ubiquitous game in real time. The uGASP[8] (ubiquitous GAming Service Platform) server [PEL 10] maintains the overall state of the game being played from the events produced by the actions of the players (players' locations in the park, clue collection, sound collection, sound objects being found that exist in the virtual 3D audio universe, and sound assembly) and deduces the advancement of concurrent requests. The AudioScape [WOZ 06] server manages the sounds and performs the sound synthesis from the 3D audio scene according to the state of the game and the advancement of the teams.

Developed in Java language, the uGASP server takes up the service-oriented architecture of multiplayer games, proposed by the Open Mobile Alliance[9], and

---

5 www.nintendo.com.
6 http://maps.yahoo.com.
7 http://maps.google.fr.
8 http://gasp.ow2.org/ubiquitous-osgi-middleware.html.
9 www.openmobilealliance.org.

extends it by adapting it to ubiquitous games [PEL 09c]. It is based on OSGi (Open Services Gateway Initiative) technology, which supplies a software architecture through components with a dynamic component charge made possible thanks to iPOJO. The Audioscape server, meanwhile, is dedicated to providing audio and graphic contents of interactions into mixed reality due to the ubiquitous context of the game. It allows the location of audio sources to be modelized from the events received through the uGASP server, in virtual space as well as in real space as 3D audio and graphic representations. This server manages the overall state of the virtual 3D world and calculates the spatialized rendering of the sound for each player in real time and for a PC. The sound effects aim to give more realism to the 3D audio scenes of virtual space. They include the direction of the sound according to the position of the source, attenuation according to distance, reverberation, the Doppler Effect (the sound frequency is affected by the source's movement when the hunter brings the sound back to their base). Finally, a PC displays visual and sound animation generated by Audioscape in real time for the whole virtual scene of the game which can be seen by the public. Our graphic designer T. Pietkiewicz has done a lot of work in representing the SoundPark game as a video animation, which makes the game pleasant to look at and improves the immersion factor for the public.

This project brings many challenges: creating a simple game that is easy to understand and immersive, integrating very different technologies, and elaborating a prototype in less than three months. To develop a simple game within this timeframe, we were inspired by Zagamore[10], an open air collective game that we simplified while keeping two classes of players who complete with each other, that is whose missions require distinct competencies and collaboration. On the other hand, the fun dimension was retained. More generally, collective games represent an interesting source of inspiration for the elaboration of ubiquitous multiplayer games. In addition to the specialization and to the technical and scientific skills of developers, the uGASP [PEL 09c] middleware brings some valuable advantages. The OSGi/iPOJO [ESC 08] framework plays a decisive role both to integrate the game services to the heterogeneous network/hardware technologies we needed. The ease of integration advocated the reuse of uGASP in the "PLUG: Paris Night University" ubiquitous multiplayer game, another "serious game" in the *Musée des arts et métiers* in Paris.

On a design level, SoundPark is characterized by its wish to immerse the player in a virtual world in which their avatar goes on a quest to collect sounds in a 3D audio environment. The link between the game design and the player is initiated

---

10 http://fr.wikipedia.org/wiki/Zagamore.

through this quest. Then, it naturally pushes us to ask the question: how can it be ensured that a player can converse with the game designer and influence the course of the game?

12.2.1.2. *Physiological sensors*

In the context of pervasive games, the sensors selected do not aim to supply contextual information (temperature and degrees of humidity) as is the case in the field of home automation, but rather to provide information on the player. Thus, movement detectors are currently being integrated into devices for games. Another class of sensor is biomedical sensors, also known as physiological sensors. Once moved away from their initial use, these sensors allow the player to take center stage. They allow some raw bio-feedback coming from the players to be integrated into the game to better immerse and interact with them. Being able to associate physiological information with emotional states is one of the aspects allowing game designers to understand the user's current state. To this end, the development or use of devices that capture affective expressions is made necessary. Among existing physiological sensors, the choice must involve miniaturized, painless, non-invasive sensors; this selection being the only guarantee of the player having accepted it. The sensors that we consider are placed in contact with the skin in such a way as to allow surface electrodes to sense physiological signals emitted by the player. During the field tests that we will describe afterward, they have been well accepted by the players and have not caused apprehension on their part. The following are the sensors:

– An electrocardiogram that records electric waves emitted by the heart. Obtained by placing jellified electrodes on the player's skin. This data is not fully reliable because it is subject to variations coming from the player's movements.

– An electromyogram that records very weak electric currents emitted by muscles and nerves. It allows the motor function of muscles and nerves to be studied, particularly during sporting activity.

– An electroencephalogram which gathers electric waves emitted by the brain. Traditionally used in neurology or in cognitive neurosciences, it allows a better understanding of how the brain works.

– A sensor that takes the dermal temperature from a part of the body that is not exposed to ambient air. This temperature varies according to mental activity, autosuggestion or visualization.

– A respiratory frequency sensor that allows the rhythm (number of inhalations and exhalations made by the player per minute) and their magnitude to be measured.

– A sensor that detects pressure in the arteries on the inner wall of vessels.

– An electrodermal resistance sensor, also known as a psychogalvanic response sensor.

– An inertial sensor.

In order to test these sensors and quantify the player's emotional state, an experimental protocol has been specified and ran by 15 men and women of different ages. In practice, this protocol consists of broadcasting images selected according to their ability to provoke reactions and emotions that are recorded. To calibrate the system, a relaxation phase precedes the emotionally charged images (e.g. images of a disaster), themselves alternated with more peaceful images. To manage this experiment, software has been developed. It fulfills three functions: broadcasting a test video, signal acquisition[11], and recording these signals.

As we have seen, from these tests it emerges that the acceptance of the sensors was totally agreed by users. First of all, the subjects who were chosen for this experiment implicitly accepted that the physiological (and therefore highly personal) data was collected. Moreover, the miniaturized and non-intrusive character of the sensors played a central role. This experiment allowed sensors to be selected pragmatically, based on the following criteria:

– The robustness, the ease of use for the players, and the non-intrusive character. To obtain respiratory rhythm, the sensor used on an elastic belt requires the ribcage to be squeezed. And yet, given that players have different chest sizes, adjusting the sensor device and its calibration turns out to be difficult. The respiratory rhythm was therefore replaced by thoracic impendence obtained from the electrocardiogram. The electroencephalogram, which is difficult for a mobile player to carry, has been discarded. Same is for the arterial pressure sensor.

– The range of signal variation and the ability of the sensor to enrich the game design. The temperature is characterized by its relative stability compared, for example, to an electrocardiogram that is particularly reactive to stimulation. This stability is a drawback to information on the player's emotional state. Then, the temperature and arterial pressure sensors have been disregarded.

As a consequence, only two sensors, the accelerometer and the electrocardiogram (Figure 12.3), have been selected and integrated in the thoracic belt in such a way that they can be easily worn by players [FRO 09].

---

11 A video of the players has been recorded to correlate the signals, gestures, and expressions of players.

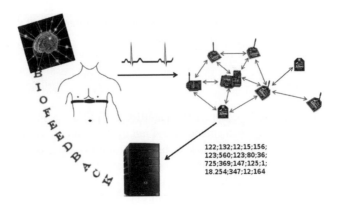

Figure 12.3. *Capturing signal via an electrocardiogram*

12.2.1.3. *Summary*

In this section, we have illustrated our vision of pervasive games by presenting two games "PSM" and "SoundPark", and by defining how physiological sensors can enrich game design. Our approach has been to share our experience, to document the problems encountered and more importantly to give hints how to solve them. And yet, robustness, reliability, trust, security, and tolerance to faults have not been considered while describing these games: we focused on fun, satisfaction, and player immersion. And yet, the ability of a game to function despite the occurrence of faults is fundamental, and the acceptance by players and the future of pervasive games depend on this ability. Games are based on "on-shelf" components, GumStick, physiological sensors, NFC telephones, and shifting them from their regular uses. This rises the question: How can a pervasive game run safely from unreliable components? How can the availability of the game be guaranteed while users from WPAN and WLAN networks share uncontrolled frequency bands and when WMAN connectivity is not guaranteed in a closed space? Solving these issues is the only issue that drives a pervasive game from a proof of concept to real product with a wide acceptance. Part of the answer have been found:

– By developing a distributed/shared solution, "PSM – the game where you are the network" branches out from a wireless network.

– By supporting several short-range connectivity sources that are adapted to closed environments (Zigbee and Wifi), uGASP software allows the game availability to be increased.

– By being based on a modular solution through OSGi-iPOJO coupling, SoundPark avoids errors being propagated to the whole of the architecture. Moreover, it makes on-the-fly insertion and suppression of components possible by making it easier to test them.

– By pooling a set of basic services, the OSGi-uGASP ensures that unnecessary manual coding error sources are not recalculated. Thus, reuse of this middleware in the "PLUG: Paris Night University" game increased efficiency.

– By providing adapted packaging of the sensors and/or by discarding sensors judged to be intrusive, acceptance from the point of view of user is higher.

The set of the practices put in during development of the material and software platforms has allowed sensor and game reliability to be improved. However, the safety of how critical ubiquitous application work embraces a set of wider attributes, among which are security, availability and robustness, which deserve to be studied as such and also to understand how robustness of pervasive game can be improved.

12.3. Critical ubiquitous applications

Faults affect the robustness of any application (e.g. a ubiquitous game). They represent a particular challenge for critical applications where a breakdown could have disastrous consequences, particularly in terms of human life. That was the case with two critical applications that we have chosen to present here. The first aim is to facilitate diagnosis of road accidents by providing a system of distributed black boxes on communicating vehicles. The second aim is to guide firefighters toward artwork that needs to be saved during a fire in a museum. These two applications have their critical character in common, and their specification and design is therefore subject to particular attention and extensive experimentation for the former (the other still being at the design stage).

12.3.1. *Distributed black box*

It is particularly difficult to analyze the causes and factors that led to a traffic accident due to the lack of contextual information (vehicle speed and atmospheric conditions at a given moment). An extensive diagnosis requires contextual information. Therefore an effective and safe way to store contextual information is needed. Based on the model of avionic black boxes, we propose a black box for mobile vehicles in the context of the European HIDENETS project[12]. This project offers a service that records the history of critical parameters of the cars of the system (positioning and speed) in such a way to be able to analyze, if there is an accident, the events having taken place before impact. In contrast to a "classic" black box which can only provide information when it is damaged, a distributed black box opportunely uses resources that are available close by, replicating

---

12 STREP-26979, http://hidenets.aau.dk.

information and making them available after impact. The challenge is twofold: guaranteeing that security functioning properties (integrity, coherence, availability, reliability, robustness, and authenticity) are verified during exchange of and storing the contextual details, and that, despite the instability of the environment due to the (high) mobility of vehicles, and therefore the dynamic nature of the wireless network. The stated objective is to guarantee the security functioning properties, which leads us first to ask ourselves the following question: How can the situation be evaluated?

Figure 12.4. *Experiment laboratory*

While the majority of algorithm evaluations designed for ubiquitous and mobile systems are performed by simulation, we propose to complete them by designing an experimentation platform of mobile systems. In order to represent a system composed of mobile communicating entities in a laboratory of only 100 m², the scale of the system was reduced by a factor of 50. Moreover, we use miniature care equipped with a precise interior positioning system (to the centimeter) and a short-range communication system (1–2 m). The design of such a platform raises three challenges:

– Generating a mobility model. The movement of miniature car has been constrained by black lines traced on the ground that the cars follow. This approach is currently being extended by a programmable platform that aims to develop models of particular mobility "*à la carte*".

– Location inside is difficult to obtain because of the expectations (a precision to the centimeter is required). Following several unsuccessful trials (MIT Cricket and movement capture systems), the infrared ultra-wide band coupling system was chosen.

– Short-range communication is obtained by using WiFi maps whose emission power has been reduced following the intercalation of a signal attenuator between the antenna and the network map.

In a disparate and complex map like the map proposed, in which distributed and mobile black holes must be emulated and stimulated, it is vital to break the application down into simple subsets known as services, in which a single task is performed. This modularity (Figure 12.5) guarantees increased reuse, configurability, maintainability, and testability. Moreover, by inserting an additional layer (middleware) which provides the set of basic software services by decoupling this software layer of the material layer, the code of the distributed black box is made more portable, which, on the one hand, facilitates its use on simulation and experimentation platforms that have been used to validate the proposed solution and, on the other hand, circumscribes the necessary code modification, a desirable property during evaluation/experimentation. The focus of this experimental platform is twofold. It allows the approach to be validated experimentally, thus complementing the validations made via a simulator. We should note that the work done by Gaëtan Severac, an engineer at IMERIS, has enabled the experimental platform to be operational [KIL 10]. This operational platform also has shown us that simulators are optimistic at the level of emulating the network interface. In particular, communication is highly asynchronous (connection–disconnection).

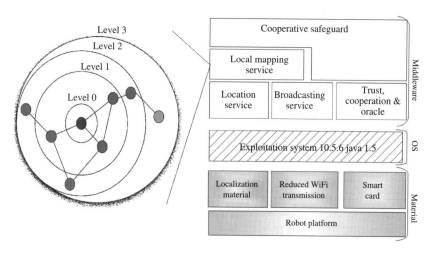

Figure 12.5. *Distributed black box*

If we now distance ourselves from the material contingencies inherent to using two hardware platforms to concentrate on service-oriented middleware (Figure 12.5), we observe that two services (the local mapping service and the location service) enable nearby vehicles to be discovered. To this end, each node is geolocalized (location service) and has a local map which allows the network to be circumvented. This network is updated by the topographical service in the following way: a system node (level 0) periodically broadcasts its local map toward its neighbors. While it is receiving the local map, a node updates its local map by fusing information: level 0 information is placed in level 1, and information from a higher level is also kept if it is more recent, up to a level defined by the service's user application. Thus, each network node has a map from which it can select nodes toward which information must be replicated. During this replication and more generally during all transmission, a modification, accidental or deliberate, must be detected. Such detection requires, on the one hand, to evaluate the degree of trust that an entity can have toward another entity (evaluation service based on a smart-card and trust trilogy-based mechanism, cooperation, and oracle) and a reliable point-to-point connection (error corrector code technique). Thus, by using the set of aforementioned services, the collaborative safeguard service, the proposed distributed black box can reliably record data (e.g. the speed of the vehicle), by replicating it onto various nodes.

12.3.2. Safeguarding heritage

Among other application domains, ubiquity has a place in dangerous environments and security assistance during disasters. Thus, the solution for tracking and safeguarding heritage and firefighters (SURPAT) [SAI 09] proposes to implement it to help and make firefighters safer while they are on duty. Musée des arts et métiers has been the study context of the project. The richness of its collection, 80,000 objects of which 4,000 are exhibited, its mission, to safeguard major techniques of the past for education purposes, and its status, Conservatoire National des Arts et Métiers (CNAM) is related to the French government. This project, initiated by the museum and which gathers together institutional (CNAM/CEDRIC, ENSTA) and private (Taztag, Aguila Technologies and SAIC Conseils) partners proposes a solution that safeguards the museums' collections by helping firefighters to not only locate and identify a target in a building during a fire, but also locate themselves and get around in a smoke-filled environment. To reach this objective, SURPAT integrates new pervasive technologies that are smart-RFID and predicts its installation with each of the objects to be safeguarded as well as the walls of the building. These smart-RFIDs will be equipped with an open, two-directional network protocol, which thus creates a mesh able to reconfigure itself that is linked via an external infrastructure network at the fire surveillance post. Its supervision constitutes a surveillance system that monitors not only the state of the fire but also the firefighters. The information conveyed by this network serves to enhance an assistance system that aims to optimize the whole system and to guide the firefighters.

During an intervention, a firefighter is equipped with a terminal linked to the smart-RFID network. By moving inside the building, this firefighter encounters smart-RFID and the information exchange between its terminal and the smart-RFID is used to triangulate the firefighter's position [PIC 10]. This position is then displayed on the firefighter's terminal and on the security's PC, which allows the location of any firefighter to be known at all times. In order to design a pleasant-looking display (and more generally a user-friendly interface), Game Maker[13] software was used. This software allowed us to develop a game that integrates a 2D graphic interface displaying a plan of the museum and of the pieces to be safeguarded, with sound effects letting the fire fighter how near he or she is to a piece that should be safeguarded, and animations (firefighter movements and direction borrowed from the firefighter). This interface allows the zone in which a firefighter finds himself to be indicated to everyone, depicting an estimate of the precision (here, a red zone of varying diameter) centered on the firefighter's position. Thus, a firefighter almost becomes an interacting player, with a security PC as the game master; all of the necessary interactions being performed in multiplayer (multi-firefighter) mode between the distant devices, and above an IP network.

At the same time, the network regularly sends supervision information signaling that a smart-RFID has disappeared. This information is used by optimization algorithms to redefine a new, safer route for the firefighter. Once they are in the room where the object is situated, the firefighter is directed to the object by the object itself that sends a signal at regular intervals. The object can then be protected or evacuated according to the defined emergency procedures.

The particularly perilous and difficult application context brings numerous risks, primarily indoor geolocalization and its unreliability. Indeed, using an RFID to locate someone in environments disturbed by water or fine dust particles poses challenges for the reliability of the method. Situating the firefighter in a room that is different to the room they are really in can lead it to propose a dangerous route and therefore endanger life. Moreover, if an accident occurs, it is vital to know the exact position of the firefighter so that help can be provided if required.

Another critical point of this project is the reliability of the information received by the firefighter. Although they keep their free will, the direction they receive must help them choose their way. And yet, the reliability and the availability of this information depend on how correct the optimization algorithms are and the robustness of the network. Therefore, it is not only the decision assistance system

---

13 www.yoyogames.com/gamemaker.

but also the whole network that play a decisive role. Firstly, the robustness of the smart-RFID: the more a tag resists the fire, the more independent it will be and the longer the network will be operational, hence the importance of the choice of communication protocol (IEEE 802.15.4 and 6LowPAN which do not consume much energy). On the other hand, research will be carried out during the project on the smart-RFID's plastic to increase its resistance to fire. The robustness of the network comes from its capacity to pass its data regularly to the decision assistance system. The chosen protocol allows the creation of a multi-hop network, to ensure eventual dynamic reconfiguration and offers a large number of possible routes to move what is carried. But it is its supervision that will really ensure the quality of the network. It is this information that will allow the decision assistance system to offer other ways to send data. Its robustness remains a crucial point that must be solved, that SURPAT proposes to study, along with a distributed architecture.

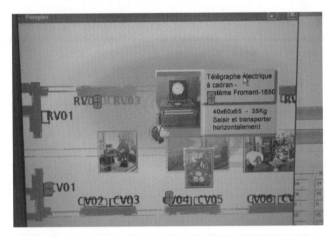

Figure 12.6. *Location of the electric telegraph in the CNAM Museum*

12.3.3. *Summary*

How securely things work has long been an issue that critical applications have to confront. This also goes naturally for pervasive and critical applications. Wireless communication, in particular, means that pervasive applications pose new challenges in terms of robustness and reliability. The highly asynchronous character of communications (section 12.2.1) and the extent of radio disturbance in an indoor environment (section 12.3.2) show us the difficulties linked to developing reliable solutions from wireless components. In this context, it is crucial to facilitate the development of secure pervasive functioning applications that allow potential errors to be detected as early as possible in the development process, by offering support to the evaluation of the reliability of future deployment. We should note that such an approach is proposed in the context of the ANR Murphy project, which aims to define a mechanism that injects faults to accelerate the occurrence of faults and a system that detects errors or dysfunction. Thus, this system could allow the user to be guided to improve the reliability of critical and pervasive application like those we have just studied.

12.4. Conclusion

Illustrating our vision of pervasive games has to led us to present two games "PSM" and "SoundPark", and to identify how physiological sensors can improve a player's immersion. The amusement and the motivation of the player depend on this immersion, and these are real cornerstones of the game that all game designers aim for. To this end, the "PSM" game (particularly) uses quizzes, which on the one hand gives it an educational dimension and on the other hand encourages a constant back-and-forth on the part of the player between the game (virtual world) and the works of the museum (real world). The SoundPark game, meanwhile, motivates the player by offering them a quest through which a character called a scout looks for clues that they give to a hunter to allow him to locate and collect sounds which together form a piece of music. In these two games, a player has to develop a strategy according to their character/profile, hunter or scout in the SoundPark game, or even curious, civic, cheater, collector, collaborator with the "PSM". The player occupies this central place and can find himself or herself comforted by physiological sensors, which capture an emotional state and physical reactions of the player, which allows the events of the game to be influenced and its realism to be improved. Thus, the interations between the player and designer are strengthened. Acceptance and therefore adoption of the physiological sensor depend on their painless and non-invasive (minituarization and ease of use for the player) character, and on their ability to enrich the game design. We should note here that the signals coming from the sensors and the emotions caused by playing the game for the user coming together are a research area that is still open, and which requires deeper thought from the scientific community. Moreover, at this level, WPAN wireless technologies play a central role by offering the player a spontaneous (and therefore non-intrusive) connection all the while giving the game its ubiquitous character. On the other hand, the lack of reliability that comes from sharing the uncontrolled frequency bands in particular or even the disturbances to the radio signal in a closed space poses questions (on robustness, reliability, or even tolerance to these faults) which are not part of what is usally thought of when considering games, though the ability of a pervasive game to function in spite of faults is vital. More generally, here it is a question of managing software and material failure at the game level, as well as accommodating heterogenity of all the network layers without altering the game, how it looks, or how enjoyable it is. To reach this objective, several approaches, and not just those limited to the domain of games, have been proposed. This similar approach followed during the development of critical applications and games is illustrated through the development of a distributed/shared solution applied to the "PSM" game to branch out from the wireless network, or even in the context of black boxes distributed with information between the nodes nearby to improve tolerance to faults. By supporting several short-range connectivity sources that are adapted to closed environments (Zigbee and Wifi), the SoundPark game and the SURPAT solution allow both to offer increased availability. Finally, the modular solution promoted by SoundPark (the distributed black box respectively) through OSGi-iPOJO coupling (a service-oriented approach respectively) facilitates the test. Moreover, reuse of components (services respectively) made available by uGASP middleware (service-oriented middleware adjacent to a distributed black box respectively) in the "Paris Night University" game (at the simulation platform level and the experimental test level of a distributed black box) allows development efforts to be factorized while limiting the risk of introducing faults. The whole of these practices put in place during development of these material and software platforms has enabled the reliability of the critical applications and games we have presented to be improved. However, although faults affect the robustness of any application (a ubiquitous game for example), in the field of pervasive games they only represent a challenge if the credibility of the game is affected by it. Thus, the data collected by physiological sensors (electrocardiogram) have become worse by limiting the bandwidth used. On the other hand, in a medical application context, a clear diagnosis depends on the precision of the traced mark coming from the electrocardiogram. In this case, and more generally as is very often the case in the context of critical applications, the solution cannot be made worse without possibly having disastrous consequences, and with in an environment that is potentially hostile (accident and fire). Thus, the games are evaluated according to metrics that are different to those found in pervasive applications, like, for example, the freedom the player has to develop strategies enabling them to win and the ability of the game to inspire in the player the wish to play again multiple times.

12.5. Bibliography

[AHA 91] Ahamad M., Hutto P., John R., "Implementing and programming causal distributed shared memory", *ICDCS 1991*, Arlington, Texas, USA, pp. 274–228, 1991.

[ARM 07] Armenio F., Barthel H., Burstein L., Dietrich P., Duker J., Garrett J., Hogan B., Ryaboy O., Sarma S., Schmidt J., Suen K., Traub K., Williams J., The EPCglobal architecture framework, technical report, GS1 EPCglobal, (version 1.2), September 2007.

[ESC 08] Escoffier C., iPOJO: Un modèle à composant à service flexible pour les systèmes dynamiques, thèse de doctorat d'informatique, Joseph Fourier University, Grenoble, France, December 2008.

[FRO 09] FROMENT S., GINIBRE M., MADER S., SARAFIAN A., SCHWARTZ A., SORIANO D., TOPOL A., DUPIRE J., "AZ66 how can we play with emotions?", *ICEC'09, Int. Conf. on Entertainment Computing*, Series LNCS, Springer, Paris, France, pp. 2, September 2009.

[GEN 09] GENTES A., JUTANT C., GUYOT A., SIMATIC M., "Designing mobility: pervasiveness as the enchanting tool of mobility", *Proceedings of the 1st International ICST Workshop on Innovative Mobile User Interactivity (IMUI)*, San Diego, CA, USA, 2009.

[HÖF 07] HÖFELD A., "In and out of reality: janus-faced location awareness in ubiquitous games", *Journal of Software*, vol. 2, no. 6, pp. 86–92, December 2007.

[IEE 06] IEEE STANDARD FOR INFORMATION TECHNOLOGY, Telecommunications and Information Exchange Between Systems – Local and Metropolitan Area Networks – Specific Requirements Part 15.4: Wireless Medium Access Control (MAC) and Physical Layer (PHY), IEEE Computer Society, 2006.

[JUA 02] JUANG P., OKI H., WANG Y., MARTONOSI M., PEH L.S., RUBENSTEIN D., "Energy-efficient computing for wildlife tracking: design tradeoffs and early experiences with zebranet", *Proceedings of the 10th International Conference on Architectural Support for Programming Languages and Operating Systems (ASPLOS-X)*, San Jose, CA, USA, pp. 96–107, 2002.

[KIL 10] KILLIJIAN M.O., ROY M., SÉVERAC G., ARUM: a Cooperative Middleware and an Experimentation Platform for Mobile Systems, WiMob'2010, Niagara Falls, Canada, pp. 8, 11–13 October 2010.

[KOS 04] KOSTER R., *A Theory of Fun for Game Design*, Paraglyph Press, pp. 256, 2004.

[PEL 09a] PELLERIN R., BOUILLOT N., PIETKIEWICZ T., WOZNIEWSKI M., SETTEL Z., GRESSIER-SOUDAN E., COOPERSTOCK J.R., "SoundPark: exploring ubiquitous computing through a mixed reality multi-player game experiment", *Proceedings of NOTERE'09 International Bilingual Conference*, Montréal, Canada, 2009.

[PEL 09b] PELLERIN R., BOUILLOT N., PIETKIEWICZ T., WOZNIEWSKI M., SETTEL Z., GRESSIER-SOUDAN E., COOPERSTOCK J. R., "SoundPark: towards highly collaborative game support in a ubiquitous computing architecture", *Proceedings of 9th IFIP DAIS International Conference*, Lisbon, Portugal, 2009.

[PEL 09c] PELLERIN R., Contribution à l'ingénierie des jeux multijoueurs ubiquitaires, Doctorate thesis, CNAM Paris, September 2009.

[PEL 10] PELLERIN R., BOUILLOT N., PIETKIEWICZ T., WOZNIEWSKI M., SETTEL Z., GRESSIER-SOUDAN E., COOPERSTOCK J.R., "SoundPark: exploring ubiquitous computing through a mixed reality multi-player game experiment", *Studia Informatica Universalis*, vol. 8, no. 3, pp. 25–45, October 2010. http://studia.complexica.net/Art/RI080302.pdf

[PIT 10] PITREY C., Surpat: sûreté du patrimoine, Mémoire ingénieur du CNAM Paris, September 2010.

[ROG 94] ROGERS F., SHARAPAN H., "How children use play", *Education Digest*, vol. 59, no. 8, pp. 13–16, 1994.

[SAI 09a] SAILHAN F., ASTIC I., MICHEL F., PITREY C., UY M., GRESSIER-SOUDAN E., GERBAUD P., FORGEOT H., "Conception d'une solution de localisation et de surveillance, à base de RFID actifs, défis et perspectives", *INFORSID GEDSIP Workshop*, Lyon, France, 2009.

[SAI 09b] SAILHAN F., ASTIC I., MICHEL F., PITREY C., UY M., GRESSIER-SOUDAN E., GERBAUD P., FORGEOT H., Sauvegarde du patrimoine en cas de sinistre : conception d'une solution de localisation et de surveillance à base de RFIDs actifs, défis et perspectives. 2ème Atelier sur la Gestion des Données dans les Systèmes d'Information Pervasifs, Atelier sur la GEstion des Données dans les Systèmes d'Information Pervasifs (GEDSIP) au sein de la conférence INFormatique des ORganisations et Systèmes d'Information et de Décision (INFORSID), pp. 1–15, January 2009.

[SIM 09] SIMATIC M., "RFID-based replicated distributed memory for mobile applications", *Proceedings of the 1st International Conference on Mobile Computing, Applications, and Services (Mobicase)*, Seattle, USA, 2009.

[SOU 10] SOUNDPARK, www.audioscape.org/srewiki/bin/view/Audioscape/SoundPark, May 2010.

[WOZ 06] WOZNIEWSKI M., SETTEL Z., COOPERSTOCK J.R., "A paradigm for physical interaction with sound in 3-D audio space", *Proceedings of International Computer Music Conference (ICMC)*, New Orleans, LA, USA 2006.

[WOZ 07] WOZNIEWSKI M., SETTEL Z., COOPERSTOCK J.R, "AudioScape: a pure data library for management of virtual environments and spatial audio", *PureData Convention*, Montréal, Canada 2007.

[YAN 07] YAN C., Jeux vidéo multijoueurs ubiquitaires adaptatifs: principes de conception et architecture d'exécution, Doctorate thesis, CNAM Paris, 2007.

[ZIC 11] ZICHERMANN G., CUNNINGHAM C., "Gamification by design", O'Reilly, 2011.

Chapter 13

Intelligent Transportation Systems

13.1. Introduction

Nowadays, vehicles, more specifically cars, are among the most sophisticated tools that are available to us. In fact, the car today is a mix of computing involving multiple processors (vehicles are using processors that are more and more powerful and capable of more complex calculations), mechanics (involving pieces that turn at great speed with maximum safety and reliability), and even pyrotechnics (with airbags or seatbelts).

Beyond vehicles, the whole field of transportation has experienced a profound change and increasing computerization, with the emergence of GPS receivers and smartphones, and has equipped many users (whether they are pedestrians, train users, conductors, or deliverers) who are now able to communicate and perform important operations.

Currently, all mobile constructors are working on advanced solutions, whether they involve infrastructures or not. For example, we can quote the trials that aim to calculate optimal speed by arriving at a set of traffic lights when they change to green to save fuel (Audi, Figure 13.1) or even the WiFi On-Board system proposed by PSA, which ensures a connection to the mobile network and also serves as a WiFi connector for all the passengers in the vehicle.

Chapter written by Mikael Desertot, Sylvain Lecomte, Christophe Gransart and Thierry Delot.

Figure 13.1. *Audi's "green wave" application for going through green traffic lights*

Naturally, these tools are best used to offer services that aim either to promote public transportation or to promote safety and reduce the harmful effects of vehicles on the environment.

In this chapter, we will present a set of solutions by focusing on the services offered, which come from research projects involving laboratories that have been to the "ambient intelligence" CNRS school and more specifically to the "intelligent vehicles" workshop.

13.2. Software architecture

13.2.1. *For what sort of applications?*

In [SCH 08], the authors categorized applications linked to vehicle networks into four large categories: active safety, public services (emergency/intervention services or toll schemes), assistance with driving, and work/leisure. Although this categorization was done for driving applications, these categories also apply to guided transportation.

According to the type of application, the service quality constraints and safety level are different. For example, for information for the traveller (getting a train timetable, for example), the user can tolerate a delay of a few dozen seconds or even a few minutes, while for active safety applications (such as avoiding a collision, informing a pedestrian that she/he is in a driver's blind spot, etc.) no delay can be tolerated. Moreover, communication links must be 100% reliable.

These constraints therefore have an impact on the middleware (including communication, service discovery system, automatic deployment tools, etc.) that is used by these applications. In the following section, we will show the importance of the context in the transportation domain.

13.2.2. *Importance of the context*

According to Dey [DEY 99], the context refers to all information that can be used to characterize the situation of an entity, which can be, for example, a person (place, movement, age, disability), a town or city (network coverage, climate, density), or even an object that is used to interact between a user and an application (telephone, smartphone, car, etc.)

All mobile applications, which are in dynamic environments, undergo changes that are important to varying degrees according to the context. For example, this context can concern:

– surrounding environments; for example, sensor data (temperature or sound, e.g.);

– personal information, like the user's timetable, their user display preferences, their priorities with regard to types of information, etc.;

– services available nearby and much more.

The first thing to do is to define the context so we can describe the rules of transformation/adaptation between different "versions" of a service. However, it is extremely difficult to establish a "general" context. In the context of applications dedicated to the transportation domain, it has therefore been necessary to establish a specific context. The work presented in [GRA 09] and [DES 10] breaks the context down into several elements, which will be introduced later.

As Figure 13.2 shows, the field of transportation has some specific characteristics such as the degree of mobility of its users (for example, pedestrians, train, or bus passengers, etc.), the dependence on the driver (for example in the city, on a highway), or even the characteristics of the unstable communication network (for example, losing connection to an infrastructure, change of neighbors).

The aim of this context model is to be used in a context-aware architecture (i.e. a software architecture capable of dynamic adaptation according to the context changes). It is also vital to consider elements linked to the platform such as those presented in Figure 13.3.

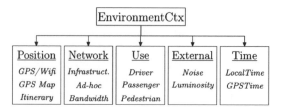

Figure 13.2. *Execution environment context of a "transportation" application*

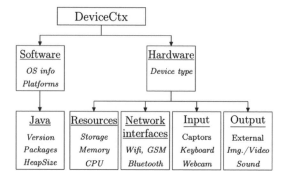

Figure 13.3. *Development context of a transportation application*

Finally, other elements are also required (specific to user preferences, for example) but in the interests of brevity they are not listed here.

13.2.3. *Services provided by the platform*

Offering services around the system means that communication, discovery and service deployment functions are made available to the domain applications. As a consequence, these applications must take into account the constraints linked to the transportation domain.

13.2.3.1. *Communications*

A lot of research has taken an interest in intervehicle communication networks in recent years. Many protocols have been created to allow vehicles to exchange information taking into account the constraints imposed by this type of specific communication. The constraints are mainly linked to the high level of dynamism and to the network support. In fact, the most constraining characteristic in the context of intervehicle networks is the high level of mobility of peer exchanging information. The speed the vehicles move at not only makes transmitting information between them difficult, but also makes the data that is received obsolete very quickly. With regard to networks, a lot of research has focused on the use of short-range networks (for example, IEEE 802.11, Ultra Wide Band, etc.) to create services to assist drivers. These networks allow two vehicles that are close to each other (i.e. a few hundred meters away from each other at most) to exchange information when they are able to communicate. Mobile phone networks (for example, 3G) allow this proximity constraint to be overcome, but require the use of an intermediary service while transmitting information. This leads to longer communication times that can turn out to be too much in certain cases (for example, communicating an emergency stop to vehicles that are behind).

It is possible to distinguish two modes of communication in the context of intervehicle services. The first, called *ad hoc* mode, consists of exchanging data directly between vehicles that are close to each other by using short-range networks. The second solution consists of exploiting a communication infrastructure, thanks to which vehicles can broadcast and/or receive information. If they generally allow the routing of information to vehicles to be greatly simplified, such infrastructures laid throughout the length of all roads cannot be envisaged in the short term. Direct communication between vehicles therefore offers an interesting alternative to deploy the first inter-vehicle services. Eventually, two solutions can turn out to be complementary. The VESPA approach, which will be described in the rest of this chapter, proves that it is possible to go without architecture, especially for notification of events that are taking place near the user. This absence of an architecture allows the reactivity of the system to improve (as it foregoes using a server that is more delicate to update). However, to access more distant services, using elements that are fixed in the architecture (for example, base stations) brings better management and a better supply of information.

13.2.3.2. *Services discovery*

To be able to discover available services is a classic function of service architectures. In fact, either a known service, having a registering role, is available (for example a UDDI directory), or applications that broadcast or collect information relating to available services, and construct *ad hoc* directories according to the results of listening to the network. The role of protocols like SLP (*Service Location Protocol*) is then decisive in this context.

If discovering services is needed and necessary, an important issue remains in intelligent transportation. The nodes (or vehicles) of the network under consideration are highly mobile. Consequently, a discovered service will not necessarily be able to be used (Figure 13.4). For example, this service may no longer be available when it could be useful to the application. If the request to the service was able to be carried out, there is thus no guarantee that the response will arrive completely or partially, if the connection is lost before the result is received.

Two solutions can help deal with this problem:

– having mechanisms that allow services to be chosen, which can be used while ensuring their availability. This can be carried out by relying on the context properties linked to the material that is calling on the service. As we have mentioned before, the context then becomes vital;

– using the service or data that the application will directly need with the user's terminal. In this way, the call will be made when the service is used.

Unfortunately, no complete and functional platform currently allows problems to be answered using the first solution. The second solution, meanwhile, can be implemented, on the condition that the specific nature (i.e. the high degree of mobility) of the environment is taken into account and managed.

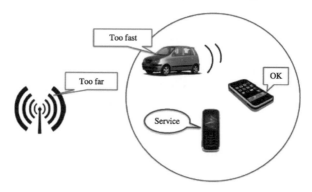

Figure 13.4. *Searching for services*

13.2.3.3. *Deployment of services*

The constraints linked to the vehicle's environment make the deployment, updation and application maintenance processes delicate. And yet, if we are to stand up to the changing nature of protocols and security updates or to simply allow the dynamic deployment of software components by the various parties, this issue becomes vital. In the case of ambient computing, all mobile terminals used to control or interact with their environments frequently find themselves connected to a fixed terminal so that the battery can be recharged. Therefore, it is possible to take advantage of this period of time when the device is connected to the network to update or install new applications. In the context of vehicles, this is no longer the case. The vehicle does not need to be recharged and therefore does not need to be connected to the network. It is regularly situated a good distance away from where its owner lives. It is therefore impossible to rely on the existence of a high-speed, reliable, and durable connection to carry out a set of operations that a user would wish. Use and maintenance must consequently rely on specific architectures, designed to be in this very dynamic kind of environment, and at the same time authorize access to the platform. The rest of this section presents both the needs and different solutions to this problem.

13.2.3.3.1. What deployment needs are there?

The deployment needs identified for vehicle applications and environments are two-fold:

– it is necessary to be able to update all systems present in the vehicle. In fact, certain basic software packages are obligatorily embedded to serve the minimum bootstrap required for the set of applications and services to be used. These basic packages usally accompany a set of basic services, which make implementing future applications easier. They must be able to benefit from evolutions when they are available and therefore it must be possible to update them dynamically;

– intervehicle communication allows parties to exchange information, services or resources. This exchange includes transfer, but also installation and starting up. Therefore, adding new parts of the application must be made possible. Moreover, this must be possible in the heat of the moment and must be able to withstand variations in connection quality. For example, if resources are shared by vehicles going anti-clockwise, the exploitable connection time will be extremely short and the whole transfer might not be able to be completed. The ability to restart this transfer when another source can be reached is the responsibility of the platform. For example, the next vehicle that can be reached that has the resource might be able to be exploited by it to end the transfer.

These two needs involve a certain number of issues, some of which have already been dealt with in other fields. It is therefore possible to benefit from "off-the-shelf" solutions to solve most problems. Among the main issues to address, managing the versions of elements is a priority. It is vital to know if an element must be updated or not, on the one hand to avoid pointless transfers, and on the other hand to avoid any risk of making the system unstable and introducing an incomptabile element. The management of versions therefore introduces another need: knowing the versions of modules that are necessary. In fact, intervehicle applications are made of a set of modules interacting with each other. Assembly remains subject to rules of interfacing and strict combinations, dictated by the nature of each component. Moreover, there is another difficulty in the possibility of defining dependencies in terms of resources and in terms of versions for the modules deployed. If a software service is deployed and requires a third service in a specific version, it must be possible to:

– make clear these dependencies and identify the version to carry out a deployment plan;

– know the status of the embedded software in the vehicle at all times so it is not used redundantly;

– know where and how to recover the right versions of each element.

This issue has already been addressed for the deployment of applications in distributed environments, but must be adapted for the vehicle's context. In fact, the constraints of the environment mean to be able to manage partial deployment. But, this type of requirement does not exist in an environment where the network connection is considered to be reliable and continuous. Moreover, in our context, and to benefit from the maximum number of services, it is important to be able to take advantage of all services or data as soon as they are available. Deployments can become competitive if two services depend on the same module when they request installation. This eventuality must be managed and the system must be able to respond to this type of request. Opening up the possibilities to different parties to be able to deploy resources or send data to the vehicle's application platform is a new source of complexity. Such deployment must not adversely affect applications that are already being executed. The arrival of new services or data must be carried out reliably or not at all. This reliability can be unintentionally adversely affected without wishing to harm anyone, but can also be the the result of malicious behavior. This is why, as in the case of distributed systems, security is necessary to guarantee such an architecture. It is vital to be able to certify that the recovered data is produced by parties who can be trusted. Moreover, it must be possible to be able to broadcast without fearing that sensitive information will be captured and that no malicious code can be found in the services used. Different solutions can be used to resolve all these issues using different deployment mechanisms that exist currently.

13.2.3.3.2. Available deployment mechanism

Deployment can be broken down into four important steps:

– the expression of deployment-related needs. For all resources or services to be deployed, its needs must be known in terms of third services or execution environments;

– the assembly or dynamic treatment of different services or data deployed;

– the conditioning of elements to be deployed. To be able to transmit and recover the information necessary for deployment, different data must be packaged in a format that can be understood by everybody;

– deployment itself, i.e. the effective transfer of the deployment unit from the emitter to the receiver.

The first two points must be offered by the architecture of the implemented platform, while the two latter points are dependent on the model used by the platform.

13.2.4. *Example of a platform*

The choice of execution environment is for now limited to packaged linux, .Nct, or Java environments. These are the most widely used in mobile terminals (while we perhaps await new standards during the democratization of computing embedded in vehicles). They are portable and adapt to many types of environment.

Among the different standards available, the OSGi platform appears to be the closest to meeting the needs mentioned. It is Java-oriented, relies on an event-based model, has a service register, and is easy to administer. If these properties can be found in other architectures, the OSGi platform has an asset that can make it stand out from others. It deals with the physical (conditioning and loading) as well as the logical (services) layers. Moreover, it has been designed to execute in constrained environments.

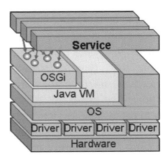

Figure 13.5. *Platform OSGi*

The OSGi Alliance is an independent, non-profit organization. It gathers together a large number of manufacturers, members or contributors. It proposes a set of specifications that offer a component-based and service-oriented environment that allows the lifecycle of the software to be managed in a standard way. This environment is based on Java (Figure 13.5). During its updates, the specification of the platform's core has not changed massively. It is extended, but has done so by increasing its range of standard services available. These are useable on the basic platform, but are not necessary to execute it. This allows a minimalism for the canvas to be guaranteed and ensures that it is easily executable on embedded materials. In fact, OSGi intially targets platforms like set-top boxes and residential or network links. These materials have limited memory and execution capacity. They have more stringent constraints regarding the lifecycle of software components as in these areas components must be able to be deployed and assembled dynamically during execution, without any interruption of existing services. With the emergence of new fields such as cellphones and computing embedded in vehicles, specification offers particular behavior for those specific environments. These features added to the specification are proposed by dedicated groups of experts. It should be noted that there is a group of experts in the context of vehicles. OSGi platforms have become the standard of dynamic Java service-oriented platforms.

OSGi therefore has all the concepts relating to service-oriented architectures. The canvass proposes a register in which services are recorded when they start. They are referenced by a service contract (in this context, a Java interface) and a set of properties (version, seller, language, etc.) that allows more in-depth searches for a service, thanks to LDAP filters. The platform also relies on an event-based system. It allows the notification of components executing on top of OSGi to manage their life cycle dynamically according to the actions performed on the platform.

OSGi allows remote deployment, execution, administration and uninstallation of software services. OSGi is made of two distinct layers: a plhysical layer that deals with deployment issues relating to conditioning units and code dependences, and a logical layer that allows service components to be described, then to be assembled, and their dynamic behavior to be managed. OSGi is therefore an abstraction layer, above the Java virtual machine that offers an execution environment to dynamic services. This architecture recovers all properties that allow modularity and the dynamic component connection to be increased. Although this platform offers the basic functionalities necessary to put in place services and intervehicle communications, it does not meet all the needs mentioned above and must therefore be personalized. Apart from its design that aims for scalability and dynamism, it is possible to accomplish personalization quite easily. In fact, as is illustrated in the following section, it is possible to compensate for the limits found in extending the framework.

The use of the platform in the context of vehicle services is illustrated in section 13.3.2.1 in the context of the VESPA project.

13.3. Dedicated transportation services and mode of communication

As mentioned previously, aspects relating to communications are among the most problematic in the area of transportation. Applications can be divided into two distinct categories: those that use a communication infrastructure and those that are able to do without it.

13.3.1. *Transportation-oriented services that use an infrastructure*

Communications used during exchanges between vehicles and an infrastructure can be divided into two large categories according to the communication coverage: short-range communication for point-to-point exchanges (for example, electronic tolls) or uni-directional communication in broadcast mode.

13.3.1.1. *Systems based on DSRC*

DSRC (Dedicated Short Range Communications) is a communication mechanism between a vehicle and a ground infrastructure. This mechanism can be uni- or bi-directional. It can be qualified by a short- or medium-range communication protocol (going up to 1,000 m). ETSI has allocated a band of 30 MHz in the 5.9 GHz frequency band for traffic telematic applications. The most well-known application is the electronic toll that allows toll barriers to be passed through at reduced speeds without even stopping (speeds of 30 km/h).

13.3.1.2. *Info-traffic services*

Info-traffic services rely on using a uni-directional broadcast link to cover a wide geographical area and thus reach all vehicles in this zone. Among the different protocols available, we can cite DAB and RDS–TMC. This traffic information is directly used by embedded GPS receivers in vehicles and enriches geographic data coming from positioning systems.

13.3.2. *Exchange services between vehicles*

As we have seen before, the services cited require an infrastructure to be put in place (for example, at the edge of the road) which is often quite burdensome and costly. To remedy that, new services are appearing that only use vehicles taking part in the service.

This technique is mainly used to exchange information between vehicles to inform users as quickly as possible (which is not the case when information must stay in an infrastructure).

In fact, despite the many efforts made to reduce it, the number of people killed on the roads remains very high, mainly due to the human factor (behavior that causes accidents, too long a response time, etc). To try to reduce the number of accidents, many programs rely on using wireless communications which has started to be used in Europe, Japan and the United States to study "intelligent transportation systems" (ITS). Such systems use information and communication technologies, and more specifically wireless networks, to allow vehicles to exchange information and thus warn drivers of danger (accident, emergency brake, etc.)

In the rest of this section, we will concentrate on systems that assist drivers using vehicle-to-vehicle communication. Thanks to recent progress in mobile computing and short-range wireless networks (IEEE 802.11, Ultra Large Band (ULB), etc) [LUO 05], a vehicle can thus receive information produced by close neighbors or even others who are farther away, thanks to multi-jump techniques that use intermediary vehicles as vectors. Exchanges between vehicles do not rely on any fixed infrastructure here. Vehicles directly exchange with each other according to the possible connections.

13.3.2.1. *VESPA*

The VESPA (*Vehicular Event Sharing with a mobile Peer-to-peer Architecture* [DCI 10]) Project, conducted at the University of Valenciennes, in collaboration with the University of Zaragoza in Spain and the Telecom Institute in Evry, aims to propose a system that allows information to be shared between vehicles. The originality of this system is that it offers a generic approach to allow different types of information to be shared. Today, existing solutions in the context of inter-vehicle communication are in fact dedicated to sharing a type of particular information or event:

– information sharing about available parking spaces [XU 04];

– information exchange about emergency brakes [BRU 04, MOR 03];

– information exchange about traffic in real time [ZHO 08].

Today, there are many events, about which it is interesting to exchange information between vehicles to improve driver safety or reduce their environmental footprint (for example, accidents, traffic jams, emergency brakes, parking lots, emergency services vehicles, special convoys, etc). The events can be generated by sensors embedded in the vehicles (for example accident, emergency brake) or signaled by drivers (for example, traffic jam, obstacle on the road). It is clearly unthinkable for a driver to use different systems for each type of information that they are interested in. The aim of the VESPA system is therefore to facilitate information sharing between vehicles that is related to all sorts of events, whether the vehicles are mobile or not (for example, a vehicle with faulty back lights), whether they are of potential interest to all surrounding vehicles (for example, an available parking space), or only those driving in a particular direction (for example, an emergency brake). Figure 13.6 illustrates how the VESPA system is used to locate an available parking space.

In the rest of this section, we will look at two essential functions of the VESPA system: evaluation of the relevance of events and their dissemination into the vehicle network.

Figure 13.6. *Use of the VESPA system to search for a parking space*

13.3.2.1.1. Estimation of the relevance of events

Thanks to the VESPA system, each equipped vehicle can receive a certain amount of information on events happening nearby. However, not all of this information is necessarily relevant to the vehicle that receives it and/or is interesting to the driver. Mechanisms are therefore necessary to filter information and not to saturate the driver with pointless information.

To determine if an event is relevant to a vehicle, VESPA calaculates a probability for each event it receives. This probability allows it to estimate whether the vehicle will encounter the event or not. Carrying out such an estimation is not unimportant. The destination of each vehicle is in fact unknown. Unlike GPS navigation systems, it is unthinkable for assistance systems like VESPA to impose on its users to systematically tell their destination. By communication alerts to drivers, the system is always useful, for all journeys, including daily journeys for which the driver does not want to state their final destination.

The probablity of encountering such an event can be calculated in different ways [DEL 11]. For example, when digital maps are available, the probability can be calculated using short paths, by comparing the time needed for the vehicle to reach the event, and the duration of the event.

13.3.2.1.2. Dissemniation of information in the ad hoc inter-vehicle network

The objective of the dissemination protocol is to forward the data that describe the events observed to the vehicle/driver couples for which they are potentially relevant. As with many existing dissemination protocols, the protocol used by the VESPA system limits bandwidth use. In fact, when some information has to be shared, only some of the vehicles must relay the corresponding message or the network will be overloaded. To avoid that, only the farthest vehicle re-broadcasts the message. More information on the mechanics implemented to reach this objective is available in [CEN 08].

Moreover, the main specificity of VESPA's dissemination protocol is to adapt the dissemination channel in response to the event. In fact, unlike existing solutions, VESPA supports dissemination in the network of different types of events. And yet, these different types of events must not be broadcast in the network in the same way. For example, information regarding a parking space must be communicated to all surrounding vehicles, wherever they are going. However, a message describing an emergency brake or a traffic jam is concerned only with vehicles traveling toward that event who are likely to encounter it.

To implement such a mode of dissemination, the protocol used in the VESPA system also uses this probability. Thus, when a vehicle receives a message that must be relayed, it will only be relayed if the probability calculated for the corresponding event is higher than a fixed threshold. The basic principle of the dissemination mechanism used in fact is that a relevant message for a vehicle is probably also relevant for its neighbors.

13.3.2.1.3. VESPA architecture

The general architecture of VESPA is optimized to take advantage of the properties of the OSGi service model (Figure 13.7) presented in section 13.2.4. Management of basic transport-oriented services is delegated to the platform. VESPA connects the location or time services that are appropriate at the time. The modes of communication are also adapted and changed according to need. Different services that facilitate the collection and broadcasting of information add an adaptation layer that allows pre- or post-treatment of raw information. These components can be updated to benefit from new functions.

The core of VESPA is a component that manages the collected data and takes appropriate decisions according to the context. Different foundations that rule behavior are assembled and can evolve. A component allows advanced services to be managed, like a protocol for reserving parking spaces, i.e. to deal with information received by the different parties looking for a free space signaled by another user. Another component allows the probability of finding one to be estimated. From the data received, it allows relevance to be estimated with regard to the vehicle's context. Finally, different services allow each type of data collected to be managed and treated. These services can of course evolve and be updated. Moreover, new services that support new types of data can be added dynamically. Thus, if the vehicle arrives in a specific environment, it is able to receive the software brick necessary to extend its capacity and interact with its new environment. Finally, VESPA connects a graphic interface service to give the driver the information that has been collected and treated, like the directions to a parking lot or signaling an accident.

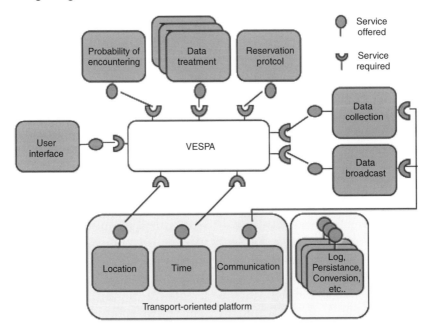

Figure 13.7. *VESPA architecture*

13.3.2.2. *RouVéCom*

The RouVéCom (Roads and Communicating Vehicles) Project aims to create an environment of communication between vehicles as well as between roads and vehicles. It uses new technologies in the field of radiofrequency communications.

This project is from a multi-laboratory project team at CNRS (EPML) that groups together electronic and microelectronic laboratories that specialize in hyperfrequencies (IEMN, IETR, Telice), a computing laboratory (LIFL), and a research institute dedicated to transportation (INRETS).

Different study scenarios have been defined in the context of this work:

– Broadcasting location information among close vehicles: some vehicles are equipped with a location system (for example of a GPS receiver). This location information can then be shared with surrounding vehicles so that a vehicle that does not have a location system can know its approximate position compared to its environment. This information improves and completes the functioning of the current intelligent gait.

– Communication between the vehicle in front and the rest: the idea is to use the vehicle's particular and favorable perception at the front to inform the other vehicles [HED 01]. The objective is to contribute to the anticipation of the driving task.

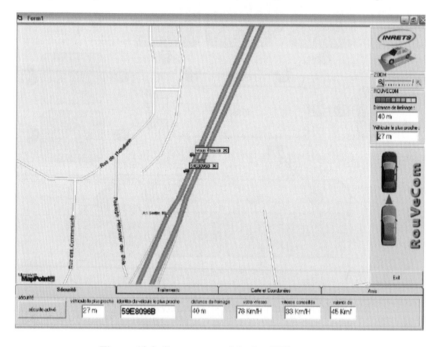

Figure 13.8. *Screen copy of the RouVéCom system*

The authors depart from the theory that every vehicle is equipped with a GPS receiver associated with map software. With such a system and with such a unique referential in common, each vehicle is capable of positioning itself on a map. Thanks to communication circuits, each vehicle peridiocally broadcasts its position and receives the position of surrounding vehicles. This system allows the vehicles that precede and follow it to be located. The interface of the system developed in the framework of the. RouVéCom project is presented in Figure 13.8.

According to the information received from other vehicles, each vehicle can determine whether they are in a dangerous situation or not. The system can then warn the driver (for example, if they are approaching at great speed a vehicle driving more slowly than theirs).

13.3.2.3. *The CALM architecture*

The CALM architecture (*Continuous Air-interface Long and Medium range*) and associated standards aim to best use the radio resources available. CALM offers a multi-layered architecture that allows communication between the infrastructure and vehicles as well as between vehicles to communicate among themselves.

The services that can be built using CALM are either linked to road safety or oriented toward commercial applications. The list of services can be found in the Calm Handbook [ISO 06].

CALM is based on IPv6 and the work coming from the IETF working group on NEMO (*NEtwork MObility*).

13.4. Public transportation services

Services dedicated to transportation are not limited to individual vehicles or roads. Many services can be imagined in the context of public transportation. They mainly aim to offer services that assist the traveler before or after they makes their journey.

13.4.1. *ICAU*

Currently, users of public transport suffer from a lack of information to guide them during their journey. When this information is available (for example, when it is displayed), accessing it is not always practical (for example, being sat away from where information is displayed), unpersonalized (for example, for the visually-impaired), and often under used (for example, there is no alert for distracted or busy users).

The ICAU application (information/cooperation with users) allows users to be told automatically and individually as soon as a bus approaches a stop they want to get off at [RIO 04a]. A material prototype of this example has been carried out and patented [RIO 04b].

Going from this experience, we can express the characteristics of this application as follows:

– A user has a PDA communicating terminal. In this terminal, a software is deployed that provides information relating to the urban network that it uses, a plan of the transportation network, and the theoretical timetable stating when buses should be at the various stops.

– The stop's notification service allows the user to choose the stop they wish to get off at on their terminal. This notification service communicates via WiFi with the calculator embedded in the bus. This calculator, via a geolocation system like GPS, always knows its position on the transport network. When the bus approaches a stop on the line, the embedded system sends users in the bus information regarding this stop (for example, the stop's name). Each terminal user compares this information with the wish expressed by the owner of the terminal. If the information corresponds, the terminal tells the owner by sounding an alrm of their choice (for example, audio, visual, vibrating, etc.) that they must prepared to get off.

Therefore, we can see in these needs that certain functions (plan, timetable) will always be available on the user's terminal while the notification service only functions in a bus equipped with a location service and the notification application.

Figure 13.9 presents the software architecture in the form of components.

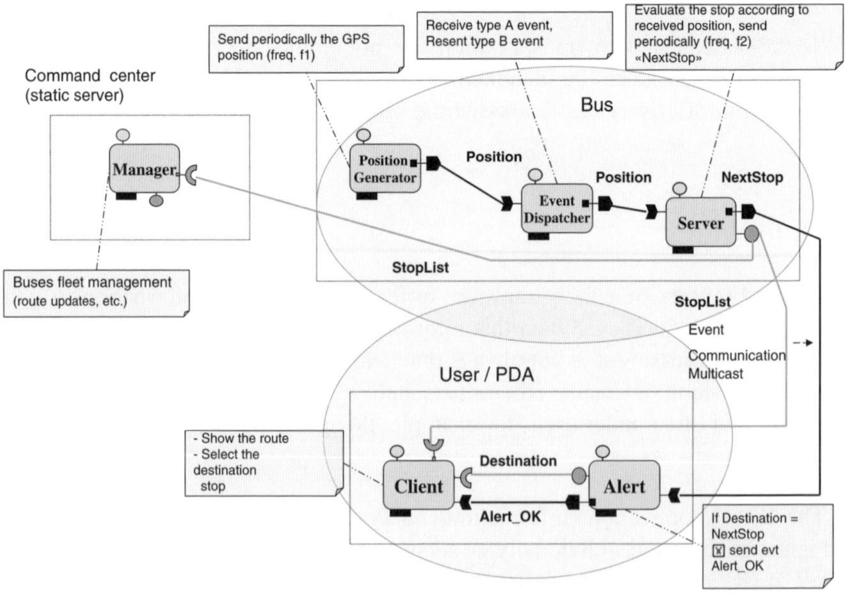

Figure 13.9. *Service software architecture*

13.4.2. *Internet access on trains*

More and more train companies are offering Internet access on trains. Almost all solutions are based on communication via satellite. In fact, the satellite offers complete coverage of a territory without having to deploy communication infrastructure on the ground. However, the main technical difficulty consists of permanently keeping connectivity with the satellite whatever be the environment. If in the open country there is no difficulty, the problem becomes more complicated with regard to towns where the satellite can perhaps be obscured by buildings or even in a mountainous area. If a tunnel is being traveled through, the link is also broken.

To make up for this loss of connectivity, many solutions are possible: move on to another form of communication (WiFi or UMTS) if this is deployed and available, or even delay/buffer the exchanges until the connection is re-established with the satellite [BOC 07]. This is ubiquitous Internet access.

13.5. Conclusion

In this chapter, we have addressed different aspects of the design of applications dedicated to making different forms of transportation safer, more pleasant, and more fun. Current areas of research for services dedicated to transportation involve several issues:

– design platforms and deployment of services: putting in place services on heterogeneous material platforms is a real challenge in making sure that the use of such services is successful;

– communication infrastructures are also an important aspect. The important question is "can we go without an infrastructure?". Current research and standardizing at a communication protocol level make the absence of an infrastructure possible. As we have tried to show in the part on intervehicle communication, this opens up new fields of applications;

– a final theme that has not been addressed here because it has been taken up in another chapter of this book is interfaces, and particularly their adaptation and acceptance by the users of these services.

The field of research is therefore an important field, with many specialities touching on ambient computing.

13.6. Bibliography

[BOC 07] BOCQUET A., GRANSART C., "Multi-model architecture for ITS software design improvements", *Telecommunications, 2007, ITST '07, 7th International Conference on Intelligent Transport Systems Telecommunications*, IEEE, pp. 1–6, 2007.

[BRU 04] BRUIN D.D., KROON J., KLAVEREN R., NELISSE M., "Design and test of a cooperative adaptive cruise control system", *Intelligent Vehicles Symposium (IV'04)*, IEEE Computer Society, pp. 392–396, June 2004.

[CEN 08] CENERARIO N., DELOT T., ILARRI S., "Dissemination of information in inter-vehicle ad hoc networks", *Intelligent Vehicles Symposium (IV'08)*, IEEE Computer Society, pp. 763–768, June 2008.

[DEL 10] DELOT T., CENERARIO N., ILARRI S., "Vehicular event sharing with a mobile peer-to-peer architecture", *Transportation Research Part C: Emerging Technologies*, vol. 18, no. 4, pp. 584–598, 2010.

[DEL 11] DELOT T., ILARRI S., CENERARIO N., HIEN T., "Event sharing in vehicular networks using geographic vectors and maps", *Mobile Information Systems*, vol. 7, IOS Press, 2011.

[DES 10] DESERTOT M., LECOMTE S., POPOVICI D., THILLIEZ M., DELOT T., "A context-aware framework for services management in the Transportation Domain", in SOCIETY I.C. (ed.), *10ᵉ Conférence Internationale sur les nouvelles technologies de la répartition (NOTERE'2010)*, Tozeur, Tunisia, May 2010.

[DEY 99] DEY A.K., ABOWD G.D., "Towards a better understanding of context and context-awareness", *LNCS*, vol. 1707/1999, pp. 304–307, 1999.

[GRA 09] GRANSART C., LECOMTE S., "Utilisation du contexte dans l'adaptation d'applications dédiées aux transports", Atelier Inforsid GEDSIP, Toulouse, France, 2009.

[HED 01] HEDDEBAUT M., RIOULT J., KLINGER M., MENHAJ A., GRANSART C., "Microwave radio coverage for vehicle-to-vehicle and IN-vehicle communication", *8th World Congress on Intelligent Transport Systems*, Sydney, Australia, October 2001.

[ISO 06] ISO working group on Intelligent Transport Systems, TC 204, "The CALM Handbook" (Communication Access for Land Mobile), 2006. http://www.tih.org.uk/images/c/c7/ The_CALM_Handbook.pdf.

[LUO 05] LUO J., HUBAUX J.P., "A survey of research in inter-vehicle communications", *Embedded Security in Cars – Securing Current and Future Automotive IT Applications*, pp. 111–122, Springer-Verlag, Berlin, 2005.

[MOR 03] MORSINK P., HALLOUZI R., DAGLI I., CSEH C., SCHAFERS L., NELISSE M., BRUIN D.D., "CARTALK 2000: Development of a cooperative ADAS based on vehicle-to-vehicle communication", *10th World Congress on Intelligent Transport Systems and Services*, Madrid, Spain, 2003.

[RIO 04a] RIOULT J., GRANSART C., AMBELLOUIS S., "Zut, j'ai loupé mon arrêt! Un nouveau service d'aide aux déplacements", *Les nouvelles technologies dans la cité*, Rennes, France, 2004.

[RIO 04b] RIOULT J., GRANSART C., AMBELLOUIS S., Détermination de l'arrêt souhaité, French patent application no. 04 12856 déposé le 3 décembre 2004, ALL/HC 116.623, 2004.

[SCH 08] SCHOCH E., KARGL F., WEBER M., LEINMULLER T., "Communication patterns in VANETs", *Communications Magazine*, IEEE, vol. 46, no. 11, pp. 119–125, 2008.

[XU 04] XU B., OUKSEL A.M., WOLFSON O., "Opportunistic resource exchange in inter-vehicle ad hoc networks", *Fifth International Conference on Mobile Data Management (MDM'04)*, IEEE Computer Society, 2004.

[ZHO 08] ZHONG T., XU B., SZCZUREK P., WOLFSON O., "Trafficinfo: an algorithm for VANET dissemination of real-time traffic information", *Proceedings of the 15th World Congress on Intelligent Transport Systems*, New York, NY, USA, November 2008.

Chapter 14

Sociotechnical Ambient Systems: From Test Scenario to Scientific Obstacles

14.1. Introduction

Scientific advances have led to an explosion in the number and functions of electronic devices used in everyday lives, throwing us into the world of ambient intelligence, as defined by Weiser 20 years ago in 1991 [WEI 91]. In this context, systems' designs presuppose movement from a centered point on multifunction machines toward a set of devices with varying interactions that are distributed and dispersed in the environment, which can be accessed by interfaces, thrusting the user into increasingly realistic and mixed worlds. As a result, the individual and her/his social, physical and organizational contexts are at the heart of considerations in the design of these systems, which must be adapted to users' needs and behaviors. This human-machine coupling must be intuitive in correlation with the content of exchanges and multimodality. Some processes may also need to occur on demand in the network (system coupling) without the users' outside control and must, in addition, be implemented by embedded autonomous entities acting collectively. These systems, consisting of human beings and components continuously interacting, may be physical entities or distributed devices. They are autonomous and have the ability to adapt to a human being's task and to the available digital physical resources.

In the field of ambient systems, the current design covers a spectrum ranging from dedicated *ad hoc* systems, to open and evolving systems. On the one hand, a system specific to one application may be implemented by an ambient system, like for example, the followup of a package by an RFID tag. A standard design focused around

Chapter written by Georges DA COSTA, Jean-Pierre GEORGÉ and Marie-Pierre GLEIZES.

this kind of scenario results in an *ad hoc* system, which is highly efficient but may be difficult to use in another context. On the other hand, ambient systems in the future will not be completely specified but complex, distributed and open. Designers will no longer have the ability to completely control them and create them in the standard descending way.

To relieve the challenge of designing these systems, interdependent and interdisciplinary research must solve these related problems:

– at a collective level: this entails studying interactions (between artificial and/or human agents) and the means of obtaining coherent and adapted collective behavior despite complexity and dynamics;

– at the human level: we need to understand the user's needs and behavior;

– at the level of the artificial agent: it is necessary to study its different aspects such as decision-making, autonomy, and adaptation;

– at the environmental level: we need to know how to represent and recognize the environment to adapt to it;

– design methods and tools: future designers need to have access to a series of models, methods, and tools to deploy these systems.

This chapter focuses on the preliminary design stage for ambient socio-technical systems that are not designed for a specific application, but a more general application that is described by one or more scenarios. The aim here is partly to examine tests led in the workshop on ambient systems, which have been undertaken at ETIA (Ecole Thématique Intelligence Ambiante, Villeneuve d'Ascq, 2009)[1]. The 21 participants in the workshop mostly consisted of researchers (PhD students and researchers) in computer science working on different sub-fields such as human–machine interaction, information systems, networking, etc. The aim of the workshop was to examine a mockup of an ambient socio-technical system in the form of software and/or material building blocks and to define the main challenges facing researchers in ambient intelligence today.

14.2. Definitions and characteristics

Ambient systems are designed to provide adapted services that respond to an individual, collective or social requirement [COU 08]. Their "ambient" components must consist of physical entities (PDAs, sensors, etc.) or distributed software. These entities are known as AmID (*Ambient Intelligence Devices*) in this chapter. AmIDs, have, by default, the ability to interact (perception and action), a more or less

---

1 www.univ-valenciennes.fr/congres/etia09.

"intelligent" autonomous behavior and may have the ability to adapt themselves to the user's current task and the available digital and physical resources.

The development of ambient systems requires the use of different technologies and/or tools. The latter are described in the form of a stack (Figure 14.1), called AmiLab (*Ambient Laboratory*) where the lowest levels represent the most basic components and the highest levels describe more complex elements designed using lower levels. In AmiLab, considered levels are as follows:

– components that are basic electronic entities;

– sensors and effectors capable of collecting data and adapting to their environment, respectively;

– AmIDs that correspond to an augmented entity (either sensor or effectors, which are, for example, capable of perception, decision-making, and action);

– network functions that allow an AmID to communicate with at least one other AmID;

– *middleware* that provides functions relating to discovery, interaction, and dynamic composition of functions and sensory-motor devices;

– user services that correspond to the "intelligent" level where the most relevant function to the user is carried out, the interaction with the user.

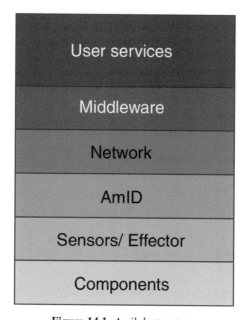

Figure 14.1. *Amilab structure*

The basis of ambient systems relies on the notion of interaction (human-system or system-to-system) and on the local autonomous component of AmIDs. Indeed, interaction increases the action capabilities of system components. As a result, the challenge of designing such systems is based on the hyper-interaction capabilities between human and/or artificial components. It implies that components in these systems must be able to interact with other components that are not known in advance by humans/users. These interactions can take place between digital entities (agent, processing capabilities, etc.), physical entities (such as medication, patient beds, PDAs, classrooms, etc.) and environmental elements (such as light levels and temperature in the home, weather on campus, etc.) or a collection of all or some of these entities and environmental elements. In addition, because components are autonomous and mobile, they must be able to judge the most relevant means of interaction and find other entities with which they can interact according to their environment.

The central and original point here is to provide AmIDs with the means of adapting to their context, either by knowing to choose the adapted interface, or to carry out the correct action to satisfy the needs of users while being transparent for the user. To respond to these challenges, among others, new grounds must be explored. It is necessary to gradually abandon finality during the AmID design stage. The AmID designer therefore does not know the role the design will play in its projected ambient system and its initial function may be changed. The mobile phone, for example, is used today as a mirror or flashlight that is completely different to its original function. At the design stage, it is necessary to account for essential conditions according to which AmIDs must function:

– An AmID ignores the explicit collective finality of the AmID network in which it is located. This sets it apart from standard programming for which the adjustment of a collective finality assimilate to *feed-back* in cybernetics. An AmID's specification is, as a result, incomplete.

– An AmID ignores the languages of others, that are not of the same kind and ontologies are not initially shared. This is one of the presumptions in ambient systems because a component at its design phase will not have been specified to interact during its life with all other AmIDs.

– Each AmID is generally able to perceive actions in the environment (including humans or artificial systems) by itself via an interface. This interface must adapt to the context.

– Each AmID must have action capabilities in the environment using effectors or communicating via interfaces.

– An AmID must be informed of the actions of AmIDs around it, notably via messages and sensors.

The design of these systems requires a different approach to that of standard systems and software because, as they are open, incompletely specified, complex and distributed, designers therefore no longer have the ability to completely control them and design them in descending order. Collective functions must therefore be developed [DIM 05].

In addition, systems can no longer be designed by a single design team at the same time. This indicates that the designer no longer has access to the completely formalized final needs of a client. The previously cited design approach for ambient socio-technical systems entails defining and modeling a general basic inoperable architecture, which is open and can be extended. This technological basis enables the introduction and development of complementary, multi-use and reusable building blocks that are vital for the creation of innovative applications for roaming users. A primary example is that of collecting environmental information and the user's context, security, and protection of private life are essential points of this.

14.3. Real-life scenario: *Ambient Campus*

To design this kind of system, it is tempting to simply combine the different technologies related to ambient systems. It is more pertinent to base this on different scenarios, even if they are currently prospective to more precisely evaluate genuine needs and constraints. The *Ambient Campus* scenario shows what we can reasonably expect from the development of these technologies in just a few years' time. A university campus, for example, integrates multiple infrastructures and interdependent services that come into their own when they have a continuous and considerable flow of information. The campus is a large-scale ambient system whose infrastructure includes rooms, buildings, and services in close interaction with users such as students, teachers, administrators, or management.

5th September 2029. Neo has just arrived on Paul Sabatier Corp (PSC) campus. His personal digital AMI has taken care of every aspect of administration and Neo only has to send his electronic signature to PSC to confirm as well as accept his course fees. For this verification, as for any transaction over $1,000, Neo's identity is biometrically confirmed.

When he exits the metro, his AMI sends a campus map to his mobile phone. This map, made available by BIG, the campus information system, is specifically generated for Neo when his location on the campus and profile are detected, and specific elements have been highlighted (its the first day of registration for Neo in his License degree). BIG contacted AMI to transmit this map.

The screen on Neo's phone is quite small and retinal projection systems are still expensive. One of the campus information screens offers to display the map between two advertisements. Neo accepts and without any effort on his part, the map is displayed. In addition, these screens are fitted with intuitive control interfaces and Neo can easily use this map for additional information, etc.

Figure 14.2. *View of an ambient campus*

19th October. Neo is outside his next class with the students from his group. The secretary changes the room at the last minute. The students are notified of this change and an itinerary is provided to go to the new room as quickly as possible. This information is also sent to Professor Smith, their lecturer. Unfortunately, the second room is already being used (after all, room planning in 2029 is not so different from 2012). This time, PRO, Professor Smith's personal agent, searches for an alternative. A neighboring room, detecting itself empty and having all the necessary requirements, responds to PRO.

The lesson starts and Neo comes to the board to solve an exercise. Meanwhile, Professor Smith studies the information BIG has sent him about Neo. He can see his mixed track record (after all a student in 2029 is not so different from one in 2012), as well as his former education that explains a gap in his knowledge, making the exercise more difficult. Professor Smith compares this with the other students and decides to change the lesson slightly to adjust and provide the missing knowledge.

Unfortunately, a fire alarm goes off. Is it real or a drill? As a research team from the computing research laboratory is testing a crisis management system, alerts increase but in cases of doubt, it is always best to evacuate. Students have also received a map on their phone based on their current position, which indicates the evacuation route toward the nearest assembly point.

2nd December. Neo is having a few difficulties with one subject, but is not alone. AMI puts him in contact with four other students experiencing the same problems (in the same way Neo has been put in contact with a number of friends). They meet in a revision room reserved for them by their AMIs. These rooms are particularly well technologically equipped for learning and the real work can begin. Their activity is analyzed and compared with a database of work sessions. The system gradually suggests supporting materials and other electronic resources.

At lunch time, the students decide to eat. Their AMIs notify them as usual of the occupation of the three university cafes. This data collected in real time reflects the estimated waiting time fairly precisely. One of the cafes is less busy and their AMIs suggest this. The same mechanisms are also used to collect the statistics of campus use to foresee new investments. The university is therefore one of the first to have paved paths, which students actually walk on!

Neo's friends from his favorite online role-playing game also appear on his screen with their position. If authorized, Neo can find them quickly and know their availability and the best means of contacting them. The authorizations can be managed according to categories (friends, colleagues, students) and can be dynamic (i.e. change over time, workload, etc.). Information is collected as and when by their AMIs, location via Wifi (average precision), RFID in rooms (high precision), availability given per person (interface on a mobile phone or PDA), or deduced (class room, IT rooms, meeting rooms, offices, on the phone, at the computer, etc.). However, unfortunately, the location alert functions ("you are 20 m from Mr X who you urgently need to see to get a signature") and the prediction of path overlaps must be paid for. However, this was the precondition for SmallBrother investing in PSC campus (as well as sitting on the board of directors).

Neo can manage a list of people in this same way. It has therefore given his mobile phone the ability to go into "available" mode (where he can meet anyone) to "ninja" mode (where he is invisible on campus, particularly useful when he wants to see his girlfriend).

13th February. Neo is surprised when his AMI suggests a new service, apparently, produced independently by a collection of services by the AMI/PRO/BIG collective on campus. Finally, the "killer-app" he has been waiting for which will push him to finish his studies!

14.4. Intuitive architectures

In an ambient system, AmIDs interact and even cooperate together with their environment. In the almost opposite manner to the completely distributed and ubiquitous entities that are AmIDs, this environment can be either completely centralized (such as the management of geographic data in Android [BIS 03]) or non-existent (if we consider AmIDs to be self sufficient). To work on these different hypotheses during the workshop, the *Ambient Campus* scenario (section 14.3) was given to participants. Their goal was to propose a supporting infrastructure for this scenario. Objectives were also to understand the multi-disciplinary aspect of these problems and to highlight scientific challenges.

14.4.1. *The building blocks of the Ambient Campus scenario*

As a first stage, the majority of groups in the workshop identified the need to define the entities involved in the scenario. The main types of non-human entity collected were: BIG, Paul Sabatier Corporation, Rooms, AMI (one or more per student), and PRO. AMIs and PRO were entities that enter and exit the ambient system considered.

The groups then focused on the concept of services. Two types of service were identified in this scenario:

– services specific to the application such as subscription management, map management, room bookings;

– generic services such as locating an individual via their *smart phone*, authentication of new arrivals, management of access rights, data security (payments), respect for private life, managing profiles and roles, adapting information content to means of communication between entities, implementing information systems, and managing communication between entities.

These different services and entities use shared information of different types, ranging from the state of a room light to the set of students' trajectories during a crisis situation. The central question concerns the type and form of infrastructure allowing the management and communication of this information between services and entities.

14.4.2. *Limitations of simplistic infrastructures*

Initially, it appears that the two extreme solutions (AmIDs alone or a completely centralized structure) were unusable. As we will see in the next section, a shared infrastructure is necessary to enable AmIDs to offer authorizations (building and data access for instance). In addition, a totally centralized version is impossible as it would entail too much communication when deployed on a large scale.

Let us first consider the limitations of systems without a support infrastructure. To operate, AmIDs must collect information on their environment (temperature, proximity to other AmIDs, etc.). It is therefore necessary to be able to identify AmIDs to manage their access rights to this information, but also actions they may make. A student can therefore not cancel all her/his lessons for a day, but a personal tutor can. It should be noted that there is a fine line between some fixed AmIDs and some infrastructure elements. A door can therefore be considered in the two roles depending on the exact definition of the chosen infrastructure.

With regard to centralized systems, they can only be used when we want a localized and autonomous system, such as a museum, for example. If we want an open system such as on a campus, it is costly and complex to centralize and manage all the information produced by the different elements in the infrastructure. In any case, centralizing all the information in a system is not useful in itself. While it is interesting for an AmID managing a blind to know the exact light levels inside and outside a room, centralizing the two values for all the rooms on a campus has little meaning and is highly costly in terms of communication.

14.4.3. *Context and role bubbles*

AmIDs are situated in a complex environment, with each in turn interacting with different elements. In one room, interaction can take place with other AmIDs as well as with another AmID on the same floor (a coffee machine or printer, for example) or even in the same country (verification of the status of a bank account, for example).

Context bubbles can be defined as the set of coherent contexts (in terms of scope and meaning). For example, a person is her/his own closest bubble. A second bubble is the room in which s/he is in. Its building is then next, followed by its campus and so on, etc.

Equally, role bubbles refer to AmID roles in relation to their context. A user can have a role as a *teacher* as well as another role as a *student*. However, away from their establishment, these roles do not define users. Roles are strongly linked to context bubbles and it is possible to have several roles simultaneously. A student can therefore be a first-aider and thus can become the person responsible if someone is feeling faint during a course.

Every AmID is therefore immersed in a constant interaction between context and roles:

– a context is an overlap of several different contexts (interrelated geographic bubbles);

– a change of context is therefore a geographic movement;

– a change of role follows a change in context, but can also a be a logical change (i.e. obtaining a first-aid certificate);

– infrastructure (centralized or even completely distributed) manages roles and transmits context.

Infrastructure therefore manages data effectively, whether on a global or local level. However, managing data does not necessarily involve transmitting them. A fundamental objective of infrastructure is the detailed management of data by:

– Adaptation: when AmIDs do not have the same needs and characteristics (more specifically from the perspective of communications), it is necessary to adapt data before sending it to AmIDs. A *smartphone* does not need the same video flow as a television and transmitting a non-adapted HD video flow to a *smartphone* would generate a network overload and reduce its autonomy while still displaying a miniature version. Equally, the service needs of different AmIDs are different and adaptation means that these can be adapted as needed. One of the most common uses is that of marketing, service research, or personalization.

– Aggregation: transmitting aggregated data reduces the amount of processing needed for an AmID while reducing the number of communication resources used. As a result, to find a free room with a video projector, it is simpler for an AmID to directly ask for the aggregated response rather than ask for the state of all rooms. The same also applies when we are interested in an average value such as the temperature or humidity of a building.

– Synthesis: this is one of the most complex aspects because it is related to the effective use of data introducing a vast range of possibilities. Adaptation and aggregation are elements that react to the infrastructure while synthesis can be seen as a more proactive aspect. Depending on its context and specific rules, it can produce new data. Synthesis can therefore detect several students having the same difficulties and put them into contact with one another.

This logical view of hierarchical context bubbles allows us to design an ambient supportive infrastructure away from technical constraints.

14.5. Scientific challenges

This logical vision is not directly and simply transposable to reality. There are two kinds of scientific challenges that emerge from a logical perspective concerning bubbles and roles' parameter, and from a technical perspective with regard to the hardware and software structure, which provides this logical infrastructure.

However, ambient intelligence is, by its very nature, multi-disciplinary and raises a number of other scientific challenges in each of the disciplines concerned within social and human sciences or ICT. We will focus here on the levels involved in software research ranging from AmIDs to services within the field of ITC. Difficult challenges will be treated at each level, between AmIDs, the network, and the aspects of behavior, and the decisions to examine the challenges of the ambient systems presented in section 14.2. The most significant scientific challenges for an ambient system are:

– System acceptability and respect for private life are challenges that must condition any development of the application and must be ensured at the four levels of Amilab: AmID, networks, *middleware*, and services. In the *Ambient Campus* scenario, people on campus must be able to easily use this new system. However, students' private data such as their location outside of class hours must not be accessible by teachers.

– Reliability entails ensuring that the system functions correctly. The mechanisms implemented must be reliable at all levels. This problem is not specific to ambient computing, but is dominant because these applications are centered around humans and must be reliable at all levels.

– The system's reactivity allows it to intervene in real time within an acceptable timeframe for the situation in question. For instance, Neo, arriving for the first time on campus, must have a map sent to him within a reasonable timeframe so that he can use it to get around.

– Discretion supports an embedded system, which is less intrusive and therefore more acceptable. This challenge requires the system to have self-* properties [KEP 03], which ensure system autonomy and therefore as little intervention as possible by the user. The ambient campus applications therefore do not mean that students have to wear special clothing filled with sensors. In this scenario, the technology exists and is familiar to users.

– Adaptation and auto-adaptation allow a system to adapt independently to context and to its user(s). Adaptation can be treated at the AmID level which, through its learning capabilities, can modify its future behavior to adapt itself. The network can adapt to maintain its level of service by, for example, ensuring connections. In terms of *middleware*, adaptation allows components to exploit their environment. Human-machine interaction must also be able to adapt to user's conditions. Adaptation refers to the system's cognitive abilities or the system's learning capacity, i.e. the ability to test and improve its behavior. Adaptation results in a more robust system, i.e. it is more resistant to malfunction. In this scenario, adaptation is necessary to allow adapted labeling to support interaction with the campus map. It is also required to manage an event such as changing rooms and lack of availability. Auto-adaptation is manifested by creating new services proposed by the collective at the end of the scenario.

– The management of context relates to the representation, memorization and use of elements (environment, other human or artificial actors, etc) with a potential impact on the execution of one or several tasks. The notion of context is important at all four levels of Amilab. Its model is complex since its environment with constantly changing actors is highly dynamic. Context is necessary due to its use in processes such as adaptation, personalization, information transmission and interaction. Managing context is necessary throughout the scenario so that entities consider the most pertinent decisions such as, for instance, helping students by suggesting supporting materials based on students' current activity and their educational profile.

– Optimality in the system's function is linked to its ability to efficiently manage resources such as energy, memory, or resources related to the application and therefore is evaluated at all levels of Amilab. Resources such as university cafes are more commonly used and provide users with more satisfaction.

– The opening of the system by accepting new entities in the system. The arrival of new AmIDs into the ambient system requires the design of models and mechanisms for introducing new elements into the network, *middleware*, and services. The system must be able to deal with a large number of situations that are unforeseen during design. On a campus, it is clear that entities such as mobile telephones and laptops must enter and exit, as is the case when Neo arrives on campus for the first time.

– Interoperability between all the systems is also necessary to obtain an open system, knowing that the whole system is either designed by a single person nor with a single technology. This challenge strongly affects the deployment of such systems and must be taken into consideration at the four levels of Amilab. There are different types of AmIDs in this scenario: mobile phones, laptops, billboards, library management systems, etc. and they must be able to interact with one another.

These several transverse challenges are not the only scientific challenges raised by ambient system. Many other, more specific challenges are involved in the development of well-performing ambient systems. The rest of this section will therefore focus on detailing the major challenges in computing research highlighted in the workshop. These scientific issues are described in terms of Amilab's major aspects.

14.5.1. *AmID*

The aim is to create AmID entities using low-level sensors and effectors (see Figure 14.1). We will focus on the perception aspect of the AmID, which has two large challenges: processing information and analyzing and structuring video data.

14.5.1.1. *Data processing*

This consists of processing, in real time, flows of sensory data (video, audio, RFID, laser, etc.) collected by fixed or embedded sensors. The capabilities of fixed sensors must be improved and provided with processing capabilities to limit network bandwidth [BER 11]; each sub-system receives data and analyzes it to detect events (such as a person or vehicle) and some behavior (human interactive gestures, dangerous situations such as falls, risks of collision, aggressive attitudes, etc.) and sends alarms on the network to neighboring sub-systems (to control it) and to a control station (to merge with other information, etc.)

14.5.1.2. *Analysis and structure of video data*

The analysis and structure of video data can entail camera data, which may be equipped with micros. There are two types of camera used: fixed (*webcam style*) or hand held (as in the ANR Blanc 2009 IMMED project: Indexing Multimedia Embedded Data for diagnosing and monitoring dementia treatment, which studies the behavior of patients predicted to develop Alzheimer's). It is today possible to extract and identify the different people appearing in a video [ZHA 10]. To achieve this, the visual and audio data associated with these people is used. However, this raises a number of challenges, which include:

– Adaptation to context: recognizing people (or objects) is made difficult in low light, long distance from the camera (problems of scale), and camera angle. In the case of hand-held cameras, there is the additional problem of the carrier's movement. Audio sensors are also occasionally unusable (due to too much noise). This therefore requires additional post-production to adapt the signal (controlling the camera according to the quality of images, detection, location, and extraction of audio sources, etc.).

– Real-time processing: applications in robotics, transport, and video-surveillance require reactivity. A number of functions (detection, monitoring and identification of people, detecting obstacles, etc.) are already executed in real time (from 10 to 20 Hz). For more complex algorithms, the transition from flow processing to real time processing is a veritable challenge because it requires re-thinking parameterizations and modeling methods to ensure both quality and density.

– Decentralization: the ability to interpret complex situations with a series of heterogeneous "intelligent" sensors and ensure that sensors cooperate and coordinate with de-centralized filtering to model imprecision and uncertainty, etc.

– Integration: this requires the design and development of communicating integrating wireless sensors, which are compact and energy independent (e.g. batteries) so that they can be easily deployed.

14.5.2. *Network level*

Networks are a basic element of embedded distributed systems and can be classified according to two sets, core networks and access networks. Access networks are networks of sensors or *ad hoc* networks, i.e. dynamic networks with mobile routers. A significant challenge is that of the management and security of open networks. How can AmIDs obtain and verify the identity and certification of other previously unknown AmIDs [GAM 11]? At the root of this question is the problem of ensuring trust in a constantly changing environment. Current solutions [STR 11] hypothesize on the prior knowledge of identity/accreditation providers, which cannot be guaranteed in an ambient context. Communication management must therefore be seen from both an individual and collective perspectives:

– Identifying and characterizing local surveillance and analysis mechanisms in a communication context continuously. An AmID, in particular, must be able to deduce and characterize its potential dependencies with regard to other AmIDs. For example, two AmIDs may communicate relying on one or several other AmIDs, which relay their communication. Equally, such an AmID relay must be aware of its role.

– Providing some of the information that will be used in the inference of AmID behavior and its interactions, therefore favoring adaptation to user context.

– Envisaging control and communication mechanisms that adapt to interaction priorities with a view to increasing the quality and continuity of users' preferred services and potentially adapting a cooperative attitude with other AmIDs to maintain a communication context as well as manage some aspects specific to security:

- before being able to communicate, each AmID must prove its identity to others. It is therefore necessary to provide relevant authentication mechanisms in a context where only the interaction between agents can provide a solution;

- communication security mechanisms also require research. Indeed, each AmID has different abilities in terms of processing power (like the processor, memory), autonomy (power, battery), supported security protocols, etc. It is therefore important to study whether standard security protocols (IPsec, SSL, etc.) can be used in this kind of environment or if a specific approach should be developed.

14.5.3. *Middleware level*

To design ambient applications, the *middleware* layer is central. *Middleware* represents the level of abstraction between applications and mechanisms (operating systems, networks) charged with executing them. The main challenges are modularity and extendability, on the one hand, because applications are not completely specified and evolutive, and on the other, accounting for software and material heterogeneity [GRA 11]. Heterogeneity is notably considered in the FP7 ICT FET CONNECT project [GRA 11].

14.5.3.1. *Automatic code generation*

Software platforms allow increasingly heterogeneous applications to be executed (virtual machines, Java machines, mobile OS, etc.) and evolve highly rapidly. Software developers want to move away from this evolution to allow the optimal and rapid adaptation of their applications. In this context, model-driven engineering must be further improved at the level of abstraction required when developing the system. This technological challenge therefore entails using languages, models, and approaches based on models allowing the automatic generation of specific "on the fly" codes, i.e. auto-adaptive codes.

14.5.3.2. *Engineering models*

Model-driven engineering (MDE) bases system design on the notion of models. As a result, it defines modeling languages (DSML, *Domain-Specific Modeling Language*)

[FUE 06] specific to the problem while being sufficiently flexible to integrate the necessary tools into the development process to account for global problems (system approach).

With regard to identifying specific modeling languages, the difficulty lies in the capacity to define AmId models and architectures adapted to ambient intelligence, which can be interoperated with heterogeneous AmIDs. Current models essentially account for task aspects while neglecting adaptation-related aspects. The highly dynamic and heterogeneous nature of these applications raises modeling problems that MDE models can effectively solve. The second point relates to the systematic approach for designing ambient intelligence applications [VER 11]. In this kind of application, a model must be produced to account for system heterogeneity, i.e. both the material environment (sensor, effectors, machines, etc.), the virtual environment (network, operating system, communication, etc.) as well as entities within the application (AmID). The contribution of MDE integrates methods and tools related to each point of view (human-machine interaction (HMI), ergonomy, architecture, etc.) or task (specification, design, simulation, prototyping, etc.) within a complete and homogeneous development.

14.5.4. *User service level*

In the context of mobility and volatility in ambient systems, the availability and quality of services varies. Due to the simultaneous and co-localized presence of component services, new (emerging) services must be constructed automatically and dynamically via composition and adaptation. The ambient system must therefore adapt and control the component to disturb its users as little as possible.

14.5.4.1. *Service auto-adaptation and autocomposition*

There is a certain complexity in the definition, experimentation, and evaluation of software technologies in the auto-adaptation and auto-composition of ambient services. Within this context, the following scientific challenges can be highlighted:

– When should a service be adapted? Identification, characterization, and strong evolution in services' context of use. The context use by a service may be acquired directly by this service (direct context) or constructed dynamically by a combination of contexts directly provided by a series of other services. The latter case introduces a challenge of context interoperability as well as respect for data confidentiality. Interoperability must allow each service the possibility of choosing how it wants to describe and model its own *direct* context. The challenge of using these contexts often raises the issue of modeling and the dynamics of the elements composing this context (modeling other services, users, resources, etc.).

– What should be adapted? Identifying the elements in a service that could be adapted in a given context. This adaptation can lead to a delegation to one or several other services in all or part of the initial service so that it corresponds as best as possible to all constraints. It is also necessary to refine automatic services and dynamically and automatically compose these services within ambient systems by allowing services to organize themselves to produce an "emerging" service.

– How should it be adapted? Identifying the mechanisms used to compose, delegate, and identify services allows us to respond to a specific need. As a result, an orchestration problem arises due to the power that some services can have in relation to others. Services must improve over time and therefore adapt by considering previous experience. This can raise problems directly related to service heterogeneity and their volatility and therefore requires deep reflection on what can be exchanged as characteristics on different accessible services and is part of the challenge related to the exchange of data between services.

For the design of services for users, we will focus on the following fields of research in computing: *context-aware computing*, multi-agent systems, and human–system interaction.

14.5.4.2. *Context-aware computing*

The notion of context is not new, but the uncertainty that is prevalent in ambient intelligence brings new challenges. Context is generally defined as any information that could be used to characterize entities at a given moment (people, places, objects) that have or could have an effect on the interaction between user and system, which are themselves part of context. Data can concern the place of interaction, the identity, and the state of groups/individuals and objects (whether computing or not) in the environment. To sumarize, context can be defined as the range of information that may impact on the execution of a task by an entity. A number of contextual models rely on centralized conceptualization such as Context Toolkit [DEY 01, CHE 04] or ontology management [CHE 04, EUZ 08]. Other distributed approaches cannot adapt to context during execution such as the COSMOS system [ROU 08]. The previously proposed models are not completely adapted to use within an ambient system because a contextual model for ambient systems needs to respect distribution criteria, openness, and accounting for the dynamics autonomously. Context management requires overcoming challenges regarding the following points, firstly the design of acquisition capacities for contextual information and modeling this information, i.e. their potential transformation, representation, update and, lastly, their use.

14.5.4.3. *Multi-agent systems*

Multi-agent systems [FER 99] are systems consisting of autonomous agents that interact in a shared environment to solve a shared task. The agents in these systems can be associated with the AmIDs [GEO 07]. The different challenges in multi-agent systems in designing an ambient application are as follows:

– Interoperability between the autonomous and heterogeneous agents (in terms of type, aim, and capability) in an ambient intelligence system. The whole range of electronic devices possible as well as humans within the system introduce a vast amount of diversity (objectives, limitations).

– The ability to account for a lack of knowledge about the design of the system's global aim. This lack of knowledge is due to the multi-objective, fluid, and therefore widely and incompletely specifiable nature of this aim.

– The fact that the system is located in a real and mixed environment (human and machines), that it is physically distributed and has specific limitations (response time, connectivity) and that it must be able to withstand being subject to failure and malfunction.

– Openness in the system with the introduction and disappearance of agents during operation as well as the adaptation of agents to their environment.

– The dynamics of the environment and the need to treat situations that were unpredicted by the designer, creating continually adaptive systems.

– The automatic deployment of such systems and the ability to scaleup.

The main aims of the projects in the FP7 Proactive Initiative: *Self-Awareness in Autonomic Systems* (AWARENESS) consist of creating systems capable of optimizing resources and their performance by adapting to context and internal changes [2].

14.5.4.4. *Human-machine interaction*

In ambient systems, HMI is not just limited to studying the basic keyboard–mouse–screen interaction. HMI currently focuses on three major aspects:

– multi-modality for effective and relevent communication between a system and user by using several interaction modalities;

– adaptation to account for changes in the interaction environment (task, platform, user) while guaranteeing usability of the interactive system. The adaptation of the interface to the user is an as-yet unresolved problem [CAL 03, KAM 11];

– mixed systems that facilitate human activities overlapping physical objects in daily life and computing capabilities.

Since technologies in interactions are no longer limited to a simple technical device, their description is complex. They should, in particular, integrate a description of the role of the user's physical environment, potential side effects and specific constraints. The definition of a context-specific interaction model is therefore required to provide a concise and usable description of these interaction agents.

---

2 cordis.europa.eu/fp7/ict/fet-proactive/aware_en.html.

Studying the characterization of the juxtaposition of different interaction techniques throughout an activity constitutes a second challenge to guaranteeing coherence throughout interaction techniques. It is therefore necessary to rely on an interaction model and complementary considerations in terms of HMI.

Finally, the last challenge identified lies in the implementation of mechanisms that can deduce a software structure from this model, which allows this technique to be implemented as well as possible anchor points with the agents composing the application's functional node.

As Joëlle Coutaz has said: "the new challenge is no longer simply providing finalized products for tasks and given activities, but to provide tools so that the user becomes the designer, 'creator of its own objects' and, by extension, the inventor of her/his own ambient system" [COU 08].

14.6. Conclusion

This chapter has traced the experimentation of initial forays into scenario-based ambient systems in the form of the ambient campus. The first stage of this process entailed identifying the software and/or material building blocks involved in the system. The briefness of the workshop (a few hours only) did not provide highly detailed design blocks. However, it did raise a number of questions and highlighted a number of scientific challenges. The main issues centered around the level of centralization or decentralization required to create an ambient system and, on the other hand, the notion of context.

The diversity of scientific fields involved in ambient systems has been clearly identified and are found at different levels in Amilab, as shown in section 14.2. The major scientific challenges raised such as acceptability, respect for private life, reliability, openness, and interoperability, reflect the complexity of designing these systems. In addition, these challenges characterize future ambient systems.

Overcoming these challenges requires integrated inter-disciplinary research ranging from HSS, ICT, and the areas of application concerned. Design must be multidisciplinary to construct not only reliable and effective ambient systems that are accepted and therefore used by people, but it is also important to implement and formalize a methodology that could take the form of a collaborative and technological platform between all the disciplines concerned. Its role is to ensure coordination of the greatest possible number of those involved in the project, supported by a design and decision-making system to ensure that:

– needs are well identified;

– the implementation of technical processes is carried out well, is economical, and conforms to techno-scientific, legal, and ethical constraints;

– decisions are taken on the basis of sufficient and objective knowledge;

– evaluation is carried out on the basis of recordings and predefined guidelines.

The collaborative aspect is ensured by experts from different disciplines and systems' end users. This platform must breath life into inter-disciplinary research using a range of methods such as different technologies while ensuring that the issue is thoroughly examined and that the solutions are studied from as many perspectives as possible. The technological aspect corresponds to a series of software and/or material building blocks available to designers. It is important to reduce the complexity and length of the design process so that designers of ambient applications have access to general building blocks at all levels of Amilab.

The design of systems and software is not a new activity but the creation of ambient systems introduces other constraints. For example, design is, by its very nature, multi-disciplinary and is not based on the whole system since we do not know its final use, which therefore introduces new issues during its design.

14.7. Acknowledgments

We would like to thank GDR I3 and ASR from the CNRS for organizing the ETIA (Ecole Thématique Intelligence Ambiante) summer school as well as Paul Sabatier University for their support with the AmIE (*Ambiant Intelligent Entities*) project and the IRIT laboratory for their support with the strategic "ambient socio technical systems" aspect. We would also like to particularly thank Rémi Bastide, Marie-Françoise Canut, Emmanuel Dubois, Pierre Glize, Christine Sénac and Philippe Truillet, and researchers at IRIT, for their participation in examining the scenario used in this chapter.

14.8. Bibliography

[BER 11] BERGÉ L. P., BRIAND C., DE BONNEVAL A., LEFEBVRE O., TAÏX M., TRUILLET P., "SysCARE : Système de Communication et d'Assistance Robotisée (poster)", *Journées francophones Mobilité et Ubiquité (UBIMOB)*, Toulouse, France, 6–8 June 2011.

[BIS 03] BISWAS P., CHATTERJEE R., Location aware application development framework, US Patent 6,594,666, 15 July 2003.

[CAL 03] CALVARY G., COUTAZ J., THEVENIN D., LIMBOURG Q., BOUILLON L., VANDERDONCKT J., "A Unifying reference framework for multi-target user interfaces", *Interacting with Computers, Special Issue on Computer-Aided Design of User Interface*, vol. 15, no. 3, pp. 289–308, 2003.

[CHE 04] CHEN H., FININ T., JOSHI A., "A context-broker for building smart meeting rooms", *Proceedings of the Knowledge Representation and Ontology for Autonomous Systems Symposium*, AAAI Press, 2004.

[COU 08] COUTAZ J., CROWLEY J., Plan "Intelligence Ambiante": Défis et Opportunités, Document de réflexion conjoint du comité d'experts "Informatique Ambiante" du département ST2I du CNRS et du Groupe de Travail "Intelligence Ambiante" du groupe de concertation sectoriel (GCS3) du ministère de l'Enseignement supérieur et de la Recherche, DGRI A3., 2008.

[DEY 01] DEY A., ABOWD G., SALBER D., "A conceptual framework and a toolkit for supporting the rapid prototyping of context-aware applications", *Human-Computer Interaction*, vol. 16, no. 2, pp. 97–166, 2001.

[DIM 05] DI MARZO SERUGENDO G., GLEIZES M., KARAGEORGOS A., "Self-organization in multi-agent systems", *The Knowledge Engineering Review*, vol. 20, no. 2, pp. 165–189, 2005.

[EUZ 08] EUZENAT J., PIERSON J., RAMPARANY F., "Dynamic context management for pervasive applications", *The Knowledge Engineering Review*, vol. 23, pp. 21–49, 2008.

[FER 99] FERBER J., *Multi-Agent Systems – An Introduction to Distributed Artifical Intelligence*, Addison-Wesley, Boston, 1999.

[FUE 06] FUENTES L., JIMÉNEZ D., "Combining components, aspects, domain specific languages and product lines for ambient intelligent application development", *International Conference on Pervasive Computing*, Dublin, Ireland, 2006.

[GAM 11] GAMBS S., KILLIJIAN M. O., DEL PRADO CORTEZ M. N., "GEPETO*: towards a platform for evaluating privacy aspects of mobility data", *Journées francophones Mobilité et Ubiquité (UBIMOB)*, Toulouse, France, 6–8 June 2011.

[GEO 07] GEORGÉ J., CAMPS V., GLEIZES M., GLIZE P., "Ambient intelligence as a neverEnding self-organizing process: analysis and experiments", *Artificial and Ambient Intelligence convention (Artificial Societies for Ambient Intelligence) (AISB-ASAMi 2007)*, Newcastle, UK, 2007.

[GRA 11] GRACE P., GEORGANTAS N., BENNACEUR A., BLAIR G., CHAUVEL F., ISSARNY V., PAOLUCCI M., SAADI R., SOUVILLE B., SYKES D., "The CONNECT architecture", *11th International School on Formal Methods for the Design of Computer, Communication and Software Systems: Connectors for Eternal Networked Software Systems*, vol. 20, no. 2, Bertinoro, Italy, pp. 27–52, 2011.

[KAM 11] KAMMOUN S., ORIOLA B., TRUILLET P., JOUFFRAIS C., "Conception et évaluation d'un système de dialogue pour un dispositif de suppléance pour déficients visuels", *Journées francophones Mobilité et Ubiquité (UBIMOB)*, Toulouse, France, 6–8 June 2011.

[KEP 03] KEPHART J., CHESS D., "The vision of autonomic computing", *Computer*, vol. 36, no. 1, pp. 41–50, IEEE, 2003.

[ROU 08] ROUVOY R., CONAN D., SEINTURIE L., "Software architecture patterns for a context-processing middleware framework.", *IEEE Distributed Systems Online*, vol. 9, no. 6, 2008.

[STR 11] STREITZ N., "Smart cities, ambient intelligence and universal access", *Universal Access in Human-Computer Interaction. Context Diversity*, vol. 6767 of Lecture Notes in Computer Science, Springer Berlin, Heidelberg, pp. 425–432, 2011.

[VER 11] VERGONI C., TIGLI J. Y., LAVIROTTE S., REY G., RIVEILL M., "Construction bottom-up d'applications ambiantes en environnements partiellement connus a priori", *Journées francophones Mobilité et Ubiquité (UBIMOB)*, Toulouse, France, 6–8 June 2011.

[WEI 91] WEISER M., "The computer for the twenty-first century", *Scientific American*, vol. 265, pp. 94–104, 1991.

[ZHA 10] ZHANG P., "Complex wavelet feature extraction for video-based face recognition", *Proceedings of the IEEE SoutheastCon 2010 (SoutheastCon)*, Charlotte, North Carolina, USA, March 2010.

List of Authors

Georges AKHRAS
Centre for Smart Materials
and Structures
Royal Military College
Kingston Ontario
Canada

Dana AL KUKHUN
IRIT
Paul Sabatier University
(Toulouse 3)
France

Isabelle ASTIC
Musée des arts et métiers
Paris
France

Coline AUNIS
Musée des arts et métiers
Paris
France

Lionel BALME
Grenoble Informatics Laboratory
Joseph Fourier University
Grenoble
France

Anne-Marie BENOIT
CNRS
Laboratoire PACTE
Grenoble
France

Gaëlle CALVARY
Grenoble Informatics Laboratory
Grenoble Institute of Technology
France

Jean CARLE
LIFL
University of Lille 1
Villeneuve d'Ascq
France

Joëlle COUTAZ
Grenoble Informatics Laboratory
Joseph Fourier University
Grenoble
France

James L. CROWLEY
Grenoble Informatics Laboratory
Grenoble Institute of Technology
France

Georges DA COSTA
Laboratoire IRIT
Paul Sabatier University
(Toulouse 3)
France

Thierry DELOT
LAMIH
University of Valenciennes
France

Alexandre DEMEURE
Grenoble Informatics Laboratory
Joseph Fourier University
Grenoble
France

Anne-Marie DERY-PINNA
Laboratoire d'Informatique
Signaux et Systèmes
de Sophia Antipolis (I3S)
University of Nice Sophia Antipolis
France

Mikael DESERTOT
LAMIH
University of Valenciennes
France

Jérome DUPIRE
Laboratoire Cédric
Conservatoire National des Arts
et Métiers
Paris
France

Nicolas FERRY
Laboratoire d'Informatique
Signaux et Systèmes
de Sophia Antipolis (I3S)
University of Nice Sophia Antipolis
France

Yoann GABILLON
LAMIH
University of Valenciennes
France

Viviane GAL
Laboratoire Cédric
Conservatoire National des Arts
et Métiers
Paris
France

Jean-Pierre GEORGÉ
Laboratoire IRIT
Paul Sabatier University
(Toulouse 3)
France

Sylvain GIROUX
Laboratoire DOMUS
University of Sherbrooke
Canada

Marie-Pierre GLEIZES
Laboratoire IRIT
Paul Sabatier University
(Toulouse 3)
France

Christophe GRANSART
IFSTTAR
Villeneuve d'Ascq
France

Eric GRESSIER-SOUDAN
Laboratoire Cédric
Conservatoire National des Arts
et Métiers
Paris
France

Michaël HAUSPIE
LIFL
University of Lille 1
Villeneuve d'Ascq
France

Vincent HOURDIN
Laboratoire d'Informatique
Signaux et Systèmes
de Sophia Antipolis (I3S)
University of Nice Sophia Antipolis
France

Stéphane LAVIROTTE
Laboratoire d'Informatique
Signaux et Systèmes
de Sophia Antipolis (I3S)
University of Nice Sophia Antipolis
France

Sylvain LECOMTE
LAMIH
University of Valenciennes
France

Nathalie MITTON
Inria Lille-Nord Europe
Villeneuve d'Ascq
France

Audrey OCCELLO
Laboratoire d'Informatique
Signaux et Systèmes
de Sophia Antipolis (I3S)
University of Nice Sophia Antipolis
France

Hélène PIGOT
Laboratoire DOMUS
University of Sherbrooke
Canada

Christophe PITREY
Laboratoire Cédric
Conservatoire National des Arts
et Métiers
Paris

France
Tahiry RAZAFINDRALAMBO
Inria Lille-Nord Europe
Villeneuve d'Ascq
France

Philippe RENEVIER
Laboratoire d'Informatique
Signaux et Systèmes
de Sophia Antipolis (I3S)
University of Nice Sophia Antipolis
France

Gaëtan REY
Laboratoire d'Informatique
Signaux et Systèmes
de Sophia Antipolis (I3S)
University of Nice Sophia Antipolis
France

Matthieu ROY
LAAS – CNRS
Toulouse
France

Françoise SAILHAN
Laboratoire Cédric
Conservatoire National des Arts
et Métiers
Paris
France

Florence SÈDES
IRIT
Paul Sabatier University
(Toulouse 3)
France

Michel SIMATIC
Institut Mines-Télécom
Paris
France
David SIMPLOT-RYL
Inria Lille-Nord Europe
University of Lille 1
Villeneuve d'Ascq
France

Marie THILLIEZ
LAMIH
University of Valenciennes
France

Jean-Yves TIGLI
Laboratoire d'Informatique
Signaux et Systèmes
de Sophia Antipolis (I3S)
University of Nice Sophia Antipolis
France

Alexandre TOPOL
Laboratoire Cédric
Conservatoire National des Arts
et Métiers
Paris
France

Emanuel ZAZA
Tetraedge game
Montreuil
France

Index